POPULAR TRANSLATIONS OF NATIONALISM BIHAR, 1920-1922

Popular Translations of Nationalism

BIHAR, 1920-1922

LATA SINGH

PRIMUS BOOKS

PRIMUS BOOKS
An imprint of Ratna Sagar P. Ltd.
Virat Bhavan
Mukherjee Nagar Commercial Complex
Delhi 110 009

Offices at CHENNAI KOLKATA LUCKNOW
AGRA AHMEDABAD BANGALORE COIMBATORE DEHRADUN GUWAHATI
HYDERABAD JAIPUR KANPUR KOCHI MADURAI MUMBAI PATNA RANCHI

First published 2012

ISBN: 978-93-80607-13-9

Published by Primus Books

Laser typeset by Digigrafics
Gulmohar Park, New Delhi 110 049

Printed at Sanat Printers, Kundli, Haryana

For
Mammi and Papaji

Contents

Preface

THIS IS AN in-depth study of the Non-Cooperation Movement, that gave a new turn to the national movement in Bihar. During and after the Non-Cooperation, the national movement no longer remained confined to the educated sections of society but assumed a mass character. The available writings on the national movement in Bihar do not, however, address its complexity. K.K. Datta's three-volume work, *History of the Freedom Movement in Bihar*, provides valuable information on different aspects of the political movement but it tends to be a narrative of systematically arranged, chronological events and a simple descriptive account of the freedom struggle. The P.N. Ojha-edited *History of the Indian National Congress in Bihar, 1885-1985*, too offers a general account of the movement. The account of nationalism revolves around recounting of certain 'well known', historical events. However, nationalism was not monolithic; it was constituted by multilayered facets and dimensions. But these studies weave events into a chronological account, where nationalism is projected as rising and progressing towards a pre-determined point. Besides, their focus is largely on the role of the Congress leaders thereby marginalizing popular participation in the national movement.

Some significant works have of course been produced on the national movement in Bihar: Papiya Ghosh's *The Civil Disobedience Movement in Bihar* is a full-length study of the Civil Disobedience Movement in Bihar, which examines the strength and weakness of the Bihar Congress and its mobilization efforts. Vinita Damodaran's *Broken Promises: Popular Protest, Indian Nationalism and the Congress Party in Bihar 1935-1946* examines the nature of the national movement in Bihar during the period when the Congress underwent a transition from being a movement of opposition to a party in power. Damodaran's study analyses the dynamics and shifts in the relationship between a movement that had been based purely on agitation and the constraints that were faced when its leaders, the Congress, formed the ministry in Bihar in 1937. However, these works focus on the later phase of national movement. Since there is no intensive study on the earlier phase of the movement, this study of non-cooperation becomes important. Besides, a study of this phase also becomes significant for revisiting the historiography on nationalism as non-cooperation marked the period when national movement moved from the confines of educated section and assumed a mass character. This study is aimed at highlighting the nature and character and the complexity of popular nationalism.

The Non-Cooperation Movement in Bihar was very significant because it constituted diverse facets and streams and unleashed a variety of protests. The movement was marked with mass articulation of nationalism. People became associated with the Non-Cooperation Movement with a variety of hopes and desires, bringing their aspirations and expressions to it. People related, assimilated and adapted nationalist ideology to their own social and political needs based on their own world views and experiences. The Non-Cooperation Movement marked resistance at different levels. However, to locate the different kinds of resistance one needs to broaden the concept of resistance, so that it can be applied to a wider range of socio-cultural practices. To focus on resistance only in its more traditional sense, i.e. always conscious and organized protest, would mean not to consider the very processes by which power is often questioned and eroded by the actions of the subordinate groups. Resistance needs to be perhaps seen as behaviour and cultural practices of the subordinate groups that contest hegemonic social formations and challenge domination; 'consciousness' need not always be essential to its base. Seemingly inoffensive behaviour can have unintended, yet strong, consequences for the objective of the dominant or the shape of a social order. In fact, one has to consider the very processes by which colonial power is often challenged and eroded by the actions of the subordinate groups. Very often commonplace actions within the bounds of legality or legitimate expression undermine ideological and hegemonic structure. It is the context and the consequences that render certain actions contentious. During the Non-Cooperation Movement in Bihar, people in a variety of positions adopted a wide range of steps, not necessarily consciously organized resistance, but they contributed to the disruption of the working of colonial power.

The movement was marked by a series of popular protests. Peasants were in the forefront of nationalist agitation. Unfortunately, the issue of the agrarian basis of the nationalist agitation has not been central to most studies on the national movement in Bihar. In general, a lot of work has been done on peasant movements and nationalist politics in Bihar. One can cite here the studies of A.N. Das, Walter Hauser, Rakesh Gupta and Jacques Pouchepadass. However, much more remains to be delved in the field of peasant politics within the broader framework of nationalist politics in Bihar. In actual fact, the upsurge and the forms of popular protests were not peripheral or merely connected to the nationalist agitation but were significant aspect of it. This book investigates the contours of peasant consciousness in its interactions with nationalism at different levels.

Stephen Henningham, in his *Peasant Movements in Colonial India, North Bihar, 1917-42*, has attempted to bring the peasants to the forefront. But his concern has been to highlight the nationalist/agrarian dichotomy, as well as what he sees as dual nationalism. He talks of two streams in nationalism: one, of the rich peasants and landlords, and the other, of the poor, low caste peasants. In his delineation, the politically motivated 'nationalist revolt' overlapped with an economically motivated 'rebellion of desperation'. According to him, nationalist conflict was distinct from agrarian conflict. Peasant action is seen merely as an economic response rather than as a political process. His study not only denies subjectivity and consciousness to the peasants, but also denies them any political voice. This study makes an attempt to break out of the binary of elite/subaltern nationalism and focuses on the complexities associated in the interaction of nationalism with popular pressures.

The Non-Cooperation Movement made considerable impact in the tribal belt, intensifying agrarian agitation. The tribals perceived swaraj as a millennium which would end all exploitation and oppression. This study also adopts a critical approach towards most of the historiography related to tribal struggles that operates with the assumption that the tribal communities were monolithic and/or the tribals were incapable of being exploitative. Scholars who have studied tribal protests in Chotanagpur have remained, despite their significant contributions, constrained by their suppositions that see tribal conflicts resulting out of the infiltration of non-tribals into the tribal territory. Consequently, the tribal movement is read as the resistance of 'aboriginals' against 'non-aboriginals' or of 'insiders' against 'outsiders'. This makes these scholars locate the tribals as almost homogeneous communities, who were united in opposing alien and unacceptable elements that had entered their land. The present study, besides recognizing the importance of tracing tribal opposition to the zamindars, banias and the British, suggests that conflict needs to be also located within the internal hierarchy of the tribal communities.

Besides the peasant and tribal resistance, the Non-Cooperation Movement in Bihar heralded resistance at different levels. But most of the works on nationalism have focussed on the struggles and insurgencies of subaltern groups. The resistance by state subordinates still remains unexplored. In fact there is a dearth of studies on the relationship between the bureaucracy and the national movement. Even if some references are made to it, that is confined to very small and exclusive administrative elite. A large number of Indians who occupied subordinate ranks in the colonial bureaucracy are not brought into the discussion. The Non-Cooperation Movement in Bihar was marked by protest by the lower rungs of police personnel. However, episodes such as polices protests have never been the focus of historians' attention. In fact, the absence of such studies give the impression that the state subordinates were normally very effectively integrated into the structure of the colonial state that was a formidable, autonomous force, when it came to controlling subordinate groups. The writings have concentrated on the contributions that the state subordinates have made to the formation and functioning of the colonial state. The subordinate's relationship is portrayed as relatively stable and unaffected by any inner conflict or contradiction. However, this is generally a history with resistance largely left out. This work highlights that there was a continuous effort on the part of the subordinate police personnel to contend and frustrate efforts of the state systems. By foregrounding such resistance, this study in a way throws light on the restraint faced by the colonial administration, and consequently, questions the formidable character of the colonial state.

The resistances during the non-cooperation become meaningful when one looks at the nationalist struggle also as a hegemonic struggle. Many studies have highlighted how the British rule was based not merely on force but was semi-hegemonic in character. The British rule in India relied greatly on the acquiescence of the Indian people in that rule. For over a long period of time, it was carefully inculcated that the foreign rulers were benevolent and just, that they were *mai-baap* of the people, and were economically, socially and culturally developing or 'modernizing' India. In fact, it is in the weakening of the legitimacy or hegemony of the existing colonial order that one can best understand how certain phases of the nationalist agitation impacted the world of subalterns. The colonial power perceived that the undermining of its hegemony was a great threat to its power. It is in the context of forefronting nationalism as a counter-hegemonic struggle that the boycotts, which were important programmes of non-cooperation, become significant. There have been studies on boycotts in which detailed accounts or descriptions of them (the boycotts) have been given and their political and economic aspects highlighted. But the significant aspects of boycott, i.e. their ideological and hegemonic bearings, still remain unexplored in studies on nationalism. However, the boycotts played not only some important role in the counter-hegemonic struggle of nationalism vis-à-vis the colonial power but they were also interwined with contest for hegemony within Indian society. Thus, giving prominence to nationalism as a hegemonic battle broadens the notion of nationalism which does not remain merely a political encounter but also becomes a cultural encounter with the colonial power. Nationalism becomes a quest to redefine and retrieve 'Indian' cultural space vis-à-vis British cultural and ideological onslaught. Although reclaiming homogeneous 'national' culture would have its ideological bearings on the subalterns and minority. Besides in the sketch of cultural nationalism the underbelly of every attempt towards identity was the description of women. Gender becomes the structuring principle of nationalism. Thus by throwing light on some of these issues, this work moves beyond the conventional 'political' paradigm and highlights the different dimensions and complexities of Non-Cooperation Movement in Bihar.

New Delhi LATA SINGH

Acknowledgements

THERE ARE many who have helped me see this book to fruition. My gratitude goes to Maitreyi College, University of Delhi, for its support towards my academic work. I am greatly indebted to the staff of the Nehru Memorial Museum & Library, National Archives of India and Central Secretariat Library in New Delhi; and the Bihar State Archives, CID Record Room, Police Archives, and Sinha Library in Patna, Bihar. I would like to thank the University Grants Commission for its research grant, which facilitated my fieldwork in Bihar. I would also like to acknowledge the Nehru Memorial Museum & Library for the jacket illustration.

During the course of my work, I received immense help from my friends. First and the foremost, I would like to express my special thanks to my friend, Biswamoy Pati whose consistent support and encouragement have been the moving forces behind this book becoming a reality. Other friends, at different levels—both personal and intellectual—have helped in the shaping of this work. I know I cannot thank all of them enough but I would like to make special mention of Indrani Sen, Amar Farooqui, P.K. Shukla, Shashank Sinha, Sadhna Arya, Ranjana Padhi, Laxmi Murthy, Gargi Chakravartty, Rachna Jain, Anurita Jalan and P.N. Singh. Also, this book with its focus on Bihar brings back fond memories of Papiya Ghosh with whom I had intensive discussions on my field visits.

The primary attraction of my field visit to Bihar was an opportunity to meet my grandfather. In fact, much of the fieldwork there was made comfortable because of the warm welcome provided by my uncles and aunts, Anil Singh, B.K. Singh, Gopal Singh, Sarita Singh and Sangeeta Singh. The company of my cousins, Sharad, Saurav, Puja, Rewat and Surabhi had made my tour of Bihar very enjoyable. My sister, Niva, has been a great moral support in my research journey. The company of her children, Shivam and Srijita, provided the ideal break from the rigours of research. Personally, I do not have enough words to thank my mother and father, who have stood by me in all my scholarly pursuits. It is their encouragement which has inspired most of my academic work. I take the pleasure of dedicating this book to my parents.

New Delhi LATA SINGH

CHAPTER ONE

Bihar Politics: Locale of Non-Cooperation Movement

SIGNIFICANT aspect of Non-Cooperation Movement in India has been its regional specificity and the salience of local issues. Hence, in order to highlight the characteristics of the Non-Cooperation Movement in Bihar, there is a need to throw light on the nature of politics in Bihar preceding it. Bihar in the early twentieth century was a strong belt of political movements. It was then a locale for peasant struggles. It also witnessed a strong agitation for autonomy from Bengal. This chapter briefly sketches the political issues which permeated Bihar politics preceding the first mass-based Gandhian movement there. Before delineating the political terrain, the territorial and social configuration of Bihar has been briefly mapped.

Territorial and Social Contour of Bihar

Bihar was a province of the Mughal Empire in the early eighteenth century and after the Battle of Buxar in 1760, it became a part of the British administered Bengal Presidency. In 1911, the British separated Bihar from the Bengal Presidency and along with Orissa it formed the province of Bihar and Orissa. In 1936, Bihar and Orissa were separated and a separate province of Bihar was created. Bihar was bound on the north by Nepal, on the west by present-day Uttar Pradesh and Madhya Pradesh, on the south by Orissa and on the east by Bengal. The river Ganga flowing across it from west to east divided it into two unequal parts with the southern part almost twice in area of the northern part. Bihar was commonly described as comprising three parts: the land north of the Ganga or north Bihar; the plains south of the Ganga or south Bihar; and the uplands in the extreme south known as Chotanagpur. Chotanagpur region, which was about half of the total area of the province, was hilly and forested, and was not, therefore, particularly suitable for agriculture. Nevertheless, it was very important because of its mining and industrial wealth. Chotanagpur was also the home of the tribal population of Bihar.

In 1912, Bihar was constituted into four divisions—Bhagalpur, Patna, Tirhut and Chotanagpur. Bhagalpur division comprised Bhagalpur, Monghyr, Purnea and Santhal Pargana districts. Patna division included Gaya, Patna and Shahabad districts. Champaran, Darbhanga, Muzaffarpur and Saran districts formed part of Tirhut division. Chotanagpur division comprised Hazaribagh, Manbhum, Palamau, Ranchi and Singhbhum districts. Darbhanga, Saran, Muzaffarpur, north Monghyr, north Bhagalpur and Purnea districts constituted north Bihar; and Patna, Gaya, south Monghyr and south Bhagalpur districts were part of south Bihar.

With an area of 1,74,000 sq. km., or 5.3 per cent of the total geographical area of India, Bihar accounted for 10.3 per cent of the total population of the country. South Bihar alone had three-fourths of the state's population.[1] The population in Bihar was predominantly Hindu. The four upper castes—Brahmins, Bhumihars, Rajputs and Kayasthas—comprising nearly 15 per cent of the total population, were the major landholding castes. Majority of the landholders belonged to these castes. In the middle rank, there were about a hundred different castes, among whom the Yadavas, Kurmis and Koeris were the most numerous. They were largely tenants. The lowest castes, mostly untouchables, accounted for nearly 15 per cent of the population and they were predominantly agricultural labourers.[2] Some Yadavas, Kurmis and Koeris, whose landholdings were too small to provide them subsistence, also worked as agricultural labourers. Some members of the untouchable castes, such as Chamars, Musahars and Dosadhs, often performed field labour for which they were paid wages in kind. These castes were distributed more or less evenly throughout the state, barring certain areas of Gaya and Palamau, where they accounted for nearly one-third of the population.[3] As a consequence of the convergence of the twice-born ritual status, concentration of land rights and legitimization of the social hierarchy by Brahminical ideology, Brahmins, Bhumihars and Rajputs held sway over the Bihar society for almost a millennium. The Kayasthas, as small caste groups, were also accorded elite status primarily because of their occupation as 'writers' or 'court scribes'.[4]

It was difficult to disentangle the economic and social basis of upper caste dominance at the village level. Grierson, writing in the 1880s, found that in the villages a clear distinction was made in the treatment of high caste and low caste tenants that subordinated the economic definition of their ranking to that of ritual status. Tenants of high and low castes were referred to by different generic names; they lived in separate quarters of the village and were granted unequal terms of tenure. Commonly, high-caste tenants were assessed at a lower rate, or received remission of part of the rent. Moreover, cultivators belonging to high castes were not required to do *begar* or unpaid labour on the landlord's fields, although they were expected to send their own field labourers for such work; low caste tenants customarily performed *begar* and were more subservient.[5]

The same rough correspondence between caste and class applied among the urban population in most towns. Government servants and professionals belonged largely to the upper castes (predominantly Kayastha), and upper status Muslims. Most of them had links with landlords and rich peasants in the villages. Banking and trade were the preserve of Marwaris and other traditional mercantile castes. Most of the small shopkeepers and artisans were low-status Muslims, while unskilled labourers were of a low or untouchable caste.[6]

The tribals were mainly concentrated in Chotanagpur. Only a comparative handful of tribals were found outside Chotanagpur in Purnea, Bhagalpur, Monghyr and in Champaran district in the Terai forest bordering the Himalayas.[7] The Muslim population was scattered throughout the rural areas, accounting for less than 10 per cent in south Bihar and Chotanagpur, and between 10 and 16 per cent in north Bihar. In Purnea, the Muslims constituted one-third of the population.[8]

Peasant Struggles: Issues and Concerns

The early twentieth century witnessed a strong peasant agitation in Bihar. In fact, at that period peasant agitations overshadowed the nationalist agitations in Bihar. Peasants discontentment could be seen in the context of the Permanent Settlement which provided the setting for the development of agriculture in Bihar till the first half of the twentieth century. The Settlement was in reality the culmination of a long series of endeavours to adjust the share of the state in the produce of the soil and to perpetuate the friendship of a class of collaborators, the landlords, to buttress the nascent British Empire. The Settlement, which made the zamindars the landowners, is viewed as a decisive point in the history of changes in land rights.[9] Instead of offering provisions for the protection of the class of actual cultivators, the Settlement armed the zamindars with more power to enable them to realize their demands on the tenants so as to secure the public revenue payable by the zamindars.[10]

The firm support the Imperial Government provided to the zamindars through the Permanent Settlement made the latter complacent and arrogant. They demanded exorbitant rents from the peasants. Under Regulation VII of 1799, the landlords were even empowered to distraint the crop, cattle and personal property of their tenants and, in certain cases, to arrest them for non-payment of rent, without reference to any court. Tenants were never presented *pattas*, i.e. a document given to the revenue payer indicating his obligations, so that they could know the exact sum payable by them. Before the Permanent Settlement, the peasants had in theory at least a definite right to cultivate and a definite share in the produce of the land, but over the next hundred years the peasants became tenants at the zamindars' will.[11] Apart from this, the increasing indebtedness of the zamindars made them extract more and more from the tenants, or transfer much of their proprietary rights to moneylenders and usurers, who were ruthless in their methods of extracting surplus from the tenants. The increasing land values, the stability of income from landed property, and the diminishing rigour of sale laws attracted moneylenders and usurers to the activities of land transactions.[12] In addition to the economic exploitation based on the system of rent, the zamindars perpetrated many types of extra-economic coercion. They extracted several types of labour rents and illegal payments (*abwabs*). *Abwabs* were collected on such flimsy grounds as marriage in the zamindar's family, education of the zamindar's son abroad, the purchase of elephants by the zamindars or the celebration of the Holi festival. Illegal cesses levied on the peasantry, for matters such as the transfer of occupancy holdings of tenants, were another important source of exploitations.[13] The high caste zamindars even imposed restrictions on ritual observances by lower caste tenants. As the zamindars got alienated from the village social structure and settled in the cities, they became even more oppressive and harsh.[14]

The size of the zamindaris in Bihar was by and large small, with the exception of a few mammoth estates like Darbhanga, Bettiah, Banailie and Dumraon. Darbhanga raj dominated Darbhanga and Muzaffarpur, and exercised control (through relations and gomastas, agents) over substantial estates in the northern parts of Bhagalpur, Monghyr and Purnea. Hathwa raj owned the northern part of Saran district and controlled smaller estates in Champaran, Shahabad, Darbhanga and Muzaffarpur. Bettiah raj held its dominance in Champaran and the Dumraon estate wielded control in Shahabad. Ramgarh raj was a princely state in Chotanagpur. There was a close alliance between the colonial state and the big landlords which was further strengthened after the 1857 Revolt. The Revolt had made the British more dependent on the local rajas and zamindars. The bigger zamindars were conferred titles such as Maharaja Bahadur, Raja Bahadur and Rai Bahadur, and they were associated with local governments as honorary magistrates and as members of municipal councils and district boards. The first Indian appointed to the Lieutenant Governor's Executive Council was Rameshwar Singh, the younger brother of the Maharaja of Darbhanga. In addition, the landed interests enjoyed a dominant position in the Legislative Council. The Bihar Landholders' Association was formed in 1878, with the Maharaja of Darbhanga as its President. It welded together local elite of separate regions, castes and religious communities in conscious defence of their shared economic interest against the tenants' demand for the amendment of Bengal Tenancy Act for which a strong pressure had been building up in Bihar. In fact, right up to the pre-war period, the close relationship between the government, big zamindars and upper castes created an almost complete overlap between dominance at the level of society and power in the realm of the state.[15]

As stated earlier, with the exception of a few big zamindars, Bihar was primarily dominated by small zamindars. But the predominance of small zamindars in Bihar did not necessarily imply better and more personalized management. Direct participation of the zamindars in matters of management of estates was considered by them to be demeaning. The average landlord maintained elaborate establishments with officials' equivalent to secretaries, money changers, record keepers, messengers, constables, rent assessors and rent collectors. Amongst the officials the *amlas,* who looked after a zamindari, were particularly very oppressive and dishonest,[16] and this was one of the common grievances aired by the peasants.

The zamindars hardly invested anything in increasing production. Their reluctance to spend anything on the upkeep of the indigenous irrigation works, once the produce rent was commuted to fixed cash rent, led to large-scale decay of the irrigation system and this affected the production. Many tenants, unable to produce enough to be able to meet the rent, lost large parts of their holdings in rent-decree sales.[17]

The position of the peasants further deteriorated after 1850 with the increase in population. Increase in population led to a rapid increase in the partition of estates and with that arbitrary rent enhancements were effected by large numbers of petty landlords, intent on maintaining their position. Following the increase in land values and the increasing population pressure on land, the zamindars began to evict tenants from their holdings on flimsy pretexts and settled these with other tenants at higher rents and *salamis* (initial payments).[18]

Legislation to protect the rights and interests of the tenants did not come until the Act X of 1859 and the Bengal Tenancy Act of 1885 were passed. These Acts abolished the landlords' power to compel their tenants to attend to their offices when summoned to do so, protected the tenants from summary eviction, guaranteed the continued occupancy of tenants, who could prove that they had rented the land from a zamindar for a period of twelve successive years, and required zamindars, who wished to raise rents, to prove legally that their claim was reasonable.[19] Legislation alone could not secure the position of the tenants. It was indeed very difficult for a tenant to prove his occupancy right on land because he did not possess any documentary evidence as rent receipts were seldom granted. Moreover, the tenants were not aware of their legal rights. In legal battles the zamindars often emerged victorious since they wielded influence and commanded more resources, legal struggles being tests of financial endurance.[20]

Even the survey settlement operations work did not benefit the tenants. The settlement operations, which provided the record of rights, indicated a predominant class of occupancy tenants with important tenancy rights. But the occupancy rights were recognized only in theory. Widespread litigation was resorted to by the landlords in civil courts in order to defeat the object of the record-of-rights, while the publication of survey settlement operation was still in progress, and the litigation continued even after the record was published. Many tenants gave up the fight and agreed to the demands of the landlords, in spite of incurring heavy expenses in law courts.[21]

The First World War had the effect of worsening the condition of the peasants.[22] The War brought about economic dislocation, increasing the prices of consumer goods. In the early twentieth century, there was a tremendous rise in population in Bihar, leading to scarcity of land, timber and grazing areas for cattle. Rights to resources became increasingly contentious. The zamindari system impinged upon the peasants with even greater force because of demographic pressure. The zamindars competed with their tenants for control over land, collected their rents rigorously and intensified their exaction of *abwabs*. Population increase intensified disputes over the possession of holdings and tempted the zamindars to rent out even 'wastelands' that had formerly been used for grazing. The demand for land had also created a market in land tenancies. Rich villagers acquired occupancy rights as an investment and then profited by subletting the holdings to sharecroppers and short-term tenants. Landlords benefited from the transfer of tenancies by levying mutation fees on transfers by sale and transfers by inheritance. Mutation fees were widely resented because they obstructed the taking over of land by the poor and also interfered with the investment strategies of the well off. With the destruction of large tracts of standing timber for building and fuel, wood assumed an unprecedented scarcity value and disputes over rights in timber escalated. Some of the grievances of the peasants were related to interference by the zamindars in what the tenants regarded as their right both in the light of long established custom and under the provisions of the Bengal Tenancy Act of 1885, to wastelands, mutation fees, disputes over rights in timber, occupancy rights, exactions and oppression of *amlas*. Peasants also strongly resented interference by the management of bigger zamindars, especially of Darbhanga raj, in what the tenants regarded as their rights.

In 1919–20 a strong agrarian unrest developed in north Bihar. There were peasant protests even before 1919 but they were sporadic, small-scale and localized. The movement in 1919 and 1920 involved a larger number of peasants and covered a wide area. Peasants' campaigns were mainly concentrated in Darbhanga, Champaran, north Bhagalpur, north Monghyr, Muzaffarpur, Samastipur and Purnea. The development of peasant movement owed much to the leadership and organizational skills of Swami Vidyanand, an important peasant activist of Bihar.

The campaign began in June 1919. It was initially concentrated in Darbhanga district, where several meetings were held in the villages of Madhubani subdivision. In Narar village in Khajauli, meetings of peasants were held on 27 to 29 June and were presided over by Jainath Singh of Narar. Vidyanand addressed these gatherings. A large number of peasants from the neighbouring villages attended these meetings.[23] These meetings provided forums to the peasants to air their grievances. Along with addressing the peasants' grievances, the peasant leaders also emphasized the importance of education and the need for the establishment of schools.[24] Following these meetings, petitions were sent to the government. In July, the inhabitants of Narar addressed a petition to the Lieutenant Governor of Bihar and Orissa, which stated that their landlord denied them their customary rights to the fruits and timber of the trees; that mutation fees were charged when their holdings changed hands; that the landlord unjustly resumed some of their lands; that they were forced to supply, without remuneration, labourers, ploughs and carts for the cultivation of the zamindar's land; that the 'well-to-do people of the village', who refused to supply labour and utensils, were denied any grazing land because the former grazing lands were settled for cultivation; and that 'even in days of fearful scarcity' the *amlas* pressurized the vendors of oil and *ghee* to give them a free supply of these commodities.[25] There was also a request in the petition for the appointment of a Commission to look into the peasants' grievances.[26]

This petition was followed by a long series of similar petitions. Many other villages also sent their petitions. The petitions varied in detail but they usually focused on grievances relating to the tenants' rights in trees, the disappearance of grazing lands, the levying of mutation fees, the infringement by the landlord of occupancy rights, and the exaction and oppressions of *amlas*.[27]

Peasant agitation rapidly spread in Darbhanga where Braja Kishore Prasad was very active.[28] The peasants no longer sought the help of the zamindars to settle disputes among them, but resolved them through their panchayats, which were formed in a number of places.[29] In Champaran, tensions mounted over grazing rights. Gorakh Prasad was very active in Champaran.[30]

Vidyanand prepared and printed a pamphlet in which he vividly described the oppression of the Tirhut tenants by the landholders. It also included petitions and memorials, which the tenants had addressed to the Viceroy, the Lieutenant Governor, and other high ranking officials. This pamphlet was circulated not only among the Tirhut tenants but also among the tenants of other districts so as to publicize their grievances and to educate them about their rights and privileges.[31] Vidyanand planned to set up Kisan Sabhas in every district in the province.[32]

The campaign soon spread to other districts and attempts were made to draw peasants of Bhagalpur into the movement. In November 1919, Vidyanand was scheduled to address a meeting in Supaul subdivision of north Bhagalpur, but the officials of the Darbhanga raj, in collusion with the local representatives of the British administration, deterred him from doing so.[33] In December 1919, Vidyanand visited the Sonbarsa area to inquire into the grievances of the local peasants. A campaign was launched against Grant, a European planter and a big landed proprietor of Bhagalpur district.[34] In Alamganj also a campaign built up against the zamindar.[35]

On 25 January 1920, the Bihar Provincial Peasants' Conference was held in Muzaffarpur where a number of resolutions were passed.[36] In February 1920, Vidyanand toured the Supaul subdivision of Bhagalpur and a meeting was held on 5 February which was attended by nearly 20,000 people.[37] A number of demands were put forth at this meeting. The demands were that rents should not be increased in the Permanent Settlement areas, that common grazing lands should be provided in all villages, that peasants should have an unrestricted right to all the trees in their holdings and that peasants should be allowed to build houses and dig wells in their occupancy holdings without taking any permission from the zamindar.[38] By March 1920, peasant protests spread to Purnea and Madhepura.[39]

The peasant movement drew extensive support. Peasants attended the meetings in large numbers. One of the meetings in Darbhanga was attended by around 10,000 people[40] and another meeting in Supaul was attended by around 20,000 people.[41] The support for movement came from a broad spectrum of the peasantry and social hierarchy.[42] Many peasant activists toured different villages. Vidyanand planned to institutionalize peasant activism through the creation of an extensive organization of peasants with branches in every village. However, his plan did not come to fruition.[43]

Apart from addressing meetings, the leaders also made efforts to raise the peasants' problems in other platforms. A large number of tenants of Darbhanga raj attended the Bihar Provincial Conference held at Laheriaserai on 17–18 August 1919. Their spokesperson addressed the assembly enumerating the grievances against the management of the raj and in particular against the assertion by the raj of rights over the timber of trees growing on the tenants' land.[44] A leaflet was circulated at this Conference which highlighted the grievances of the tenants of Pargana Bucchaur of the Darbhanga raj.[45] Accompanied by 200 peasant delegates, Vidyanand attended the Amritsar session of the Congress in December 1919 and voiced the peasants' grievances at this forum. Before attending the Congress session, Vidyanand had met some prominent political leaders in Patna and requested them to take up the grievances of the Tirhut tenants in the Congress session at Amritsar.[46] He also convened a meeting in Bhagalpur district to discuss representations of tenants grievances at this Congress.[47] Vidyanand strongly advocated appropriate representation of the tenants in the Legislative Council so that the amendment of the Bengal Tenancy Act could be pursued in the Council.[48]

The government viewed the emergence of the peasant movement with increasing concern. Echoing the fear, one government report stated, 'Vidyanand's frequent attacks on the police and on European landlords are instigating some villagers to lodge unfounded complaints against the police and their landlords'.[49] The Darbhanga raj expressed apprehensions about the peasant agitation. The administrators of the Darbhanga raj adopted a variety of coercive methods to dissuade people from supporting the movement. They were assisted in their efforts by the police and officials.[50]

It is this strong tradition of peasant agitation that sharpened with its convergence with the Non-Cooperation Movement in Bihar.

Struggle for Regional Autonomy

Another movement that dominated early twentieth-century Bihar was the politics of regional autonomy, the demand for separation of Bihar from Bengal. Bihar had been a part of Bengal Presidency. A strong anger and resentment had been building up in Bihar against Bengal and the Bengali community in Bihar, who were seen as dominating the people of Bihar. The Bengalis, contrary to their small proportion of population in Bihar, held larger share of seats in the provincial and subordinate services, as they were more educated compared to the Biharis. Very few Biharis had taken to English education. By the end of nineteenth century, when the population of Bihar was around twenty million, less than 800 students were enrolled in the six colleges of Bihar. And of these a large proportion of students were Bengalis, while Kayasthas and upper-status Muslims accounted for the rest. The domination of Bengalis in matters of public employment and in the grant of funds for various purposes was highly resented by the Biharis. The movement for separation of Bihar from Bengal underlined the discrimination faced by the Biharis. The movement also stressed that Bihar was ethnically, culturally and linguistically different from Bengal. History was also appropriated to buttress claims for a separate identity. It was argued that administration based in Calcutta would not ensure the interest of Bihar and that the local government in Bihar would be more responsive to the needs of the people of Bihar.[51]

The struggle for the separation of Bihar had begun around 1870. Public associations and newspapers ventilated the grievances of the local people, pointing out the incongruity of the union of Bengal and Bihar, and the adverse effects on the people of Bihar resulting from the union. These bodies played a significant role in the construction and articulation of the separate identity of Bihar.[52]

The first opportunity for raising the demand for a separate state arose in 1894, when the colonial government planned to make territorial rearrangements in the Presidency of Bengal for reducing the administrative burden on the Lieutenant Governor of Bengal. The leaders of the movement argued that the best solution was to separate Bihar, as it was a homogeneous territory and it did not want to be a part of Bengal.[53] The second opportunity arose when the government contemplated the partition of Bengal again for the sake of reducing the administrative burden of Bengal. The leaders repeated the same arguments emphasizing that it would be fair and proper that Bihar be separated rather than that Bengal be divided.[54] They argued that administrative efficiency would improve if the size of the reunified province is reduced and a separate province of Bihar and Orissa is created, rather than partitioning Bengal.[55] In fact, when the Swadeshi Movement was launched in 1905 against the colonial government's proposal of partitioning Bengal, Bihar consciously distanced itself from the Swadeshi Movement. The people in the movement for separation of Bihar did not want to alienate the colonial government by joining swadeshi agitation as they felt the government would not be sympathetic to their cause and that their demands would be neglected. During the swadeshi phase, they continued their agitation for separation and expressed their loyalty towards the government.[56] The British who wanted to consolidate their support amongst the educated sections of Bihar, who had demonstrated their loyalty to British government by refusing to join the nationalist agitation against partition, became somewhat receptive to their ideas. Once the colonial government became sympathetic to their cause, even the big landholders of Bihar, who till then had kept aloof from the separation movement, joined it.[57] Thus, the partition of Bengal brought the support of other sections in the movement, who had earlier distanced themselves from it. The movement, which till then had been dominated by the Hindu educated class, was also joined by the native aristocrats and upper-class Muslims.[58] In 1908, the three leading public associations of Bihar—the Bihar Landholders' Association, the Bihar Provincial Conference, and the Bihar Provincial Muslim League—submitted a joint memorial to the Lieutenant Governor of Bengal, stating the grievances of the 'entire Bihar community'.[59] In 1911 at the Delhi Durbar, the Viceroy annulled partition of Bengal and constituted Bihar and Orissa as a separate province. The seat of government was also transferred from Calcutta to Delhi. A separate Governorship in Council was created to administer the new province of Bihar and Orissa.[60]

In fact, the movement for separation of Bihar had drawn major support from the high caste, middle class and educated elite. For these groups, the creation of the new province signalled fresh opportunities for both private professional advancement and public, social and political activity.[61] The Kayastha community participated in this movement in large numbers and the Bihar Kayastha Provincial Sabha played a leading role.[62] Eminent Muslim lawyers, like Ali Imam and Mazharul Haq, were actively involved. They organized the Bihar Provincial Conference, which, at its first session in Patna in 1906, passed a resolution supporting the separation of Bihar from Bengal.[63] The movement did not have a base among the masses. In fact, the movement had little or no impact on the lives of the vast majority of the inhabitants.[64]

Charting the Terrain of Early Nationalism

The Swadeshi Movement and the Home Rule Movement[65] did not have much impact in Bihar. When Gandhi visited Champaran in 1917, he found 'the Congress practically unknown' in Bihar. Stating the Congress affair in Bihar, Rajendra Prasad, an important nationalist leader from Bihar, said that even those, who had heard the name of the Congress, desisted from joining it or mentioning it.[66] Political activity was largely confined to passing resolutions in Provincial conferences, attending annual sessions of the Congress, contributing to the Congress fund, writing articles in newspapers and participating in debates, and asking questions in the Legislative Council. If public meetings were ever held, they were held in towns, and speeches were usually in English. The Congress was not in touch with the masses.[67] As a party, Congress organization was still loose. There was no constitutional procedure for enrolling Congress members, and anybody who wished to become members of the Congress had simply to declare their intention. If the organization was lax, the claim for different posts in the party structure was practically non-existent. The election of representatives to the Indian National Congress and members of the All India Congress Committee (AICC) depended upon the availability of persons, who would be prepared to serve in these capacities.[68]

Most of the members of the Congress in Bihar were either small zamindars or lawyers. The occupations/professions of delegates from Bihar to the Allahabad Congress Session, 1910, show the social base of the Congress in Bihar:[69]

Occupation(s)	*Number of delegates*
Zamindar	12
Landholder[70]	3
Zamindar and lawyer	6
Banker and zamindar	2
Lawyer	14
Member, Servants of India Society	1
Not known	1
TOTAL	39

The bigger zamindars had kept themselves aloof from the Congress, since they did not want to alienate the government. They did not want to jeopardize their beneficiaries like securing titles and appointments to official positions from the government.[71]

The Rowlatt agitation changed to some extent the prevailing political scenario in Bihar. The call for Rowlatt agitation, the first nation-wide protest, was given by Gandhi in February 1919 against the unpopular legislation that the British threatened to introduce. The bill, known as the Rowlatt Bill, which aimed at severely curtailing the civil liberties of Indians under the guise of curbing violence, was introduced in the Legislative Council. This act of the government was perceived by the Indians as a grievous insult, especially as it came at the end of the First World War when substantial constitutional concessions were expected as India had helped the British in winning the war. Initially, constitutional methods of protest were resorted to but when such protest did not have the desired effect, Gandhi mooted the idea of satyagraha. The form of protest finally agreed upon was the observance of a nationwide hartal, along with fasting and prayer. In addition, it was decided that civil disobedience would be offered against specific laws. It was agreed that the satyagraha would be launched in April 1919. Satyagraha Sabhas were set up to campaign against the bill. The members of the Satyagraha Sabha took a pledge to disobey the act and to court arrest and imprisonment.[72]

However, even before the Satyagraha Week, protest against the Rowlatt Bill was mounted in Bihar. A meeting was held in the Town Hall in Patna on 16 February 1919, and around 200 people, including leading pleaders and zamindars, attended it. Resolutions were passed opposing the bill.[73] Protest meetings were held in Muzaffarpur on 16 February 1919[74] and in Mansurganj on 27 February 1919.[75] In Bettiah Estate in Champaran, bazaars remained closed on 6 February 1919 as a mark of protest.[76] In Monghyr and Chapra, protest meetings were organized.[77] A huge mass meeting was held at the Qilla Ground in Patna City on 23 February and people came from as distant place as Gaya to attend the meeting.[78] A protest meeting was organized in Gaya on 22 February.[79] The Bihar Provincial Association and the Bihar Provincial Congress Committee (BPCC) held a joint meeting in Bankipore on 2 March to protest against the bill. Zamindars and lawyers were present at this meeting in large numbers.[80]

The Rowlatt agitation had a strong impact in Patna.[81] On 4 April at a meeting in Patna City, which was attended by around 10,000 people, it was decided to participate in the hartal on 6 April to mark the day as that of 'humiliation and prayer'.[82] Rajendra Prasad, Mazharul Haq, Rai Bahadur Purnendu Narain Sinha and Hasan Imam addressed this meeting. According to an official report, this meeting was attended by a large number of 'baniyas, shopkeepers and labourers'.[83] Another mass meeting was held in the evening of 5 April at the residence of Mazharul Haq to outline the programme for 6 April. Around 3,000 people, including a large number of students, 'baniyas' and shopkeepers, were present at that meeting.[84] Hindu-Muslim unity was emphasized in these meetings.[85]

In all these meetings, the leaders exhorted 'Indians to awaken from the slumber and work for the good of the country, and [to] no longer remain the slaves of Europeans'.[86] While addressing the meeting held at the residence of Mazharul Haq on 5 April, one of the leaders said:

> Indians were the sons of heroes and it was not proper for them to sleep, when the foreigners were enjoying all the benefits of their country. India was the birthplace of Rishis and heroes like Buddha, whose followers the Japanese had taught a lesson to the Russians during the late Russo-Japanese War. Indians, who were once reckoned to be great heroes, were now becoming slaves of Europe. Foreigners were sucking their blood, while they were sleeping.[87]

On 6 April, almost all the shops in Bankipore and Patna City remained closed, and all business, including traffic, was suspended.[88] Two arches were erected near the chauk in Patna. Since the early hours of 6 April people of all classes walked bareheaded and barefooted to the ghat. They carried with them

Bande Mataram flags and shouted slogans such as *Bande Mataram*, *Ram Chandra ki jai*, *Mahabir ki jai* and *Mahatma Gandhi ki jai*. After bathing in the Ganga, they offered prayers at various temples for deliverance from the difficulties which had befallen them following the enactment of the Rowlatt Act. Muslims also offered prayers in various mosques. Most of the Hindus and Muslims observed fast. So did most of the students. At 4 p.m., a procession was taken out to the Villa. The people in the procession throughout kept shouting *Bande Mataram*, *Shri Ram Chandra ki jai*, *Mahabir ki jai*, *Mahatma ki jai*, and *Allah-o-Akbar*. According to a government report, nearly 75,000 people participated in the procession.[89] Most of the students of Patna were present in the meeting and took part in other celebrations of the day. A large number of people from the *mufassil* were also present. A large number of Marwaris of the city too participated in these activities. Proscribed literature was hawked and unregistered newspapers sold.[90]

Satyagraha Day was observed in other places as well.[91] In Bihar Sharif, all shops remained closed. Large number of people kept fast. A mass meeting was held, attended by around 1,500 people, which included both Hindus and Muslims. Both communities participated in the prayer of Maghrib Namaz and the *havan puja* at Dhaneshwar Ghat. They paid their homage to Bari Dargah, the tomb of Makdum Sharfuddin.[92] Satyagraha was observed in some of the villages of Bihar Sharif as well.[93] In Hajipur, a meeting was held and around 3,000 people attended it. This place had not witnessed such a big meeting before. In fact, most places had not witnessed such large meetings before. Lalganj, Mahnar, Bhagwanpur, Sarai and nearly all the important villages in the interior of Hajipur observed satyagraha. All the shops were closed and business remained suspended. People from all sections of society observed satyagraha.[94] In Muzaffarpur, all shops and businesses remained closed. Shops near the railway station and the dharamshala too remained closed. Not even eatables including fish, meat and vegetables were available. No hackney and *ekka* plied. A mass meeting was held on the ground of Town Hall and 20,000 people from all classes attended it. The people were bareheaded and barefooted.[95] Satyagraha was observed in Chapra and shops remained closed in Sahibganj, Katra and other places. A large procession under the leadership of Mahatma Kirpa Ramji marched to Sarju River. The numbers swelled to thousands as the procession reached the river bank where prayers were offered and the leaders addressed them. After taking a dip in the river, a general prayer was again offered. Later, the procession, shouting slogans like *Bharat Mata ki jai*, marched through Sahibganj and Dahiawan to Datra Bazaar.[96] In Danapur, shops in the town, Nizamat and Cantonment remained closed. *Ekkawalas* (coach driver) and *ghariwals* (vehicle driver) did not ply. Even farmers suspended their activities. All commercial activity came to a halt. In the morning, a large number of people went to the Digha Ghat and in the evening, a meeting was held on the river bank.[97] In Buxar, a mass meeting was held near the chauk, which was attended by a large number of Mahajans and Marwaris.[98] In Fatwah, many women observed a fast and after bathing in the Ganga offered prayers to the sun god for protection of their sons and husbands from the impending disaster.[99] In Gaya, people observed fast and offered prayers at the Vishnupad Temple after bathing in the Phalgu River. Many women of 'respectable families' also observed the fast.[100] In Jharia, 5,000 people attended the protest meeting.[101] At Bakhara in Muzaffarpur, shops remained closed and the 'leading men' of the village delivered speeches in various areas.[102] In Motihari, the market remained closed but the tehsildars of Bettiah Estate and Motihari factory, aided and abetted by the police, threatened the shopkeepers to open their shops. Despite these threats the shops remained closed.[103] Ranchi was also strongly affected by the Satyagraha Movement and groups of young men went all around Ranchi shouting *Gandhiji ki jai*.[104] A meeting was held at Siwan in Saran on 21 April and nearly 2,000 people of Siwan and the neighbouring villages attended it.[105] A meeting was organized in the interior of Shahabad district to further the satyagraha agitation against the Rowlatt Bill. Under the leadership of Mithila Saran Singh a satyagraha meeting was held at Massaurhi in Patna district.[106] One sanyasi from Punjab was active in Barharwa; explaining satyagraha to people, who travelled in steamers.[107] At a public meeting in Bhagalpur in May 1919, the Bihar Landholders' Association and the Domiciled Bengali Association voiced their protest against the bill.[108]

Many people, including students, affixed their signature to the satyagraha vow.[109] Prominent among them were Mazharul Haq, Parmeshwar Lal, Chandrabansi Sahay, Nageshwar Prasad Singh, Syed Hasan Imam, Braja Kishore Prasad, Rajendra Prasad and Devaki Prasad Sinha.[110] Many people in Patna, Arrah and Gaya, which included students, pleaders, mukhtars, and vakils, signed the pledge.[111]

The Rowlatt agitation marked the beginning of different political era. It heralded to some extent a change in the social base of the Congress. From around 1919, the membership of the Congress organization broadened. Merchants and businessmen, particularly Marwaris, began to participate in the movement. Rich peasants and small landlords were also associating with the Congress.[112] In one of the government reports it was recorded how 'the local zamindars were anxious to know particulars regarding the act and were under the impression that some great *zulum* had been done'.[113] A large number of lawyers and students played an active role in the movement.[114] Despite the widening of the Congress base, the movement was largely confined to urban centres. In urban centres, the lower middle class and artisans played a more active role than did the industrial workers.[115] The leadership of the Congress continued to be dominated by the upper, highly educated strata of society. These leaders had taken recourse to the constitutional methods of agitation.[116] The big landholding section had not only kept itself aloof from the movement but the Bihar Landholders' Association, in a meeting held at Patna on May 1919 presided by Darbhanga Maharaj, condemned passive resistance and asked the people to cooperate with the government in maintaining law and order.[117]

The Khilafat Movement

In this section is given a brief account of the impact of Khilafat Movement in Bihar. Khilafat Movement, initiated by the Muslims in 1919, was against the adverse terms imposed on the Ottomon Empire (Turkey) by Britain and its allies after Turkey had been defeated in the First World War. Britain and its allies partitioned Turkey and took away Thrace from Turkey proper. This was in violation of the earlier pledge of the British Premier, Llyod George, who had declared, during the First World War, that they were not fighting to deprive Turkey of the rich and renowned lands of Asia Minor and Thrace, which were predominantly Turkish race-wise.[118] The Sultan of Turkey was also the Khalifa, i.e. the temporal and spiritual head of Muslims of the world. After the war, he was deprived of his Khalifadom, and he could no longer exercise control over his empire's holy places. All this enraged the Muslims and their discontentment led to the Khilafat Movement.[119]

A Khilafat Committee was formed under the leadership of the Ali brothers, Maulana Azad, Hakim Ajmal Khan and Hasrat Mohani, and a country-wide agitation was organized.[120] Branches of the Khilafat were established all over India to act as a pressure group for securing the retention of the temporal powers of the Sultan of Turkey as Khalifa and ensuring his continued suzerainty over the Islamic holy places. Resolutions opposing the dismemberment of Turkey and the Khilafat were passed.[121] In Bihar also a Khilafat Committee had been formed, which worked in close association with the Congress. Mazharul Haq, Abdul Sami, Ghulam Imam and Narul Hasan played an active role in the movement in Bihar.[122]

17 October 1919 was observed as an All India Khilafat Day. On this day, all business came to a halt. Prayers were offered for the safety and preservation of the integrity, dignity and power of the Turkish Empire and Khilafat of the Sultan of Turkey.[123] Khilafat Day was observed at many places in Bihar. The hartal in Patna was very successful. It brought business to a halt.[124] Most of the shops in Patna City and suburbs remained closed. In the evening, a mass

meeting was held on the grounds of the Madrasa mosque which was presided over by Nawab Sarfaraz Hussain Khan. A large number of Muslims, Hindus and Sikhs attended the meeting. Hafiz Ahmad Ghani led the prayer. A resolution was passed to maintain the honour and integrity of the Khilafat.[125]

In Darbhanga also all business was suspended. Even the butchers restrained from slaughtering and the *thika garis* (cart carriages) stopped plying. In the evening a public meeting was held in the precincts of the Darbhanga Trading Company, which was attended by around 6,000 people, and in it was passed many resolutions.[126] Muslims offered prayers at the Idgah, Killaghat and Badshai mosques and Hindus offered prayers at various temples.[127]

Gaya, Bihar Sharif, Chapra, Monghyr, Ranchi and Bhagalpur—all observed Khilafat Day. Both Hindus and Muslims took part in the agitation in large numbers and resolved unanimously to maintain the honour and integrity of the Khilafat.[128] In Bihar Sharif, a public meeting was organized after the Juma prayer. Nearly a thousand Muslims offered the Juma prayer. In Bhagalpur, a large number of Muslims kept fast. There was a public meeting after the Juma prayer at the Talarpur mosque. In Phulwari Sharif, men and women kept fast and recited the Koran. Shops remained closed and, after the Juma prayer, a mass meeting was organized which was attended by a large number of maulanas and priests. Shops remained closed. A large number of Muslims offered prayers in mosques for the protection of the Khalifa. Prayers were offered in such remote places as Gudri and Salempore. In Gaya, shopkeepers, businessmen and legal practitioners suspended their business. Many Hindus and Muslims observed fast. In the afternoon, more than 2,000 Muslims assembled at the Jama Masjid to offer prayer. This was followed by a public meeting which was attended by a large number of Hindus as well.[129]

In November 1919, a call was given by Gandhi to boycott the peace celebrations following the treaty of the First World War as a protest against the British government's betrayal of Muslim sentiments.[130] Meetings were held at many places in Bihar and several resolutions were passed, seeking an honourable peace settlement with Turkey and integrity of the Khilafat and holy places of Arabia. Mazharul Haq, Hasan Imam and Wasi Ahmed were the main organizers of the anti-peace celebration and the Khilafat agitation.[131] Leaflets and posters issued by the Delhi Anti-Peace Celebration Publicity Board and the Calcutta Khilafat Committee were distributed.[132] A public meeting was held on 30 November 1919 at the Anjuman Islamia Hall in Patna, which was presided by Maulana Shah Rasheedul Haque. A large number of Hindus and Muslim leaders were present in this meeting.[133] Maulana Shah Suleman reiterated Gandhi's appeal not to participate in any celebration of victory or peace.[134] Hasan Imam thanked the Hindus for their support. Sarfaraz Hussain Khan added that the Muslims could not rejoice, when their Khalifa was in distress. A large number of maulanas were present in this meeting.[135] M.A. Jinnah, S.A. Sami, Mazharul Haq and Hasan Imam resigned from the Peace Celebration Committee in protest, stating that they could not observe the death anniversary of the Khalifa.[136] In Patna, Vidyanand was actively involved in the anti-peace celebrations.[137] The lawyers in Patna boycotted the celebration.[138]

In Ranchi, the Muslim community did not participate in the celebrations. Their houses were not illuminated and their boys did not take part in the school sports. Many shops remained closed. On the night of 14 November, the Muslims went round the bazaar telling the people of their grievances and asking them to boycott the celebrations. Though 13 December was a holiday at the Madrasa, the students attended the school wearing black bands on their arms. The government attributed the success of the programme to Maulana Abul Kalam Azad, who had considerable influence in Ranchi.[139] Anti-peace celebrations were observed by both Hindus and Muslims in Bhagalpur, Monghyr, Madhubani, Darbhanga and Muzaffarpur.[140] In Gaya in a mass meeting, attended by thousands of people, it was resolved not to participate in peace celebrations.[141] The lawyers of Gaya boycotted the celebrations.[142] The police in Gaya took strong action and searched many places and seized Khilafat posters.[143]

It was decided that the second Khilafat Day and an all-India protest against the dismemberment of Turkey would be held on 19 March 1920. This day was observed as the day of 'National Mourning'—a day of fasting, prayer and hartal.[144] Hartals and meetings were held all over Bihar. Resolutions were passed which stated explicitly that Hindus and Muslims recognized the Sultan of Turkey as the Khalifa and that for Muslim loyalty it was imperative that the peace terms with the Sultan of Turkey be strictly in accordance with the injunctions of Islam. In Arrah, prayers were offered and shops remained closed and a meeting was held, which was addressed by Motilal Nehru and C.R. Das. In Pachamba, too, shops remained closed and business was suspended. The meeting in Pachamba was attended by a large number of Hindus and Muslims. A large number of labourers of the neighbouring coal mines did not work. Chapra witnessed a complete hartal and the Hindus joined the prayer at the Jama mosque (known also as Kazi Saheb's mosque) after the Juma prayer. A special meeting was organized in the Chainpur Haat. A large meeting was held in Bhagalpur which was attended by over 10,000 people. All shops were closed and business came to a halt. The Muslims in Gaya, numbering around 5,000, offered prayers at the Jama Masjid. Krishna Prakash Sen Sinha presided over a mass meeting of around 25,000 people. In

Barh, even the title holders and Honorary Magistrates participated in the meeting. A mass meeting was held in a mosque in Madhepura. Aurangabad, Giridih and Hazaribagh also observed Khilafat Day. In Bihar Sharif, prayers were offered in all the temples and mosques. Business came to a halt in Sabzi Bazaar in Bihar Sharif. Nearly 2,500 people attended the meeting in Daltonganj. In Muzaffarpur, printed notices, signed by 'leading' Muslims and Hindus, were issued giving a call for the hartal. All shops remained closed. Even articles like vegetables, meat and fish were not available. Hackney carriages and *ekka* ceased to ply and the *golas* (rice market) were shut. The meeting at Muzaffarpur was attended by almost 10,000 people.[145] The hartal was very successful in Patna where Md. Sami, the Secretary of the Provincial Khilafat Committee, played a leading role.[146] Khilafat Day was observed in Ranchi and Darbhanga, where meetings were held and resolutions passed against the peace terms.[147]

In April 1920, Shaukat Ali visited Bihar at the invitation of the Khilafat leaders, Mazharul Haq, Dr Mahmud and Md. Sami.[148] Shaukat Ali, while addressing meetings on 24 and 25 April in Patna, told the government to resolve the Turkish issue on honourable terms and warned that if it failed to do so the Muslims would boycott and non-cooperate with the government. He also gave indication of resorting to Hijrat and Jihad.[149] Maulavi Narul Hasan, a lawyer of the Patna High Court, also gave a stirring speech. Shaukat Ali visited Gaya and Monghyr, addressing large meetings.[150] At the meeting in Gaya, Krishna Prakash Sen Sinha announced that he had returned to the Collector his certificate of honour, which was granted to him in recognition of his services for recruitment during the war.[151] At these meetings, Hindu-Muslim unity was emphasized and the Hindus were thanked for their support and the Muslims were advised to abstain from cow slaughter. Shaukat Ali addressed a meeting of over 5,000 people in Monghyr on 27 April. He expressed apprehension that if the Khilafat question was not resolved, Muslims, would be reduced to slaves. He urged young Muslims to follow the mandate of God and declare Jihad if the demands of the Indian Muslims were not met.[152] In Patna, Shah Badaruddin renounced his title of Shamsul-Ulema as a mark of protest.[153]

The turning point in the Khilafat Movement came with the publication of very harsh terms of the Treaty of Sevres with Turkey on 14 May 1920. The Treaty of Sevres made it amply clear that the dismemberment of the Turkish Empire was complete.[154] This further intensified Muslims' anger. After this, the nationalist leaders seriously considered the idea of non-cooperating with the government. One of the strong proponents of non-cooperation was Gandhi who was sympathetic to the Khilafat cause and was in close touch with the Khilafat leaders. In fact, Gandhi looked upon the Khilafat agitation as a golden opportunity for cementing Hindu-Muslim unity and drawing the Muslim masses into the national movement.[155] Early in 1920, he had declared that the Khilafat issue overshadowed that of the constitutional reforms and the Punjab wrongs, and announced that he would lead a movement of non-cooperation, if the terms of peace with Turkey did not satisfy the Indian Muslims.[156] Soon, Gandhi became one of the leaders of the Khilafat Movement.[157]

A conference of the Ulemas was held at Phulwari in Patna on 15 and 16 May 1920. Maulana Azad Sobhani, Maulana Abdul Bari, Hasrat Mohani and Shah Mohiuddin were among those who spoke in the conference. Maulana Kadir Azad Sobhani, Maulana Abdul Mazid and the Ulema from Kanpur and Mathura also attended the conference, in which it was resolved to continue the movement for another six months.[158] On 5 June 1920, Abdul Sami, Khwaja Abdul Majid and Syed Mahmud organized a mass meeting at Bankipore Maidan to offer prayers for the success of the movement.[159] Maulvi Etmad Hussain and Pesh Imam of Bakerganj mosque attended the meeting.[160] A signature campaign to present a memorandum to the Viceroy was organized in Patna, Monghyr, Gaya, Bhagalpur and Muzaffarpur. Anti-government leaflets and booklets were distributed throughout the province.[161] Maulana Shah Badruddin prepared a *fatwa* appealing to the Muslims of Bihar to follow non-cooperation and to renounce all titles and honours bestowed upon them by the government.[162] On the Id day printed leaflets and posters sent by the Central Khilafat Committee of Bombay stating the Muslims' obligations to the Khilafat and appealing to them for funds were distributed in Patna. Ghulam Imam of Patna City delivered speeches at various places, advocating non-cooperation and condemning the peace terms.[163] Maulvi Zamir-ud-din Haidar, the Honorary Magistrate of Gaya district, resigned from his post.[164]

On 9 June 1920, the Khilafat Committee at Allahabad unanimously accepted the suggestion of non-cooperation and asked Gandhi to lead the movement.[165] A four-stage non-cooperation was announced which included boycott of titles, civil services, police and army, and non-payment of taxes. Gandhi began to press the Congress to launch a similar campaign around three issues—the Punjab wrong, the Khilafat wrong, and Swaraj.[166] In July, Shaukat Ali wrote a letter to the Bihar Provincial Khilafat Committee, urging it to mobilize people for active and all-out non-cooperation. The Bihar Provincial Khilafat Committee met at Patna to discuss this letter and decided to give full support to the movement.[167] A meeting was held at the Madrasa mosque in Patna City on 25 July 1920, where Mazharul Haq, Rajendra Prasad and others explained the principles and ideas of non-cooperation and of the Khilafat Movement.[168] Mohammad Shafi undertook a tour of Muzaffarpur district during which he explained to the people the scheme of non-cooperation.[169] In Bhagalpur, the Khilafat Committee met at the residence of

Deep Narayan Singh to discuss issues related to the Khilafat and non-cooperation.[170] On 30 July 1920, at a meeting in Patna conducted by Mazharul Haq full faith was reposed in Gandhi.[171] The next day, the BPCC appointed a committee comprising Mazharul Haq, Hasan Imam, Ganesh Datta, Rajendra Prasad, and Ayudhya Prasad, and the committee adopted the programme of non-cooperation as the only way for the redressal of Muslim grievances.[172]

The Khilafat Committee formally inaugurated non-cooperation on the Khilafat Day on 1 August 1920. A hartal was observed in the entire province.[173] A public meeting was held in the Madrasa mosque in Patna City under Mazharul Haq who explained the purpose of non-cooperation and urged the people to maintain national unity.[174] Around 2,000 people, many of them from nearby villages, attended the meeting. A large number of people from educated sections from Bankipore, Phulwari and Patna City, students and 'bazaar people' also attended that meeting.[175] Meetings were also held in Muzaffarpur and Darbhanga.[176] A hartal was observed in Arrah, Chapra, Monghyr, Bhagalpur, Ranchi, Gaya, Palamau, Hazaribagh and Daltonganj.[177] On 4 August, Maulana Atanullah of Amritsar delivered a speech at Mazharul Haq's house in Patna. Around 500 people attended the meeting amongst whom a large number were local students.[178]

Resignations of titles and honorary offices were announced on Khilafat Day. Shah Badruddin Saheb of Phulwari renounced the title of Shams-ul-ulema, Nurul Hasan resigned from his membership of the Provincial Legislative Council and he appealed to his countrymen to follow suit. Maulana Shah Suleman of Phulwari relinquished his honorary magistracy's position.[179] In Monghyr, Muhammad Zubair, a leading barrister, gave up his lucrative practice at the bar.[180]

What was called 'Bihar mourning' was observed after Tilak's death. On 6 August, a procession led by Mazharul Haq, Rajendra Prasad, Hasan Imam and Nurul Hasan was taken out in Patna to mourn Tilak's death. In this procession the people joined in bare head and foot.[181] There was mourning in other places in Bihar and the people pledged to follow non-cooperation.[182] The Tilak Memorial Committee, comprising Mazharul Haq, Hasan Imam, Sarfaraz Hussain, Ganesh Dutta, Rajendra Prasad and others, was set up to collect funds.[183] In Gaya, Abu Mohammad Hasan resigned from his post of Honorary Magistrate, and Malik Mukhatar renounced his title and honour.[184]

In August 1920, many Muslims migrated from the British Raj to Darul-Islam (Afghanistan) under the Hijrat Scheme.[185] On 15 August 1920, a meeting was convened at the house of Mazharul Haq to form the Hijrat Committee with Shah Mohiuddin as its president. The objective of the committee was to enable Muslims to migrate to Afghanistan.[186] To maintain unity and co-operation, Maulana Shah Suleman urged the Muslims not to slaughter cows on the eve of Bakr Eid. In Gaya, Maulvi Fazlur Rahman and Khwaja Mohammad Noor also exhorted the people to stop cow sacrifice and maintain communal unity.[187] Mazharul Haq announced his withdrawal from the Council election and his letter of resignation published in the *Searchlight* on 19 September declared:

> I, as a Mussalman, can never cooperate with the government, which was bent upon destroying Islam. As an Indian, I cannot work with the government, whose hands were stained with the blood of many countrymen of the Punjab.[188]

A large number of students, including Mohammad Sher, Abdul Bari and Mohammad Saqi, who became active in later Bihar politics, left schools and colleges. Several of them did not sit for their final metric examination. Maulana Shah Badruddin and Syed Ali Nabi renounced the title of Khan Bahadur. As many as 44 lawyers gave up their legal practice, half of them were Muslims.[189] Students of Nurul Huda also left school and expressed their desire to serve the Khilafat cause.[190] Khilafat meetings were held in Sitamarhi, Giridih, Monghyr, Fatwah, Kako, Sasaram, Champaran, Gaya, Muzaffarpur and Bhagalpur, where people in large numbers adopted the principle of non-cooperation.[191]

Mazharul Haq and others undertook an extensive tour of Bihar and Orissa, and delivered stirring speeches on non-cooperation and the Khilafat agitation.[192] At a meeting in Hilsa on 27 October 1920, Shah Ghafoor compared Mazharul Haq with Lord Krishna. He said that as 'Lord Krishna was born at the time of distress, similarly Mazharul Haq was born to help us in trouble'.[193]

The Congress became sceptical of any possibility of political advance through constitutional means and seriously considered the option of non-cooperating with the government. When the Congress met in September 1920 at Calcutta, it accepted non-cooperation as its own programme and, once the Non-Cooperation Movement gained momentum in Bihar, the Khilafat Movement merged with it. The Non-Cooperation Movement would mark the shift in political base and character of the movement.

Notes

1. Nirmal Sengupta, 'Agrarian Movements in Bihar', in *Agrarian Movements in India: Studies on 20th Century Bihar*, ed. Arvind N. Das, London: Frank Cass, 1982, p. 16.
2. Ibid., p. 17.
3. Ibid.

4. F.R. Frankel, 'Caste, Land and Dominance in Bihar: Breakdown of the Brahmanical Social Order', in *Dominance and State Power in Modern India: Decline of a Social Order*, vol. I, eds. F.R. Frankel and M.S.A. Rao, New Delhi: Oxford University Press, 1989, p. 46.
5. A. George Grierson, *A Bihar Peasant Life*, Patna: Supdt., Govt. Printing, 1926, p. 326.
6. Frankel, 'Caste, Land and Dominance in Bihar', p. 55.
7. Sengupta, 'Agrarian Movements in Bihar', p.17.
8. Ibid., p.14; Frankel, 'Caste, Land and Dominance in Bihar', p. 54.
9. Kaushal Kishore Sharma, *Agrarian Movements and Congress Politics in Bihar,* New Delhi: Anamika, 1989, p. 17.
10. Sengupta, 'Agrarian Movements in Bihar', p.18.
11. Ibid., p. 20; Sharma, *Agrarian Movements and Congress Politics,* pp. 22–3; Arvind N. Das, *Agrarian Unrest and Socio-Economic Changes in Bihar, 1900–1980,* New Delhi: Manohar, 1983, p.198.
12. Sengupta, 'Agrarian Movements in Bihar', pp. 18–19.
13. Ibid, p. 19; Das, *Agrarian Unrest and Socio-Economic Changes in Bihar,* p. 44.
14. Ibid.
15. Frankel, 'Caste, Land and Dominance in Bihar', pp. 59–66.
16. Manoshi Mitra, 'A Review of the Role of Zamindars in Bihar vis-à-vis the Agrarian Economy', in *Proceedings of the Indian History Congress,* 37th Session, Calicut, 1976, special issue, papers presented by teachers and research students of the University of Delhi, pp. 114–29.
17. Sengupta, 'Agrarian Movements in Bihar', p.19.
18. Stephen Henningham, *Peasant Movements in Colonial India, North Bihar, 1917–42,* Canberra: Australian National University, 1984, p. 71.
19. Sharma, *Agrarian Movements and Congress Politics,* pp. 29–30.
20. Henningham, *Peasant Movements in Colonial India,* p. 71.
21. Sharma, *Agrarian Movements and Congress Politics,* p. 37.
22. This paragraph and the next are based on Henningham's *Peasant Movements in Colonial India,* pp. 70–89.
23. Bihar and Orissa Police Abstract of Intelligence, 1919, 5.7.1919, Bihar State Archives (hereafter BSA).
24. Ibid.
25. Fortnightly Report of Bihar and Orissa for the first half of October 1919, Home Department (Political) File no. 14/1919, National Archives of India (hereafter NAI), 'Copy of note by the Criminal Investigation Department on Kisan Sabhas'.
26. Fortnightly Report of Bihar and Orissa for the second half of November 1919, Home Department (Political) File no. 5/November/1919, NAI.
27. Henningham, *Peasant Movements in Colonial India,* p. 75.
28. Fortnightly Report of Bihar and Orissa for the first half of September 1919, Home Department (Political) File no. 59/ September/1919, NAI.
29. Bihar and Orissa Police Abstract of Intelligence, 1919, 28.10.1919, BSA.
30. Fortnightly Report of Bihar and Orissa for the first half of September 1919, Home Department (Political) File no. 59/1919, NAI.
31. Bihar and Orissa Police Abstract of Intelligence, 1919, 13.12.1919, BSA.

32. Ibid.
33. Henningham, *Peasant Movements in Colonial India,* p. 76.
34. Fortnightly Report of Bihar and Orissa for the second half of December 1919, Home Department (Political) File no. 44/1919, NAI.
35. Ibid.
36. Fortnightly Report of Bihar and Orissa for the first half of February 1920, Home Department (Political) File no. 88/February/1920, NAI.
37. Ibid.
38. Ibid.
39. Fortnightly Report of Bihar and Orissa for the first half of March 1920, Home Department (Political) File no. 90/March/1920, NAI.
40. Henningham, *Peasant Movements in Colonial India,* p. 79
41. Fortnightly Report of Bihar and Orissa for the first half of February 1920, Home Department (Political) File no. 88/1920, NAI.
42. Henningham, *Peasant Movements in Colonial India,* p. 81.
43. Bihar and Orissa Police Abstract of Intelligence 1919, 13.12.1919, BSA.
44. Fortnightly Report of Bihar and Orissa for the second half of August 1919, Home Department (Political) File no. 44/August/1919, NAI.
45. Ibid.
46. Bihar and Orissa Police Abstract of Intelligence, 1919, 13.12.1919, BSA.
47. Fortnightly Report of Bihar and Orissa for the first half of January 1920, Home Department (Political) File no. 41/January/1919, NAI.
48. Bihar and Orissa Police Abstract of Intelligence, 1919, 22.11.1919, BSA.
49. Fortnightly Report of Bihar and Orissa for the second half of June 1920, Home Department (Political) File no. 97/1920, NAI.
50. Henningham, *Peasant Movements in Colonial India,* p. 85.
51. Narendra Jha, *Aspects of Regional Consciousness in Bihar, 1870–1912,* M.Phil. dissertation, Jawahar Lal University, 1991.
52. Ibid., pp. 65–74.
53. Ibid., pp. 81–91.
54. Ibid., pp. 91–112.
55. Ibid., pp. 92, 96.
56. V.C.P. Chaudhary, *The Creation of Modern Bihar,* Patna: Yugeshwar Prakashan, 1964, p. 91; Jha, *Aspects of Regional Consciousness in Bihar,* p. 97.
57. Frankel, 'Caste, Land and Dominance in Bihar', pp. 64–5.
58. Chaudhary, *The Creation of Modern Bihar,* p. 91; Jha, *Aspects of Regional Consciousness in Bihar,* p. 97.
59. Ibid., pp. 103–13.
60. Frankel, 'Caste, Land and Dominance in Bihar', pp. 64–5.
61. Chaudhary, *The Creation of Modern Bihar,* pp. 200–5.
62. Frankel, 'Caste, Land and Dominance in Bihar', p. 64.
63. Ibid.
64. Henningham, *Peasant Movements in Colonial India,* p. 93; F. Tomasson Jannuzi, *Agrarian Crisis in India, The Case of Bihar,* Austin: University of Texas Press, 1974, pp. 107–16.

65. K.K. Datta, *History of the Freedom Movement in Bihar,* vol. I, Patna: Bihar Government Press, 1957, pp. 112–16.
66. Mahatma Gandhi, *Autobiography or Stories of My Experiments with Truth,* Ahmedabad: Navajivan, 1927, p. 411; Ramashray Roy, *Study of the Bihar Pradesh Congress Committee,* University of California, Berkeley, Ph.D. thesis, 1966, pp. 93–4.
67. Rajendra Prasad, *Bapu Ke Qadmon Me,* Aligarh: Anjuman Taraqqui Urdu, 1954, pp. 74, 95.
68. Prasad, *Autobiography,* p. 51.
69. Datta, *History of the Freedom Movement in Bihar,* pp. 526–31
70. The term 'landholder' is generally used as a synonym for a tenant or to refer to a lessee or proprietary rights. In this instance it probably refers to lessees.
71. Frankel, 'Caste, Land and Dominance in Bihar', p. 67.
72. Ravinder Kumar, ed., *Essays on Gandhian Politics: The Rowlatt Satyagraha of 1919,* London: Oxford University Press, 1971, pp. 1–4.
73. Bihar and Orissa Police Abstract of Intelligence, 1919, 17.2.1919, BSA.
74. Ibid.; *Searchlight,* 23 February 1919.
75. Bihar and Orissa Police Abstract of Intelligence, 1919, 28.2.1919, BSA.
76. Ibid.
77. *Searchlight,* 23 February 1919.
78. Ibid., 27 February 1919.
79. Ibid.
80. Ibid., 6 March 1919.
81. Freedom Movement Papers, SCRO 57, BSA, 'Note on Satyagraha, DIG to Commissioner, 6 April 1919'.
82. *Searchlight,* 6 April 1919.
83. Freedom Movement Papers, SCRO 57, BSA, 'DSP, Patna City to SP, Patna, 5 April 1919'.
84. Ibid.; *Searchlight,* 6 April 1919.
85. Freedom Movement Papers, SCRO 57, BSA, 'Note on Satyagraha, DIG to Commissioner, 6 April 1919'.
86. Ibid.
87. Ibid.
88. *Searchlight,* 10 April 1919.
89. Freedom Movement Papers, SCRO 57, 'Satyagraha Movement'.
90. Ibid.; *Searchlight,* 10 April 1919.
91. Ibid.
92. Ibid.
93. Ibid.
94. Ibid.
95. Ibid.
96. Ibid.
97. Ibid.
98. Ibid.
99. Ibid.

100. Ibid.
101. Ibid.
102. Ibid.
103. Ibid.
104. Ibid., 26 April 1919.
105. Ibid., 19 April 1919.
106. Bihar and Orissa Police Abstract of Intelligence, 1919, 12.4.1919, BSA.
107. Fortnightly Report of Bihar and Orissa for the first half of May 1919, Home Department (Political) File no. 48/1919, NAI.
108. *Searchlight,* 8 May 1919.
109. Bihar and Orissa Police Abstract of Intelligence, 1919, 17.5.1919, BSA.
110. *Searchlight,* 1 April 1919.
111. Ibid., 9 March 1919.
112. Rajendra Prasad, *Mahatma Gandhi and Bihar: Some Reminiscences*, Bombay: Hind Kitab Limited, 1949, p. 75; G. McDonald, 'Unity on Trial: Congress in Bihar, 1919–39', in *Congress and the Raj: Facets of the Indian Struggle, 1917–1947,* ed. D.A. Low, London: Arnold-Heinemann, 1977, pp. 293–4.
113. Bihar and Orissa Police Abstract of Intelligence, 1919, 24.5.1919, BSA.
114. Freedom Movement Papers, SCRO 57, BSA.
115. Ibid.
116. Roy, *Study of the Bihar Pradesh Congress Committee*, pp. 96–7.
117. Fortnightly Report of Bihar and Orissa for the first half of May 1919, Home Department (Political) File no. 48/1919, NAI.
118. B. Pittabhi Sitaramayya, *History of the Indian National Congress, 1885–1935,* Bombay: Padma Publications, 1946, pp. 318–19.
119. Gail Minault, *The Khilafat Movement: Religious Symbolism and Political Mobilisation in India,* New Delhi: Oxford University Press, 1982, p. 74.
120. *The Indian Annual Register,* 1919, p. 250.
121. Minault, *The Khilafat Movement,* p. 74.
122. Muzaffar Imam, *Role of Muslims in the National Movement, 1912–1930, A Study of Bihar,* New Delhi: Mittal Publications, 1987, pp. 128, 131.
123. *Searchlight,* 16 October 1919.
124. Ibid., 19 October 1919.
125. Fortnightly Report of Bihar and Orissa for the second half of November 1919, Home Department (Political) File no. 5/Novement/1919, NAI; *Searchlight,* 19 and 23 October 1919.
126. Fortnightly Report of Bihar and Orissa for the second half of October 1919, Home Department (Political) File no. 16/October/1919, NAI; *Searchlight,* 23 October 1919.
127. Bihar and Orissa Police Abstract of Intelligence, 1919, 25.10.1919, BSA; *Searchlight,* 23 October 1919.
128. Ibid.
129. Ibid.
130. Ibid., 6 November 1919.
131. Fortnightly Report of Bihar and Orissa for the second half of November 1919, Home Department (Political) File no. 5/1919, NAI.
132. Ibid.

133. Bihar and Orissa Police Abstract of Intelligence, 1919, 2.12.1919, BSA; Fortnightly Report of Bihar and Orissa for the second half of December 1919, Home Department (Political) File no. 45/1919, NAI; *Searchlight,* 4 December 1919.
134. Ibid.
135. Ibid.
136. Fortnightly Report of Bihar and Orissa for the first half of November 1919, Home Department (Political) File no. 5/1919, NAI.
137. Ibid.
138. Ibid.
139. Fortnightly Report of Bihar and Orissa for the second half of December 1919, Home Department (Political) File no. 45/December/1919, NAI.
140. Ibid.
141. *Searchlight,* 11 December 1919.
142. Fortnightly Report of Bihar and Orissa for the first half of December 1919, Home Department (Political) File no. 44/1919, NAI.
143. J.C. Jha, 'The Khilafat and the Non-Cooperation Movement in Bihar (1919–22)', in *History of Indian National Congress in Bihar,* ed. P.N. Ojha, Patna: K.P. Jayaswal Research Institute, 1985, p. 198.
144. P.C. Bamford, *Histories of the Non-Cooperation and Khilafat Movements,* New Delhi: Deep, 1974, p. 150.
145. *Searchlight,* 25 March 1920.
146. Ibid.
147. Fortnightly Report of Bihar and Orissa for the second half of March 1920, Home Department (Political) File no. 91/March/1920, NAI.
148. Fortnightly Report of Bihar and Orissa for the second half of April 1920, Home Department (Political) File no. 92/April/1920, NAI.
149. Ibid.; Imam, *Role of Muslims in the National Movement,* p. 130.
150. Fortnightly Report of Bihar and Orissa for the first half of May 1920, May 1919, Home Department (Political) File no. 94/May/1919, NAI.
151. Ibid.
152. Bihar and Orissa Political Special File no.143/1920; Fortnightly Report of Bihar and Orissa for the first half of May 1920, Home Department (Political) File no. 94/May/1920, NAI.
153. Imam, *Role of Muslims in the National Movement,* p. 130.
154. Minault, *The Khilafat Movement,* p. 90.
155. Bipan Chandra et al. *India's Struggle for Independence 1857–1947,* New Delhi: Penguin, 1989, p. 185.
156. Sitaramayya, *History of The Indian National Congress,* pp. 322–3.
157. Jha, 'The Khilafat and the Non-Cooperation Movement in Bihar', p. 198.
158. Fortnightly Report of Bihar and Orissa for the first half of May 1919, Home Department (Political) File no. 95/May/1919, NAI.
159. Imam, *Role of Muslims in the National Movement,* p. 130.
160. Ibid.
161. Fortnightly Report of Bihar and Orissa for the second half of June 1920, Home Department (Political) File no. 97/June/1920, NAI.

162. Fortnightly Report of Bihar and Orissa, July 1920, Home Department (Political) File no. 105/July/1920, NAI.
163. Fortnightly Report of Bihar and Orissa for the first half of June 1920, Home Department (Political) File no. 97/June/1920, NAI.
164. Fortnightly Report of Bihar and Orissa for the second half of May 1920, Home Department (Political) File no. 95/May/1920, NAI.
165. Chandra et al., *India's Struggle for Independence*, pp. 184–5.
166. Bamford, *Histories of the Non-Cooperation and Khilafat Movements,* pp. 14–15.
167. Fortnightly Report of Bihar and Orissa for the first half of July 1920, Home Department (Political) File no. 106/July/1920, NAI.
168. *Searchlight,* 4 August 1920.
169. Fortnightly Report of Bihar and Orissa for the second half of July 1920, Home Department (Political) File no. 106/1920, NAI.
170. Imam, *Role of Muslims in the National Movement,* p. 131.
171. *Searchlight,* 1 August 1920.
172. Ibid.
173. Ibid., 4 August 1920.
174. Ibid.; Fortnightly Report of Bihar and Orissa for the first half of August 1920, Home Department (Political) File no. 111/August/1920, NAI.
175. Bihar and Orissa Political Special File no. 242/1920, 'Copy of a Special Branch Officer's Report regarding a hartal and Non-Cooperation meeting held at the Madrasa Mosque, Patna City on the 1 August 1920'.
176. Ibid.
177. Ibid.; *Searchlight,* 6 August 1920.
178. Bihar and Orissa Political Special File no. 242/1920, 'Copy of a Special Branch Officer's Report dated the 5 August 1920'.
179. *Searchlight,* 4 August 1920.
180. Ibid.
181. Ibid., 11 August 1920.
182. Ibid., 6 August 1920.
183. Ibid., 11 August 1920.
184. Ibid., 6 and 15 August 1920.
185. Imam, *Role of Muslims in the National Movement,* p. 132.
186. Fortnightly Report of Bihar and Orissa for the second half of August 1920, Home Department (Political) File no. 112/August/1920, NAI.
187. *Searchlight,* 20, 29 August and 3 September 1920.
188. Ibid., 19 September 1920.
189. Ibid., 22 and 29 September 1920.
190. Fortnightly Report of Bihar and Orissa for the second half of October 1920, Home Department (Political) File no. 66/October/1920, NAI.
191. Imam, *Role of Muslims in the National Movement,* p. 134.
192. *Searchlight,* 3 and 6 October 1920.
193. Qeyamuddin Ahmed and Jata Shankar Jha, *Mazharul Haque,* New Delhi: Publication Division, Government of India, 1976, p. 55.

CHAPTER TWO

Contouring the Non-Cooperation Movement in Bihar: 1920–1922

IN SEPTEMBER 1920, the Indian National Congress launched a strong political campaign against the British administration of India. The Congress led by Gandhi denounced as inadequate the British constitutional concessions granted under the Montague-Chelmsford Reforms and demanded swaraj or self-rule for India. The Congress decided to put pressure on Britain to grant freedom to India by mobilizing Indians to refuse to co-operate with the alien rule. Gandhi finally believed that British rule was based on the active collaboration of some Indians and the acquiescence of the rest, and, if Indian cooperation was withdrawn, the British Empire would collapse. The programme of non-cooperation was designed to ensure the collapse of the British Empire through the boycott of forthcoming elections to the provincial and central legislatures, the boycott of government schools, colleges and courts, abandonment of titles, resignation of honorary offices, and government jobs, and the boycott of foreign goods. Later, the programme also called for the boycott of liquor. The movement eventually culminated in active civil disobedience: the refusal to pay cesses, taxes and land revenue, and complete non-cooperation with the authorities in order to paralyse the administration.[1]

An overview of the Non-Cooperation Movement in Bihar in its different phases is presented here. Various issues—national and local—taken up by the movement, as it intensified, are examined. The impact of the movement in different areas and the government's response to the movement are also critically assessed.

In Bihar, the pressure for launching the Non-Cooperation Movement had been mounting much before an official decision was taken by the Indian National Congress at the Nagpur Session in December 1920. The Bihar Provincial Congress Committee (BPCC) approved the principle of non-cooperation for the redressal of national wrongs and decided to support the Khilafat Movement at its meeting on 31 July 1920 at the *Searchlight*[2] office in Patna.[3] Many senior members of the BPCC, such as Sachidanand Sinha and Syed Hasan Imam who strongly believed in constitutional methods of struggle, opposed the resolution and expressed strong doubts and apprehensions about the strategy of launching such a movement. The resolution could be passed only with the support of students and other members and that, too, when these senior members had left the meeting in 'disgust'.[4]

The resolution was discussed again in the last week of August at a Provincial Political Conference meeting held in Bhagalpur.[5] Rajendra Prasad, who presided over this Conference, strongly pleaded in favour of it. Some of the senior leaders again opposed the resolution. Despite their opposition, the resolution was passed. For the first time, delegates other than those from the professional classes attended this Conference. A large number of peasants were present and it was largely due to their support that the resolution was passed.[6] The peasants, who had been agitating against the zamindars in some areas under the leadership of Swami Vidyanand, joined hands with the Congress and participated in large numbers in meetings of the Congress as they found it a viable platform for the redressal of their own grievances. Swami Vidyanand, who was a staunch supporter of the Non-Cooperation Movement, toured the province preaching non-cooperation.[7]

A committee, comprising Rajendra Prasad, Mazharul Haq and Shah Muhammad Zubair, was set up to formulate a practicable scheme, suited to the conditions of this province, to give effect to the principle of non-cooperation.[8]

At the special session of the Congress held in Calcutta in September 1920 the resolution was passed by 1885 votes against 873. The delegates from Bihar were in favour of the resolution; and the peasants' support again proved significant.[9] Even before the Congress met at Nagpur to ratify the resolution on non-cooperation, local leaders in Bihar had undertaken a tour of the province to advocate non-cooperation.[10] The base of the Congress began to expand beyond the educated sections of the people, and as the movement would spread, the base would further enlarge.

Election Boycott

The boycott of the Council elections scheduled for December 1920 was an important aspect of the movement. Even before the ratification of the resolution by the Congress at Nagpur, the nationalist leaders were faced with the forthcoming elections to be held under the Montague-Chelmsford Reforms. The BPCC asked all the candidates to withdraw their names. It also gave a call to the electorate to boycott the elections.[11] In connection with the election boycott campaign, Rajendra Prasad and many other leaders toured different parts of the province and addressed several meetings.[12] College and school students were mobilized and organized into bands of volunteers to assist in the campaign. In Monghyr, two groups of volunteers, one comprising Hindus and the other Muslims, with captains and lieutenants duly appointed, were formed.[13] The advocates of non-cooperation carried out a signature campaign among the electors for boycotting the elections,[14] and they succeeded in their efforts to a large extent.[15] Only 27.3 per cent of Hindus and 12 per cent of Muslims in the urban areas cast their vote. In contrast 41.8 per cent of Hindus and 28.3 per cent of Muslims voted in the rural areas.[16] The voting pattern was a reflection of the spread of the non-cooperation campaign, which was initially active in the urban areas and had not yet made headway in the rural areas.[17] The campaign was very intensive in the Tirhut Division where the turn out of electors was the lowest, only 13 per cent. Tirhut Division also had a strong tradition of agrarian protest. In Chotanagpur, where the Non-Cooperation Movement had not yet spread, the turn out of electors was the highest.[18]

However, advocates of non-cooperation did not meet with the same kind of success in dissuading candidates from withdrawing their nominations. A large number of candidates had filed their nominations from all the constituencies, despite the decision of the Congress that it did not want representatives either in the Provincial or Imperial Legislative Assembly or in the State Council. The Congress also made it clear to the candidates that if they were elected, the Congress would not consider them as its representatives.[19] The limited success on this front was taken cognizance of by Rajendra Prasad and other leaders of the Congress.[20]

The failure of the Congress to dissuade candidates from contesting can be partially explained by examining the social base of the candidates. Most of the candidates belonged to bigger landlord families which maintained close links with the government and were opposed to the movement. The returning officer classified most of them as moderates, some of them as zamindars, and a large number as having no politics at all.[21]

However, Swami Vidyanand and other peasant leaders contested the election from Bhagalpur and north Darbhanga districts, despite their claim to be strong supporters of Gandhi. They believed that being elected to the Provincial Council would help the peasants' cause.[22] The campaign in these areas mainly revolved around the question of the landlord-tenant relationship and brought into focus some of the issues for which the peasants had been fighting.[23] All the four peasant candidates won in the election and their victory was very significant because until then the zamindars had enjoyed a monopoly in the Council. These candidates had built up a strong base amongst the peasants. They had taken up peasants' grievances and had fought for their cause against the zamindars. Besides, many people in the rural areas were not aware of the Congress as the Congress campaign had not yet become visible in the rural areas.[24] There was a sharp rift between the Congress and these peasant candidates because the latter did not abide by the Congress' call for election boycott, and Gandhi even disclaimed them. What is significant is that these candidates, despite the Congress' disassociation from them, proclaimed themselves disciples of Gandhi and strong advocates of the Non-Cooperation Movement.[25]

The election boycott campaign broke the political lull to some extent. Many districts, where the non-cooperators were active in organizing political meetings, could successfully agitate popular feelings against British rule and create a wider social base for political movements in the immediate future. This election was held under the Montague-Chelmsford Reforms that had widened the base of the rural electorate. Landholding peasantry was brought into the fold of the rural electorate. The campaign against the election was primarily taken up amongst them.

Emergence of Gandhi as a Phenomenon

The Non-Cooperation Movement initially made limited progress in Bihar.[26] As for boycotting courts by lawyers, very few of them resigned to join the movement.[27] Further, few people surrendered their titles. The boycott of foreign goods, swadeshi and recruitment of volunteers achieved modest gains. The leaders pinned their hopes on Gandhi's visit to Bihar in December 1920 to arouse enthusiasm amongst the people for the movement.[28] In the wake of Gandhi's visit, a number of meetings were held in various places. The government, alarmed by the large attendance at these meetings, warned the nationalists that if such 'objectionable meetings' continued even after Gandhi left Bihar, it would be forced to extend the Seditious Meeting Act to certain areas.[29]

Gandhi was accompanied by Maulana Shaukat Ali and Maulana Abul Kalam Azad.[30] Apart from addressing public meetings, Gandhi met a large number of students.[31] In his programme of triple boycott—boycott of foreign goods, boycott of law courts and boycott of government controlled colleges and schools—he laid maximum emphasis on the last.[32] His visit led to the establishment of many national schools. Many government schools repudiated their affiliation to the University, which were under government control, and became national. These schools refused to accept grants-in-aid from the government.[33] In Bhagalpur district and Santhal Pargana subdivision Gandhi's visit led to the launching of the anti-liquor movement.[34]

Gandhi's visit to Bihar stimulated the Congress workers and kindled new hopes among the urban intelligentsia. The report of the District Officer of Madhubani subdivision vividly highlighted the impact of Gandhi's visit to Madhubani in Darbhanga, a district which later emerged as one of the strong centres of the Non-Cooperation Movement. Giving an account of this district, he wrote that initially, despite the exhortations of nationalist leaders like Braja Kishore Prasad and Dharnidhar of Darbhanga, people were not enthusiastic to join the movement. The leaders' attempt to persuade the lawyers to give up their practice was not successful. Elections passed off successfully. A Congress branch was set up in Madhubani but there was not a single man to take charge of the office. The District Officer wrote how Gandhi's visit to Darbhanga district infused enthusiasm amongst the people. Gandhi's visit was followed by rumours that he was not an ordinary human being but an avatar, a superhuman, who had come to relieve the sufferings of mankind. His visit coincided with a reduction in the prices of cotton, sugar, salt and other articles of daily consumption in Darbhanga district. People attributed the fall in prices to his visit. This infused the Gandhites, who organized volunteers, and went around the district with them, singing songs in praise of Gandhi and attributing divine qualities to him. They distributed printed leaflets and exhorted people in Gandhi's name to wear khadi and dissociate themselves from government institutions.[35]

Congress leaders regularly urged people to 'pay respect' to Gandhi or 'follow the mantra' of the Mahatma when they appealed to people to support programmes like khadi, boycott of government-funded schools and elections. In fact, a large number of rumours centring around Gandhi circulated. Some of these rumours attributed super-human attributes to Gandhi. One of the beliefs, very common amongst the people, was that when the British arrested Gandhi he escaped from the jail in an invisible manner. There was another rumour that in the jungle of Nepal a large army of Gandhi was ready. Even the newspaper reported rumours around him. In one of the newspapers it was reported, how one day a floating cloud was changing its shape in the sky and that at first it appeared as the four-armed Vishnu and then assumed the shape of Gandhi before disappearing.[36]

In fact, the development of the Non-Cooperation Movement revealed how Gandhi had emerged as an important phenomenon and an alternative centre of power. When Gandhi was not physically present at the scene, the non-cooperators made sure that he was present symbolically. They organized innumerable occasions to pay homage to him. 'Gandhi days' became monthly events.[37] The public speeches associated with such occasions often focused on reciting Gandhi's virtuous qualities: how much he loved people, bore sufferings for them, worked for the upliftment of the downtrodden and the removal of animosity and differences amongst the people.

Gandhi *chalisa* was often recited in the meetings. *Chalisa* eulogizes and attributes divine qualities to a person, thus transforming him to a divine person. Non-cooperators frequently told stories from Gandhi's life as illustrations of his greatness. Often these took on a mythical quality or assumed the aura of morality tales. Gandhi was compared with the hero of *Ramayana*. The nationalists said that victory would come to them as Gandhi, epitome of dharma, was with them, since nationalist struggle was a *dharmic yudh* (religious war). The nationalists often said, 'Don't fear the waves (for) there is with you Gandhi the tester of truth and dharma.'[38] It was further added that by promoting dharma, Gandhi opened the door of heaven for people, made *kalyuga* the *satyuga* and gave them *amrit*. One nationalist pamphlet stated, 'When your boat being in the middle of the river, you have a helper like Gandhi. . . the crew consists of nine and the boat is of satyagraha. God himself is the sailor why the star would not shine then.'[39]

Gandhi was projected as the repository of knowledge. It was said that before him, there was darkness and ignorance and it was he who had shown light to the people. People were told not to fear as Gandhi, the *veeron ka sardar* (the epitome of strength) was with them. It was further added that, since people were fortunate to have Gandhi with them, they should sing the qualities of Gandhi and pray to God so that he may live long. It was wished that Gandhi's fame should spread all over the world and that people should hear and recite to others his instructions selflessly.[40] Some nationalist songs were almost like prayers, requesting Gandhi to shower his blessing upon them. The following is one such example:

> Make a gift of the dust of your feet to me. O great leader of India, ocean of learning, wise one and destroyer of vanity. O crown of India, destroyer of crooked policies save the wretched persons from ignominy and establish (the peace of) the rule of Rama.... I bow low, with all reverence, to Gandhi who is the home of kindness, whose fame is eternal and who is the dispeller of the darkness of ignorance.[41]

The nationalists urged people to be like Gandhi. One of the songs, 'Shri Gandhi Chalisa', appealed to the people. It said, 'come dear heroes of India, let us too be like Gandhi'. It underlined how one Gandhi was doing so much work and with all his might removing the wretchedness of India and serving the country with a selfless motive. Gandhi was said to be firm in truth, did not fear death and looked upon his body as trifling. The song further said that if there be one Gandhi in every family, who would undergo all sorts of hardships for the sake of truth, dispel ignorance by spreading education in every family, bring happiness in India and destroy miseries, that person would be the true hero.[42]

Such polemic around Gandhi served several political ends simultaneously. First, it confirmed Gandhi's significance in people's eyes, perpetuating his reputation as a leader of tremendous stature. Besides, it furnished people with a sense of privilege in having such an extraordinary leader. It attempted to render Gandhi's authority superior to that of either the British or the established leaders of public life and thus break the hold of deference that these figures exerted. At times, the non-cooperators suggested that Gandhi's claims to the support by his followers were inviolable.

Initial Impact in Rural Areas

Till December 1920, the movement had not made much headway in the rural areas.[43] Only some villages, lying in the northern belt of Champaran, Bhagalpur and Monghyr districts, with a strong tradition of anti-planter and agrarian protest, were impacted by the Congress propaganda. Non-cooperators were equally active in these areas and many local leaders played an important role in the non-cooperation campaign. Despite this, the District Officer of Champaran reported that in the villages of north Champaran there was no overt sign of hostility against the government till December 1920. At the same time, the official expressed concern about the development of an independent attitude amongst the villagers, who openly talked of swaraj. Villagers said that as swaraj was coming, the lesser connection people had with the government, the better it was for them. In one place in Champaran, the villagers expressed their hostility against the British by wiping off census numbers on many houses. In some villages of north Champaran like Shikarpur, Harinagar and Ramnagar, committees were set up with members calling themselves 'raiyat volunteers'. These volunteers settled disputes amongst the villagers and also played important roles in the spread of the Non-Cooperation Movement. In north Bhagalpur, Swami Vidyanand was very active. Though the villages of Patna district were least impacted by the movement, yet at times some impact became visible. Following a non-cooperation meeting in Hilsa, the Kurmis and Koeris of Karai Parsurai and the adjoining villages of Diawan decided to boycott foreign cloth and began to cultivate cotton. In Chotanagpur, the movement did not make any inroads.

However, the movement initially had not made much impact in the rural areas. Only agitators, like Swami Vidyanand, who was the leader of peasant agitation, succeeded in building a base among the people. While campaigning for the Non-Cooperation Movement, Swami Vidyanand linked it up with peasant's questions. The Congress leaders had yet to build up their base as the Congress was still a new force in rural areas.

The government asked its different district officers to assess the extent to which the movement had made an impact in the rural areas. The general impression of the officers was that the non-cooperation propaganda had till then not succeeded in 'engendering any feeling of hostility or bitterness against the government'; but they simultaneously expressed anxiety that continuation of anti-government propaganda was leading to a certain amount of 'uneasiness, doubt, insecurity and loss of confidence amongst the people as it was difficult for ignorant villagers to follow the change in the government policy which allowed people of no consequence to rave against and abuse the highest officials of government'. The officers apprehended that 'such propaganda, coupled with the prevailing high prices for which the government would be blamed by the non-cooperators, would stir up feelings of hostility against the government and prepare the way for Gandhi's propaganda of non-cooperation as being the best means of attaining swaraj, when, it was claimed, all difficulties would be removed'.

Nationalist Propaganda: Metaphors and Symbols

The nationalist leaders undertook extensive tours of the province. A number of meetings were held which were attended by many people.[44] Between 25 January and 5 February 1921, no less than 56 meetings were held in Muzaffarpur district alone.[45] Often these meetings were held at haats, bazaars and fairs where large numbers of people gathered for business.[46] Most often before the meetings prayers were offered in different temples and mosques. Meetings were often held at river banks, temples and madrasas as these places had sacred significance and provided sanctity to the meetings.[47] In Chapra, local leaders like Rahul Sankrityayan[48] and Nagnarayan even seized an opportunity of festival like Chhath (worship of sun god) to spread the message of non-cooperation.[49] Meetings of women were held at night.[50] Traditional elements associated with nationalist meetings served to add to the enthusiasm. Biguls or signals of war were sounded to publicize the venue of a meeting. Drums were commonly used to disseminate nationalist news of all kinds. Leaders often used local dialect to address these meetings. Meetings began with the singing of patriotic songs. Alas and dolas, bhajans and ghazals became integral part of public meetings.[51]

Press played important role in nationalist propaganda. Extensive reporting of nationalist activities, meetings and hartals by itself had become a form of political protest. Congress committees at different levels published notices of meetings, circular letters, resolutions and general information for Congress workers in the columns of newspapers. The facts of daily arrests of leaders, vast processions, injuries to Congress volunteers, who had come into conflict with the police, were all displayed in bold types in the press. In fact, newspapers and journals by adopting the simple technique of reiteration created continuous and persistent propaganda and in the process greatly helped Congress mobilization. People became aware of the day-to-day political activities in different places. Newspaper reporting compounded the sense of humiliation felt by the readers in their everyday lives. It gave articulation to the anti-British sentiments which was no doubt latent in the minds of most Indians. Perhaps this aspect of the potency of the newspapers for the mediator of disaffection has not been appreciated to its fullest. Newspapers also played an important role in weaving together everyday events and nationalist activities and putting them in perspective. It generated debates, provided strong ideological basis to the movement and powerfully shaped the trend of nationalist politics. The contents of newspapers were seen to affect the authority and prestige of the government and led colonial officials to evolve ways of monitoring 'native' newspapers by starting the system of the 'Native Newspaper Reports' which kept officialdom informed of the tone of the vernacular press.

Alongside newspapers, another important component of public discourse was vernacular non-periodical literature which included nationalist pamphlets, leaflets, songs, Congress news-sheets, cyclostyled and handwritten materials, books and posters. Much of this literature was produced by underground printing presses and distributed through clandestine channels to avoid proscription. Such literature flourished, especially during periods of censorship and press control.[52]

Besides, the pamphlets were written in such a language that even a schoolboy reading in class II was able to read it out and illiterate villagers could easily follow what was said. The periodicals were also very cheap. People could have a copy of a pamphlet for 2 paise and they were at liberty to print further copies of it themselves. It was hoped that Congress committees would use such pamphlets in village propaganda. Non-periodical literature also contained important nationalist resolutions and messages. The government regarded such literature to be subversive in nature and strict control was exercised over the circulation of such literature.

The number of periodicals that directly supported the Congress programme or were openly sympathetic with it increased since the early 1920s. However, circulation figures could be deceptive as the number of buyers do not necessarily indicate the actual readership. Vernacular papers can be, and are, read to illiterate hearers by their literate neighbours in town, villages, railway carriages, public meetings and so on. Only some kind of geometric progression, then, would give us an idea of the number of buyers, readers and listeners reached by the press. The example from the story of Rambriksha Benipuri,[53] 'Chita Ke Phool', would highlight this aspect. There is a character in the story, Ramu, from the poor family. Ramu could not pursue education because of lack of resources and was also expected to help his father. He used to collect grass everyday for the cattle. He eagerly looked forward to every Friday because that was the day Bhujawan Dada of the village would get his newspaper. Ramu had keen interest in national movement. He was also interested in international news. Every Friday, he would go to Bhujawan Dada's place. Even Bhujawan Dada eagerly looked forward to his coming. Many people collected at Bhujawan Dada's place on Friday. In winter, Bhujawan Dada lighted fire in front of his house. People sat around it and listened to Bhujawan Dada reading the news.[54]

Lantern slides were also used to illustrate the impact of the British rule. These lantern slides portrayed British rule as impoverishing the country and leading to an enormous drain of wealth.[55]

The nationalist used popular idioms in campaign, with which the people could easily relate and identify with. Meetings began mostly with the singing of national songs. Most of the songs highlighted the adverse impact of foreign rule on India. One of the songs, 'Firangia', portraying drain of wealth, became very popular. It depicted how the rich land of Bharat had become a cremation ground, where wealth, men, strength and wisdom had been destroyed. It further highlighted how the drain of wealth reduced the country to famines, where people were starving. It further stated that at the juncture when the country was becoming very poor there was increasing imposition of taxes on everything.[56]

Metaphor of garden was often used in nationalist songs and speeches for the prosperous country. British rule was said to have ruined and deserted the garden. London was said to be turning into Nandan Kanan (Eden) and Alkapuri (the fabulous place of Kubera, god of wealth) due to the influx of wealth from India. Another metaphor 'Shakuni' was used for the British ruler. Shakuni was a character in the *Mahabharata*, who, through various intrigues, brought about the destruction of the country.[57]

One of the most popular images projected of the British rule was that of 'jalim', the perpetrator of atrocity. The imposition of martial law and the atrocity at Jallianwala Bagh in Punjab was a recurring theme in many nationalist pamphlets. One of the songs, 'Oppression of Dyer', brings out the atrocity perpetrated by the British. It highlighted as to how Dyer in Jallianwala killed the helpless children, young and old with bullets and as to how the soil was still drenched with the blood of children. The pamphlet also highlighted that Dyer's atrocity 'spoilt the honour of dear and devoted wives'.[58]

British rule was often depicted in the nationalist songs and pamphlets as based on falsehood, treachery and evil passions. British institutions like courts, bureaucracy, government schools and colleges, etc. were projected as institutions meant to instigate evil passions, crush people's soul and their noble ideas and to make them slaves of money. 'Devil, demon, oppressive, dishonest, shameless, destructive and unjust' were some of the common epithets frequently used by the nationalists for the British.[59] Many pamphlets depicted how the British came to India as guests and then created troubles amongst the people and finally grabbed India. The British were also said to have displayed false affections and gradually deprived Indians of everything. It was also said that guests were entertained only for a few days and not for centuries. The English nation was often compared with crow for its cunning character. One of the pamphlets said that the British came to India in the guise of a magician and made the people dance like monkeys.[60] The campaign also highlighted how the British cheated and looted those very people who had helped them. In a pamphlet was narrated a story drawing analogy to this side of the British character. The story was of a king who had gone to forest for hunting with his soldiers. When the king was very hungry a shepherd fed him. In order to express his thanks the king gifted the shepherd 60 villages by writing the gift on a *peepal* leaf. Later the king regretted what he had done: giving him 60 villages just for a piece of bread. When the shepherd went to drink water the king cunningly got the *peepal* leaf devoured by a goat.[61]

The British were accused of ruling India by the divide and rule policy. One of the pamphlets referred them as 'shopkeepers who had come to India and fed the people a kind of sweetmeat that had brought about a rift between the Hindus and Muhammadans'.[62] Another pamphlet highlighted how 'before the coming of the British the people were passing their mornings and evenings in tranquility but when the British came, they created a bustle in vain, kindled the fire and killed the Indians, having turned them into majnum'.[63] The British rule was referred to as 'yams'. It was also said that because of people's 'slumber' the foreigners had managed to become the rulers of the country.[64]

The impact of British rule on India was perceived as having not only adverse effect on its economy but also having adversely affected Indian society and culture. The nationalists emphasized how India which had a glorious civilization, was, under the British rule, becoming devoid of its spirituality, individuality, manliness and strength. The nationalists also underlined how, under the British rule, Hindu and Muslim religions had come under threat. Hence, the nationalist struggle did not remain merely confined to extermination of the British, a political struggle, but broadened to become an ideological and cultural encounter with the British. The struggle got linked with the question of saving India's glorious civilization from the cultural onslaught by the British. It was a call to save the religion, the honour and the spirituality of the nation. The past greatness of India was strongly emphasized. India was projected as the birthplace of a glorious civilization and as the locale of different forms of knowledge, arts and religions. It was also underlined that

India, not only at the level of ideas but even in material terms, had a highly developed past. It depicted India as the land that contained 'great' prosperous cities, huge dwelling places, ports, temples, gardens, centres of learning and arts. The nationalists bemoaned that the past greatness of India no longer existed. It was regretted that under the British rule India had reached its 'fallen' state, where Indians had become lazy and lost their self-confidence, their spirit and strength. British rule was held to be responsible for the decline in Indians' character.[65]

The country was often referred to as mother. It was often highlighted how under the British rule Bharat Mata had to undergo different tortures.[66] Appeal was made to the people to sacrifice their lives for the cause of the mother nation. Dying for one's country was considered to be the greatest sacrifice for the nation. One of the pamphlets highlighted that those alone realized a little of the pleasure of dying in the world who died in the service of their country and nation. It further said that it was better to die than to lead a life of slavery and that those 'who die live and those who live die'.[67]

In fact, the centrality of the idea of self-sacrifice in Gandhian scheme of things became pervasive. It began to be expected from all the rank and file of Congress workers. Local followers of the movement drew upon this vocabulary with considerable frequency. Special appeal was made to the youth to sacrifice their lives for the cause of the nation. The call was made in the name of the mother country and also to save religion and chastity of women. It was said that youths who had 'hot' blood would smilingly sacrifice their lives for Bharat Mata as the place of mother was higher than that of heaven. One of the pamphlets exhorted the youth in the following manner: 'O dutiful and gallant heroes, rise. Mother India is calling, O youths! Forsake your fascination for wives now to preserve the honour of the country.'[68]

In another pamphlet relationship of a mother and a son was highlighted. Country was frequently referred to as a motherland. Since country was a motherland, one was expected to be its faithful son and make sacrifices for it. One should 'bow, salute, sing song in praise of motherland and devote body, mind and riches to her'.[69]

The nationalists even invoked the vocabulary of honour and shame in spurring local residents to abandon their association with the British. The non-cooperators linked up the involvement in Congress politics and the local preoccupation with respectability. It promoted a sense of identification with country by suggesting that family honour and shame were dependent upon non-cooperation. Those who did not observe nationalist strictures might become subject to serious social sanctions similar to those faced by persons who had violated the injunctions of caste organization. The leaders of non-cooperation regularly berated their audiences for failure to observe expected behavioural standards. It was also repeatedly said that to be an acceptable member of one's own community, one must devote oneself to the larger collectivity of Indians. In this way, the nationalists were attempting to create a sense of the inescapability of involvement with non-cooperation.

The nationalists also expressed the apprehension that the British rule had been gradually destroying the religion of the country. One of the pamphlets stated 'the religion has now departed. There is no truth in the Kshatriyas, the Brahmans have turned rustic, the pandits have all turned beggars and call at each door'.[70] It was pointed out how the British had 'encroached upon Islam by breaking their pledges' and how they had even 'expunged the orders of God and had got the fatwa of the Ulema proscribed'.[71] It was also emphasized that the 'Britishers had slaughtered lakhs of cows and fed the troops daily with them. Hides were turned into boots. Dyes were manufactured by red blood and threads prepared by the fat'.[72] In fact it was frequently invoked that under the British rule the 'sacred' cow was under threat, signifying that the nation was in peril. People were asked to remove the misery of the mother cow. One of the pamphlets said: 'Bhagwati (mother cow) is the direct outcome of the generosity of God. Serve it. Give to mother cow a place in every household. Health, beauty and wealth would shine and the nation would become powerful.'[73] Another pamphlet emphasized that in order to protect sacred cows it was the religious duty of the Hindus to non-cooperate with the Government. For the nationalists purchasing foreign cloth and yarn was tantamount to committing sin like cow slaughter. The pamphlet further stated that 'if there is any regard for the Hindu religion and Choti (tuft of hair on the head), all the Hindus should become non-cooperators by the Gopashtive (8th of Kati K, 2nd fortnight)'.[74]

The nationalists also repeatedly drew upon the vocabulary of purity and pollution, central element of Indian religion, in describing satyagraha. Satyagraha, which entailed sacrifice, was seen as a step leading to internal self-cleansing. Use of the purity motif suggested a whole series of political conclusions: that the continued acceptance of British rule polluted India and its people, that wearing foreign clothes or continued participation in legislative councils and government-funded schools was a worldly attachment that perpetuated impurity, and that removing India's condition of impurity required acts of penance. Khadi would not only bring wealth but would also purify mother's body.[75] Non-cooperators regularly stressed the atonement of self-purification that would accrue to those who distanced themselves from colonial institution and commitments. They said 'at first you may not really like wearing khadi since you may find it rough and ugly in appearance, but its internally purifying character will make the thoughts of your mind pure'.[76] Ritually, this theme was symbolized by the purificatory baths that often preceded public meetings and processions. The idiom of purity and pollution further encouraged non-attachment to family and worldly possession that might inhibit the willingness to engage in bold action. Here again, there was sometimes an effort to pre-empt the possibility of non-involvement.

Joining the agitation was like sharing a religious mission. It was a 'deshpuja' and 'deshdharma', extracting the notion of duty. Country was elevated to the status of a mother god, demanding highest sacrifice from all. Over and over speakers at public meetings stressed that the national movement was a dharmic battle. 'Those who die for their religion are not dead even though they die. They get immortality who never fear death'.[77] In fact, dharma had been one of the central motifs in the rhetoric of local Gandhians. Over and over again speakers at the public meetings stressed that dharma was involved in the struggles to redress the Punjab and Khilafat wrongs and to bring an end to colonial rule. To wear khadi was to protect one's 'svadharma' for Hindu and Muslim alike. It was the 'deshdharma' of Hindus to support Muslims in the Khilafat Movement. The word dharma continued to carry with it the meaning of a sacred and inescapable set of ethical obligations incumbent on individuals by virtue of their position in life. Having been born Indians the people, it suggested, had no other choice but to participate in the national cause if they were to remain morally upstanding persons. The term had an almost coercive quality, it attempted to prevent the possibility not only of opposition but also of apathy and inaction. By suggesting that principles of the highest order were at stake, non-cooperators also provided participants with a sense of moral ascendancy over the British, who were portrayed in profane and worldly terms. They talked of moral truths and the spiritual and political principles espoused by the Mahatma, such as *ahimsa, satya, tyag* and *tapasya.* In this way, the battle was lifted to a moral plane.[78]

The nationalists often drew metaphors from mythologies, particularly from the great Hindu epics *Ramayana* and *Mahabharata*. British government was defined as a modern Ravana while terming non-cooperators as incarnations of Ram. The nationalist struggle was also paralleled as a war between Kauravas and Pandavas, the two arch opponents of the *Mahabharata*, implicitly associating the British with the former and the nationalists with the later. Mythological metaphors contributed to drawing the lines between right and wrong in contemporary struggle in particularly stark terms. They provided those who were ready to make sacrifices for the nation with a sense of involvement in a privileged and sacred moment on a historical scale that reached back into mythological time. These kinds of arguments attempted to eliminate the possibility of aloofness from the Congress cause. They isolated those who remained apathetic or who opposed non-cooperation as obstacles to the creation of new society of mythical proportions.[79] This kind of propaganda, thus, had a strong impact. The key to the success of the non-cooperators lay in their ability to generate and employ expressions with a metaphor-like function. Metaphors can play a crucial role in shaping perceptions of reality. By bringing together concepts drawn from distinct conceptual domains, metaphors create mental linkages between concepts that are difficult to understand, unfamiliar, and distant, and those that are easily comprehensible and evoke powerful feelings of passion, anger or excitement. It injected into public culture a vocabulary that originated particularly in the domain of religious practice and personal honour. Such motifs played a major persuasive function in deflating colonial hegemony and offering powerful new cultural meanings that would inspire or even coerce participation in public politics. However, it should also be pointed out how such counter colonial hegemony of the nationalists laid down at the same time the foundation of mainstream nationalist hegemony, with its implication for caste, class, gender and minority in society.[80]

The First Phase of the Movement: Its Spread in Different Districts

By January 1921, the movement made considerable headway in both urban and rural areas. In addition to gaining support among professionals, students and the urban poor in towns, the movement rallied support among a broad spectrum of society in the countryside. The boycott of educational institutions, which initially elicited little response, received, before long, an enthusiastic response once alternative national educational institutions were set up. The other programmes of the Congress, however, the call to surrender titles and to resign from honorary positions and posts of lawyers, teachers and government servants elicited only a lukewarm response. The boycott of government courts met with greater success. Panchayats were set up in several places.[81] One movement that became immensely popular, even though that was not a part of the original agenda of the Congress, was the anti-liquor movement. By January 1921, it reached its height in most districts.[82] There was unrest also among the lower rungs of the police force and they threatened to go on strike unless their pay was increased.[83]

By January 1921, the movement made deep inroads in Tirhut Division[84] and in the northern belt of Bhagalpur and Monghyr districts.[85] In Tirhut Division, the movement drew strength from a whole network of organizations. Sabhas and seva samitis were set up in many places in Champaran, Muzaffarpur and Darbhanga districts.[86] The sabhas, also known as peasant sabhas, were an indication of the spread of the movement among the peasantry. The village was the unit of the sabha, and the panch was appointed from amongst the sabhas. In some parts of the Tirhut Division, circles comprising a number of villages were set up, with head panches and treasurers. These organizations played a significant role in the spread of the movement. The sabhas organized weekly meetings to discuss non-cooperation, to settle disputes amongst the villagers and to collect funds; they were assisted by the panchayats. Disputes over land, loans and grazing were settled by these panchayats which frequently resorted to social boycott to enforce their order. The sabhas were also assisted in their functioning by seva samiti volunteers, who were generally referred to as peons by the peasants. The volunteers collected funds to meet the recurring expenses of the Congress organization. The main source of funds was *muthia,* a system in which a handful of grain was kept aside every day by a householder and this was collected weekly by the volunteers. In fact, *muthia* evokes the image of village women, who before putting rice into the pot, kept aside a handful of rice with great devotion and faith in the name of Gandhi Baba. Such moment was for them overwhelmingly emotional. They sacrificed a part of their daily wages, thus depriving their children of fuller meals, forcing them to remain partly hungry.[87] The expenses for running these organizations were met through this system till it was later augmented by the Congress membership of 4 *annas*. This also shows how the tradition of giving alms to the Brahmin assumed a modern form of fund raising in the movement. The sabhas attained a considerable degree of organization in the villages of Motihari, Madhuban, Lauriya and Segauli in Champaran district.[88]

The movement in Tirhut Division was mainly carried forward by the peasant sabhas. As a result, the government could not enforce the Seditious Meeting Act to suppress the movement.[89] Even the zamindars were apprehensive of the establishment of sabhas and panchayats for settling disputes among the peasantry. They perceived it as a threat to their power and authority, and also as an erosion of their hegemony. The zamindars had not yet recovered from the peasant agitations that had preceded the Non-Cooperation Movement: those agitations kept haunting them.[90]

In Tirhut Division, the movement drew strength from agrarian and social tensions that had crystallized during the anti-indigo agitation and peasant protests preceding the Non-Cooperation Movement.[91] In Madhubani sub-division, peasants, who had previously protested against the Darbhanga raj, actively participated in the Non-Cooperation Movement.[92] The movement kindled the expectations of peasants, whose desires and aspirations got linked with the demand for swaraj. The anti-planter struggles intensified and relations between the planters and peasants became very strained. Many factory managers had to confront problems from their labourers and servants.[93] Those

Europeans, who had settled in large numbers in Muzaffarpur district, faced resistance from their servants.[94] Agrarian tension also mounted against the Indian zamindars. The tenants of the Ramnagar raj disputed the claim of the raj over grazing and wood cutting in the forest, the payment of rent and other claims of the zamindars. These areas had earlier witnessed agrarian agitations against the Bettiah raj, the Ramnagar raj and other zamindars.[95]

Many cases of the looting of haat were reported from Muzaffarpur and Darbhanga districts. Between 10 and 14 January 1921, there were ten such cases in Muzaffarpur district and three in Darbhanga. Shops were looted to the accompaniment of shouting of the slogan, *Gandhiji ki jai*.[96] An official comment on the question of haat looting stated that the evidence in the possession of the government left no doubt that haat looting was directly connected with the state of 'excitement' and 'unrest' fomented by the non-cooperation agitation. The person, who started the loot first asked the price of rice, cloth, vegetables and other articles and when the price was mentioned alleged that Gandhi had given the order that the price should be usually a quarter of the current market rate. According to the official, when the shopkeepers refused to sell at lower prices, they were abused and beaten and their shops looted.[97]

The Provincial Congress leaders were extremely critical of these incidents. Many of them immediately rushed to the areas where such incidents happened, and distributed leaflets and handbills condemning these activities and requesting the people to remain non-violent, which they explained was very crucial for the success of the movement.[98] According to Tirhut Division Commissioner, incidents like haat looting intensified because of 'the growing currency amongst the masses of the belief that the forces of law and order were weakening and that swaraj was imminent'.[99]

By January 1921, Monghyr and Bhagalpur districts became the strongholds of the movement.[100] In Monghyr district, northern Monghyr, Begusarai and Sadar subdivisions, which lay along the north of the Ganga River, were particularly affected.[101] This was another belt which had witnessed strong peasant agitation against the Banaili raj and Darbhanga raj under the leadership of Swami Vidyanand.[102] The 'agitators' toured the district and organized meetings.[103] Maulavi Muhammad Zubair was one of the prominent leaders. School boys from Patna and Monghyr, who withdrew from their schools, helped in the mobilization by organizing meetings in different places. A large number of Marwaris in this district participated in the movement. There was a total hartal in the city when the Governor visited Monghyr in January 1921. Shops remained closed. The anti-liquor movement was strong in this district and excise sales declined sharply. Cases of haat lootings were reported from certain areas. In Kharagpur, Singheshwar Choudhari attempted to mobilize the people against the Darbhanga raj. The Santhals in the hills were told by the non-cooperators to stop collecting sabai grass for the Darbhanga raj. The government expressed concern over the development of the movement in Monghyr because it perceived this district to be the only one in Bhagalpur Division as having 'population of sufficient virility to give trouble'. The government's apprehension was based on a strong tradition of peasant protest in this area.

In Bhagalpur district, the movement made a strong impact, especially in areas which lay to the north of the Ganga.[104] This was another belt where peasant agitation had been strong.[105] Nationalist meetings were frequently held in a number of places.[106] In this district the Marwaris also participated in the movement in large numbers. Deep Narayan Singh, a prominent local leader, regularly toured the district and addressed several meetings. The movement affected excise sales. Santhal Pargana was influenced by the movement since its very inception, and here the movement primarily took the form of a no-rent campaign. There were cases of haat lootings in some parts of Bhagalpur district.

In Patna Division, the movement reached the intensive phase only in Shahabad district.[107] A definite programme was launched here for propaganda work. The whole district was divided into four parts according to its subdivision for carrying out propaganda work. These subdivisions were: (a) Arrah: Arrah Town, Arrah *mufassil* and Piru; (b) Buxar: Buxar and Dumraon, (c) Bhabua: Bhabua and Mohania; and (d) Sasaram: Sasaram, Dehri, Kargarh and Bikramganj. Each subdivision was to be under a chief organizer known as a supervisor and a team of volunteers was to carry out propaganda work. These supervisors were expected to organize subcommittees in their areas. Many meetings were held in different places and a large number of teachers and students associated themselves with the movement.[108]

At a public meeting in Dumraon in Shahabad district on 13 November, the call for the boycott of liquor was made for the first time.[109] This district also faced problems with the settlement of cattle pounds.[110] Pounds could be settled with great difficulty, and, that too, at considerably low fees, as people amicably settled trespass cases in the villages and did not take cattle to the pounds.[111]

In the Chotanagpur belt and the Purnea district, the pace of the movement was slower even though efforts had been on since November 1920 to spread the movement in Chotanagpur. It was only in late January 1921 that non-cooperators succeeded in establishing contact with the Tana Bhagats in Ranchi.[112] The Tana Bhagats responded in large numbers to the appeals made by the non-cooperators and their support gave a fillip to the movement. The movement amongst the Tana Bhagats primarily brought forth their animosity against the landlords and trading community.[113]

Motilal Nehru, Rajendra Prasad, Mazharul Haq and Swami Biswanand toured Chotanagpur area and addressed a number of meetings.[114] In Jamshedpur, a large number of industrial workers attended these meetings.[115] The movement gained a strong foothold in Giridih which was easily accessible to 'agitators' from other areas. There were many panchayats in this region and the volunteers were well organized.[116] The liquor boycott was very effective in Chotanagpur. The non-cooperators successfully prevented the settlement of excise liquor shops.[117] Another activity related to the anti-liquor protest that was very popular in this region was the 'illicit' distillation of liquor.[118] Under the new excise policy, the government had banned private distillation of liquor. The protest flouted the government policy.

The Congress campaign in Purnea was launched only in late February 1921 and it gained momentum following Rajendra Prasad's tour of the area.[119] Non-cooperators from Patna and Bhagalpur organized meetings in different parts of the district to mobilize people for the movement.[120] Also many 'local enthusiasts cropped up trying to spread the movement assiduously at haats and other convenient centres'.[121] A large proportion of the population in this district were Muslims, who were actively involved in the movement.[122] The Congress campaign in this district gave an impetus to the movement and, once the movement gathered momentum, local issues were linked up with it, strengthening it.

The movement had a strong impact on Sadar and Araria subdivisions in Purnea district.[123] Here anti-liquor movement was very strong and excise shops were picketed. The people were hostile towards the police and excise officers, who found it difficult to get accommodation in the *mufassil*.[124] Sabhas played an active role in the movement, particularly in the Araria subdivision.[125] The boycott of cattle pounds was one of the distinctive features of the movement in Purnea district. Ferry farmers and pound keepers in the Kishenganj subdivision boycotted auction settlements.[126] The relations between the planters and peasants were strained as Purnea district had a strong tradition of anti-planter and agrarian protest.[127] On 13–14 February 1921, a Kisan Mahasabha meeting was held in Madhubani which was attended by around 8,000 cultivators.[128] Another Kisan Sabha meeting was held in one of the *qasbas* (a small town).[129] All this strengthened the forces at work against the zamindars and indigo factory owners. In some places, tenants delayed rent payment. According to the district officer, 'it seems as though they were taking time to see what would happen when the promised swaraj comes. In some parts, the belief was that Gandhi raj was timed to come in *chait* (Hindu calendar month), till which payment of rent was withheld, but when *chait* came and went without swaraj they began to pay'.[130]

Hostile atmosphere was building up against the chaukidars (night watchmen).[131] The chaukidars were an auxiliary body, who acted in support of the trained police force, and were significant figures in the maintenance of public order. Their duties included guarding the villager's crops, houses, and possessions against theft, reporting deaths, births, crimes and unusual events to the local police station, and assisting the police in the investigations of crime and the apprehension of criminals. In pre-British times chaukidars were hereditary village servants through whom the landlords traditionally exercised their policing functions. They were appointed by the landlords primarily to protect life and property in the village, although their services were frequently utilized by the zamindars as labourers on their estates. They worked under the close supervision of the landlords, who were also responsible for their well-being. They were regarded as the 'natural police' of the country and were part and parcel of the village community. They were maintained by the people and remunerated either in land assignments or in grain contributions from each household. Their menial duties suggest the low social status of chaukidars. They were members of economically 'depressed' families and socially 'depressed' castes (Dusadhs, Ahirs and Chamars). Their low social status is also illustrated by their petty wages.[132]

Gradually the British removed the police from the control of the zamindars. The government strengthened its links to the village watchmen by the Bengal Act VI of 1870, the Village Chaukidari Act. It created chaukidari panchayats of three to five villagers, intending to control the appointment, dismissal and maintenance of village watchmen. This legislation aimed at correcting what was considered to be the primary reason for the inefficiency of the system: the irregularity of watchmen's pay. This act sought to recast him as a servant of the village community rather than of the malik. The chaukidar's role was transformed from actively apprehending suspects to being mere informants. However, this attempt to reorganize generated problem. For the village watchman to function as a government connection, he had to be extricated from close ties to the local control structure, whether emanating from the estate or the village. The administration selected the members of the chaukidari panchayats from among landlords, rich peasants and from European landlords and sugar planters. Local panchayat members often used the chaukidars as their own private police. The collectors of the chaukidari tax often acted oppressively. It was their custom to greatly harass the poor people and assess whatever tax they liked. Thus the official's attempt to co-opt the chaukidari system was not successful. Structural changes had to be made at a level of local society. Notwithstanding official efforts to oversee the workings of the village watchmen, they remained bound to the local control system. As one commissioner of Patna noted, they were so entirely the creatures of the village authorities that they often accepted whatever wages the later chose to pay and acknowledged payment in full for their wages. Where the panchayat members were Bhumihar Brahmins or Rajputs, they assessed themselves and their friends lightly and the poorer and more dependent classes with undue severity in order to make up the deficiency. Distraint was frequently resorted to and partiality was shown not only in the assessment but even in the collection. Moreover, raiyats were charged twice; they not only paid the levy imposed by the chaukidari panchayats, but also customary chaukidari cess to the zamindar, which, in many cases, had become consolidated with the rent.[133]

People opposed the payment of chaukidari taxes. Activists in the anti-chaukidari campaign urged people to stop paying the taxes levied for the support of their local chaukidars, urged chaukidars to resign, and urged members of the chaukidari panchayats, which held the responsibility for the collection of chaukidari tax and the recruitment and direction of chaukidars, to relinquish their positions. The call for a campaign against the chaukidari system found a receptive audience. It was the most hated tax. No villagers liked this tax for the simple reason that the chaukidar was more an oppressor than a friend to the village folk. Congress supporters supplemented persuasion with limited violence to get chaukidars to resign their positions. Since the chaukidars came from the lower sections of society, they were easily subjected to pressure. Uncooperative chaukidars were refused access to village wells, and their womenfolk were harassed whenever they went out into the fields to relieve themselves. In some instances they encountered physical violence and complete social boycott.[134]

The Congress workers also made intensive efforts to win over the local chaukidars to the nationalist cause. Chaukidars resigned, and many others stopped performing their duties. The chaukidari system was vulnerable because the chaukidars were only incompletely under official control and protection and hence could be subjected to pressure within the villages.[135]

There was also discontentment amongst the chaukidars over their pay. In payment they received a miserly Rs. 3 to Rs. 5 a month. Not only were they meagrely paid but the pay of the chaukidars was in arrears for periods varying from six month to two years. In 60 per cent of the cases in Saran, warrants had to be served on the panchayats before they would pay their chaukidars. Chaukidars were becoming discontented. Their responsibilities were large and remuneration very small.[136] The post of a chaukidar was becoming less attractive and in several districts, in official's own words, 'only men of inferior type and character were forthcoming to fill it'. The colonial officials had a poor opinion of their capabilities and credentials, and could never trust them by vesting in them any real responsibility. They lashed out at chaukidars as 'the most debased class of the inhabitants', describing watchmen in particular as 'the leader of criminal gangs'. Such frequent official criticism and ridicule was a reflection of the souring of the relationship between the Raj and its local functionaries.[137] Although some of the traditional authority of these men had by then been eroded, they still possessed enough formal power to be able to coerce their neighbours and thus be a political threat to the government. In the considerable archival evidence that is available regarding peasant unrest and Congress activities in the villages, the chaukidars and mukhias hardly figure as effective instruments of authority at the local level of the colonial power. It can thus be concluded that due to a range of factors the colonial power could no longer rely on its local functionaries to act as agents or order and authority on its behalf.[138]

By February 1921, the boycott of educational institutions began to lose momentum and students returned to their institutions. The call for renouncing titles had little effect, it was soon realized that no political mileage could be drawn from this or from the resignation of professional and government posts. The liquor boycott received maximum impetus.[139] When the boycotts began to lose momentum, the nationalists turned their attention towards the formation of organizations like sabhas, panchayats and seva samitis. These organizations spread across rural areas and gave strength to the movement. The government also feared the development of these organizations.[140]

Panchayats became very popular in Bihar as people were familiar with them. Every community and caste had its own panchayat. Panchayats were established in a large number of villages in Saran, Muzaffarpur, Champaran, Darbhanga, Patna, Gaya, Shahabad, Bhagalpur, Hazaribagh, Ranchi and Palamau districts. Saran district, in particular, had a large number of panchayats.[141] Many seva samitis were set up. The nationalists laid great emphasis on the recruitment of volunteers. Volunteers emerged as the special task force for the organization of the movement at the grass roots level, spreading nationalist ideology, mobilizing the masses, helping in the organization of processions, advertising political meetings and assisting the Congress leaders in their propaganda activities. The Congress penetrated into the villages through the organizational network of these 'pracharakas'. In many villages, volunteers assisted the peasant sabhas and local arbitration courts. In March 1921, around 6,000 people had offered themselves as volunteers. By April 1921, their numbers rose to 7,860, and by June to 10,319. Many of these volunteers were from lower classes and castes. In Saran and Champaran, a large number of Doms were enrolled as Congress volunteers.[142] It was fairly clear that the national movement was no longer confined to a few people in the educated sections of society but had widened its social base, which gave it strength and a militant character.

Next Phase of the Movement

From April 1921 onwards, the Non-Cooperation Movement entered its next phase. As the boycott programme failed to produce the desired effect, the Congress was compelled to launch other programmes. It met at Bezwada in April to discuss the programmes around which the next phase of the movement was to be organized.[143] At this meeting, the feasibility of including civil disobedience in the Congress programme was mooted. The delegates from Bihar were strongly in favour of civil disobedience but most of the delegates from other provinces opposed it. However, Rajendra Prasad, the Congress leader from Bihar, opposed it on the grounds that Bihar was not yet ready for civil disobedience as the lawyers in Bihar had not wholeheartedly accepted the doctrine of non-cooperation and had not forsaken their practice. Unless the lawyers did so, he said, 'the masses, if aroused, would be without leaders'.[144] In the absence of any leader, he feared, the anger of the masses would be directed against their landlords, leading to bloodshed and would thus justify government intervention, resulting in the complete suppression of the movement.[145] Gandhi also did not endorse civil disobedience programme. However, he said that if in future civil disobedience was to be launched, it would be in Bihar as its leaders had given ample evidence of their capability and could be trusted to steer the movement successfully.[146] The fear underlying the opposition to civil disobedience reflected the deep-rooted agrarian tensions in Bihar. The nationalist leaders feared that the peasants, who were the mainstay of the movement, would translate the call to air their grievances against the zamindars. The Civil Disobedience Movement, they believed, would sharpen their confrontation with the zamindars.

The Congress decided to develop a constructive programme. A resolution was passed exhorting the people to concentrate on three tasks: (1) collecting Rs.1 crore for the All India Tilak Swaraj Fund, (2) enrolling one crore members for the Congress, and (3) introducing 20 lakh charkhas in the villages and cities. The deadline for these tasks was 30 June 1921. Each province was asked to contribute in proportion to its population.[147] In addition to this, the period from 6 to 13 April was to be observed as Satyagraha Week.[148] The resolution also stated that both the local and district boards as well as municipalities should be brought under nationalist control.[149]

It was decided that a hartal would be observed on 6 and 13 April. On 6 April the Rowlatt Act was passed and on 13 April the Jallianwala Bagh incident took place in Punjab. During the Satyagraha Week, all business would be suspended, all shops would remain closed, people would observe *roza* and *brata* and offer prayers in temples and mosques for attaining swaraj. Besides, people were enjoined to abstain from 'intoxicating' substances. Moreover, the Congress reiterated the task of collecting money for the All India Tilak Swaraj Fund during this week.[150] The programme imparted a sacred aura to the Satyagraha Week.[151] In Bihar, notices for the observation of the Satyagraha Week were printed and distributed in various places, accompanied by the beating of drums. Also processions were taken out in different places, with people singing national and religious songs. In many places, meetings were held in the evening. On the whole, the hartal was peaceful in most places in Bihar.[152]

The District Officer of Patna, who had been a witness to hartals on earlier occasions in Patna, described the hartal on 6 April as the most successful and peaceful.[153] In Patna, most of the shops remained closed and processions were taken out, with people singing patriotic and religious songs. These processions occasionally drew up in front of shops in order to explain why the hartal was being observed and having done this, continued to move down the road.[154] In the evening, a procession of around 300 men, largely students, set out from Mahendru with a Mahavir Jhanda and gathered at the compound of Mazharul Haq in Bankipore, where a public meeting was held. It was attended by nearly 600 people.[155]

Hartals were observed in other places as well. In Giridih, coolies working in the colliery absented themselves from work on 6 April. As a mark of protest, coolies at the railway station in Bhagalpur remained away from work on 13 April. In Purulia, most of the pleaders and *mukhtars* did not attend court. However, the lawyers, the elite section of the town and the big shopkeepers distanced themselves from it. The speakers who addressed the meetings dwelt primarily on the collection of funds and the formation of Congress committees.[156]

The Congress also focused on contesting elections to the local bodies. Even though the Congress advocated the boycott of election to the Council yet it was in favour of contesting elections to the local bodies as these bodies could play significant role in furthering the cause of the national movement. These bodies could expand the nationalist base because of the power they enjoined at the local level. These bodies often convened and addressed political meetings, presented address of welcome to the non-cooperators on their visit to their districts and emerged as the main promoter of constructive programme. Besides, these bodies, despite their circumscribed powers, set out to raise the quality of life of the people. The Congress fared well in the municipality election in Muzaffarpur held in April 1921.[157] In a real sense, if there was any contest, it was in Ward 1 in Muzaffarpur. Despite the contest, both the candidates elected from this Ward were non-cooperators. In other Wards, opponents of non-cooperators could not secure any votes unless they signed the pledge agreeing to the terms of non-cooperators. The pledge was that if elected in the municipality then the contestant would carry on the work as ordered by the District Congress Committee by giving votes and would consider it his religious duty to try to attain swaraj.[158]

Baijnath Prasad Singh, Sheo Bux Marwari and Shamnandan Sahay were elected only after they signed this pledge. Non-cooperators, who stood in opposition to these candidates, withdrew from the contest once these candidates had signed the pledge. Of 12 elected members in the Tirhut Division municipality, seven were 'avowed non-cooperators'.[159] Three other candidates also signed the pledge, agreeing to the non-cooperators terms. The remaining two candidates, Gajadhar Prasad and Khwaja Abdul Majid, who were elected from Ward 5, were described by both non-cooperators and others as their sympathizers. The Congress also won the municipal elections in Motihari, where four staunch non-cooperators, Gorakh Prasad, Debi Lal Sahu, Kedar Nath Sahu and Ramdayal Prasad Sahu, were elected. The non-cooperators' candidates pledged not to accept grants from the government for any purpose, to convert government schools into national schools, to abolish water tax, and to increase the salaries and wages of municipal employees.[160]

While the Congress concentrated on these programmes, a marked trend was emerging in May 1921: demonstrations by the masses outside the courts when non-cooperators faced a trial or when they were driven from the court to the jail.[161] For example, Giridih witnessed a serious 'riot'-like situation. There was tension when a cultivator was ordered prosecution by the police for an alleged assault committed by him to give effect to an order of social boycott passed by the panchayat. This order infuriated the people and thousands of them followed the 'accused' to the Magistrate's court. When he was taken to jail, the crowds pelted the police with stones and besieged the police in the Jail Warden's quarters. Later, they hurled bricks at the thana and assaulted the sub-inspector. When the sub-inspector attempted to disperse the crowd by threatening to shoot them, they attacked the thana.[162] A similar demonstration was held in Gaya when two non-cooperators were tried in the Magistrate's court. The police attempt to drive the non-cooperators to jail in a private vehicle was foiled by the crowd. Eventually, the Deputy Superintendent of Police had to escort them to the jail on foot followed by nearly 400 people, which included many young boys, youths and people from the lower class and castes.[163] In Bhagalpur, a large crowd followed a non-cooperator, who was tried and convicted. The police seemed powerless to prevent the demonstration.[164] In Bettiah, when a case under Section 144 of the Criminal Procedure Code was heard in the court, around 4,000 people gathered outside the court of the Sub-Divisional Officer and behaved in a 'very noisy manner'.[165]

Such demonstrations not only undermined British authority but also eroded the power and prestige of the legal system. When the police arrested the non-cooperators, they were often attacked. People no longer viewed arrests and trials as attempts to maintain law and order, rather they perceived such acts as coercion to uphold the power of the Raj. Those among the people, who appeared as criminals in the eyes of the British, were regarded as heroes by the masses, who expressed solidarity with them. In fact, it was through institutional and ideological authority that the British had tried to consolidate their hegemony and this hegemony was shaken up by the impact of the movement.

The Decline: Perceived as a Temporary Phenomenon by the Government

By May 1921, the movement began to lose momentum. Few meetings were held and those that were had poor attendance. Meetings were mostly organized for collecting money for the All India Tilak Swaraj Fund. Panchayats and seva samitis declined. The anti-liquor campaign lost its fervour and the sale of liquor increased. The enrolment fell in national schools.[166] The response to the All India Tilak Swaraj Fund was lukewarm.[167] The movement declined in the Tirhut Division. The European planters were no longer nervous and they had few problems regarding labour or rent collection. They also ceased to worry about their personal safety or the adequacy of internal security schemes.[168]

However, from the government's viewpoint, this decline was only a temporary phenomenon. The government feared that the nationalist leaders were busy making preparations for the revival of the movement with more vigorous and better organized agitations. The revival, according to government officials, would be easier as the organizational network was strong. They believed that these organizations would be ready to spring into action on receipt of a fresh mandate from Gandhi. Though the movement suffered a setback in all the provinces yet the Government of India was not confident enough to relax its policy vis-à-vis the movement.[169]

The government's fear that the movement could be revived easily did have some basis. As mentioned earlier, the movement was no longer confined to a few persons in the educated sections of the society; it had a broad base. It was clear that once the masses were organized and politicized, and their desires and aspirations were linked with the movement, the movement would acquire its own dynamics. It would follow its own rhythm and momentum, often independent of the nationalist leaders, with the masses bringing up their own agendas to the movement.[170]

Preparation to Revive the Movement

In July 1921, the Congress made attempts to revive the movement. The AICC, at its Bombay Session in July 1921, discussed the issues around which to organize the next phase of the movement. The Congress leaders decided to concentrate on the boycott of foreign cloth.[171] However, this programme failed to make an impact in Bihar. It gathered momentum only by late September 1921. It had some impact in Darbhanga, Champaran and Muzaffarpur districts.[172] Gandhi Kutir at Malkhachak in the Dighwara Thana of Saran district emerged as an important khadi centre.[173]

The issue of civil disobedience came up for discussion at the Bombay Session but the Congress leaders decided to defer it as they believed that the country was not yet ready for it. The AICC, nevertheless, instructed its members to begin preparations for it so that it could be launched in the near future.[174] A resolution was also passed by the BPCC to the effect that the conditions were not favourable for civil disobedience.[175] In Bihar, however, civil disobedience was discussed in most meetings and the local leaders at these meetings reiterated the probability of launching it in the near future.[176] Many of these meetings were attended by a large number of people. For instance, the meeting held at Mansurganj in Bhagalpur on 16 November was attended by nearly 1,500 people.[177]

In Bihar, a strong pressure was building up from below favouring this programme. For instance, campaigns were launched by local non-cooperators for the non-payment of chaukidari and municipal taxes as well as rent to the zamindars. In many areas, processions were taken out and meetings were held in contravention of the provisions of the Police Act and Section 144 of the Criminal Procedure Code. Many persons summoned under the criminal law declined to accept the summons and even tore them. The police and the chaukidars came under pressure not to report for work as Gandhi raj had dawned.[178]

The Congress viewed these trends with apprehension, for it wanted the movement to be strictly within the confines of non-violence. At the peak of the movement, Gandhi said that the nation must be disciplined to handle mass movements in a sober and methodical manner.[179] When the Congress was planning to launch the Civil Disobedience Movement, maintenance of non-violence and discipline was considered very important. Masses were not only to be mobilized for civil disobedience but they were also to be integrated into the specific forms of Gandhian Non-Cooperation, i.e. maintenance of peace. For this, the necessity of well-trained volunteers was realized.[180] In Bihar, the Congress volunteers of the early phase of non-cooperation were modelled largely on the patriotic karmi or sewak of the pre-war period, who had functioned as a controller of crowds at swadeshi meetings as well as at fairs and festivals. As the movement spread, a large number of people offered themselves as volunteers. The Congress felt that they were not disciplined and trained, as they often resorted to social boycott and intimidation to spread the movement. They defied authority in every manner and prevented others from approaching the police or the courts for lodging their complaints. Such activities were in sharp contradiction to the Congress policy.[181]

Gandhi was of the view that these volunteers were not trained enough and reliable as they had repeatedly failed to enforce order. He believed that they tended to merge in a crowd instead of standing apart and disciplining it. He said: 'volunteers often become demonstrators instead of remaining people's policemen'.[182] Gandhi wanted to change the character of the Congress volunteers by making them trained 'handlers' of the mass movement. No 'raw volunteers' were to be allowed to assist at the larger demonstrations. All volunteers were to be reviewed prior to a demonstration and issued specific instructions as suitable for the occasion. They were expected to carry a book of general instructions about their work at railway stations, public meetings and street marches, while escorting 'heroes' through a large gathering, regarding signalling of messages, protection of women, etc. Volunteer corps were to be set up for the purpose of disciplining the public and maintaining order.[183] Drill training and other exercises were organized for volunteers, in order to instil in them a sense of discipline. Rules were to be formulated for making 'people's policemen out of Congressmen'.[184]

At the Bombay Session of the AICC in July 1921 decision was taken to reorganize the volunteer corps throughout the country. The committee passed a resolution that all volunteers should be brought under central control and be known as the National Volunteer Corps. They were expected to take the pledge of non-violence and obey the command of their superiors, and be prepared to face risks in the discharge of their duties. Their duties were clearly defined and special emphasis was laid on good conduct, non-violence and social service. In Bihar, the National Volunteer Corps known as the Qaumi Sevak Dals were formed, comprising seva samiti members, Khilafat workers and Congress workers. A central board of control was set up with its headquarters at Muzaffarpur.[185]

Revival and Intensification of the Movement

Not only did the Non-Cooperation Movement revive in September 1921 but it also became intensive. Tirhut Division again emerged as a strong centre of the movement. The movement made strong impact in Sitamarhi in Muzaffarpur district where numerous meetings were held. People openly defied the

Magistrate's order, prohibiting any meeting within 300 yards of the *kachahari*.[186] In the night of 16 October, they broke open the office of the munsif's court and burnt the title suit register, rent suit register, execution register, miscellaneous register, statistical register of rent suit, etc.[187] Whenever a non-cooperator was arrested, large crowds carrying drums, trumpets and flags followed him.[188] The movement was equally successful in Champaran district where Congress 'national thanas, with their subdivision of circles', were set up.[189]

As the movement revived in Tirhut Division, the anti-planter campaign intensified. There was tension between tenants and planters over grazing rights; the latter complained that the peasants grazed cattle over their reserved grass.[190] In many areas, the tenants boycotted the bazaars of the planters and parallel bazaars were set up. District-level Congress leaders in Motihari disclaimed any responsibility for the boycott and tried to dissuade the people from it.[191] The Chauterwa factory (a planter's factory) was burnt on 2 November 1921 to the chants of *Gandhiji ki jai*.[192] In some areas, tensions mounted against the zamindars. In the villages of Champaran, many meetings on agrarian issues were held and the local non-cooperators played a key role in these campaigns. There were protests against the Union Committee in Bagaha in Champaran. The assessment of union taxation faced problem.[193]

At the national level, the arrest of the Ali brothers in September 1921 brought to the fore another issue. The Ali brothers were arrested for their speech at the All India Khilafat Conference at Karachi on 8 July. In that speech, they had proclaimed that it was against religious law for Muslims to serve in the British army and they insisted that this message be conveyed to every Muslim in the army.[194] Their arrest was condemned by Gandhi, who along with other leading Congressmen, issued a manifesto covering Muhammad Ali's speech and added that every civilian and member of the armed forces should severe connections with the repressive government.[195] On 5 October, the Congress Working Committee also passed a similar resolution in Bombay.[196] The Bihar Provincial Conference endorsed the Karachi resolution at a meeting in early October.[197]

In Bihar, meetings were held in Patna, Muzaffarpur, Champaran, Darbhanga, Bhagalpur, Monghyr, Manbhum and Palamau areas where Khilafat Committees were strong, as a mark of protest against the arrest of the Ali brothers.[198] At these meetings the Karachi resolution was read out and *fatwas* were distributed, exhorting the police and the army to resign from service.[199] In Tirhut Division, a large number of meetings were held in Madhubani in Darbhanga district, in Bettiah, Madhuban and Motihari in Champaran district and in several places in Muzaffarpur district in October 1921.[200] Nearly 5,000 people attended the meeting held in Motihari in

Muzaffarpur district on 23 October 1921. The local non-cooperation committees played crucial role in mobilizing people for this meeting. Following the distribution of *fatwas* many constables resigned from the service on the ground that it was *haram* to work for the government.[201]

The visit of the Prince of Wales to India in November sparked off protests in many areas. The agitation against the visit of a member of the British royal family can be seen as a contest for hegemony, a fight for prestige, between the nationalists and the colonial rulers. Gandhi emphasized the fact that the presence of a royal personage in the midst of his subjects was symbolic of imperial authority.[202] The colonial rulers, however, argued that the visit was a purely non-political gesture on the part of the Prince of Wales to keep in touch with his Asian subjects.[203] Gandhi opposed the visit vigorously and campaigned against it. In justification of his opposition, he said that it was his duty to educate the public about the truer perception of the meaning of the proposed Royal visit. 'Truer', because it would refute the not so true claim made by the administration about the visit being beyond politics. Contrary to what the British claimed in public, the government wanted to draw political mileage out of the proposed visit to demonstrate to the world that India was happy and content under the Raj. Gandhi, on the other hand, concluded that the Prince's visit was an attempt to uphold the prestige of the colonial government. Interpreting the visit as politics calculated to demonstrate the might and glory of the Empire, Gandhi called for counter-demonstrations. The protest was to take the form of a hartal throughout the land to coincide with the Prince's arrival on 17 November 1921, followed by local boycott of all ceremonies, receptions and other activities organized in honour of the Prince.[204]

The resolution to boycott the visit of the Prince of Wales was passed at several meetings from the AICC to various provincial level committees.[205] On 17 November, the day the Prince landed in Bombay, there was total hartal in Bihar.[206] The hartal was very successful in Patna. Attempt was made for a complete closure of all activities in Patna—to stop all provisions, *ticca gharries*, coolies, municipal service and visitors to the city. In the large number of meetings held in Patna, which were attended by a large number of people, appeals were made to government servants to resign from service, to washermen to refuse to wash the clothes of Europeans and to *ekka* drivers to refuse to ply persons wearing foreign clothes.[207] In Dumka, there was a total hartal and many Congress workers were arrested.[208] In Bhagalpur, too, the hartal was very successful. All shops were closed, business suspended and labourers stopped work. No conveyances plied. Even a marriage party had to do without a carriage and *baza* (trumpet) and were expected to shout *Gandhi ki jai*.[209] In Dumraon, the Maharaj used his influence to convince the shopkeepers to open their shops but failed in his attempt.[210] At the Dahari Fair in Balia, the hartal was total and the Deputy Collector visited the fair site to review the extent to which the people heeded the call for the hartals. When he asked a shopkeeper to give him a paan, he was refused. Later when he asked an old lady selling bangles for some bangles, she snubbed him and he immediately left the site.[211] The hartal at the Sonepur Fair was equally successful. A large number of volunteers, estimated to be 18,000 according to a government report, visited the fair. According to Nirsu Narayan Sinha, a member of Bihar and Orissa Legislative Council, who was in Sonepur on the day of the hartal, the shopkeepers observed the hartal voluntarily and were not under any pressure to do so. The shopkeepers told him: 'if other people were making sacrifices they would also make a sacrifice by closing their shops for a day'.[212]

The non-cooperators made preparations for a hartal on 22–23 December to coincide with the Prince's visit to Bihar. In Patna placards announcing the hartal were pasted in all public places and also on the compound walls of houses, including those of the Europeans.[213] When the Prince visited Patna, he was given a warm welcome by the moderates and loyalists but there was a total hartal in the city, particularly in the bazaar area. The hartal was on the whole peaceful.[214] Hartals were held in Purulia, Manbhum, Gaya, Santhal Pargana and Dhanbad districts.[215] On 22 December, there was a total hartal in Barh and a *havan* was performed in the evening on the banks of the Ganga.[216] The government expressed its surprise at the presence of a very small crowd. It was recorded with surprise: 'the unlettered masses, whom not only their traditional loyalty to the Crown, but even natural curiosity would in normal circumstances have attracted in tens of thousands to see the King Emperor's heir had not turned out in large numbers. Later on the same day at polo ground and on the next day at a garden party given by the landowners of the province a very small number of cultivators and poor classes were present. Very few people from Patna and its neighbouring districts participated in the function that welcomed the Prince'.[217]

Government Policy vis-à-vis the Non-Cooperation Movement

The discussion so far has focused on the development of the movement in its different phases and areas. It is equally significant to note how the government responded to the movement. The way the movement developed was a source of anxiety to the government as it had not faced before such a concerted effort. The movement was unprecedented; it encouraged defiance in many directions.

So far, the Government of India had followed a policy of non-interference vis-à-vis the movement. Underlying the rationale for this policy was the belief that the Montague-Chelmsford Reforms would succeed, progressive opinion in Britain had to be placated, the sympathy of the moderates for the regime had to be won and law and order had to be preserved. It feared that undue repression, as revealed by the aftermath of the Amritsar massacre, would produce a political backlash. In addition, it wanted the administration to appear as an impartial arbiter. The government was hopeful that the Congress would eventually withdraw from the movement.[218] But when the movement began to intensify in January 1921, the government reconsidered its policy of non-interference. It was concerned about the potential effects of Gandhi's campaign on the 'masses of urban elements and on large bodies of tenants'.[219] However, after much deliberation the government reached the conclusion that it would be inopportune to rescind the policy of non-interference.[220] Through further reappraisals of the policy, over the next six months, the Government of India continued to adhere to this policy. The Bihar government, however, was not happy with this decision of the Government of India. It could not comprehend why such a subversive movement was allowed to continue unhindered by the government.[221]

Local government officials in Bihar were of the opinion that this policy of restraint had negative consequences. They stated that 'allowing the Congress campaign to gather momentum, undermined the prestige and authority of the colonial administration and caused doubts and hesitancy amongst its servants and loyalists'.[222] They believed that this inaction of the government was leading to the 'impression amongst the ignorant masses that the government was either careless and indifferent or else afraid to put it down, leading to further excitement and unrest'.[223] They felt that not only had the people lost faith in them because of the government's inaction but also had doubt as to whether the government seriously intended to enforce the law.[224] They wanted the government to explicitly state its policy that the movement was 'dangerous, tending to lawlessness, and ultimate anarchy and that it was prepared to support all reasonable measures taken to prevent such lawlessness'.[225] Continuation of the movement was interpreted by the local officials as an erosion of their authority.

It is clear that if the Government of India had at any point of time during 1921 adopted a policy of active repression, the local government would have promptly taken the necessary action. Some members of the Viceroy's Council expressed similar sentiments. The Finance Member, Sir Malcolm, remarked in January 1921 that the government's attitude of tolerance did not have the desired effect as was hoped. He stated that the movement had stirred up feelings in a hundred directions, sometimes taking 'racial' turn and sometimes a direction not very different from 'Bolshevism'. Further voicing apprehension, he said, that if such forces continued unimpaired the classes which formed the backbone of their administration would not remain unaffected.[226] He emphasized that success of administration, besides being dependent on the definite enforcement of statute law and the working of the administrative machinery, depended as much on the maintenance of a general atmosphere of obedience to authority and acceptance of the existing order of society.

In November 1921, the Government of India was forced to reconsider its policy as conflicts escalated in some parts of the country, and the Congress planned to launch civil disobedience and organized opposition to the Prince's visit. On 24 November 1921, in a long letter of instruction, the Government of India informed the local governments that 'a stage has now been reached at which action on a more drastic and comprehensive scale than has hitherto been required be taken'.[227] The provinces promptly initiated action against the movement. The Bihar Government issued a notification under the Criminal Law Amendment Act on 10 December 1921, declaring various volunteer associations unlawful.[228] The Bihar government justified the action, saying that 'for nearly two years the government had adopted a policy of mildness (some even called it inaction), trusting to the good sense of the educated classes for a rejection of the Non-Cooperation doctrine'. It felt that this course of government was justified in so far as the 'tangible' results achieved by that movement was concerned, as resignations of titles, boycott of schools and courts had not made much impact and very few government servants had resigned. But the government underlined its anxiety stating that the real danger lay when non-cooperators had turned from the educated sections, whom they had failed to gain over, to mobilization of masses and organization of volunteer organizations in every districts.

It apprehended most the taking up by the non-cooperators 'the dangerous programmes like refusal to pay taxes, rent or revenue, and reduction of the allegiance to army and police'. It further stated that so long as 'the non-cooperators confined themselves to picketing of liquor shops, cloth shops, collection of muthia, etc., no great harm was done and any actionable excesses had been dealt with as breaches of the ordinary law'. The government underlined that 'now it feared that the minds of the masses were being steadily impregnated with contempt for authority and being prepared for the last stages of the campaign, that is, the civil disobedience' and this was considered by it as the greatest danger. In such situation the government stated that it could not 'afford to sit idle and see volunteer organizations perfected, merely because refuge was taken under the plea of non-violence, which it felt would be flung aside when civil disobedience would be enforced and when attempts would be made as threatened to march on government buildings, call out government officers and take their place with bands of volunteers'.[229]

Following this notification there were numerous proscriptions, arrests and prosecutions.[230] However, this did not dampen the spirit of the non-cooperators. Dying for one's country was considered to be the greatest service to the nation. The nationalists said that it was the moral duty of people not to support tyrannical government.[231] They reiterated that no amount of repression by the British would be able to silence the people, who had resolved to fight to the end. There were a large number of pamphlets and songs which stressed the strength and ability of people to face boldly any kind of threat and repression from the British. In one of the pamphlets it was said let the British commit as much atrocities as they wanted to but people would not recede till swaraj was obtained. People were asked not to sigh or recede till swaraj was obtained even if the 'police blindly beat them with batons, shower gunshots, massacre men, women and children, loot away their properties, torture them in jails, clamp martial law in towns and villages, or there be the situation of Jallianwala Bagh in every corner of India'.[232] In another pamphlet, the British were challenged, saying 'gladly oppress us to your heart's content. You will see the result of your tyranny. Such a time has come that you will see with your own eyes that the jails will be filled up soon. India has become ready to sacrifice her life and in return she will get freedom tomorrow if not today'.[233]

Repression was considered a temporary phenomenon. The nationalists said that 'for a time, the enthusiasm for freedom may possibly be stopped under the threats of jails, handcuffs, scaffold and bullets, but it is possible that the fire of freedom which is lying hidden under the ashes may, with the lapse of time, break out in the form of a horrible revolution and may reduce the military administration to ashes'.[234] They further added that the movement which has kindled 'Swantrata ka junoon' could not be suppressed and that there were thousands of Gandhis and Muhammads in this country.

Even the moderates openly expressed dissatisfaction with the government policy which they perceived as unduly repressive.[235] On 13 December, a deputation of the members of the Legislative Council of Bihar met the Governor and requested him to withdraw the Act. They pointed out that the step was 'unwarranted by the circumstances of this province and moreover highly inopportune and inexpedient because non-cooperation in Bihar had so far been characterized by non-violent methods of work'.[236] They added that 'at a time when the Province was awaiting the visit of His Royal Highness, the Prince of Wales, on a mission of peace, goodwill and sympathy, it was essential that the people should be free from any sense of panic or any feelings of bitterness due to repression actual or apprehended'.[237] They urged the government to withdraw the notification temporarily or till the civil disobedience campaign was launched, when it would be necessary to take action under the Criminal Amendment Law Act. They believed that such a step would relieve the situation and would not further alienate the supporters of the government.[238] The government did not want to alienate the moderates, and feared that its action would push the moderates towards the Congress. It decided to revoke its orders in the hope that the moderates' counsel would prevail. The government was also keen to extend a warm welcome to the Prince and did not want any disturbance at that time.[239]

The Chief Secretary sent a circular on 18 December 1921 to the district officers relaxing its policy though he recognized the grave objections which existed to any modification of the instructions issued only a week ago. However, he considered that the notification had already served its purpose as a warning and as justification for the house searches, which placed local officers in possession of information regarding the volunteer organizations. In particular, he believed that it checked the decision to enter immediately upon civil disobedience. Hence the Chief Secretary did not think that any harm would be done if further action in the way of arrest and prosecution under the special Act be deferred till Christmas week. It was represented to the Governor that such relaxation of policy would have beneficial effect on the situation at Patna. The Governor considered it desirable to accept the risk and the misrepresentation involved in the modification of recent orders, if such step contributed to the success of Prince's visit. Instructions were issued to officers not to take action under the Criminal Law Amendment Act without previous reference to Government.[240]

However, the government's relaxation of its policy was not received favourably by the local officials. According to them, the withdrawal of the Act gave the impression that the government was not earnest in its attempt to suppress the movement as well as the volunteer organizations. This, they believed, emboldened the people, who came forward in large numbers to become volunteers and court arrest. They feared the erosion of their base. Further expressing their anxiety, they said that the gentry class and the leading men from rural areas, who were their supporters, were wondering if they had backed a wrong horse by sticking to the government and were seriously considering whether it was not advisable to become high priests of the charkha cult as they had several times been asked to do. The local officials believed that the arrests of the non-cooperators under the Act had intimidated them, and if the policy had not been withdrawn, it would have benefited the government immensely.[241] The local police, in particular, had to cut a sorry figure as the people viewed the warning as a mere hoax and realized that no real attempt was made to uphold authority.[242] Contrary to the government's expectations, the preparations for the hartal continued and in many places it was very successful. After this, the movement again gained momentum and gave a jolt to the British apparatus.

Challenging the British Apparatus: Erosion of Respect for Authority

The government-issued a notification under the Criminal Law Amendment Act which raised another agenda before the movement. The nationalists perceived the notification as a curtailment of their basic democratic right to freedom of speech and organization. As this issue assumed paramount importance, the other issues receded to the background. To oppose these laws became the foremost priority of the Congress.[243] Gandhi declared that the Congress no longer intended to launch satyagraha as announced earlier but to struggle for the right of freedom of speech and organization. This right, he said, was not only of the Congressmen, but also of all parties.[244] In defiance of the Act, the BPCC gave a call to the people to recruit themselves as volunteers.[245] Thus, the Act, instead of dampening the spirit of the nationalists, further emboldened them to mobilize the masses. Even after action to be taken under the Act was deferred, the general drive for the recruitment of volunteers continued.[246]

This clearly reveals how the nationalists turned every situation in their favour. When the government was a passive spectator, the situation was interpreted as an erosion of its hegemony, but when action was initiated there was a hue and cry about the government being repressive and depriving people of even their basic civil rights. It was a no-win situation for the government.

Small processions carrying national flags and shouting *Gandhi Maharaj ki jai* became a commonplace occurrence in most places. The imminence of swaraj charged the atmosphere.[247] This phase of the movement was primarily directed against the British apparatus. There was open defiance of British authority and the symbols of British power, i.e. the courts, jails and police, which came under severe attack. Processions were taken out in defiance of government orders. Pressure was brought upon government employees to resign from service.[248] In north Bihar, the movement against the planters intensified once again.[249] The British had to openly resort to the use of armed forces to maintain their authority.

In Bhagalpur, even before the notification under the Criminal Law Amendment Act was revoked, there had been considerable activity in the *mufassil* in connection with the organization of the Qaumi Sevak Dal and the formation of new Thana Congress Committees. Government action gave a tremendous impetus to this activity and the non-cooperators doubled their efforts and many places which were untouched earlier were overrun with volunteers. In the town, however, the activities of the volunteers ceased immediately after the proclamation of the act.[250]

In Monghyr, too, volunteers were highly organized and wielded great influence among the masses. The notification drove 'the majority of Indians who were previously sitting on the fence into the arms of the non-cooperators'. Pleaders and *mukhtars* suspended practice. Foreign cloth was consigned to flames.[251]

In Gaya, recruitment of volunteers continued, even after the notification had been revoked.[252] Volunteers frequently marched around the town picketing the courts. When the courts reopened after the vacation on 3 January 1922, a large group of volunteers gathered outside and tried to disrupt the functioning of the courts.[253]

In Patna, bands of boys paraded singing national song. In the *mufassil*, volunteers were secretly recruited[254] and many members of the Bar enrolled themselves as volunteers.[255] At a large public meeting in Barh, the speakers challenged the government to arrest as many as it could. They pointed out that for every worker imprisoned hundreds of thousands of men would offer themselves as volunteers. The meeting ended with bonfire of foreign cloth. All present pledged to wear khadi and many people recruited themselves as volunteers.[256]

In Chapra, too, a large number of people offered themselves as volunteers.[257] In Shahabad district, there was disturbance in the towns of Buxar and Sasaram. In Buxar, the volunteers who were arrested shouted slogans and sang patriotic songs on their way to the jail. The Sub-Divisional Officer of Buxar reported that 'the political prisoners in Buxar had formed a happy family in the central jail and used to work each other up to a high pitch of enthusiasm'.[258] On 17 December, house searches and arrests of some leaders led to tension in Sasaram. When the accused were taken to jail, a large and excited crowd followed them. On 21 December, in defiance of the government order, a large procession carrying the Khilafat flag marched to the court and on the way appealed to all government servants to resign from service.

There was tension in Champaran too, where a large number of volunteers were recruited. The non-cooperators hailed the withdrawal of the notification as their victory.[259] In Dhanah, there were clashes between the people and the police.[260]

The situation in Purnea also was tense. According to the Superintendent of Police in Purnea, 'the government proclamation declaring volunteer associations unlawful and carrying the warning that persons, who persisted in disregarding the law would be prosecuted, having been followed by no action, whatsoever, had produced a very bad effect'. The police official said that the local police found themselves in a 'thoroughly false position as the people saw that the warnings apparently were mere bluffs and that no real attempt was made to uphold authority'.[261] A large number of volunteers were recruited, especially in Araria. In Forbesganj, large bands of volunteers marched around the town shouting slogans and singing patriotic songs. They informed the police on duty that they were not required to patrol the town any longer. In interior areas of this district, particularly in Araria, there was intensive picketing of liquor shops. The non-cooperators not only put pressure on the chaukidars to resign from service but also on the Tahsildar Panches to stop collecting chaukidari tax.

On 8 February 1922, around 300 people demolished a pound in Dhanaha and raised a swaraj flag over it to the chants of *swaraj ho gaya*. Rumours were rife in Purnea district that swaraj had been or would be realized soon. This led to 'outbreaks of lawlessness'. The sub-inspector and the police were defied by one of the parties in a land dispute in Rupauli and were forced to leave the spot. The party looted the disputed crops shouting *Mahatma Gandhi ki jai*. The police managed to arrest the accused with much difficulty, amidst hostile demonstration.

In Baisee, the warrant and the subsequent producing of people in court accused of intimidating chaukidars sparked off demonstrations and slogan shouting in the court compound. In Araria, when the police and chaukidars arrested three picketers, accused of assaulting and robbing a customer in a liquor shop, they were attacked by a large crowd shouting non-cooperation slogans. Even though the nationalist leaders in Purnea had cautioned the volunteers to refrain from 'more objectionable features of the agitation such as picketing, interfering with the chaukidars, taking out of processions and demonstrations outside the court and thana', their advice went unheeded.

The situation was extremely tense in Muzaffarpur district, which had the highest number of volunteers. Numerous meetings were held for the purpose of enlisting volunteers. The Superintendent of Police of Muzaffarpur reported that a large number of volunteers were daily sent from rural areas and 'given good feed' at Shafees house. The volunteers were told that they would not be arrested as the jail was full and, even if arrested, would be released on 31 December 1921, when swaraj would be obtained. The police superintendent further reported that these volunteers loitered on the streets whole day 'shouting and yelling and making themselves a general nuisance'. Only the ringleaders were selected for prosecution.[262]

Muhammad Jalil, who resigned from the position of clerk in the Commissioner's office, played an active role in mobilizing volunteers in the

Muzaffarpur subdivision. In the Sitamarhi subdivision, 21,000 volunteers were enlisted. Bajrangi Singh in Paru, and Birjnandan and Rajmangal Sahi in Baruraj were actively involved in recruiting volunteers. Maulvi Magful was active in Shakera, where 9,000 volunteers were enrolled. In Deoria and Motipur, Hirdey Narain and his younger brother enlisted volunteers. Ali Bux and Akhtar were active in Sadar and Minapur where 400 and 700 persons respectively became volunteers. Katra, Mahua and other thanas also had large numbers of volunteers. In Hajipur, a majority of volunteers were from the *mufassil.* They patrolled the streets, singing patriotic songs and reciting *fatwas.* Sitamarhi, with its large posse of volunteers, was the most affected in the movement. These volunteers willingly courted arrest and went to jail which was considered a place of pilgrimage. The volunteers organized processions in many villages of Muzaffarpur district. They marched shouting *Gandhiji ki jai* and other slogans.[263]

During this phase, the anti-planter campaign intensified. The factories of the planters were picketed and their employees pressurized not to work for them. There were frequent demonstrations outside the factories.[264] In Baruraj, Brijnandan and Rajmangal Sahi led a large procession with 'elephants, flags and swords'. They passed the factories of Muraripur and Thikaha on the way and informed the people that 'swaraj had come and they were now going to take over from the British'.[265] There was agitation outside the Deoria factory in Paru, and the Bhagwanpur factory in Shewhar.[266] On 4 January 1922, large crowds surrounded the Belsand factory shouting *Gandhiji ki jai.*[267] Demonstrations were held outside the Bowarrah factory. Meetings were held on the grounds of Sursand raj in defiance of the orders of the factory owners. When the manager sent peons to disperse the crowd, not only did the people refuse to move but they jeered at the peons.[268] Finding themselves under threat, the factory owners sent their families to the town. Both Europeans and Indian supporters of the British, expressed their disappointment at the failure of the government to take adequate measures against the movement.[269]

This phase, too, was marked by a large number of demonstrations, often held outside thanas, the quarters of the sub-deputy magistrate and munsif, and the court compound. It was common for the 'accused' to abuse the Magistrate. On 23 December 1922, when alms were being distributed by government officials to 800 beggars in the court compound in Hajipur, some non-cooperators, led by ex-head constable, Ramdutta Singh, ex-sub-inspector of schools, Deep Narayan Singh, national thana sub-inspector, Madanmohan Sahay, and the headmaster of the national school, Bulaki Sahu, arrived carrying a swaraj flag and told the beggars that it was *haram* to accept alms from government officials. Jails were overcrowded with non-cooperators. The undertrials openly advocated defiance and insubordination of authority to their companions in jail. They ignored and openly flouted the jail warden's attempt to enforce order and discipline. When the Magistrate visited the jail, the volunteers refused to stand up but remained seated as a mark of protest; and they often shouted and insulted him. According to the local officials, the sub-jail was in a 'state of mutiny'. In his memoir, Bajrang Sahay, described how the jail had become a site of struggle for the nationalists. When the Jail Superintendent came for his weekly round of visit to the prisoners they were expected to stand up and salute him. Bajrang Sahay in his memoir wrote how they refused to respond to 'sarkar salam' in jail. When the Superintendent would come close to the prisoners, each prisoner was expected to keep his left hand lifted and with the help of his right hand to show his teeth to the Superintendent to convince him that the prisoner was not using smuggled tobacco. But this practice the prisoners refused to observe. When the Superintendent took an offence to it, Bajrang Sahay handed him his history ticket pointing out that he had been jailed for spreading disaffection and hatred against the government. So 'how could [the] Superintendent expect him to respect him in the name of that very government and that if he was expected to respect him then there was no need for him to be in jail'.[270]

The lack of respect for authority, especially among the lower classes, was a major concern for the government.[271] In fact, it is interesting to note the dwindling authority of the prison in the popular psyche. Cautious efforts were undertaken by the nationalists to destroy the traditional belief that jails were only for the criminals. Amongst the middle class there was an initial fear of the colonial jails as public institutions that subjected them to infamy and disgrace. In fact, the growth of middle class consciousness about jails was centrally associated with its own claim to a non-criminal identity.[272]

Credit must go to the Gandhian vision of equipping people with fearlessness. To achieve independence people were not to be bowed down with fear of jail. In fact, prison as a disciplining institution had lost its teeth in the time of nationalist struggle. Going to jail became a badge of honour, a matter of pride, one of the certificates to prove one's involvement in the freedom struggle. Epithets like 'a pilgrimage to Swaraj Ashram', 'Royal Hotel' were enthusiastically employed as euphemisms for going to jail. It was projected as a place of pilgrimage. In fact, jail going was exhorted in these words: 'Go to the place of all divine avtars from lord Sri Krishna to Mahatma Gandhi, that is, jail. Is not that temple of salvation dearer than bearing the cut-throat system of administration.'[273] To go to jail for the national cause was an expression of renunciation and penance. Those who willingly performed the jailyatra rose quickly in prominence and power in local public life. When a person was arrested huge crowd used to gather to see him off to prison. Speakers at a huge meeting after his arrest used to praise him for his *atmabal* (soul force) and termed his arrest a *deshyagna* (holy sacrifice for country). It was seen as offering the sacrifice of self to the tyrannical administration. Consequently, jail went through a change of trajectory in the nationalist era—from a grim evil place, where no 'respectable' class would willingly go, to a pilgrimage site which accorded a badge of honour. Thus, the jail as a sign system went through a reversal of role: from a symbol of British rule, authority, and terror, it became a site where nationalist forces routinely mocked the imperial insignia and demonstrated their increasing influence in day-to-day life.

As mentioned earlier, the police was a major target of attack.[274] On 26 December 1921, around 200 volunteers accompanied by a large and noisy mob, carrying swaraj flags, forced their way into the Sonbarsa thana compound in Sitamarhi. The volunteers told the police to resign from service. On 23 December 1921, 100 sevak dal volunteers paraded in front of the Hajipur police station hurling abuses at the police and shouting *sarkar ki nokri karna haram hai*. A clash followed between the police and these sevak dals, who were supported by a mob of 2,000 people. In another incident, nearly 300 volunteers marched to the Raghupur Police Station and informed the sub-inspector that on 1 January 1922, they would hoist the swaraj flag in the compound and take over the police station. In Mahua, the volunteers abused and insulted the police and in Hajipur the car of the Superintendent of Police of Muzaffarpur was attacked.[275]

The widespread hostility and frequent attacks on the police demoralized the police force and greatly undermined the prestige of the government. The letter of Muzaffarpur District Magistrate to Inspector General of Police highlighted his concern of constant erosion of British hegemony. The letter stated how in the past, the establishment had been able to meet the requirements of the district because of its great prestige and prestige of the government behind it. It said that because of the organized agitation against the police and the government, the prestige greatly diminished. As a result, it stated, that the police had to rely more on a show of strength where formerly prestige alone precluded opposition. It said that the strengthening of the armed guard had become unavoidable.[276] The government now relied openly on military and police force. This laid bare the alien and unrepresentative character of the British rule. In many places, military and additional police force were posted.[277] For example, Sitamarhi Police Station had a force of 50 additional armed police and mounted military police which patrolled in Bagaha, Dhanaha, Lauria and Jogapati in Champaran district. A squadron of the 11th/12th Cavalry dispatched from Meerut in December 1921 was in the Muzaffarpur district, when a company of the 5th Northumberland Fusiliers arrived in Muzaffarpur town for winter training. Half a squadron of the cavalry was 'engaged in a route march through the Sitamarhi subdivision'.[278]

The nationalist leaders did not approve of direct confrontation with the British in the form of picketing of thanas and demonstrations outside the courts or police stations. They strongly believed that such direct confrontations with the British authority would lead to official repression. They wanted the volunteers to desist from such activities and dispatched telegraphic orders to that effect to Gaya, Hajipur and Sitamarhi. They warned that such a confrontational attitude with the authority would alienate the moderate elements.[279] The nationalist leaders made determined efforts to win the support of the moderates, and to rally popular opinion to their side in defence of freedom of speech and the right of association for political purposes.[280] The BPCC passed a resolution on 12 January 1922, stating that volunteers were strictly prohibited from saying in a court or a thana that government service was forbidden by religion, from reading *fatwa* and making any sort of 'noise' there. They were also prohibited from picketing or assembling on the road outside court and jail and making 'noise' or 'crying' loudly.[281]

These instructions were sent to all volunteer associations. In addition, nationalist leaders made attempts to enlist as volunteers men of a 'better type', who would give the government no grounds for arresting them otherwise than as members of proclaimed associations. A set of rules was also drawn up for the organization of volunteers where the emphasis was now on non-violence.[282]

At this juncture, an incident took place at Chauri Chaura in Gorakhpur district of UP. On 5 February 1922, members of a non-cooperation procession massacred a group of policemen. Gandhi and the AICC reacted to the massacre by calling off non-cooperation on the grounds that if it continued it would lead to widespread violence. The suspension of non-cooperation and repressive measures by the police brought the movement to an end. [283]

Thus this chapter gives an overview of the Non-Cooperation Movement. The movement had stirred up feelings in many directions. In many areas, the movement received an impetus from the Congress campaign, but it extended its parameters beyond those of the Congress programme and took on a local colour from its surroundings as it was shaped in each locality. The nature of the movement was fluid, taking up a variety of issues in different areas. It received an impetus from social tensions, agrarian tensions, anti-indigo protest, and it also provided a vehicle for the expression of a variety of grievances. In many areas, it led to agrarian protests. In north Bihar, the movement led to a strong anti-planter campaign. In fact, once the desires and aspirations of the masses were linked up with the movement, it followed its own rhythm and dynamism, throwing up different agendas, both national and local. Institutions of British authority were challenged and British symbols of power came under attack. Thus, though the movement did not achieve its declared object of forcing the British to allow Indians to govern themselves, it gave a rude jolt to the apparatus of British authority. The following quote from Rambriksha Benipuri aptly describes the basic impact and character of the movement:

> When I recall non-cooperation era of 1921, the image of a storm confronts my eyes. From the time I became aware, I have witnessed numerous movements; however, I can assert that no other movement upturned the foundations of Indian society to the extent that the Non-Cooperation Movement did. From the most humble huts to the high places, from villages to cities, everywhere there was a ferment, a loud echo.[284]

Notes

1. Sitaramayya, *The History of the Indian National Congress*, pp. 353–87; Chandra et al., *India's Struggle for Independence*, pp. 184–7.
2. A local newspaper of Bihar.
3. *Searchlight*, 4 August 1920.
4. Fortnightly Report of Bihar and Orissa for the first half of August 1920, Government of India, Home Department (Political) File no. 111/1920, NAI; AICC Papers, File no. 1920, Part 11.
5. *Searchlight*, 3 September 1920.
6. Ibid.
7. Fortnightly Report of Bihar and Orissa for the second half of September 1920, Government of India, Home Department (Political) File no. 84/1920, NAI.
8. *Searchlight*, 15 October 1920.
9. Bihar and Orissa Political Special File no. 143/1920, 'Copy of a Special Branch Officer's Report dated 10 September 1920'; Judith Brown, *Gandhi's Rise to Power: Indian Politics 1915–1922*, London: Cambridge University Press, 1972, p. 260.
10. Datta, *History of the Freedom Movement in Bihar*, pp. 306–9; *Searchlight* of October and November 1920.
11. Rajendra Prasad, *Autobiography*, Bombay: Asia House, 1957, p. 120.
12. Ibid.
13. Bihar and Orissa Political Special File no. 346/1920, 'Copy of a Special Branch Officer's Report dated 28 January 1921'.
14. Ibid.
15. *Searchlight*, 10, 12 and 17 December 1920.
16. Fortnightly Report of Bihar and Orissa for February 1921, Government of India, Home Department (Political) File nos. 35/February/1921 and 77/February/1921.
17. *Searchlight*, 19 December 1920.
18. Fortnightly Report of Bihar and Orissa for the second half of December 1920, Government of India, Home Department (Political) File no. 77/1921, NAI.
19. Fortnightly Report of Bihar and Orissa for the first half of October 1920, Government of India, Home Department (Political) File no. 59/1920, NAI; Prasad, *Autobiography*, p. 120.

20. Ibid., pp. 120–21.
21. Fortnightly Report of Bihar and Orissa for the first half of November 1920, Government of India, Home Department (Political) File no. 74/1920, NAI.
22. Henningham, *Peasant Movements in Colonial India*, p. 40.
23. Bihar and Orissa Political Special File no. 375/1920, 'Note on the Effect of Non-Cooperation Propaganda in Rural Areas'.
24. Ibid.
25. Arvind N. Das, 'Peasants and Peasant Organisations: The Kisan Sabha in Bihar' in *Agrarian Movements in India: Studies on 20th Century Bihar*, ed. Arvind N. Das, London: Frank Cass, 1982, p. 53.
26. Fortnightly Reports of Bihar and Orissa of October and November 1920, Government of India, Home Department (Political) File nos. 59/1920, 66/1920, 74/1920 and 33/1920, NAI.
27. The various boycotts in Bihar have been discussed in detail in Chapter 3.
28. Fortnightly Report of Bihar and Orissa for the second half of November 1920, Government of India, Home Department (Political) File no. 33/1920, NAI.
29. *Searchlight*, 8 December 1920.
30. Fortnightly Report of Bihar and Orissa of the first half of December 1920, Government of India, Home Department (Political) File no. 35/1921, NAI.
31. *Searchlight*, 10, 15, 17 and 19 December 1920.
32. Ibid.
33. Ibid., 8 December 1920; Fortnightly Report of Bihar and Orissa for the first half of December 1920, Government of India, Home Department (Political) File no. 35/1921, NAI.
34. Fortnightly Report of Bihar and Orissa for the first half of December 1921, Government of India, Home Department (Political) File no. 35/February/1921, NAI.
35. Bihar and Orissa Political Special File no. 434/1922, 'Small note to Chief Secretary of My Experience of the Movement when Posted as S.D.O., Gopalganj, 15 August 1920'.
36. Suresh Sharma, *Ramvriksh 'Benipuri': Benipuri Granthavali*, vol. IV, New Delhi: Radhakrishna, 1998, p. 4.
37. Datta, *History of the Freedom Movement in Bihar*, pp. 281–466.
38. Bihar Special Branch File no. Part-I-132L/1921, proscribed song, 'Sri Gandhi Updesh Bhajanavali', CIO Branch, Patna.
39. Ibid., File no. 181L/1921, proscribed song, 'Shri Gandhi Chalisa', CID Branch, Patna.
40. Ibid., File no. 132L/131, proscribed song, 'Sri Gandhi Updesh Bhajanavali', CID Branch, Patna.
41. Ibid., File no. 181L/1921, proscribed song, 'Prayer to Gandhi', CID Branch, Patna.
42. Ibid., File no. 181L/1921, proscribed song, 'Shri Gandhi Chalisa', CID Branch, Patna.
43. Bihar and Orissa Political Special File no. 375/1920, 'Note on the Effects of Non-Cooperation Propaganda in Rural Areas—D.I.G., 20.12.20'. This paragraph and the following three are based on this source.
44. *Searchlight*, January and February 1921.

45. *Bhartiya Rashtriya Congress Ka Itihas* (District Muzaffarpur, Bihar), Muzaffarpur: Congress Shatabdi Samaroh Samiti, 1985, pp. 22–3; Datta, *History of the Freedom Movement in Bihar,* p. 329.
46. *Searchlight,* 23 November 1921; Bihar and Orissa Political Special File no. 153/1921.
47. Bihar and Orissa Political Special File no. 50/1921; *Searchlight,* January 1921.
48. Rahul Sankrityayan (9 April 1893–14 April 1963), who is called the father of Hindi Travelogue, was one of the most widely-travelled scholars of India. He became a Buddhist monk and eventually took up Marxist Socialism. Sankrityayan was also an Indian nationalist, having been arrested and jailed for three years for creating anti-British writings and speeches.
49. Kamala Sankrityayan, ed., *Rahul Vanmay: Jeevan Yatra,* vol. I, New Delhi: Radhakrishna, 1994, pp. 259–60.
50. Ibid.
51. This comes out from the various meetings addressed by non-cooperators, Bihar and Orissa Political Special File no. 44/1921.
52. This has been vividly studied by Gyanendra Pandey, *The Ascendancy of the Congress in Uttar Pradesh 1926–34: A Study in Imperfect Mobilisation*, New Delhi: Oxford University Press, 1979.
53. Rambriksha Benipuri was a great Hindi writer. He took active part in Indian National Movement and was active with Congress Socialist organization.
54. Sharma, *Benipuri Granthavali,* p. 1.
55. Bihar and Orissa Political Special File no. 44/1921.
56. Bihar Special Branch, File no. 132L/1921, proscribed song 'Firangia', CID Record Room, Patna.
57. Bihar and Orissa Political Special File nos. 242/1927 and 286/23.
58. Bihar and Orissa Political Special File no. 286/21.
59. Bihar Special Branch, File no. 132L/1921, proscribed song 'Sri Gandhi Suyash Gazal', and 'Swaraj Ke Faede', CID Record Room, Patna.
60. Ibid., File no. 145/22, proscribed pamphlet, 'Deshghatia', CID Record Room, Patna.
61. Bihar and Orissa Political Special File no. 286/1921.
62. Ibid.
63. Ibid., File no. 182/1921.
64. Bihar Special Branch File no. 163L/1921, proscribed song, 'Sri Gandhi Suyash Gazal', CID Record Room, Patna.
65. Bihar and Orissa Political Special File no. 254/1921.
66. Bihar Special Branch, proscribed song, 'Gandhi Updesh Bhajnavali', CID Record Room, Patna.
67. *Desha,* 18 October 1923, 'Martyr to the Country'.
68. Bihar and Orissa Political Special File no. 30/23.
69. Bihar Special Branch File no. 132L/1921, proscribed song, 'Sri Gandhi Updesh Bhajanavali', CID Record Room, Patna.
70. Bihar and Orissa Political Special File no. 476/22.
71. Ibid.
72. Ibid., File no. 30/23.
73. Ibid., File no. 72/29.

74. Ibid., proscribed pamphlet, 'Victory to Mother Cow: The Test of the Hindus, Be Non-cooperators'.
75. Bihar Special Branch File no. L111/22, proscribed song, 'Chhati Ka Peepar', CID Record Room, Patna.
76. Mahatma Gandhi, *Khadi: Why and How,* Ahmedabad: Navajivan, 1959, pp. 104–5.
77. Bihar Special Branch File nos. 286/23, 169L/1921 and 155L/1921, proscribed song, 'Dharma Ki Ter', CID Record Room, Patna.
78. Bihar Special Branch File nos. 169L/1921 and 155L/1921, proscribed song, 'Dharma Ki Ter', CID Record Room, Patna; Haynes, Douglas, Rhetoric and Ritual in Colonial India: The Shaping of a Public Culture in Surat City, 1852–1928, New Delhi: Oxford University Press, 1992.
79. Ibid.
80. Ibid.; Partha Chatterjee, *The Nation and its Fragments: Colonial and Postcolonial Histories,* New Delhi: Oxford University Press, 1994.
81. Fortnightly Reports of Bihar and Orissa for January 1921, Home Department (Political) File nos. 41/1921 and 42/1921; *Bihar and Orissa Annual Administration Report, 1921,* pp. 147–8.
82. Ibid.
83. *Searchlight,* 20 February and 11 March 1921; Bihar and Orissa Political Special File no. 102/1921, 'Note by DIG showing the Extent to which Unrest Among the Police has been kept up by Non-cooperators'.
84. Government of India, Home Department (Political) File no. 49/1921.
85. Bihar and Orissa Political Special File no. 400/1921.
86. *Searchlight,* 4 February 1921; Bihar and Orissa Political Special File no. 12/1921. The rest of the paragraph is based on Bihar and Orissa Political Special File no. 12/1921.
87. Fanishwar Nath Renu, *Maila Anchal,* New Delhi: Rajkamal Prakashan, 1954.
88. Bihar and Orissa Political Special File no. 12/1921.
89. Freedom Movement Papers, SCRO 53, BSA; Bihar and Orissa Political Special File no. 144/1921, 'From Chief Secretary, Bihar and Orissa, to the District Officer, 31 January 1921'.
90. Ibid., File no. 12/1921, 'District Magistrate's Letter to Commissioner, Tirhut Division, 10 January 1921'.
91. Ibid., File no. 529/1921.
92. Ibid., File no. 12/1921.
93. *Searchlight,* 28 February 1921; Bihar and Orissa Political Special File nos. 40/1921 and 12/1921.
94. Ibid., File nos. 40/1921 and 12/1921.
95. Ibid., File no. 12/1921.
96. Fortnightly Report of Bihar and Orissa for the second half of February 1921, Government of India, Home Department (Political) File no. 42/1921, NAI; Bihar and Orissa Political Special File no. 12/1921, 'Tirhut Division Commissioner's Letter to Chief Secretary, dated 17 January 1921'.
97. Ibid.
98. *Searchlight,* 28 January 1921.
99. Bihar and Orissa Political Special File no. 12/1921, 'Tirhut Division Commissioner's Letter to Chief Secretary, dated 17 January 1921'.

100. Ibid., File no. 400/1921.
101. Ibid.
102. Henningham, *Peasant Movements in Colonial India,* pp. 70–89.
103. Bihar and Orissa Political Special File no. 400/1921, 'Fortnightly Report for the first half of January 1921, Monghyr'. The rest of the paragraph is based on this source.
104. Ibid., 'Fortnightly Report for the first half of January 1921, Bhagalpur'.
105. Henningham, *Peasant Movements in Colonial India*, pp. 70–89.
106. Bihar and Orissa Political Special File no. 400/1921, 'Fortnightly Report for the first half of January 1921, Bhagalpur'. The rest of the paragraph is based on this source.
107. *Searchlight,* 27 April 1921; Datta, *History of the Freedom Movement in Bihar,* pp. 330–3; Sahajanand Saraswati Papers, personal diary, 1921, NMML, New Delhi.
108. Datta, *History of the Freedom Movement in Bihar,* pp. 330–3.
109. Ibid., p. 308; Fortnightly Report of Bihar and Orissa for the first half of December 1920, Government of India, Home Department (Political) File no. 44/1920, NAI.
110. In the villages when cattle grazed on others' field or reserved grass, they were brought to and kept in a pound. The owners could get back their cattle only after they had paid certain fines. These pounds were auctioned to the highest bidder who gave a specified amount of revenue to the government.
111. Fortnightly Report of Bihar and Orissa for January 1921, Government of India, Home Department (Political) File nos. 41/1921 and 42/1921, NAI.
112. Fortnightly Report of Bihar and Orissa for the second half of January 1921, Government of India, Home Department (Political) File no. 42/1921, NAI.
113. Bihar and Orissa Political Special File nos. 50/1921, 51/1921 and 219/1921.
114. Fortnightly Report of Bihar and Orissa for March 1921, Government of India, Home Department (Political) File nos. 65/1921 and 45/1921, NAI.
115. Datta, *History of the Freedom Movement in Bihar,* p. 339.
116. K.K. Datta Papers, 'Statement of Bajrang Sahay—My Reminiscences of the Freedom Movement in Bihar', manuscript section, NMML, New Delhi, pp.13–14.
117. Bihar and Orissa Political Special File no. 153/1921.
118. Fortnightly Report of Bihar and Orissa for the second half of February 1921, Government of India, Home Department (Political) File no. 43/1921, NAI.
119. Ibid.
120. Ibid., File No. 12/1921, NAI.
121. Bihar and Orissa Political Special File no. 173/1921, 'Copy of Personal Diary of Superintendent of Police, Purnia, for the week ending 26 February 1921'.
122. Fortnightly Report of Bihar and Orissa for the second half of February 1921, Government of India, Home Department (Political) File no. 43/1921, NAI; *Bihar and Orissa Annual Administration Report, 1921,* p. 149; Bihar and Orissa Political Special File no. 184/1921, 'Bhagalpur Division Commissioner's Report to Chief Secretary dated 1 June 1921'.
123. Bihar and Orissa Political Special File no. 173/1921, 'Copy of Personal Diary of Superintendent of Police, Purnia, for the week ending 26 February 1921'.

124. Fortnightly Report of Bihar and Orissa for the second half of February 1921, Government of India, Home Department (Political) File no. 43/1921, NAI; *Bihar and Orissa Annual Administration Report, 1921,* p. 149; Bihar and Orissa Political Special File no. 184/1921, 'Bhagalpur Division Commissioner's Report to Chief Secretary dated 1 June 1921'.
125. Ibid.
126. Fortnightly Report of Bihar and Orissa for the second half of February 1921, Government of India, Home Department (Political) File no. 43/1921, NAI; *Bihar and Orissa Annual Administration Report, 1921,* p. 149; Bihar and Orissa Political Special File no. 184/1921, 'Bhagalpur Division Commissioner's Report to Chief Secretary dated 1 June 1921.
127. Bihar and Orissa Political Special File no. 184/1921, 'Bhagalpur Division Commissioner's Report to Chief Secretary dated 1 June 1921'; Henningham, *Peasant Movements in Colonial India,* pp. 55–6, 76.
128. Bihar and Orissa Political Special File no. 84/1921, 'Note on the Kisan Conference held at Bhagalpur on 30 April and 1 May 1921'.
129. Ibid., File no. 173/1921, 'Copy of Personal Diary of Superintendent of Police, Purnea, for the week ending 26 February 1921'.
130. Ibid., File no. 184/1921, 'Bhagalpur Division Commissioner's Report to Chief Secretary, 1 June 1921'.
131. Ibid.; *Bihar and Orissa Annual Administration Report, 1921,* p. 149. The campaign against the chaukidars became very sustained and marked during the Civil Disobedience Movement.
132. Henningham, *Peasant Movements in Colonial India,* pp. 22–3; Anand Yang, *Limited Raj: Agrarian Relations in Colonial India, Saran District 1793–1920,* New Delhi: Oxford University Press, 1989, pp. 85–6, 104–5.
133. Ibid., pp. 104–10.
134. Henningham, *Peasant Movements in Colonial India*, pp. 100, 116–19.
135. Ibid.
136. Yang, *Limited Raj,* p. 109.
137. Ibid., p. 106.
138. Henningham, *Peasant Movements in Colonial India*, pp. 116–19.
139. Fortnightly Report of Bihar and Orissa for the second half of February 1921, Government of India, Home Department (Political) File no. 43/1921, NAI.
140. Fortnightly Reports of Bihar and Orissa for February and March 1921, Government of India, Home Department (Political) File nos. 12/1921, 65/1921 and 45/1921, NAI.
141. *Searchlight,* 28 January, 18 February and 16 March 1921.
142. Bihar and Orissa Political Special File no. 65/1921, 'Note on Seva Samitis and Volunteer Movement in Bihar and Orissa, Period October 1920 to October 1921'.
143. *Searchlight,* 6 April 1921.
144. Bihar and Orissa Political Special File no. 178/1921, 'Copy forward to all Superintendent of Police from 2nd Assistant to the D.I.G. of Police, Crime and Railway, 6 April 1921'.
145. Ibid.
146. Ibid.; Fortnightly Report of Bihar and Orissa for the first half of April 1921, Government of India, Home Department (Political) File no. 51/1921, NAI.

147. Brown, *Gandhi's Rise to Power*, p. 313.
148. *Searchlight,* 1 and 6 April 1921.
149. Fortnightly Report of Bihar and Orissa for the first half of April 1921, Government of India, Home Department (Political) File no. 51/1921, NAI.
150. *Searchlight,* 1 and 6 April 1921; Bihar and Orissa Political Special File no. 173/1921, 'Satyagraha Week-Notice Signed by Mazharul Haque, Chandrabansi Sahai and Jagat Narain Lal'.
151. *Searchlight,* 6 April 1921.
152. *Searchlight,* 8, 10, 13, 17, 20 and 22 April 1921; Bihar and Orissa Political Special File no. 173/1921, 'Note on Hartal on 6 and 13 April 1921'.
153. *Searchlight,* 8 April 1921; Bihar and Orissa Political Special File no. 173/1921, 'Copy of a Special Branch Officer's Report dated 6 April 1921, Regarding a Meeting held at Bankipore in Connection with the Hartal Observed on 6 April 1921'.
154. *Searchlight,* 8 April 1921; Bihar and Orissa Political Special File no. 173/1921, 'The Crime and Railways Branch D.I.G.'s letter to Chief Secretary, 8 April 1921'.
155. Ibid.
156. *Searchlight,* 10, 13, 17, 20, 22 and 27 April 1921; Bihar and Orissa Political Special File no. 173/1921, 'Note on Hartal on 6 and 13 April 1921'.
157. Ibid., File no. 224/1921, 'Extract from D.O. No. 56/P dated 28/29 April 1921 from Commissioner, Tirhut Division'.
158. Ibid., File no. 394/1921, 'Extract of Paragraph of the Hon'ble Mr. McPherson's Note dated 5 July 1921'; Fortnightly Report of Bihar and Orissa for the first half of April 1921, Government of India, Home Department (Political) File no. 51/1921, NAI.
159. Bihar and Orissa Political Special File no. 224/1921, 'Extract from D.O. No. 56/P dated the 28/29 April from Commissioner, Tirhut Division'.
160. Ibid.
161. Fortnightly Report of Bihar and Orissa for May 1921, Government of India, Home Department (Political) File nos. 63/1921 and 46/1921, NAI.
162. *Searchlight,* 3, 6 and 8 May 1921; Bihar and Orissa Political Special File no. 238/1921.
163. Ibid., File no. 214/1921, 'Extract from a D.O. letter dated 6 May 1921 from the Superintendent of Police, Gaya'.
164. *Bihar and Orissa Annual Administration Report, 1921*, pp. 150–1.
165. Fortnightly Report of Bihar and Orissa for the first half of May 1921, Government of India, Home Department (Political) File no. 63/1921.
166. Bihar and Orissa Political Special File no. 411/1921, 'Sd. H. McPherson, 5.7.21—Account of His Visit in Tirhut from 28 June to 3 July 1921'; *Bihar and Orissa Annual Administration Report, 1921*, pp. 150–1; Fortnightly Reports of Bihar and Orissa for June and July 1921, Government of India, Home Department (Political) File Nos. 64/1921 and 1/1921, NAI; Sankrityayan, *Rahul Vanmay,* p. 258.
167. *Searchlight,* 29 June 1921.
168. Bihar and Orissa Political Special File no. 411/1921, 'Sd. H. McPherson, 5.7.21—Account of His Visit in Tirhut from 28 June to 3 July 1921'.
169. Freedom Movement Papers SCRO 56, BSA.

170. Bihar and Orissa Political Special File no. 53/1921.
171. Bamford, *Histories of the Non-Cooperation and Khilafat Movements,* p. 32.
172. Bihar and Orissa Political Special File no. 538/1921.
173. *Young India,* 12 February 1925.
174. Bihar and Orissa Political Special File no. 575/1921, 'D.I.G.'s Weekly Report, 15.12.21'.
175. *Searchlight,* 5 August 1921.
176. Ibid., 11 and 30 November 1921; Fortnightly Report of Bihar and Orissa for November 1921, Home Department (Political) File no. 18/November/1921, NAI.
177. Bihar and Orissa Political Special File no. 575/1921, 'Report of a Meeting Held by D.N. Sinha on 16.11.21'.
178. Ibid., File no. 643/1921.
179. *The Collected Works of Mahatma Gandhi* (hereafter *CWMG*), vol. 20, p. 107.
180. Bihar and Orissa Political Special File no. 575/1921; *Bihar and Orissa Annual Administration Report, 1921*, p. 151.
181. Bihar and Orissa Political Special File no. 65/1921, 'Note on Seva Samitis and the Volunteer Movement in Bihar and Orissa, Period October 1920 to October 1921'; Government of India, Home Department (Political), File no. A, June 1921, nos. 248–82 and File no. 327-IV/1922, NAI.
182. *CWMG*, vol. 20, p. 107.
183. Ibid., vol. 18, p. 284.
184. Bihar and Orissa Political Special File no. 65/1921, 'Note on Seva Samitis and the Volunteer Movement in Bihar and Orissa, Period October 1920 to October 1921'.
185. Bihar Special Branch, proscribed pamphlet, L187/1921, 'Desh Ki Pukar-Kaumi Sevak Dal Ka Sangathan', CID Record Room, Patna.
186. Bihar and Orissa Political Special File no. 538/1921, 'From Chief Secretary to the Secretary to the Government of India, dated 10 December 1921, Subject: Extension of the Seditious Meetings Act to the Tirhut Division'; *Searchlight,* 13 January 1922.
187. Bihar and Orissa Political Special File no. 529/1921, 'Extract from the Confidential Diary of the Superintendent of Police, Muzaffarpur, for the Week Ending 20 October 1921'.
188. *Searchlight,* 13 January 1922; Bihar and Orissa Political Special File no. 529/1921, 'Extract from the Confidential Diary of the SP, Muzaffarpur, for the week ending 20 October 1921'.
189. Ibid., File no. 602/1921, 'From Chief Secretary, Bihar and Orissa, to All District Officers, dated 20.12.21'.
190. Ibid., File no. 538/1921, 'From Chief Secretary, Bihar and Orissa, to the Secretary to the Government of India, dated 10 December 1921, Subject: Extension of the Seditious Meetings Act to the Tirhut Division'.
191. Ibid.; *Searchlight,* 9 November 1921.
192. Ibid.; *Motherland,* 8 and 15 November 1921; Bihar and Orissa Political Special File no. 529/1921; Government of India, Home Department Political File no. 357/1921, NAI.

193. Bihar and Orissa Political Special File no. 538/1921, 'From Chief Secretary, Bihar and Orissa to the Secretary to the Government of India, dated 10 December 1921, Subject: Extension of the Seditious Meetings Act to the Tirhut Division'.
194. Bamford, *Histories of the Non-Cooperation and Khilafat Movements,* p. 37.
195. Government of India, Home Department Political File no. 303/1921, NAI.
196. Bamford, *Histories of the Non-Cooperation and Khilafat Movements,* pp. 36–8.
197. *Searchlight,* 7 October 1921.
198. *Bihar and Orissa Annual Administration Report, 1921*, p. 152.
199. Bihar and Orissa Political Special File no. 521/1921.
200. *Motherland,* 23 October 1921.
201. Bihar and Orissa Political Special File no. 538/1921, 'From Commissioner, Tirhut Division to the Chief Secretary, Bihar and Orissa, dated 9 November 1921'.
202. *CWMG*, vol. 18, p. 102.
203. 'Report of the Civil Disobedience Enquiry Committee', *The Indian Annual Register 1922–23,* pp. 65–7, 72–3; Ranajit Guha, 'Discipline and Mobilize', in *Subaltern Studies VII: Writings on South Asian History and Society*, eds. Partha Chatterjee and Gyan Pandey, New Delhi: Oxford University Press, 1992, pp. 73–6.
204. Ibid.; *CWMG*, vol. 18, p. 102.
205. *Searchlight,* 31 August and 11 November 1921.
206. *Motherland,* 22 November 1921.
207. *Searchlight,* 18 November 1921.
208. Ibid., 20 November 1921.
209. Ibid., 23 November 1921.
210. *Motherland,* 22 November 1921.
211. Sahajanand Saraswati, *Mera Jeevan Sangharsh,* Patna: Sitaram Ashram, 1952, p. 121.
212. *Searchlight,* 23 November 1921.
213. *Bihar and Orissa Annual Administration Report, 1921,* p. 156.
214. *Searchlight,* 25 December 1921.
215. Bihar and Orissa Political Special File no. 3/1922.
216. *Searchlight,* 25 December 1921.
217. *Bihar and Orissa Annual Administration Report, 1921,* p.156.
218. Bihar and Orissa Political Special File nos. 111/1921 and 144/1921; D.A. Low, 'The Government of India and the First Non-Cooperation Movement, 1920–22', in *Essays on Gandhian Politics—The Rowlatt Satyagraha of 1919,* ed. Ravinder Kumar, London: Oxford University Press, 1971, pp. 301–14.
219. Government of India, Home Department (Political) File no. 49/1921, NAI.
220. Bihar and Orissa Political Special File no. 144/1921, 'From Secretary, Government of India, to the Chief Secretary, dated 28–30 January 1921'.
221. Bihar and Orissa Political Special File nos. 12/1921 and 586/1921.
222. Ibid., File no. 586/1921.
223. Ibid.
224. Ibid., File no. 144/21, 'From Chief Secretary to the Secretary to the Government of India, Home Department, Delhi, 15 March 1921'.

225. Ibid., File no. 12/1921, 'Personal Appreciation of the Situation, Champaran S.P., 17 January 1921'.
226. Low, 'The Government of India and the First Non-Cooperation Movement, 1920-22'.
227. Ibid.
228. *Searchlight,* 11 December 1921; Government of India, Home Department (Political), File no. 49/1921, NAI.
229. Bihar and Orissa Political Special File no. 586/1921, 'Communique, Government of Bihar and Orissa, Political Department, Special Section, dated 18 December 1921'.
230. *Searchlight,* 11, 14, 16, 21 and 25 December 1921.
231. Bihar Special Branch File no. L38/1921, proscribed pamphlet, 'Swaraj ke Faede', CID Record Room, Patna.
232. Ibid., File no. L73/1921, proscribed pamphlet, 'A Vow-Swaraj Ka Danka', CID Record Room, Patna.
233. Ibid., File no. 156L/1921, proscribed song, 'Swarajpataka', CID Record Room, Patna.
234. Bihar and Orissa Political Special File no. 37/24.
235. AICC Papers, File nos. 5–6/1922; Low, 'The Government of India and the First Non-Cooperation Movement, 1920–22', p. 308.
236. Bihar and Orissa Political Special File no. 586/1921.
237. Ibid.
238. Ibid.
239. *Searchlight,* 21 December 1921; Bihar and Orissa Political Special File no. 586/1921, 'Communique, Government of Bihar and Orissa, Political Department, Special Section, dated 18 December 1921'.
240. Ibid.
241. Ibid., File no. 538/1921, 'From the Chief Secretary, Bihar and Orissa to the Secretary to the Government of India, 10 December 1921'.
242. Ibid., File no. 586/1921, 'Communique, Government of Bihar and Orissa, Political Department, Special Section, dated 18 December 1921'.
243. AICC Papers, File nos. 5-6/1922.
244. Prasad, *Autobiography,* p. 155.
245. *Searchlight,* 14 December 1921.
246. Ibid., 14 December 1921; AICC Papers, File nos. 5–6/1922.
247. Bihar and Orissa Political Special File nos. 643/1921 and 3/1922.
248. Ibid., File nos. 643/1921 and 3/1922.
249. Ibid., File no. 3/1922, 'Report for the week ending 5 January 1922'; *Searchlight,* 18 and 29 January 1922.
250. Ibid.
251. *Searchlight,* 11 January 1921.
252. Ibid., 14 December 1921.
253. Ibid.; Bihar and Orissa Political Special File no. 3/1922, 'Report for the week ending 5 January 1922'.
254. Ibid.
255. *Searchlight,* 16 December 1921.
256. Ibid., 28 December 1921.

257. Sankrityayan, *Rahul Vanmay,* pp. 260–1.
258. Bihar and Orissa Political Special File no. 3/1922, 'Report for the week ending 5 January, 1922'. The rest of the paragraph is based on this source.
259. Ibid.; *Searchlight,* 14 December 1921; Bihar and Orissa Political Special File no. 586/1921.
260. *Searchlight,* 15 January 1922.
261. Bihar and Orissa Political File no. 146/1922, 'Extract from the Confidential Diary of the Superintendent of Police, Purnea, for week ending 16 January 1922'. This and the following two paragraphs are based on this source.
262. Ibid., File no. 37/1922, 'Copy of Daily Confidential Diary of the Superintendent of Police, Muzaffarpur, 30 December 1921'.
263. Ibid., 'Copy of a Daily Confidential Diary of the Superintendent of Police, Muzaffarpur, 9 January 1922'.
264. Ibid.; Fortnightly Report of Bihar and Orissa for the first half of January 1922, Government of India, Home Department (Political) File no. 18/January/1922, NAI; Government of India, Home Department (Political) File no. 751/1922, NAI; Bihar and Orissa Political Special File no. 643/1921.
265. Ibid., File no. 3/1922, 'Report for the week ending 5 January 1922'.
266. Ibid.
267. Ibid.; Sharma, *Benipuri Granthavali,* p. 217.
268. Bihar and Orissa Political Special File no. 643/1921.
269. Ibid., File no. 37/1922, 'From Commissioner, Tirhut Division to the Chief Secretary, 24 January 1922'.
270. K.K. Datta Papers, 'Statement of Bajrang Sahay—My Reminiscences of the Freedom Movement in Bihar'.
271. Bihar and Orissa Political Special File no. 586/1921.
272. Anandita Mukhopadhyay, 'Jail Darpan: The Image of the Jail in Bengali Middle Class Literature', in *Studies in History,* n.s., vol. 15, no. 1, 1999, pp. 108–44.
273. Arun Kumar, *Rewriting the Language of Politics: Kisans in Colonial Bihar,* New Delhi: Manohar, pp. 176–7.
274. Bihar and Orissa Political Special File no. 3/1922, 'Report for the week ending 5 January 1922'.
275. Ibid.
276. Ibid., File no. 586/1921, 'Copy of a Note by the Commissioner of the Tirhut Division'.
277. Freedom Movement Papers, SCRO 56, BSA.
278. Government of India, Home Department (Political), File no. 441/1921, NAI; *Motherland,* 23 June 1922.
279. *Searchlight,* 11 January 1922; *Motherland,* 9 and 12 January 1922.
280. Ibid.
281. Fortnightly Report of Bihar and Orissa for January 1922, Government of India, Home Department (Political) File no. 18/January/1922, NAI.
282. *Searchlight,* 25 January 1922; Fortnightly Reports of Bihar and Orissa for January 1922, Government of India, Home Department (Political) File no. 18/January/1922; *Annual Administration Report of Bihar and Orissa, 1922,* p. 5.
283. Chandra et al., *India's Struggle for Independence.*
284. Sharma, *Benipuri Granthavali,* p. 38.

CHAPTER THREE

Contests, Hegemony and the Making of a New 'National' Identity: Mapping the 'Boycotts'

NON-COOPERATION was, for Gandhi, a struggle against British hegemony. It was to prove that under British rule coercion exceeded persuasion. Gandhi pointed out how the alien government had been eager to acquire prestige by recruiting collaborators, parading them as representative of Indians and flaunting their support as evidence of a rule based on consent. Institutions like law courts and legislative councils and ideological resources like educational institutions provided that collaboration and gave hegemony to the British. Withdrawal of cooperation from the Raj would demonstrate that the government did not rule by consent. Boycotts would, thus, be the most effective means of undermining the prestige of the Raj. The mobilization of the masses would destroy those structures of domination through which the colonial government ensured its hegemonic dominance.[1]

Gandhi was never tired of reiterating that the Non-Cooperation Movement was a fight for prestige. By refusing to collaborate with 'satanic' government, an epithet often used for unjust and oppressive government, Gandhi felt his compatriots might recover some of the self-respect and moral purity they had lost by allowing themselves to be subjected to foreign rule.[2] Thus, the question of hegemony emerged as an issue of central importance in the politics of non-cooperation. The nationalists also indicated their own hegemonic ambitions in the form of constructive programmes, which would create the social and ideological base for the future. The constructive programmes also tried to create a domain of cultural identity. This chapter attempts to look at the four important boycotts of the Congress programme in the context of Bihar. These were boycotts of government educational institutions, courts, foreign cloth, and liquor. The aim is to understand the nature of these boycotts, their ideological thrust, the forms of the campaigns, the manner of their spread in different areas and their impact on government authority. The chapter also looks at the furthering of the constructive programme of establishing popular panchayat courts, national schools and colleges, the spread of swadeshi goods by installing charkhas, conducting weekly or monthly fairs and encouraging handspinning and weaving. An attempt has also been made to show the significance of these constructive programmes in visualizing an alternative society. Throughout the period, Gandhi insisted on success of constructive programme as a precondition for launching the second level of non-cooperation, i.e. mass civil disobedience, which included the non-payment of all taxes to the government.

Boycott of Educational Institutions

The boycott of government educational institutions was one of the most important programmes of the Non-Cooperation Movement. At the All India Students' Conference at Nagpur on 28 December 1920, delegates from Bihar unanimously supported the resolution favouring the boycott of government educational institutions and establishment of national educational institutions. A programme of action was also laid down for the students. It included propaganda work, constructive activities and formation of seva samitis or volunteer corps. The students were also expected to help conduct primary education in villages, help in the formation of temperance unions, learn the art of weaving and handspinning and promote the same in different villages and towns.[3]

Rajendra Prasad had certain apprehensions about the boycott of government educational institutions.[4] His opinion was that this issue would not get wide support because people looked at education more as an avenue for seeking employment and earning one's livelihood, rather than viewing government educational institutions as means for establishing colonial hegemony. The main attraction of English education was that, compared to national education, it had a better chance of fetching one a job. Rajendra Prasad was not in favour of setting up national educational institutions because he felt that people would join them hoping that these would provide them with the same benefit of fetching jobs as English education did. He first wanted campaign against government educational institution to be built up, and later, depending upon the response of the campaign, to open national educational institutions. Other nationalist leaders felt that students would not boycott their schools and colleges unless alternative educational institutions were opened for them. But Rajendra Prasad was not in favour of using such incentives for promoting the boycott of educational institutions. He said that students should be directly appealed to in the name of the country and that a thorough appraisal of the drawbacks of English education should be presented to them. They should be made aware that it was a thorny path and they had to face privation and suffering. In his words, 'if the students joined the movement after understanding the implications of their participation, non-cooperation would be more enduring. But, if they joined the movement thinking that their education and their employment securing capacity would not be affected, in view of the alternative offered, the students' association with the boycott movement would be short-lived because once they saw that their hopes were falsified, they would be disheartened and would go back to their old institutions.' However, when the call for boycott of education was given, despite Rajendra Prasad's reservation, national educational institutions were simultaneously opened.

Spread of the Movement and the Different Phases

The initial boycott of educational institutions did not have much response in Bihar. Nationalist leaders in Bihar hoped that Gandhi's proposed tour to this province 'might enthuse the people on this issue'.[5] But, by November 1920, the non-cooperators succeeded to a great extent in generating a 'considerable amount of unrest' in the educational institutions in Patna and Tirhut Divisions.[6] They actively built up the campaign against the boycott of educational institutions.[7] Students of B.N. College, Bihar School of Engineering, Law College and New College in Patna withdrew in large numbers. Many of these students were accommodated in the Sadaqat Ashram in Patna.[8] The students of B.N. Collegiate School, T.K. Ghosh Academy and the Anglo-Sanskrit School in Bankipore and the Saghra Wakf School in Bihar also threatened withdrawal, if government recognition of their schools was not cancelled.[9] Government Madrasa in Patna was also affected to a great extent.[10] In the Bakerganj mohalla in Patna, a national school was opened.[11] In Nawadah also, a national school was opened.[12] The students of the Bihar National College did not take the examination.[13] A national school was opened at Phulwari Sharif, too.[14]

The leaders addressed students in a large number of meetings in Patna, exhorting them to boycott government educational institutions. On 11 November, there was a meeting in the Anjuman Islamia Hall at Pirbahore in Patna. Around 200 school and college students attended this meeting.[15] Another meeting was held in the Anjuman Islamia Hall at Bankipore in Patna on 13 November. Around 500 to 600 students attended this meeting.[16] On 14 November, a meeting, presided over by Mazharul Haq, was held in Patna. It was attended by over 1,000 students, comprising both Hindus and Muslims.[17] In another meeting, held on 16 November at Mazharul Haq's compound in Patna, a large number of students were present. According to different government reports, the number of people attending this meeting varied from 2,000 to 8,000.[18] Many students left their classes to attend these meetings. The students of the Bihar National Collegiate School repeatedly requested their headmaster to close the school so that they could also attend the non-cooperation meetings. But when there was no response to their requests, the students on their own skipped their classes on 15 November and attended the meeting.[19] Also many students, on their own initiative, organized processions and convened meetings. They even invited the leaders to address such meetings. In Patna, around 50 students of B.N. College left their classes shouting *Gandhiji ki jai*. Other students of that college also joined them. They went out in a procession to Patna College. Some of the students of Patna College even joined the procession. Around 25 students of the Patna New College also joined them. The procession carried a black flag with a white star and crescent and a white flag that depicted a portrait of Hanuman. Then the students sent invitations to Mazharul Haq, Rajendra Prasad, Deep Narayan Singh, Jagat Narayan Lal and other local leaders to address their meeting. Many more students joined the meeting after their classes were over. The number of people at the meeting increased to 500.[20]

In these meetings, the speakers mainly dwelt on the reasons underlying non-cooperation. They highlighted the enslaving role of English education and made an earnest appeal to the students to boycott their educational institutions. Students were asked to appeal to their guardians to allow them to boycott their educational institutions, but if their guardians did not agree to their appeal, they were told to non-cooperate even with their guardians. Students were asked to give serious thought to what they were going to do before quitting their educational institutions.[21] Maulana Abul Kalam Azad, while addressing one such meeting in Patna on 16 November 1921, told the students 'not to look back once they had decided to put their hands to the plough'.[22] He also said that 'they should not expect alternative national educational institutions to be ready for them as soon as they withdrew from their educational institutions'.[23] Even Jawaharlal Nehru, while addressing the students in the same meeting, said that, 'Non-cooperation did not specify that big national schools and colleges would be substituted for British educational institutions'.[24] The leaders asked those students, who had withdrawn from educational institutions, not to join the national schools and colleges but to dedicate their lives for the service of the nation. The students were asked to help in propaganda and constructive activities of the Congress.[25]

Educational institutions in the Tirhut Division remained 'disturbed'.[26] In Muzaffarpur, B.N. Collegiate School, Greer Bhumihar Brahman College and

Muzaffarpur Zila School remained greatly 'disturbed'. One of the professors of the Greer Bhumihar Brahman College took great interest in the Khilafat matters. The headmaster of the middle school in Bagaha in Champaran district also took an active part in the movement. The Chapra Collegiate High School disaffiliated itself from government recognition and developed into a national school. In the Tirhut Division, even in the villages, educational institutions were affected.

Besides the Patna and Tirhut Divisions, till December 1920, the boycott had not made much impact in other Divisions. Government high schools in the Bhagalpur Division remained largely 'undisturbed' with some exceptions[27] like T.N.J. College in Bhagalpur which remained greatly 'disturbed'. Students of the Jamtara H.E. School in Santhal Pargana boycotted their school. The boys of the Deoghar H.E. School passed a resolution demanding a national school.[28] In the Godda High School, a teacher forwarded an application asking for his son's name to be removed from the rolls. The managing committee dismissed both the teacher and his son.[29] In Chotanagpur, it was only the Ranchi Zila School that was to some extent affected.[30]

The movement declined somewhat by the end of December 1920. The government considered the winter vacation to be the main reason for this decline.[31] But by January 1921, another wave of boycott started. This can be seen as the onset of the second phase. This phase was more marked by 'picketing and intimidation' to dissuade students from attending classes, especially in Muzaffarpur and Bhagalpur.[32] The minister of education issued instructions to various District Magistrates, asking them 'to provide police protection, if asked, to those educational institutions, which were threatened with intimidation and where unlawful means of discouraging students were attempted'.[33]

Patna remained quiet in this phase, despite the persuasion of the non-cooperators.[34] But, unlike Patna Division, the Tirhut Division in this phase, too, remained 'disturbed'. The movement affected most of the high schools and colleges in Muzaffarpur in the Tirhut Division.[35] The Bhumihar Brahmin Collegiate School and Mukharji Seminary in Muzaffarpur witnessed a great degree of tension. More than 80 per cent students of these institutions withdrew.[36] In the Darbhanga district, a large number of students who had left their schools and colleges moved around different villages asking the students to boycott their educational institutions.[37] In Madhubani, a government school was converted into a national school.[38] Motihari in Champaran district was comparatively quiet.[39]

The Bhagalpur Division remained greatly 'disturbed' in this phase.[40] A large number of students of Madhepura High School and Monghyr Zila School boycotted their schools. The Head Maulavi of the Jammu High School and another Muslim teacher of the high school in Supaul actively participated in the movement. Bhagalpur was the most 'disturbed' district. The attendance in a Bhagalpur Zila School by 24 January 1921 dropped from 346 to 176.

The government took serious note of this fresh wave of boycotts. The Chief Secretary expressed his concern for allowing the non-cooperators to deliver 'violent speeches' without any restraint and 'peaceful' students prevented from going to schools. He felt that 'the nurturing of any such feeling that the ordinary processes of the law had been suspended was bound to be reflected in the discipline of the schools'. He said that in any case where the Educational Officer reports the use of force to the Magistrate action should be taken to prevent students from being forcibly kept away from schools. He wanted heads of the colleges and schools to refer all cases of withdrawal to the parents for their approval, stating that the government wanted to do their best to enlist parental support against the 'mischievous attempts'. Such 'mischievous attempts', according to him, if successful would result in injury to no one but the boys themselves. He further stated that if parents and guardians expressed their desire to remove their boys from the educational institutions, then their requests should be immediately complied with. However, he was of opinion that the majority of the parents and guardians were not in favour of withdrawal of their children from educational institutions.[41]

By February 1921, reports from most districts indicated decline in the boycott. Many students were anxious to return to their institutions. In fact, many students started returning to their schools and college, but the impact of the boycott was clearly obvious. The Commissioner of Patna admitted that 'damage had already been done to the then existing educational institutions'.[42] The government apprehended that 'for some time to come, the result of the educational boycott would be apparent in the general slackness of discipline, absence of respect of students to their teachers and loss of the habit of regular and steady application to work'.[43]

Rahul Sankrityayan narrates in his autobiography the kind of impact that the national school had on even the younger students in the village. He gave example from his village Ekama in Chapra, where he actively campaigned. This village had a Gandhi Vidyalaya. Two young students of this school, Ramchandra and Mangal, mobilized the other students, mostly of the age group 6 to 12, and took out a procession shouting slogans like *Gandhi Mahatma ki jai*, *Bharat Mata ki jai*, etc. After the procession, they held a meeting. Ramchandra presided over the meeting and Mangal addressed it. Such example, according to Rahul Sankrityayan, indicated how schools like Gandhi Vidyalaya played a very crucial role in generating enthusiasm amongst school children.[44]

Even though boycott of educational institutions started declining, the movement succeeded in affecting a large number of educational institutions.

The total decline of students in colleges and secondary schools in two years, i.e. 1921 to 1922, was 15,747. The total number of national schools on 31 March 1922 was reported to be 442 and that of pupils in them 17,333.[45]

National schools, both for the primary and secondary stages, were established in most of the districts.[46] The total number of primary school was around 250 and of secondary school around 50. Some 20,000 to 25,000 students received education in these national schools.[47] At Hussainabad the government-aided Sanskrit Tol was transformed into a national middle school.[48] Many professors and teachers resigned their posts. They either joined national educational institutions or took to national work.[49] Rajendra Prasad resigned from both the Senate and the Syndicate of Patna University.[50] A National College was established in Patna in January 1921.[51] By March 1921, 71 students enrolled in this college.[52] Bihar Vidyapith was also opened to co-ordinate, control and guide the activities of all the national educational institutions that had come up in this province.[53]

The students withdrawing from educational institutions were expected to actively participate in the movement. Most of them were engaged in propaganda activities.[54] A committee was formed in Patna to do the spadework for nationalist propaganda. Ram Binod Singh was its secretary.[55] Students in Patna went from door to door collecting students' signatures in support of the movement.[56] The nationalist leaders, while addressing the students in various meetings, urged them to engage in propaganda and the constructive programmes. Jagat Narayan, while addressing a students' meeting at Anjuman Islamia Hall in Bankipore on 29 January 1921 in Patna, told the students to organize meetings in schools and colleges. He also told them to select students for propaganda work in the *mufassil* from amongst those who had volunteered to work for the movement in the various meetings.[57] A training class for fifteen days was also started in the National College in Patna to give necessary instruction to such students. The students were also expected to learn weaving and handspinning and to promote the same in different villages and towns.[58] Many students also became members of the seva samitis. Around two hundred college students of Patna were devoting their time in the different villages, helping the Congress in its organizational work at the local level.[59]

One of the problems faced by non-cooperators in the opening of national educational institutions was paucity of funds.[60] *Muthia* was one of the ways suggested for collecting funds. Rajendra Prasad, Mazharul Haq and Chandra Bansi Sahay also put forward a suggestion to collect funds through one rupee receipts. In one of the Kisan Sabha meetings, which was held at Rajpur in Champaran, there was a suggestion to open a national school in every village and to support those schools by taking subscriptions of a handful of rice from each villager. The banias of this area provided financial support in the opening of national schools. In Shikarpur in Champaran, where most of the students of the lower primary school had withdrawn, the banias funded the opening of a national school for these students.

Gandhi's tour to Bihar in February 1921 facilitated the opening of many national schools.[61] In this tour, Gandhi collected a huge corpus of fund, which he donated for opening national educational institutions in Bihar. Gandhi was in favour of collecting subscriptions from even the poorest people. He asked the students to try to collect subscriptions of one paisa from every person. In Jharia, he succeeded in collecting a huge sum from the Gujaratis, Bengalis and Marwaris. The Bihar National College was opened in February 1921 with the support of this fund.

Education: Domain of Cultural Autonomy and Identity

The boycott of educational institutions and setting up of alternative national education institutions in its place was also an ideological battle for the nationalists.[62] The nationalists, while addressing the students in different meetings, underscored that the basis of British power was not merely physical strength but also ideological. They highlighted that colonial educational system had been playing the ideological role of legitimizing British rule. It did the work of injecting 'doses of the slow poison' of colonial ideology. It created what is called colonized minds, which acted as catalysts in percolating colonial ideology downwards and in providing an ideological justification for the continuation of British rule. Recognizing the ideological role of British education, the nationalists unleashed a systematic attack on the colonial educational system in order to free the intelligentsia from the fetters of colonial ideology.[63] At many nationalist platforms, the dominant theme in various speeches was invariably a systematic attack on the philosophy of English education, which, they thought, created crippled minds. The theme of the slavery of the mind had become one of the fundamental ideological elements of their attack.[64]

Muhammad Ali also, while addressing meetings in his tour of the province in February 1921, constantly drew the attention of students to the enslaving character of English education. In one meeting in Patna on 6 February 1921, he said, 'the middle, lower and ignorant classes have joined the movement but the educated sections, because of their slave mentality, due to their being nurtured in English education, have been most reluctant to join the movement'.[65] Bringing out the effect of English education in another meeting in Patna on the same day, he said 'when it was possible for a person to be killed with a little sugar, there was no necessity to administer poison to him.

The little sugar was added to education by the British in order that the people of India might become slaves and lose their freedom'.[66] He asked the students and teachers 'whether they would like to be among Lords Chelmsford and Reading or would want blessings from God'.[67]

While addressing the students in various meetings, Mazharul Haq, Deep Narayan Singh, Tulsi Singh and other provincial leaders also highlighted the 'crippling' nature of English education.[68] Many students and teachers, who had withdrawn from British educational institutions, also explained how they had been enchained by English education.[69]

The uniformity of this theme in their attack was apparent not only in political speeches and writings but also in their nationalist pamphlets and songs. One pamphlet, which was distributed amongst the people, titled 'Bharat Mata Ka Sandesh' brings out vividly how the nationalists viewed the education imparted in government educational institutions. It said how the Mother has sent message through Gandhi asking boys over 18 years to withdraw immediately from their educational institutions as the kind of education given in these educational institutions strengthened the bond of slavery and destroyed self-help and self-reliance. It said how the Indian history before the coming of the British was shown in dark light and the British rule was looked upon as 'messiah'. This history, it stressed, would bring about a feeling of helplessness and would generate a strong apprehension that if the British gave them swaraj or left them, Indians would fight among themselves and die, and that once again other people from outside of India would invade, conquer and rule over India. It also said that the present education was costly and poor people could not afford it and that even people with average background could afford it with great difficulty. It further pointed out that even after receiving such costly education, getting a job was difficult. It highlighted that the large universities, colleges and schools were not made for the good of the students, but they were trained there to be slaves.[70]

The boycott of colonial educational institutions could be seen as a moral and psychological war that had to precede the political battle. Jawaharlal Nehru, while addressing students in a meeting in Patna on 16 November 1920, said that as people were afraid to speak freely, they should first have moral and mental independence before achieving physical independence. He further said that people had lost their self-respect as the kind of education imparted to them in schools and colleges had enchained their souls. According to Nehru, since education inculcated in the minds of educated Indians that Europeans were superior to them, they preferred to wear English dress and imitate English style aiming to acquire English prestige.[71]

Speakers in many meetings also highlighted that receiving English education was a threat to their religion and native culture. The need was felt to preserve the distinctness of one's culture and no intrusion of the colonial government in that area was to be allowed. The nationalists advocated the spread of native languages and going back to the roots of one's own indigenous culture and traditions. A strong feeling developed that English education was not good for one's character and morality.[72] Maulana Abul Kalam Azad, while addressing students in a meeting on 16 November 1920 in Patna, told them that 'a sepoy in the Army gave his body for Rs. 12 but the students were becoming soul-enslaved free of cost and this was contrary to their religion'.[73] In one such meeting in Patna on 28 January 1921, Waris Husain, a local leader, said that, 'they would not derive any benefit from English education as it only taught them to read dog and pig, with the result that the students had forgotten their religion'.[74]

Besides, mocking attitude towards the products of educational institutions was not uncommon. One of the popular sayings was: 'Learn English and you lose your humanity'. The origins of this kind of mocking attitude towards educated Indians are not far to seek. Literacy in English that education gave, in whatever degree of proficiency, was surely a gateway to worldly success. Neither the chances of gainful employment nor the status that the knowledge of English brought with it could be sneered at. It could only be ridiculed under the familiar theme of the fallen morality of the man of success. Such ridiculing could serve as a means of relieving the collective guilt of a colonized society. The educated man served as a scapegoat in this respect: how could he deny having sold his soul (i.e. culture) for the sake of money?[75] The perception that women had remained the bulwark of India's moral strength because they had not been educated was also common.[76]

One of the weapons the nationalist intelligentsia used to spread the nationalist ideology was the setting up of a network of national schools and colleges. These were distinctly national institutions, which had their own curriculum, faculty and sources of funding. The guiding principles of the curriculum of national schools under Bihar Vidyapith were:

> (1) that the students' mind must not be stuffed with unnecessary and useless things, (2) that, along with liberal education, he should also be given instruction in things that would help him to earn his livelihood, (3) that the patriotic spirit should be kindled and fostered in him from the beginning, and above all (4) that he should be taught to be god-fearing, (5) instruction to be national must be given from the nation's point of view. The student's home and country should therefore be the centre from which it should start and whatever is taught should be taught in direct reference to it. This is specially necessary in the case of geography and history. Another point kept in view is that the instruction must proceed from the familiar and the known to the unfamiliar and the unknown.[77]

Thus, education was getting redefined. Nationalists said that the kind of education given in the schools exaggerated and rationalized the inequalities in society. They further said that such education added a pervasive feeling of dissatisfaction, moral anarchy and a licence to individual self-seeking, hypocrisy and tyranny. They pointed out that in the nationalist education institutions there was a stress on the ethical aspects of education and the need to integrate the individual within the collectivity. Human self-fulfilment was an essential aspect of this education.[78] Gandhi, while opening a national school in Champaran, said,

> I look upon our present system of education with horror and distrust. Instead of developing the moral and mental faculties of the little children, it dwarfs them. . . . The chief thing aimed at in national schools is contact of children with men and women of culture and impeachable moral character. That to me is education. Literary training is to be used merely as a means to that end.[79]

Education, for Gandhi, was to be de-linked from its main priority of providing jobs. Gandhi said, 'may not men earn their bread by intellectual labour? No. . . . Mere mental, that is, intellectual labour is for the soul and is its own satisfaction. It should never demand payment'.[80]

Character building and swadeshi were seen as integral part of the national educational system. Jawaharlal Nehru exhorted the students to take the opportunity offered by national education to build up their character and simultaneously realize the power of sacrifice, discipline and suffering.[81] According to Mazharul Haq, the main motive of the national educational institutions would be character building among the students and to inculcate in them the spirit of sacrifice and service to the nation.[82] The Bihar National College was started with a view to providing sound education to the young men of the province and to prepare them for service to the country. It was also aimed at giving instruction of a practical nature to enable the earning of a livelihood to those students, who withdrew from the government institutions.[83] National education emphasized the grounding of students in different aspects of nationalist ideology and economic programmes, like the spread of charkha and khadi. Thus, the nationalist education would perform a dual role. Firstly, it would root out the ideological justification for the continuation of British rule. Secondly, it would lay the social ideological foundations for the pattern of future socio-economic developments in the country.[84]

Thus, by attacking the prevailing system of education, Indian leaders sought to establish the role of education in idealist terms. It was a moral and psychological war that had to precede the political battle. The main thrust of the nationalist education would be to kindle patriotic spirit, build student's character and inculcate amongst them the spirit of sacrifice and service to the nation. The education was to be provided from the nation's point of view. The most significant aspect of it was to preserve the distinctiveness of India's culture and to resist the intrusion of the colonial government. In fact, the major burden of looking after the cultural dimension of nationalism fell on education, which was supposed to protect India's cultural uniqueness (which lay in her spirituality). The nationalists advocated the need to go back to the root of one's own indigenous culture and tradition. English education came to be seen as a threat to religion and native culture. Thus, the nationalists confronted the colonial education system as an agency of cultural domination and out of this confrontation arose the urge to define India's educational needs from within India's own cultural repertoire. Education became a means of reclaiming India's self-identity pushing aside the colonial masters. Studies have been highlighting the implications of seeking India's educational problems in a broader religio-cultural revival. In north India, the emphasis of shedding off foreign association of education led to the projection of Hindi as the symbol of self-identity which had its consequences for anti-Muslim consciousness. According to religion and culture, a central place meant conferring predominant position to ancient Indian texts of religion and literature which acquired a principal place in the curriculum of national education. This also had implication for non-Hindus. The educational discourse lacked adequate recognition of the problem of inequalities. There was a belief that spiritual knowledge would destroy miseries. Ideas such as the practice of inquiry within one's milieu; and the application of knowledge to solve daily problems were alien to the agenda of moral upliftment which had a central place in nationalist discourse. Educated Indians sought to improve the moral fibre of Indian society. School-related knowledge got isolated from everyday reality and cultural milieu of the child. The curriculum and textbooks were devoid of any positive symbols of the 'depressed-class' child's world. They either have no symbols representing the lower order or only negative symbols. The world view of the higher and propertied castes, interspersed with symbols of middle-class life, finds dominant representation. The history of the oppressed sections of society, the symbols of their culture, their arts and crafts, in short, anything that might present them as a people with dignity, are absent from the sanctioned school literature. Thus, the cultural autonomy and identity presented in this literature were reflections of the upper-caste vision, drawn heavily from the Brahminical tradition.[85]

Boycott of Foreign Cloth

The destruction of indigenous weaving and the influx of foreign cloth, resulting in unemployment and a huge drain of wealth, had become visible symbols of colonialism for the nationalists. The boycott of foreign cloth was an important programme of the Non-Cooperation Movement. The nationalists were promoting khadi in place of foreign cloth. The promotion of khadi can be seen as a part of the Swadeshi Movement signifying economic independence—a necessary component of political swaraj. The Swadeshi Movement enjoined total abstinence from machine made goods and asked Indians to spin their own yarn and get it woven by their own weavers. It was an attempt to revive the indigenous industry and reconstitute the basis of home consumption. Once the handspinning industry revived, the spinning wheel—charkha—emerged as an important symbol of nationalism. A concerted effort to boost home industry through a boycott of British goods was already once made in the swadeshi campaign in Bengal from 1905 to 1910.[86]

Gandhi was able to generate a huge range of beliefs, aspirations and popular symbols to enlist people around khadi and charkha. He felt that, through stimulating the production and use of indigenous cloth, he could provide supplementary employment to the masses, remove untouchability and promote self-sufficiency in the villages. It could be the basis of a new non-industrial, craft-based economic structure in independent India, which would weld together people of all religions and castes, drive out British rule by non-violent means, and introduce an improved standard of morality and a sense of national unity.[87] The charkha came to be seen as a tool of economic and political emancipation for the poverty-stricken village masses.

By 1919, Gandhi was appealing to all to adopt khadi and take a vow of swadeshi. Gandhi set about converting the nation to khadi in a systematic and structured manner. He established numerous organizations and associations for its promotion, as well as training centres for spinning and weaving. He also persuaded the Congress Party to give khadi a central place in its policies.[88] By 1920, the Non-Cooperation Movement included boycott of imported textiles and organization of pickets at the entrance to foreign cloth shops. Furthermore, all Congress workers and leaders were expected to wear white khadi.[89] While the Congress was to set an example, all Indian men and women were called upon to burn foreign cloth as part of their acceptance of the swadeshi vow. Volunteers hawked khadi through the streets, providing door-to-door collections of foreign cloth for burning.

Spread of the Movement

Even though the boycott of foreign cloth had been a part of the Congress programme, it was only from August 1921 onwards that the Congress laid special emphasis on it.[90] The boycott of foreign cloth was the main agenda for discussion at the All India Congress Working Committee meeting in Patna on 16 August 1921. It was resolved that, by the end of September 1921, an effective boycott of foreign cloth was to be brought about.[91] The BPCC set up a separate committee, with representatives from different districts, to draw a strategy for this programme. The committee decided that volunteers would collect foreign cloth by going from house to house. It also decided to spend one-fourth of the local swaraj fund for promoting handspinning and khadi. Appeals were made to the foreign cloth dealers to give up trade in foreign cloth, to dispose off their stocks and to sell only Indian-made cloth.[92] However, the government was hopeful that this programme of the Congress, as compared to liquor boycott, would not get wide support because it would affect the material interests of the Marwari community, who were the chief dealers of foreign cloth. Preventive action against picketing of liquor was rendered more difficult by the fact that a large number of people, even the moderates, supported tacitly, if not openly, the anti-excise campaign.

The government hoped that support of the campaign against foreign-made cloth would come only from a more limited section of the population, since most of the people required cloth. According to the government, unless the Indian supplies were supplemented from outside, the poorer classes would be in rags and for this reason it hoped that the cloth boycott would attract less support than the campaign against the liquor traffic. Besides this, the government considered another reason which would operate against cloth boycott: as already said above, it would not get the support of the Marwari community, the principal dealers in foreign cloth, who till then had been on the side of non-cooperation as this section would be mainly affected by the cloth boycott. The government felt that when any community was totally against the programme, the weapon of social ostracism, though so effective against individuals, would cease to operate in a wide context.[93]

Despite the government's hopes, there was a widespread campaign against foreign cloth. A large number of meetings were held in different parts of Bihar, where the speakers mainly dwelt on the boycott of foreign cloth and the need for swadeshi. In August 1921, Gandhi, along with Muhammad Ali and other leaders, toured Bihar. They addressed a large number of meetings. In these meetings, apart from Hindu-Muslim unity, they also dwelt on the need for boycott of foreign cloth and promotion of khadi.[94] On 11 August, they addressed meetings at Buxar, Dumraon, Bikramganj, Koath and Sasaram. Around 6,000 people, amongst whom were many women, attended the Dumraon meeting. The Buxar meeting was attended by 8,000 people, most of whom were from the agricultural classes. The meeting at Bikramganj was attended by 5,000 people. On 12 August, Gandhi and Muhammad Ali addressed meetings at Sherghatty and Gaya. Around 15,000 people attended the Sherghatty meeting. The Gaya meeting was attended by 10,000 people. On 13 August, they addressed meetings at Nawadah and Bihar Sharif. The Nawadah meeting was attended by 10,000 people and that at Bihar Sharif by 15,000 people. After the meetings, a large number of caps and coats were thrown away and burnt. Gandhi also addressed a private meeting of cloth sellers and weavers in Patna City on 16 August. It is significant that the meetings held in the course of Gandhi's tour in the province were not attended by people of 'Rais' class, and this in a way throws light on the base of the national movement.

Even provincial-level leaders, like Rajendra Prasad, addressed many meetings in Bihar, laying emphasis on boycott of foreign cloth. In September 1921, Rajendra Prasad toured many places and addressed many meetings, advocating boycott of foreign cloth. He addressed a large number of meetings in Tirhut Division. On 3 September, he addressed meetings in Raxaul and Motihari.[95] He also toured many places in Bhagalpur Division.[96] On 4 September 1921, he and Shah Zubair of Monghyr addressed a meeting at Begusarai, which was attended by 1,000 people.[97] In this meeting, Rajendra Prasad spoke mainly about the necessity of using home-made cloth and of boycotting foreign cloth; he also said that the only means of getting swaraj was to encourage the old charkha in every house and to produce sufficient cloth. Advising cloth merchants not to deal in foreign cloth in future, he said that swadeshi would fetch them the same profits. He asked the cloth dealers to hold a meeting amongst themselves and take a decision not to sell foreign cloth anymore. On the same day, Rajendra Prasad addressed another meeting in Begusarai. Around 1,000 people attended this meeting. After these meetings, most people, in response to Rajendra Prasad's appeal, threw off their foreign clothes and caps and made a bonfire of these.

On the evening of 4 September, a meeting of the local Marwaris and cloth merchants was held at Sri Narain Aggarwal's residence in Begusarai. Banarsi Prasad Jhunjhunwala of Bhagalpur told the merchants the disadvantages of using foreign cloth. He said that if they were true to their religion and wanted to save cows, they should give up trade in foreign cloth and take to swadeshi cloth. He explained that the British rule in India existed chiefly for trade and that the British, in order to safeguard their empire, had employed many soldiers, who killed thousands of cows every day. He appealed to them that if they would give up wearing foreign cloth, the number of English soldiers would be reduced, and thereby, many cows would be saved from slaughter. Thus he played upon the fear that under British rule the sacred cow had come under threat to arouse anger against the British. The anxiety around religion as a whole spoke of the seriousness of the situation and the urgency to oppose the foreigner. Most of the Marwaris of Begusarai signed an undertaking promising not to indent and sell any foreign cloth after their present stock was exhausted.

Rajendra Prasad and Muhammad Shah Zubair also addressed a meeting at Gogri on 5 September 1921. Muhammad Shah Zubair told the Muslims present in this meeting that if they were keen to amend Khilafat wrongs, they should wear khadi. He also told them that by inflicting financial loss on the British by boycotting their 'unholy' foreign cloth, they could take revenge on them (the British) who had done religious wrongs to them.[98] In the same meeting, Mohammad Ishaq of Barami told the Muslims

> now that your religion is at stake, give up cooperating with them. Adopt swadeshi. Do not wear foreign cloth. Do not send the 60 crore of rupees annually to England, with which weapons are made to attack your Kaba and Mecca. Don't you remember your sisters in the Punjab were beaten on their buttocks with flogs. Take a lesson and save your country. Establish swaraj. Boycott foreign cloth. Do not be ashamed to weave and spin. When Fatima, daughter of the Prophet spun, why can't you do that.[99]

On 5 September, Rajendra Prasad and Muhammad Shah Zubair also addressed a meeting at Jamalpur, which was also attended by 1,000 people.[100] They asked the local merchants to sell country-spun cloth. Mohammad Ishaq of Barami, while addressing this meeting, said that the

> British cloths are woven by English people and when your mothers, sisters and wives use them, then the hands of the English people fall on the persons of your mothers, sisters and wives. The mothers and sisters were beaten by canes in Punjab and you cannot like that the British goods should be used by your mothers and sisters, who were not respected. The Marwaris should say to the purchasers of British cloth that those cloths have insulted your mother and sisters and they should not use them.[101]

It is interesting to see how the nationalists throughout the campaign particularly played upon the sentiments of mothers and sisters being insulted under the British rule to arouse anger against the British. Modesty and chastity were looked upon by the nationalists as the main virtues of women, and they felt that it was the duty of every society to protect the honour of women most. Hence, encounter with the British did not remain merely political but got extended and became a call to protect the honour of women.

Nationalist leaders also campaigned in Bhagalpur, an important cloth distribution centre in Bihar. Lala Lajpat Rai visited Bhagalpur on 10 September 1921 and made an appeal to the people to boycott foreign cloth. Initially, the response of the Bhagalpur merchants to his call was not enthusiastic.[102] On

11 September 1921, Lala Lajpat Rai, accompanied by Rajendra Prasad, Deep Narayan Singh, Banarsi Prasad Jhunjhunwala, Prem Sundar Basu and Kamaleshwari Prasad visited Monghyr to mobilize the people for the boycott of foreign cloth and the adoption of charkha.[103] In Monghyr too, these leaders met the local cloth merchants and discussed with them ways and means of boycotting foreign cloth. Most of the local cloth merchants agreed not to buy any more foreign cloth and also to give up its sales, once the present stocks were over.[104] A meeting was also held in the evening at Choramba, which lay midway between Monghyr and Jamalpur on the Sitakund Road. 3,000 people attended this meeting.[105] While addressing this meeting, Lala Lajpat Rai, apart from dwelling on the need for swadeshi, told the Muslims that the caps, which they wore, called Turkish caps, were not manufactured in Turkey but by the Italians and Austrians at whose hands the Muslims had suffered great disgrace. He also said,

> it is not part of the duty of government servants to wear foreign caps or clothes. Their being in service does not prevent them from using swadeshi things. I will be the last person to request government servants to be unfaithful but would exhort them to be true to their salt. Just and honest, they should not be oppressive and tyrannical and must not submit false reports. I will not ask anything more of them now, as the time to do so had not yet come, but a time will soon come when we will demand more of them.[106]

While addressing the same meeting, Rajendra Prasad, apart from speaking on the need for swadeshi and the boycott of foreign cloth, also talked about the circular, which the Chief Secretary had sent to different Commissioners guiding them how to deal with this movement.[107] While discussing this circular, he said that, on the one hand, the government wanted to show that they were in favour of improving Indian industries and that for that they were spending a good deal of money by getting highly paid officials from abroad; on the other hand, when the nationalists tried to improve the home industries by advocating the use of swadeshi cloth, the government instructed its officers through circulars to oppose swadeshi on the plea that it would lead to the looting of cloth shops. Rajendra Prasad pointed out that the main fear of the British was that the Indians would obtain swaraj through swadeshi. He further said that

> the British had said the same things at the beginning of the Non-Cooperation Movement but there was very little looting, and the cause of it is well known to the officers in the areas in which it occurred, as well as to the planters. The government is appealing to cloth dealers, the Marwaris and the moderates to help them suppress the spread of swadeshi, yet the cloth merchants of Bhagalpur, Monghyr, Khagaria,

Begusarai and Santhal Pargana have already joined them in the boycott of foreign cloth and use of khadi. Those weavers, who have given up weaving for some other profession, must revert to weaving and all cloth merchants must give up dealing in foreign cloth and deal in swadeshi.[108]

On 20 September, Rajendra Prasad and Sri Krishna Singh addressed a meeting at Durga Asthan in Sultanganj attended by around 2,000 people.[109] Addressing this meeting, the latter said that 'caps which Muslims wore were made by the hands of those foreigners, who had destroyed their religion, Islam'. Appealing to the women in the same meeting, Rajendra Prasad said that, 'Mahatma Gandhi had sent message to every woman of India that they must take to charkha as a religious duty. Women should devote 2 hours a day to ply charkha and supply materials for clothing to their countrymen.' While addressing the same meeting, Maulana Muhammad Ali said that in Bihar he succeeded in securing the signatures of a number of dealers, who vowed to cease dealing in foreign cloth. He pointed out that in other countries people had to shed blood to gain freedom but in India the leaders had not asked the Indians to do so. He further said that it was incumbent on every Indian, who was true to the soil, to follow the Swadeshi Movement and to burn every piece of foreign cloth found in his house, and, if the people carried out the instructions of Mahatma Gandhi, they would obtain swaraj within ten days. The local merchants agreed not to buy and sell foreign cloth.

In Madhubani and Samastipur subdivisions in Darbhanga district also, a number of meetings were held, where the local leaders mainly dwelt on the necessity of boycotting foreign cloth and of propagating swadeshi. In Madhubani, meetings were held on 3 October at Jhanjharpur, on 14 October at Phukahi, on 15 October at Laukahi, on 16 October at Barhi, on 17 October at National School in Madhubani, on 18 October at Dhausahi, on 21 October at Dhaundiha and on 24 October in Madhubani town.[110] A large number of meetings were also held in Sadar.[111] In Samastipur, young boys went round from one shop to another and told the shopkeepers and customers that it was a sin to purchase foreign cloth. These boys carried on the campaign in a peaceful way. Even the government admitted that there was no incident of violence, restraint and criminal intimidation.[112] The campaign had such influence in Madhubani that even the cart drivers refused to carry foreign cloth from railway station to the shops.[113]

Meetings were also held in Bhagalpur. One of the meetings at Supaul in Bhagalpur, held on 6 August, was attended by 2,500 people. Deep Narayan Singh addressed this meeting.[114] In Chotanagpur Division, Sarla Devi, a niece of Rabindranath Tagore, visited several districts in October 1921 advocating khadi and charkha.[115]

Mostly after the meetings, there were public bonfires of foreign cloth. People would then throw away, with enthusiasm, their foreign cloth into the bonfire.[116] Such metaphor of cloth was used to forcefully challenge colonial authority, most visibly through the ritual of the public burning of foreign cloth. Bonfires were also held at prominent places in almost all major cities and towns.[117] The mock funeral-like atmosphere invoked by bonfires provided occasions for the dramatic display of popular sentiments and enthusiasm on this issue. It was a statement of defiance against authority, forcefully challenging British authority. Since the bonfire involved participation of a very large number of people, it became practically impossible for the police to prevent or disperse them. Usually the police force available was not adequate and their dispersal often involved the use of considerable force. The response of the authorities could only be blunt and violent to these symbolic challenges of their authority.

Local Congress Committees organized systematic campaigns of picketing to pressurise traders to stop dealing in foreign cloth. Large groups of volunteers sat on dharna outside the shops of those who refused to comply. Traders were persuaded not to place fresh orders and their existing stocks were confiscated and sealed by Congress Committees. Those traders who broke these seals or indulged in clandestine deals were forced to pay fines to Congress volunteers.[118] In addition, great deal of social pressure was put on those traders who resisted. In many instances, social boycott was also resorted to drawing upon traditional institutions of social authority like caste and traditional panchayats. The authorities found it difficult to deal with the picketing of cloth shops as the Congressmen were using informal methods to put pressure upon the traders. The authorities could intervene only when the Congressmen obstructed traffic, disrupted business during hartals or the traders complained of coercion. But the Congressmen used subtle and indirect methods to achieve their end and the police could do little to stop the campaign.[119]

The local leaders in their own languages/idioms in the campaign tried to highlight as to how import of foreign cloth drained away India's wealth to England. To give one example from a village Ghoradeyi in Shahabad where a local nationalist, poet Kailash was explaining to the people how British carried away the golden ornaments of their wives and in return gave them brass nose studs which people accepted happily. Its impact was so strong in this village that people stopped all bullock carts to check if they were carrying foreign goods.[120]

The picketing of shops of foreign cloth was very prominent in Champaran and Muzaffarpur district.[121] In October 1921, a number of Marwaris of Motihari in Champaran resolved not to indent any foreign cloth until February 1922.[122] In Muzaffarpur in February 1922, 188 cloth merchants signed a pledge not to deal in foreign cloth.[123] Even the drivers and owners of horse-drawn carriages in Muzaffarpur decided not to carry foreign cloth.[124] In Mahmar in Hajipur, the Thana Congress Committee actively picketed shops selling foreign cloth and largely succeeded in stopping its sale.[125] In Sitamarhi also, cloth picketing was very strong. No cart or coolie was available in Sitamarhi for carrying cloth. Local cart drivers there met in a meeting in October 1921 and resolved not to carry cloth any more.[126] In Patna City, the weavers and cloth sellers met Congressmen in August 1921 and assured them that they would not buy foreign raw thread.[127] On 29 September 1921, the cloth merchants and weavers of Bihar Sharif signed a pledge not to purchase foreign cloth.[128] The cloth merchants of Arrah in a meeting in October 1921 decided not to deal in foreign cloth and pledged to pay a fine of Rs.100 per bale of cloth in case of any breach of the pledge. They also said that if any one among them did not pay the stipulated fine for breach of pledge his shop could be boycotted.[129] There was a cloth merchants' meeting in Patna in February 1922, in which it was decided that fines of Rs.101 would be imposed on those who violated the pledge.[130] In Muzaffarpur, ladies also actively promoted swadeshi. Every day, they went round, with charkha, khadi and carded cotton, to different houses to promote khadi among women.[131] The cloth merchants of Bhagalpur also took a pledge in January 1922 not to deal in foreign cloth.[132] Cloth merchants of Monghyr, Khagaria, Begusarai and Santhal Pargana too joined the boycott of foreign cloth and the use of swadeshi.[133] In several districts, specific areas were distributed among 'national superintendents, national darogas', etc. for the purpose of a house-to-house appeal to give up foreign cloth.[134]

Large amounts of Congress funds were also released for the spread of spinning and weaving amongst the villagers. Weaving institutes, funded by the AICC and BPCC, were established to impart the skills of spinning and weaving, and also to promote the sales of handspun products in different parts of Bihar. Forty-eight depots were opened in eleven districts of Bihar to sell and place cotton and charkhas within easy reach of the people.[135] The Patna District Congress Committee in Kadamkuan supplied khadi and charkhas to the various subdivisions and even gave them free to the poor.[136] In the Dighwara Thana of the Saran district, there were about 7,000 spinning wheels and 5,000 to 6,000 looms in working order.[137] The Gandhi Kutir at Malkhachak, under Ram Binod Singh's guidance, played a very active role in the promotion of khadi. The Gandhi Kutir was in touch with nearly 200 weavers in the surrounding villages, to whom it supplied charkhas and yarn. The poor women of the villages found a ready market for their yarn, which gave impetus to spinning. Every spinner got at least seven rupees a month and this became a means of livelihood for many people, especially for widows.[138] The fact that the estimated income for a year, 1921, from looms in this district was Rs. 2,800 would give one an idea of the work done in this direction in Saran.[139] On 4 July 1921, at a meeting of the BPCC, it was proposed to start a Central Yarn Depot at Muzaffarpur, a Central Cotton Depot at Maharajganj in Saran and a Central Khadi Depot at Patna and small depots for yarn, cotton and khadi in every district.[140] The Maharajganj Cotton Depot claimed to have supplied raw cotton to various Congress Committees in the Province.[141] Gradually cotton depots were opened in many places in Bihar.[142] In Gaya, there was one combined weaving and spinning institution and seven weaving institutions.[143] In Patna district, weaving and spinning were taught at Sadaqat Ashram, Khagoul, Bihar Sharif, Fatwa, Gopalpur, Bahpura and Massaurhi.[144]

A large number of processions, to promote swadeshi, were also taken out in different places. A khadi procession was taken out in Patna in November 1921. In front of the procession, charkhas were carried on an *ekka* and behind it were volunteers with national flags.[145] In Arrah, a khadi procession was taken out on 1 August 1921. This was led by the Secretary of the Shahabad District Congress. The people in the procession requested the passers-by to boycott foreign cloths. In response to their appeal hundreds of caps, coats, shirts, saris and dhotis were surrendered.[146]

Even occasions like birthdays and death anniversaries of leaders were chosen to advocate khadi. Gandhi's birthday was made a special occasion to promote the charkha and sale of khadi. In Patna City, a khadi procession of about 500 men was taken out on 30 September. Most of the prominent Khilafat and Congress workers of Patna participated in the procession.[147] In front of the procession, a swaraj flag was carried which was followed by three bullock carts with charkhas. Leaders like Dr. Waris, Jagat Narain Lal and Swami Visvanand also participated in the procession. The procession terminated at Gulab Bagh and there a meeting, presided over by Rajendra Prasad, was held, where the crowd swelled to 2,500. A large number of Muslims attended this meeting. After the meeting, there was bonfire of foreign cloth.[148] On 30 September in Hajipur, on the eve of Gandhi's birthday, Congress workers and students of Gandhi Vidyalaya took out a procession. In front of the procession there was a woven swaraj flag, followed by two boys singing. The students and Congress workers requested the passers-by to boycott foreign cloth. They went from door to door requesting people to give up foreign cloth. This was followed by a meeting in the evening.[149] Tilak's death anniversary on 1 August 1921 was also made the occasion to promote swadeshi. On this occasion in Patna, foreign cloths were burnt on the grounds of a national school.[150]

Exhibitions were also held to promote swadeshi. There was a hand-weaving exhibition in Patna in November 1921.[151] In Purnea, there was an exhibition of charkha, handspun thread and handwoven clothes on

10 December 1921. After the exhibition, prizes were given to the best producers.[152] Occasions like fairs, where there were large gatherings, were often chosen by the nationalists to promote swadeshi. In Sonepur fair, which was held in November 1921, swadeshi propaganda was very intense. Postcards and leaflets advocating swadeshi were distributed. Hawkers went round the fair selling khadi. Processions were taken out and meetings were also held advocating khadi.[153]

Thus, different methods and campaigns were adopted to promote khadi. A wide range of people got associated with the khadi programme. Rich and poor, government and others, men and women all could join. Khadi exhibitions were visited by Congressmen, non-Congressmen, government officials, zamindars, lawyers, big and small merchants and, in some places, even by Europeans.[154] Khadi workers also comprised a wide range of rural people, including teenage boys who carried raw cotton, thread, and cloth along selected routes between village spinners and weaving centres: widows who spun thread for a small income. The membership of the Khadi Movement was particularly fluid: people joined for a time and then quit or moved on to other forms of political action. Some khadi workers associated their activity directly with the Indian National Congress, seeing khadi as the entrance into other forms of nationalism, while others participated in khadi production in very local terms.

Thus, khadi had emerged as an important political symbol encompassing many meanings, being multi-vocal, in what they represented to different people. It was seen as a tool of economic and political emancipation for poverty-stricken village masses. However, it was not only looked upon as saviour of wealth and an important component of swadeshi but its meaning had been expanded to encompass a broad cultural symbol of swarajya. The boycott of British goods can also be seen as part of a wider aim to sever all connections with the colonial ruling classes. It was transformed from an endangered rural craft to a powerful symbol of the moral and spiritual regeneration of India. Around this single issue got enlisted a huge range of beliefs, aspirations and popular symbols.

Economic Significance

The nationalists were highlighting the economic benefit of making and wearing swadeshi. Khadi was seen as a tool of economic emancipation for poverty-stricken village masses. According to Gandhi, to donate a wheel was an ideal form of charity, for it helped the poor without making them beggars and without robbing them of self-respect, and at the same time it was calculated to make India self-supporting in the matter of clothing and it would save India's annual drain of nearly Rs. 60 crore. He also said that stimulating the production and use of indigenous cloth would provide supplementary employment to the masses, promote self-sufficiency of India's villages and would be the basis of a new non-industrial craft-based economic structure in independent India. The nationalists were also emphasizing that khadi would supplement people's income as India was primarily an agricultural country and its land productivity was not high. The idea of handspinning was also based upon the notion that there were millions of men and women in agricultural sector, who were idle for four months in the year for want of some employment. While addressing one of the meetings in Bihar, Gandhi said that Bihar, being primarily an agricultural region with few industries, was particularly suited for khadi work. An average person in Bihar had less than three-quarters of an acre of land. From the yield of this small quantity of land, nearly four-fifths of which were unirrigated and depended upon the uncertainties of the monsoon, people had to survive and also to meet demands of the zamindars, the society and the State. The nature of agriculturalist's work was such that it allowed plenty of leisure but at short intervals. In fact, agriculture did not require more than a hundred day's labour in the year but this work was so distributed that the farmer could not leave his farm and seek work elsewhere at a distance. It is during these idle hours of agricultural production, Gandhi believed, that taking to charkha would serve the purpose. Even the scanty earnings by charkha, according to Gandhi, would provide substantial relief to poor people. Moreover in Bihar, with a large number of weavers and looms, the tradition of spinning was still extant in most parts. Gandhi was strongly of the opinion that if spinning could be revived in Bihar it would provide supplementary occupation and income to poor people.[155]

The spinners and weavers worked mostly during their spare time. In many villages, spinning was the sole means of livelihood for many women. In fact, data shows that it served 1,200 poor women in only three centres in Bihar.[156] Gandhi Ashram in Malkhachak in Bihar was an important spinning centre. Four hundred wheels plied in this village which had a population of around one thousand. Many women in this village plied wheels and on an average got Rs. 200 per month. The village had an earning of around Rs. 800 per month.[157]

In fact, many areas where khadi production picked up during this period had a long tradition of spinning and weaving, and spinning was still prevalent in many of those areas. Gandhi was emphasizing that the tradition of spinning would greatly facilitate khadi work. He said that khadi work could be extended almost indefinitely in those areas if sufficient capital, organizational and technical skills were forthcoming.[158] In his campaign in Bihar, Gandhi had emphasized that in the transition stage one must concentrate on those centres which had a tradition of spinning and through effective organization make those centres self-supporting and permanent.[159] Hence khadi activity during the national movement can be seen as a revival of tradition. In fact khadi cloth of the variety propagated by Gandhi had always been popular amongst the peasantry, for it was an extremely cool and comfortable form of dress. This rough cloth was not popular amongst the rich, who liked to dress immaculately to distinguish themselves from the peasants. Khadi cloth crumpled easily, the sleeves tended to ride up to the elbow and ironed creases soon disappeared from the trouser leg. It also shrank in the wash. In the past, the rich had worn the high quality handwoven cloth which had also been exported to Europe. It was this industry which the mills had devastated rather than the country cloth industry. Gandhi was therefore not so much restoring an almost dead industry to life, as he was giving publicity to an existing low-caste industry.[160] The report on the 1899–1900 famine stressed that 'weaving was still a flourishing country craft. However, these weavers used mill yarn. Gandhi wanted them to use handspun yarn'.[161] In Bihar khadi production picked up most in Darbhanga district which had a long tradition of spinning. Many Muslim families in this district had for years been spinning and weaving. Mostly the Muslim women in the villages of this district had taken to spinning. Women from the weaver's families used to spin and men weaved.[162] Khadi was a source of employment for many families in these villages. It provided extra income and some marginal relief to the rural poor.

Political Significance

Khadi bhandars, places where khadi were made and sold, were playing an important political role in the movement. These khadi bhandars groomed and supported nationalist workers and leaders at many different levels. They provided training and livelihood to considerable number of full-time Congress cadres. Moreover, these khadi centres were like feeders which sustained the Congress organization through periods of slackness in the nationalist campaign. They made not only financial or moral contributions to the regular Congress organization but also provided a legal cover for its activities in especially difficult times. These institutions worked in fact like a branch Congress office. Since the closing of the Congress office the local khadi bhandars had been the focus of activities of the Congress, serving as local meeting places where volunteers and bystanders discussed local politics and disseminated political information into the countryside. Khadi centres provided safe houses for political activist escaping from police. The employers received and carried about from place to place 'objectionable' literature, etc.[163]

News and information about regional and nationalist politics spread along the khadi routes, carried by the young couriers. Villages were brought into the arena of khadi centres by child-messengers. Young boys, who carried raw cotton from khadi bhandars to spinner's homes and returned with the finished thread, brought with them news of ongoing khadi boycotts. Sometimes in the process village women ventured out to khadi centres or to small groups at a relative's house in order to spin together. Women shared the information with one another in spinning circles reminiscent of *ghoors*,[164] fireside gatherings, in which women discussed religious issues or their family lives.

The khadi workers helped extend Gandhian influence considerably, spreading and keeping alive the name of the Congress in remote towns and villages. They built up rural support for Congress and above all helped in establishing Congress hegemony over the low-castes untouchables. The Khadi Movement cut across classes, incorporating weavers, who had always performed this job, along nationalists who were learning to weave for the political cause. In Bihar weavers were generally Muslims and considered by the Brahmins and Rajputs—two other castes that participated in the movement in Darbhanga district—to occupy a lower social position. Yet the khadi bhandars, centres where khadi was woven, distributed, and sold, provided a space where castes and classes mingled as rural people joined together to make cloth. Khadi bhandar had its significance for the kind of space provided there. It had in its own way provided a break from the normal routine of society. In it, the rules of the outside world about women's propriety, caste relations, or respectable occupations to some extent became blurred.[165]

Social Significance

Khadi production also became the central symbol of social change in villages. In fact, in the political conditions of the 1920s the dividing line between social and political work was a thin one. The local khadi centres acted as pivotal points for broader rural construction schemes—arbitration courts, relief work and untouchability campaigns. The Khadi Movement provided a corps of rural volunteers who worked toward social reform. These volunteers had also become essential to rural relief work in times of crisis. Khadi workers' dedication to social reform in the countryside propelled them to direct action against more conservative forces. Generally, khadi workers did not criticize authority but appealed to the admirable cause of 'social uplift'. In addition to spinning and weaving, khadi workers were the first to set up reading programmes for children and adults. They refused alcohol and boycotted the sale of intoxicants. They also performed religious plays in villages to promote, in their terms, 'morality'. Their moral imperative contributed to their authority and hinted at a zero-sum distribution of authority in the countryside. The khadi workers raised the question: could both the khadi workers who boycotted toddy and the landlord who bought toddy be moral? The Khadi Movement also provided at times the strongest stand against parda which was most commonly practised among elite women. Anti-purdah movement confronted villages on a daily basis with images of drastic changes in social rules.[166]

Thus, in a way the Khadi Movement had also provided a structure through which narrators could talk about rural society, its standards and hierarchies, and its rules for social interaction, especially because the Khadi Movement preached social reform. Participation in it revealed to khadi workers on a conscious level the nature of the social system which they had once uncritically accepted. Therefore, khadi workers chose in their lives and their narratives to break with the social system to varying degrees and in varying ways. The roles of different participants demonstrate the social breaches of the movement and the range of effects that the Khadi Movement had on its members. Their histories constructed personal social dramas for volunteers and collective social dramas for the movement as a whole.[167]

Though it is also true that the social change for which the movement stood never took hold as completely as it initially intended. The movement was seen as progressive, if not radical. The redress of the social drama was in some ways a reintegration. The programme when looked at as a solution to the social and economic problems of rural India could not be so significant. Khadi workers became known for their moderate approach to social and political change. As far as economic problems were concerned, it did provide marginal relief to the poor but was not the solution of the economic problems of rural India and neither did it provide a critique of it.[168] Village women spun khadi thread with limited participation in its larger implications.

Khadi: A Broad Cultural Symbol

Handloom weaving was gradually getting transformed from an endangered rural craft to a powerful symbol of the moral and spiritual regeneration of India. It was not only looked upon as a saviour of wealth and an important component of swadeshi but its meanings were expanded to encompass a broader cultural symbol of swarajya.[169] The nationalists tried to highlight the significance of the spirit underlying khadi: faith, patience, self-sacrifice, austerity and fellow feeling. Khadi also came to be seen as a panacea for miseries, afflictions, mental agony and fears, and would keep the banner of religion flying.[170]

Khadi came to be looked upon as sacred, and it was expected that its radiance would influence other aspects of living, and its fragrance would purify and make public life clean and wholesome. It was being emphasized that the credibility of a khadi wearer had such a great impact that words uttered by him was like wisdom of the scriptures.[171] The spinning wheel was held to be an actual member of the family. The battle between khadi and foreign cloth was represented as a symbolic encounter between good and evil. Spinning also came to be seen as an act of prayer. It was seen as a purgation of individual sin and creation of new life in the spinner and in the community.[172] Charkha was also looked upon as a saviour of dharma. It was supposed to remove *papi* and *adharmi* from the country and bring about prosperity, love and *sadbhavana* amongst the people.[173] Cloth stood alongside the symbol of mother cow. Taking to the charkha was thought to be a holy and yogic activity and people's dharma and karma.[174]

The symbol of the *sudarshan chakra* (God Krishna's armour) was frequently used for the charkha. This *sudarshan chakra*, according to nationalists, was supposed to break the chain of slavery. Hence the nationalists stressed that it was people's duty to use the spinning wheel and cut off the fetters of bondage and save Mother India from the shame of being stripped naked like Draupadi. It was to purify mother's body and fill up with wealth.[175]

Khadi was projected as the main weapon of struggle against the British and as an ideal alternative to the machine guns used by the enemy. One of the nationalist songs 'Bharat Udhar' said:

> *Do not call it charkha consider it chakra sudarsan*
> *Consider it to be the enemy of dushman*
> *Consider it to be the reason of Hind's independence*
> *This charkha itself is tope, sword and machine gun*
> *Even machine gun, sword had been defeated by it*
> *Even machine gun is afraid of its onslaught.*
> *Swadeshi paltan are bombs.*[176]

Being a khadi soldier required a spinning wheel and cotton rather than a gun. In a way, a new kind of nationalist soldier was being conceived, who would not fight with the gun but spinning wheel.[177] Rambriksha Benipuri in his memoir talks of khadi activity in Patna where every Sunday, members of the Patna Youth Association would make rounds trying to sell khadi. He further said that with bales of khadi on his shoulder and the yardstick of it in his hands, he used to feel as though he had embarked on a national victory mission. He evokes the image of new kind of khadi soldier for the country—khadi being the uniform of the warriors of national independence. Clothing a single youth in khadi amounted to the recruitment of a new freedom fighter into the army of nationalists.[178] In this battle, women would be the equal partner with men. Indeed a new kind of soldiers, women freedom fighters, who fought with their spinning wheels, had emerged.

There was also a romantic notion and aesthetic concern attached to the charkha as opposed to machines. Swadeshi was also seen as an heir to a movement of artistic revival, which sought to protect the values of indigenous craft traditions against the impersonality of mill production and the drab uniformity of chemical dyes. Modern industrial society was criticized for its destructive and alienating effects on the bodies, minds and morals of the people.[179] One of the nationalist pamphlets, 'Charkha Vinode', promoting khadi said:

> There is more art in handspun, which has a poetry behind it, than in the soulless machine made cloth. The cracking sound of the wheel seems pleasant and the chatter of the handloom is agreeable. Such sounds rouse the withered heart. Friends what a nice whirling sound of charkha appears to the ears.[180]

The notion of protection and shame associated with clothes was also used by the nationalist leaders in their propaganda of khadi. Nationalists often highlighted that the consumption of millions of rupees worth of foreign goods leaves Indian men and women poor and naked. One of the nationalist pamphlets, 'Bharat Mata ka Sandesh', said, 'the tyrants stripped off the clothes from the body of our sisters on the road. It is our duty to use the spinning wheel and cut off the fetters of bondage and to save Mother India from the shame of being stripped naked like Draupadi'.[181] In fact, the image of female nakedness and shame was a particularly powerful one for nationalists, which was very frequently used by them to arouse anger against foreign rule.[182]

The need to support khadi and boycott foreign goods was woven through with notions of neighbourliness, patriotism, purity and sacrifice, all of which provided unifying ideologies more powerful than any single call for political representation or independence. Khadi came to be seen as a saviour of native culture. Such cultural terminology was highly emotive and used to arouse mass emotions. There were stirring episodes of people pledging never to wear foreign garments and shedding them on to communal fires.

Clothing as a Political Symbol

The movement attached much economic and political significance to the issue of cloth. Wearing khadi was to become a moral duty both to the nation and to the people. It was said that the khadi wearer should recognize the full implication of the khadi spirit, 'illimitable faith', 'illimitable patience', self-sacrifice, poverty of life and fellow feeling with every human being on earth. To wear foreign cloth was to violate *dharma*. Khadi, by contrast, was projected as sacred cloth: its radiance was to influence other aspects of living and its fragrance would make public life clean and wholesome. Gandhi even suggested that people should seek *darshan* from khadi. It was also said that in order to wear khadi a person should therefore maintain a lifestyle worthy of it, for the 'outward appearance must be fit with the expression within. It was not enough for people to don khadi simply because it was coming into vogue'.[183] Gandhi constantly emphasized the purity and godliness imparted to its wearers by the homespun. The mere act of wearing khadi, according to Gandhi, was so virtuous in itself that it could purify the wearer. Foreign cloth was looked as intrinsically vile and its contact was physically and mentally defiling.[184] Gandhi also said that foreign cloth with its superficial glamour and artifice lured innocent people away from the path of truth and virtue. Foreign clothes were referred to as filthy, defiling, untouchable and people were called to cleanse themselves by assigning their garments to the sacrificial flames.[185]

A strong appeal was made to give up British attire and to wear khadi as an Indian dress. Propaganda from khadi extremists ranged from the humorous to the physically threatening public ridicule of those wearing foreign cloth. Ridicule sometimes turned from mild intimidation to physical violence. Khadi-clad pickets not only prevented those wearing foreign cloth from entering foreign cloth shops but at times even barred them from entering Hindu temples. People wearing foreign cloth were made the butt of jokes and were ridiculed in the following way:

> *Brother, look to the distress of the children of India*
> *My income is eleven pies only.*
> *I got my suits made at Whiteaway's and*
> *my spectacles from Lawrence and Mayo*
> *I use Westland pocket watch and*
> *attend Durbar with Dawson boots on.*[186]

Khadi was emerging as an alternative national dress and became an important political symbol. In his Champaran tour, Gandhi said that he wore the national dress because it was the most 'natural and becoming for an Indian'. He believed that copying European dress was a sign of their degeneration, humiliation and weakness.[187]

Once dress had attained such elaborate symbolic importance, there was no escape from participation in the battle of clothes, no matter whether a person actually wished to participate in it or not. In fact, the success of clothing as a political symbol lay in the fact that every man and woman in India wore clothing of some sort and so was drawn automatically into this national debate. What to wear became a much discussed public issue. Gandhi's particular emphasis on the morality of khadi gave the problem a new flavour. Whereas in the past it was considered morally and culturally acceptable to alter one's dress to suit the occasion or to wear a combination of Indian and European dress, it was khadi on a permanent and daily basis. Any hope of finding a neutral solution to the problem of what to wear seemed now to have been completely eradicated, since Gandhi actively encouraged people to interpret one another's clothes as signs of personal and political belief.[188]

Gandhi was encouraging all Indians to wear khadi. Gandhi hoped that khadi dress could act as a blanket covering internal differences with a facade of apparent sameness, implying national unity whether or not such unity actually existed.[189] Explaining the virtues of the khadi, Gandhi said: 'The khadi-wearer has distinctly something to his credit in as much as he serves both the poor and his country. Khadi immediately takes him up from a lower level and makes him the friend of the poor.' By suggesting that all Indians should reject foreign cloth and revert to khadi permanently, Gandhi was offering a resolution to the problem of the divided self that threatened Indian identity under British rule. For Gandhi a change of clothes was like a change of religion, it was a question of morality and belief. He even argued that the person who wears foreign cloth is no longer Indian, 'since by his dress he has become a foreigner'. And just as nationality and religion were more or less permanent features of a person's identity so the choice of khadi over foreign cloth was to represent a permanent and lifelong conversion.

Apart from anti-foreign cloth propaganda and the emotional pressure of public scrutiny, there were, as we have seen, actual rules and regulations which constrained people's choices of what to wear. This applied especially to Congress politicians and all those attending national schools, who were, according to membership regulations, obliged to wear khadi permanently. For women the pressure was less institutionalized but came instead from the authority structure of the family—a woman married to a khadi-wearing husband would generally be obliged to wear khadi herself. Although khadi activity was becoming very popular amongst women but initially there were some reluctance among them to wear white khadi as dress. Aesthetically, some feared that it would stamp out many of the decorative arts which women enjoyed. More generally, women feared the dull uniformity and sombre unattractive image that khadi represented. One even expressed the fear that by wearing khadi she might be guilty of leading her husband to 'lose his character' since he might be attracted to other more glamorous women wearing foreign or mill-cloth. Yet perhaps more poignant than any of these aesthetic considerations were the negative associations that plain white khadi evoked. For, white was essentially a colour worn by men and worse still, by widows. Since widowhood was the most feared and least respected state a woman could attain, most young women seem to have been reluctant to embrace so grim an image, however much they sympathized with Gandhian sentiments. As a result, few but the most devout ashram dwellers and some old women adopted plain white khadi saris in their simplest form. Even the most politically motivated women retained at least some form of decoration in their saris.[190]

In the dress khadi cap, also popularly known as Gandhi cap, became an important symbol of opposition to the British. It was becoming a visible mark of swadeshi and swaraj. Headwear has a symbolic importance in any society. It reveals a man's social and religious status. To the Indian this cap was a symbol, but a highly complex one. Involving a cosmological system which set the meaning of the head and its covering, it had as well an ideological referent as a critique of British rule in India and embodied to its wearer a protest against the insults and deprivations of 150 years of colonial rule. Gandhi's primary motive was to invent a form of pan-Indian headwear which anyone could afford and wear. By promoting this small khadi cap, which could be used by both rich and poor, Gandhi hoped to attain a level of visual uniformity which had never existed before in Indian headwear.[191] The cap spread quickly among his supporters and he made it an obligatory part of the Congress uniform. During the Non-Cooperation Movement, it was sold at all major political meetings and on street corners. By 1922, a substantial number of Indian male population were wearing it.

The British authorities were unhappy at this sudden mushrooming of white caps on Indian heads. It came to be seen as defiance of authority and a sign of disorder.[192] In fact from the eighteenth to the twentieth century, the British and Indians fought out a battle about the proper forms of respectful behaviour centred on heads and feet. In the conceptual scheme which the British created to understand and to act in India, they reduced vastly complex codes and their associated meanings to a few metonyms. If Indians wore shoes in the presence of sahibs, they were being disrespectful in the early nineteenth century. The European concepts of custom and superstition were means to encompass and explain behaviour and thought, and allowed the British to save themselves the effort of understanding or adequately explaining the subtle or not too subtle meanings attached to the actions of their subjects. India was redefined by the British to be a place of rules and orders, and once the British had defined something as an Indian custom, or traditional dress, or the proper form of salutation, any deviation from it was defined as rebellion and to be punished. Indians had to conform to such British constructions.[193] Wearing the Gandhi cap thus was a metonym for disorder. The British had for long been trying to control Indian headwear and they now began to clamp down on Gandhi cap-wearers by dismissing them from government jobs, fining them and at times physically beating them. The government employees were forbidden to wear the Gandhi caps in the office and risked dismissal if they wore khadi dress and caps. Pleaders were barred from wearing any cap.[194]

The significance of the khadi cap was created as much by British responses to it as by Gandhi's personal attempts to promote it. Sometimes Gandhi used to talk of the political significance of the khadi cap and at other times claimed that it was really nothing more than a beautiful, light, inoffensive part of a garment, valued for its practicality more than for its political significance.[195] This was a vital part of Gandhi's political technique. By emphasizing the apparent innocence of the khadi cap, he was able to make the government suppression of the garment appear both unnecessary and unreasonable. He went so far as to suggest that the symbolic significance of the Gandhi cap was less his own doing than a product of the government's overcharged imagination. Just as forceful as British attempts to curb the wearing of the cap through prohibition, imprisonment and sometimes the violent assault of Gandhi cap wearers were the attempts made by khadi cap-wearing Indians to remove foreign headwear from non-Gandhians and to force them to wear the Gandhi cap. Many accounts of the bonfires of foreign cloth also report the forcible seizure and burning of foreign headwear by Gandhi cap-wearers. Under the powerful intimidation of Congress volunteers, people would often hand over their foreign headwear out of a 'sense of shame'.[196]

Gandhi might be regarded as the author of the symbol, since it was he who created the khadi cap and tried to define its significance as a garment of unity for all Indians fighting the non-violent battle for swaraj. British suppression of it had also enabled him to heighten its significance as a symbol of political freedom. But neither Gandhi nor the British were entirely responsible for the symbolic developments of the cap. However, the Gandhi cap illustrates the complexity of symbolic formation and interpretation. For the British authorities, the cap posed continual problems precisely because its symbolism could not be controlled. They could, of course, have simply ignored the sudden appearance of thousands of khadi-capped heads in the Indian streets, but while this might have diminished the symbolic value of the cap, it would have done so only at the risk of allowing the number of cap-wearers to increase. An alternative policy, which was periodically favoured, was to stamp out the physical presence of the cap, but this only encouraged the symbolism of the garment which, under Gandhi's nurturing, became at times a cap of martyrdom. But if the British were not able to control the significance of the cap, nor could Gandhi himself do that. Once the cap was in widespread circulation, its meaning could no longer be centralized. Throughout this process of diffusion of Gandhi's teachings, individuals and groups picked up Gandhian symbols and injected them with their own specific values and desired meanings. Gandhi cap, despite its visual consistency, was used by different groups to represent their own interests. For, as the cap emerged on an increasing number of heads so it was subjected to an increasingly wide range of symbolic interpretations. Ultimately it participated not merely in British-Indian power struggles but also in inter-Indian struggles.[197] The Santhals wearing Gandhi caps would confront and attack the police believing that they were immune from bullet wounds as they were wearing Gandhi Maharaj's caps. To them the Gandhi cap had taken on the role of a talisman, capable of protecting its wearer.[198] For the industrial workers Gandhi cap became a symbol of unity. In Monghyr, a worker was humiliated and insulted by his foreman for wearing a Gandhi cap. When other workers came to know about this, they all resolved in protest to go to work wearing Gandhi caps. Around 300 workmen came to the work all wearing Gandhi caps.[199] Similarly, for Hindus and Muslims, fighting the Khilafat cause in 1921, the cap had been momentarily perceived as a garment of solidarity that cut across religious boundaries.[200] Thus Gandhi cap became a visible mark of swadeshi and swaraj—a cap of martyrdom.

Khadi: Rendering Women as Domestic(ated) and not Political Subjects

The message of khadi was particularly directed to women. This was one of the programmes of national movement through which a large number of women were being brought into political struggle. Gandhi was one of the strongest proponents for associating women with khadi activity. He urged women to take the swadeshi vow: the promise to relinquish foreign good and spend a certain amount of time each day spinning thread and to wear khadi. He said that it was a moral and religious duty to return to those prosperous days when thousands of women of high birth spun their own yarn and got it woven by professional weavers.[201]

Khadi emerged as one of the most popular activities amongst the nationalist women. Women were associated with different aspects of this programme. Many women picketed in front of foreign cloth stores and many bought and used spinning wheels. A large number of married women with older children were also engaged in this activity, sometimes as part of a family effort. Many widows had also taken to spinning and earned some money.[202] Mothers were telling their sons not to join government service but to take to independent trade, especially the manufacture and sale of swadeshi goods. Women's craft fairs, i.e. 'mahila silpamelas' were held in many places under the nationalist auspices. Handicrafts made by Indian women were sold in these fairs so as to promote indigenous cottage industry. A large number of khadi articles were sold in these fairs.[203] In many nationalist songs, women were depicted as making earnest appeal to their husbands to get them spinning wheels so that they could save their dharma and drive away scarcity. The following nationalist song 'Bhanda Phore' brings out the importance and symbolic value of khadi to women:

> I request you, O Lord; with folded hands and lying prostrate at your feet to bring for me a swadeshi sari. I will wear chunari. This is singar of sohagin, the saput of widows;....Fill with wealth and purify the body of mother.
>
> I will spin yarn and weave cloth as sanctioned by dharma. The excess of scarcity is now really intolerable, o dear, raise my veil a little and teach some arts to me.
>
> Don't forget the old traditions. Charkha worship is written in karma kand.[204]

Why were the nationalists particularly interested in mobilizing a large number of women in national movement, especially through khadi programme, and how were they projecting this programme? Were some special meanings getting woven into khadi, to which women could easily relate? Answer to some of these questions may throw some light on the nature of participation of women in nationalist activity and also the attitudes of the nationalists towards women participants.

One has seen how in the course of the campaign many meanings were getting attached to khadi. The participation in khadi activity was perceived as an extension of religious activity of women, since khadi was projected as religious and spiritual activity. It was considered to be a holy and yogic activity which would have a purifying and cleansing effect on society. Cloth stood alongside the symbols of mother cow. The nationalist pamphlet 'Charkha Vinode' used for mobilizing women highlighted the spiritual aspect of khadi activity. It depicted: 'the Sohagin adjusted the charkha, fitted the handloom and took to cotton ginning. When she sat on the stool and began to spin yarn, she waked up the yoginis. When she put on the newly-woven cloth and set out for the market even good women began to feel jealous of her'.[205] This conjures up an image of this activity as a spiritual quest. Spinning was particularly emphasized as the duty of every religious women. Transformation of khadi into a religious symbol helped the association of women in this activity in large numbers. In fact, nationalism being projected as a *dharmic* battle—a deshpuja (country worship) did facilitate women's participation in the movement. Since religion was a culturally decreed female domain, women could effortlessly identify themselves with politics as a religious mission.

Moreover, spinning and weaving are generally looked upon as women's activities. There has been a strong tradition of spinning among women. In India, as in many other societies, the distinction between spinning and weaving was theoretically central to the division of labour within the family. In Manu also there is a reference to it. According to the laws of Manu, unmarried girls were the spinners (spinsters) whereas after marriage they graduated to weaving (becoming wives). With the development of professional weaving castes, this distinction became less important when imported thread began to make domestic spinning redundant, among artisans themselves it seems to have persisted until the nineteenth century. Thus the renewed admiration for indigenous handicrafts during the national movement accorded recognition to an area in which women's special skills and talents were prominent.[206]

Gandhi also wanted to bring women once again into the labour process so as to augment India's productive power. India's poverty, according to Gandhi, was a direct result of abandoning indigenous crafts and becoming dependent on foreign made items. He felt that women, who were the home makers and nurturers, the key figures in India's regeneration, were ignorant of the causes of poverty. Association of women with this activity was not based on the notion of women's identity as wage-earners but Gandhi stressed that such activity would reaffirm the ancient status of women.[207] Conscious attempts to expand the scope of nationalist activity so that poor women were included in the task of nation-building were based on the image of women as nurturers rather than wage-earners. Besides, there was no attempt by the nationalist women to organize women workers. Even their few attempts at employment generation for women, made along swadeshi lines, seem to have assumed that women's wage work was subsidiary activity to supplement the male wage rather than to earn a living wage. The Patna branch of the Ghorekamini Nari Samiti founded an industrial school for women in the 1920s at which they were taught handicrafts; the objects produced were sold at annual exhibition-cum-sales. Proceeds of the sale, however, were not divided by the producers but given to charity.[208]

Thus, even though spinning was being portrayed as the traditional occupation of women, its role was merely that of supplementing family income. The rural masses, mostly women, got some extra money from cotton spinning. This little extra income through khadi was seen by Gandhi as supplementing their income and easing the economic problems in their houses. Gandhi in his Bihar tour while appealing to the women to take to khadi and spinning often said that 'every yard of khadi purchased means a few coppers in the hands of women. It is for the women of India, a large number of whom do not get even an anna per day, that I am going about the country with my spinning wheel and my begging bowl. The same money which you spend on foreign cloth may be very usefully employed in covering the naked bodies of a few of the poor sisters'.[209] Thus this activity was not built on the notion of identity of women as a worker. Women were not looked upon as a worker. Gandhi still did not have the notion of economic equality for women. In Gandhi's idealized image of women her economic activity, especially the aspects of her economic independence, is not emphasized. As the most important activity he recommended to the women spinning and weaving, both of which he considered as religious acts and conforming to the 'nature' of women. On the economic independence of women he spoke evasively. The image of modern independent career women does not fit into Gandhi's conception of the ideal woman. According to him, women in the embodiment of sacrifice and suffering, with her advent to public life would result in purifying it, in restraining unbridled ambition and accumulation of property.[210] Thus Gandhi's view of women's equality was located within a religious and the patriarchal system, projecting a concept of women's role as being complementary to that of men and embodying virtues of sacrifice and suffering. In 1921 he stated: 'To men the female sex is not the weaker sex, it is the nobler of the two for it is even today the embodiment of sacrifice, silent suffering, humility, faith and knowledge.'[211]

Participation in nationalist activity like khadi did not entail defiance of socially accepted or traditionally presented role of women. In fact, the way women's political role was conceived it finely dovetailed with her traditionally accepted role in society. The nationalists tried to draw a linkage between the so-called 'proper role' of women in society and their participation in this activity. This activity had given scope to a large number of women to participate in the national movement without jeopardizing her place at home. It was not essential to abandon home and family to work in the movement. Gandhi urged women to 'do what they could' even from the home. The nationalists most often said: 'Ply charkhas, o my sisters, whenever you get some time from your housework. Do not forget old traditions. Charkha worship is written in karma kand.'[212] Women were told that whenever they were free from the housework they should, instead of wasting their spare time in 'gossip' and 'quarrel', take up spinning. This was seen as a more meaningful way of spending time. It was said that while spinning they could even sing religious and patriotic songs. They were also told that apart from financial benefits charkhas had many other benefits. Spinning was seen as a sort of light exercise and by its use women could do some exercise. It was projected as a plaything with which women could even amuse themselves even while being at home. The following extract from a nationalist pamphlet depicts some of these images:

O dear, bring me a charkha from whatever place you can so that I may sit within my house and amuse myself with it like a play thing, so that it may save both money and dharma, so that I may chase away trouble and anguish from the mind, for it brings forgetfulness, so that I may pull down the mills of the impatient (mill owners) as with the sudarshan.... I will not waste my time by idly spending it. I will not gossip at the time of work. I will take up spinning and support my family.[213]

In this way giving up foreign cloth and using only swadeshi goods were methods of involvement that were intrinsically connected with their domestic role. This activity refurbishes her traditional role at home. Women's primary role was located at home and other roles were seen as secondary to this primary role.

Moreover, the question about gender segregation and the abolition of purdah, which were central to anti-purdah movement and critical of social reform, could be ignored by many participants in the Khadi Movement because of the flexibility that khadi production provided. In some conservative families women chose khadi as a form of political expression because they could participate in it at home without violating parda.[214] This occupation was seen as the most honourable and decent living for women. Gandhi said that, 'discarding foreign cloth and wearing handspun meant protecting the purity of women who for want of the elegant occupation of spinning were driven to outdoor occupation which exposed them to unnecessary danger'.[215] While addressing the women in one of the meetings in Bihar, Gandhi said that in a country where millions were poor and starving, and doing arduous jobs like breaking stones for the roads or carrying metals, charkha would provide them some income. Besides it would provide women, who, according to Gandhi, ought to be as dear as mothers and sisters, with dignity and independence, work outside the supervision of overseers, who were lustful and of bad character. He said that in khadi activity women would have to work under the observation of 'clean lads' who would regard their honour as sacred as their own sisters. For Gandhi what was important was the dignity of women and not whether they received more money through other professions from 'insolent' hands.[216] What comes across is that chastity of woman was a more important issue for Gandhi and the nationalists than woman's right as a worker. In fact by invisibilizing woman as a worker, the nationalists were absolved of addressing the issues and concerns of woman as a worker.

Gandhi appealed to 'prostitutes' to take to khadi as it was not a life of shame but of dignity. This throws some light on the nationalists' perception of 'prostitutes'. In fact, nationalism was not merely a political question but it has also became a quest for women's respectability, linked up with questions of women's sexuality. This led to the construction of 'ideal' and 'good' women vis-à-vis the 'bad' women. The respectability discourse stigmatized the 'prostitutes' and not only categorized them as 'bad' women but also marginalized them.

Modesty and chastity were seen as the main virtues of women and it was these virtues that needed to be protected most. The nationalists throughout the national movement have talked of the natural and social principles that provide the basis for the feminine virtues. In this context they have extensively talked of modesty. It was said that modesty or decorum in manner and conduct is a specifically human trait that does not exist in animal nature. Further, within the human species, it was said that women cultivate and cherish god-like qualities far more than men. For the nationalists women, protected to a certain extent from the purely material pursuits of securing a livelihood in the external word, express in their appearance and behaviour the spiritual qualities that are characteristic of civilized and refined human society.[217] The example for epitome of chastity was Sita. Gandhi's ideal woman was the mythical Sita, the self-sacrificing monogamous wife of the *Ramayana*, who guarded her chastity and remained loyal to Rama in spite of many provocations. Sita was promoted as the model for Indian women. Speaking frequently to women's groups, Gandhi repeated two messages: the best role model was Sita and spinning was an essential aspect of the women's work. While addressing the meetings of ladies, Gandhi often emphasized that if they wanted swaraj which was synonymous with Ramraj, they should be like Sita who was pure of heart and kept her body clean by wearing handspun and handwoven khadi. He emphasized that spinning would bring discipline amongst women, which would make them pure in their hearts and souls and bring them closer to the model woman Sita.[218]

It is with this notion of purity and chastity that a dress code was advocated by the nationalists for women. There was a strong emphasis on women to wear white khadi as a dress. Gandhians stressed that real beauty consists in making body and mind pure. They were opposed to excessive decorations and accused women of being slaves both to their own whims and fancies and to their husbands. Women were told that if they wanted to play their parts in the world's affairs they must refuse to deck themselves for pleasing men. Bright colours were considered as 'ugly spots' because it was believed to arouse passions. White khadi, Gandhi thought, was a suitable means of enabling women to enter the public political sphere without appearing sexually provocative or immodest.[219] In this way was created or constructed image of women which were endowed with attributes approved by the patriarchal society. Thus, patriarchy provided the basic philosophy for the investiture of female body: the emergence of upper-class Hindu women from the seclusion of the *antahpur* or *zenana* necessitated the mediation of their male patrons in the design of a new style of dress at once modest and appropriate to the new image of womanhood envisaged by the social reformers. This image was now marked by signs of respectability which would protect them from the unsolicited male gaze to which emancipation might subject them. This image was likewise invested with the virtues of civility, propriety and shame/modesty together creating a dominant 'feminine' ethic which worked as a powerful subjective regulator of female physicality and sexuality. Thus, attempts were made to construct women's identity through excercising control over her body and sexuality. Women were allowed little or no space for an independent, self-perceived articulation, definition or expression of their sexuality or identity. Woman's body becomes an instrument and symbol of nation's honour.[220]

Thus, if one looks at the women's participation in khadi programme one finds that their political participation was merely an extension of their domestic role. This participation was not extended to a claim for her equality in political choice and action. Her action was not linked up with any corresponding leap in domestic or family relations or with a change in her lifestyle and role outside politics. The structures developed to mobilize women, for the movement was not to politicize them or give them political agency and subjectivity. It gave limited autonomy to women in politics which valued modesty and practised sex segregation. The political tacticians had developed political activities for women that violated neither the patriarchal ideology nor the norms of segregation. The nationalists rarely sought a permanent reversal of the customary role of woman in and outside political action. Women's subjectivities were located at home. Her role as mother, nurturer, sacrificing was retained and went unchallenged. The nationalists harped on the supreme relevance of traditional roles and values and spoke of the need to develop such 'womanly virtues' as chastity, self-sacrifice, submission, devotion, kindness, patience and the labours of love. They emphasized that feminine (spiritual) virtues should not be lost even if women came out in the public domain. Apart from it, since patriotism was subsumed within religion, women's politicization fitted into the traditional cultural matrix. Politics was internalized as a special form of sacrifice in an essentially religious process. The language, imagery and idiom of the entire nationalist protest remained steeped in tradition and religion. And herein lay the paradox: such strong traditionalist moorings alone permitted the sudden political involvement of thousands of women but that in its turn inhibited the extension of radicalism to other sphere of life. The nationalists were hardly concerned with 'emancipating' or 'liberating' women from the bonds which the society imposed on them.[221]

Boycott of Court: Hegemonic Insignia of a Colonial State

The boycott of courts was an important programme of the Non-Cooperation Movement. In fact, judiciary had been an important pillar of colonial authority. Law was the state's emissary, bearing the hegemonic insignia of a colonial state. Judicial statements on a particular event were constituted by the interplay between legality and politics, where the facts were admitted into the record of events through the procedural and power grid. The constant reorganization of the hegemonic judicature was almost all the time moved by explicit considerations of promotion of revenue exaction. The minimal degree of law and order which would make colonization safe for the colonizers and provisions of rights for the Indian elite, which supported colonial governance, also had an impact on the functioning of law. Judges laid stress upon colonial order and not law alone. Colonial law attempted to forge a judicial discourse to legitimize its rule even as it punished the populace.

Judicial processes moved at a snail's pace. Implementation of laws involved protracted private litigation. Moreover, the law was complex, vague and spoke an unfamiliar language, necessitating hiring of lawyers. Litigation became a game of money from which only the rich could benefit. Men with resources manipulated the judiciary exerting undue influence for their own vested interests.[222] In the villages, the peasants were its worst victims. The tenants often knew little about their legal rights, and civil courts generally remained under the domination of landlords and moneylenders. The peasants lost their lands to them in litigation. The tangled web of procedure of the legal system put the poorer man, the less educated, at the mercy of resourceful men who chose to ruin him by litigation.[223]

The Non-Cooperation Movement built up strong anger against the courts which was projected by the nationalists as not for delivering justice but primarily for meeting the needs of the colonial state. The nationalists asked the people not to take their cases to the courts. They said that taking recourse to the judiciary would mean showing faith in the British government and increasing the prestige of the government. Lawyers were asked to withdraw from legal practice. Their remaining in this profession was seen as imparting strength to the government.[224] Many lawyers in Patna, Gaya and Shahabad suspended their practice and many amongst them joined the Non-Cooperation Movement.[225] Non-cooperation had greatly demolished the prestige of the law courts and also the prestige of the government.[226]

In their campaign, the nationalists projected the aim of courts as only that of earning money in the guise of justice. They said that through the courts the government earned many crores of rupees every year. They pointed out that the poor could not expect any justice as cases were won not on the basis of their merit and truth but only on the basis of money. Court was seen as a place where peons, clerks, *mukhtar* and touts fell upon the client as 'vulture falls upon a carcass'.[227] The nationalists further pointed out that justice was not so costly in any other country.[228] Litigation being a game of money was shown vividly in the proscribed leaflet 'Swaraj ke Faede' which was distributed amongst the people to build up the campaign for the boycott of courts. It underlined the profession as full of deception and cheats, with touts and pleaders hands in gloves. It highlighted how money was wheedled out on various pretexts and at different stages by touts, pleaders, *amlas*, peons, *peshkars* (one who submit cases). It depicted money being extracted as *peshi* (illegal fee for putting up the case) by the *peshkar*, as fees for giving service of notice or the summons by the peon, as process fees, stamp fees, fees for admitting petition, vakil's fees and bribes for the witnesses. It further stated that after paying so much, the cases often got reversed, and even if decree was prepared, the execution gave immense troubles, giving rise to fresh quarrels. Underscoring how reviews and appeals made people insolvent, it asked people to follow Gandhiji's advice, find out men fit to be panches and refer cases to them for arbitration and not take suits to the courts.[229]

The nationalists also pointed that the winning of a case did not depend upon truth but upon a 'good' lawyer and tactful litigant. Those lawyers were considered 'good' who could prove what was true as false and vice versa by the force of their speech. Justice depended upon the verbal prowess of the lawyer, upon the witnesses coached up by the *mukhtar* and upon the amount of money spent. Court came to be seen as a place of falsehood, treachery, deceit, dishonesty, human frailty, wickedness and meanness.[230] This is depicted as explained in the following quotation taken from a nationalist pamphlet:

> Somewhere witnesses are coached up, somewhere the clients are being taught to get their statements by heart like parrots, somewhere cunning moharris (clerks) are quarrelling with the litigants, somewhere public servants are settling their bribe, somewhere a vakil is cheerfully fixing his fees and somewhere again a mukhtar is running from one court to another with a number of villagers at his back. And all these artful transactions are carried on openly without any litigation. People call vakalat an independent profession and feel proud of it, so much so, that it is considered the highest ideal of education. Men with high degrees go out of the Universities with this end in view, but in fact there is no other profession so degrading and slavish. Vakils are the slaves of the courts.[231]

Courts also came to be seen as places that 'crush the people's soul, suppress noble ideas in their mind, make them slaves of money, weaken the conscience of the people and instigate evil passions amongst them'.[232] The legal profession was projected as a hated profession that led to divisiveness in society and increased family disputes. The nationalists said that the huge building of the courts and the heavy law books in the Bar Library were not meant for the people's good but were built to set one against another and to 'waste people's wealth and dharma'.[233]

Panchayats: Repository of Truth and Dharma

The non-cooperators projected panchayats as a far better alternative to government courts. They stressed the formation of panchayats and asked the people to take their cases to panchayats rather than to the courts. They said that decisions in the panchayats were impartial as justice was meted out on the basis of truth, and bribery had no place. The panchayats were projected as the saviour of people's 'dharma, izzat and wealth'. Their role in society was seen as harmonious and not divisive.[234] The government viewed the panchayats as arbitration courts but Rajendra Prasad refuted this view. He said that the scheme adopted by the nationalists did not contemplate courts on the lines of the existing arbitration courts, as it wanted all litigation to be dealt by the village panchayat or by panchayats comprising representatives from several villages.[235]

This programme of the Congress received a good response. There existed a strong tradition of panchayats among different communities. Unlike courts, which were an alien intrusion, the panchayats were from the people's milieu. The people were familiar with the language of panchayats. Most of the villages had caste panchayats which generally looked after their caste interests. However, many such panchayats were also getting affected by the nationalist movement. The Congress activists were making attempts to communicate the message of nationalism to these panchayats, which served to widen the influence and role of their panchayats. The meetings of such panchayats passed a series of resolutions to regulate the professional and social conduct of the castes, but besides it also sought to enforce novel dietary taboos, i.e. giving up of liquor, *ganja*, toddy and *bhang*. Those not abiding by their decisions would be outcast or fined. Thus the elements of the nationalist programmes were internalized by the lower castes through their panchayats. Hence, such panchayats did not remain confined to interpersonal village matters and rituals.[236] Besides, these panchayats, Gandhian panchayats were also getting established during the Non-Cooperation Movement as units of nationalist organization at the village level. Most of the members of these nationalist panchayats came from 'lower castes'.[237]

Nationalist panchayats, amounting to several thousands, were formed in Bihar.[238] They were established in a number of villages in Chapra, Muzaffarpur, Motihari, Darbhanga, Patna, Gaya, Shahabad, Monghyr, Bhagalpur, Hazaribagh, Ranchi and Daltonganj districts.[239] At Saran, Rajendra Prasad and Mazharul Haq gave personal attention to this task.[240] In Buxar, Sahajanand played a very active role in formation of panchayats in different villages.[241] In Saran alone, panchayats were formed in over a thousand villages.[242] Large number of people became members of the panchayats. Many of them came from the untouchable castes—the Doms and Chamars. The 'respectable elders' of the village had kept themselves aloof from these panchayats.[243]

A large number of cases were brought to these panchayats. In the initial months, there was a considerable decline in the minor complaints before criminal courts and civil suits.[244] In his autobiography, Rajendra Prasad, while discussing the formation of the panchayats, narrated how at one place the panchayat acquired so much authority that it worked almost like a regular court of law. People were filing cases and paying court fees.[245] However, panchayats soon started facing certain difficulties. People started bringing long-standing disputes to the panchayats, and panchayats being time-bound, could not take up these cases. This brought about disillusionment.[246] Reports from several districts also indicated that the attempts to enforce panchayat's decrees were resisted. Social boycotts were often resorted to by panchayats to enforce their decisions, which often led to clashes with the police.[247]

The nationalists in its campaign reposed a lot of faith in panchayats as alternative institutions. Nationalist panchayats were projected as institutions which would deliver fair justice to the people.[248] However, there is a need to problematize the institutions of panchayats. The traditional caste and village panchayats were not democratic as the interests of the dominant sections and castes of the villages predominated in these panchayats. The marginalized sections did not get justice from these institutions.[249] The nationalist panchayats, whose social composition was changing, as a large number of its members came from subordinate classes and castes, faced another problem. In many situations it was ineffective in the implementation of its judgement as its decision would not be followed by the dominant sections of the community, who had kept themselves aloof from such panchayats.[250] So the structure and power of the panchayats has to be seen in the wider context of community. The culture of a community creates the resources for questioning ideologies of the state however simultaneously it homogenizes the imagining of the community and silences alternative perceptions. The community is not egalitarian or neutral but remains dominated by the upper caste, and class, and writ with patriarchal oppression. It is in this context that one has to critically assess the meanings of the nationalist projection of the panchayats as the saviour of people's 'dharma', 'izzat' and 'wealth'. Society and family gets projected in these campaigns as sacrosanct, needing to be protected, and the nationalists hoped that panchayats would bring harmony in society and family and not be divisive of them. However, the question arises as to whose 'dharma' and 'izzat' needs to be protected and what kind of society and family structure needs to be protected. It may reinforce the honour of the community, reinforcing its class, caste and patriarchal structure.

Liquor Boycott: Various Dimensions

There was a strong protest in Bihar centring on the liquor boycott during the Non-Cooperation Movement. Even though liquor boycott was not a part of the official programme of the Congress when Non-Cooperation Movement started, but once this programme gained momentum, the Congress encouraged it. It had a very wide appeal. The campaign against liquor met with a large amount of support even from those who had not supported other forms of protest against the government. The government reports stated that the movement received more sympathy and support than almost any other part of the non-cooperation programme. The Deputy Commissioner of Hazaribagh, for example, stated that the movement commanded the sympathy, tacit or avowed, of many, who were otherwise totally opposed to non-cooperation, and the Deputy Commissioner of Singhbhum also had arrived at the same conclusion. The Collector of Monghyr also considered that the movement was likely to have a permanent effect. He was doubtful whether the old level of consumption would again be reached.[251] According to the government, the object of attack was well chosen as it felt 'the sympathies of the educated class, whose tastes did not lie in the direction of country spirit, were enlisted on the representation that the movement was one towards temperance'.[252]

Looking at the support to this issue, the question arises: why the history of drink and drinking during the colonial period in India has been a subject of almost complete neglect? This may seem surprising, seeing that during the later years of British rule the revenue from country drink was second in importance only to the land revenue. The brunt of taxation of drink was borne by the lower classes. Whereas high levels of land revenue were seen as crippling the 'honest agriculturalists' on whom the wealth of India depended, high taxes on drink have been commended as helping to check a supposedly pernicious habit. In the eyes of orthodox Hindus, Muslims and Jains drinking was a disreputable and degrading habit.

However, there is more to drinking than taxation alone. All the evidence suggests that drink has occupied and continues to occupy a central position in the life of large numbers of Indian peasants and tribals. For the tribals, in all spheres of their life, drink had positive associations. It was a food of the gods which possessed an element of divine power; it set a seal on negotiations and legitimized family ceremonies; it enhanced the pleasures of social gatherings and public festivities; it provided succour during times of scarcity. Thus drink lubricated the whole cycle of life of the peasants. They were acculturated into drinking at an early age, and knew how to take their drink—with moderation on the whole, but with gusto when the occasion demanded it. Hence, it was the disavowal of this element of their life which formed such an important part of the mass protest.

Before the colonial period, most of this country drink was produced in a customary manner. *Daru* and toddy making process was extremely simple and any peasant could easily make cheap country liquor. *Daru* was made chiefly from the flowers of the mahua tree. Toddy is the fermented juice of any kind of palm tree. Most of the tapping of the palm trees was carried out by the peasants who tilled the land on which the trees grew. The tapper and his family drank most of the toddy themselves and sold any surplus. As a rule, toddy trees were considered to be the property of the man on whose land the trees grew. Before the liquor laws of the late nineteenth century, peasants did not require a licensee to draw and consume toddy. If they sold any surplus, they were meant by law to sell it to a licensed toddy dealer. There were not many licensed toddy shops and often they were located far off from the villages. As toddy was a highly perishable commodity which could not be transported far in those days of poor communications, there was the practice of widespread bartering between peasants. Although this was technically illegal, the authorities made little attempt to prevent such infringement of the law. On the whole, therefore, the landowning peasants obtained their toddy free from tax.

The bonded labourers of rich, high-caste peasants were generally allowed to draw toddy freely from the trees on their master's land. Besides, the toddy sold in the shops was not expensive. The normal practice was for a customer to be allowed to drink as much toddy as he wanted for two to four pies. Being an easily obtained natural product, toddy was the most popular drink. Thus, before the colonial period, country liquor was, to some extent only, a marketed commodity. Manufacture and sale of liquor were by law permitted only to those who had been given permission by a government liquor farmer. The right to distil and sell spirits was farmed out. Toddy was taxed in some areas by a levy on toddy trees. But, the great majority of trees escaped taxation. The revenue from liquor was not large.[253]

The British took over and continued this system in its essential until the last quarter of the nineteenth century. Under this system the liquor rights for each area were sold by auction for a period of one year. The successful bidder was responsible for selecting village level liquor dealers who distilled and sold country liquor and collected and sold toddy. From them he collected the duty which they were required to pay on any liquor which they made. In practice the liquor farmer took a lump sum from the local dealer which bore little relation to the actual quantity of liquor manufactured and sold. Little control was exercised over the local distilleries, and much of the duty was evaded.[254] The British disliked this system as it provided an opportunity for widespread evasion of revenue. The obvious remedy was to ban the village-based manufacture. In 1859 a circular was sent to the provincial governments, suggesting that central distilleries should be established in all populous regions.[255] Liquor manufacture was to be confined to central distilleries, that excise duty was to be levied on this liquor before it left the distillery, that no toddy was to be drawn from trees except by permission of the collector and under licence, that each toddy tree that was tapped was to pay tax under excise, and that liquor and toddy were to be sold in licensed shops, with licenses to be auctioned as before. These measures were to be brought in gradually over a number of years.[256] In this way, drink could become a standardized commodity paying regular rates of excise. Over the next decades, the tax on drink increased by leaps and bounds as the excise on country liquor, the charge for the toddy tree rates ever rose. As a result of the ever increasing tax the price of *daru* soared over the years.[257]

The measure also strengthened the liquor dealers' position. Liquor shopkeepers enjoyed exclusive rights for the sale of liquor or toddy in a cluster of villages. The peasants had little recourse against them when they diluted and adulterated the drink and gave short measures. As the peasants were often deep in debt to the liquor dealers, who were also landowners, they hardly dared complaint. The excise inspectors and police, who were often in league with the shopkeepers, were bribed to turn a blind eye to malpractices. In fact, gradually, the liquor dealers were emerging as the great landowners. Most of the poor peasants' and tribals' lands were passing to them. Moreover, as the liquor dealers' estates became larger, they became more rapacious. They maintained their own strongmen to coerce the poor and landless into labouring in their fields for nominal payment. Any protest by the peasants was suppressed with the help of the local police.

In desperation, peasants throughout sought to obtain their drink 'illicitly'. In effect this meant resorting to 'illicit' distillation. Among the poor and landless no stigma was attached to breaking the law in this manner; rather it was considered admirable to thus outwit the liquor dealers and the police. In villages in which there were no liquor dealers, high caste peasants or other outsiders, it was possible for a peasant to make *daru* in his own house.[258] The other major way in which the liquor laws could be circumvented was by smuggling liquor and toddy from foreign territory. Poor peasants were prepared to walk miles to obtain cheap liquor in this manner, and as the borders of the different territories were much intermingled it was impossible to prevent such smuggling.[259]

Another radically different solution to the problems brought about by British policies was to give up drink altogether. In Brahminical Hindu culture abstention from spirituous drinks was considered a great virtue, and it is probable that even before the colonial era there were certain tribal and low caste peasants who refused to drink in the belief that this would raise their status in wider society. The families who tried to distance themselves from other members of their community were the more prosperous ones. Refusal for them to drink together in a community in which such drinking represented a symbol of mutual solidarity could be considered a gesture of renunciation of membership of the community. The difference between this isolated type of renunciation and the popular temperance movements which started in the late nineteenth century was that in the latter case entire communities which were undergoing a process of pauperization attempted to give up liquor and toddy. Through such radical cultural reform they hoped to save themselves from further impoverishment and also to enhance the status of their community in the region as a whole. Although this hope was not altogether realistic, the strategy had some real strengths. Faith in the old culture had been undermined and it was felt that a fresh start was required. Refusal to drink represented both a moral stand and a new symbol of commitment to the cause of communal advance. It provided a badge of solidarity in the peasant's struggle against the liquor dealer who were also landlords and, in addition, it cut the economic cord which bound the peasant to the liquor dealer.[260]

Thus the liquor boycott was not only fuelled in part by resentment against the colonial liquor laws but was also part of a widespread movement throughout India in which low status communities began to demand a status equal to that of higher social status. There was a trend of 'social reform' where certain communities were giving up drinking liquor and eating meat. Some refer to it as sanskritization, but others consider it as a form of assertion where low status communities began to demand equality with higher status communities.[261] Amongst the Oraons of Ranchi, a movement started in 1914–15, known as the Tana Bhagat, where the Oraons were enjoined by divine command to give up superstitious practices and animal sacrifices, to stop eating meat and drinking liquor, to cease ploughing their fields and to withdraw their field labour from non-tribal landowners. Through the reform, the Oraons hoped to save themselves from further impoverishment and also to enhance the status of their community in the region as a whole.[262]

During the course of the movement, an influential element among them forged an alliance with the Gandhian nationalists, thereby gaining on their side a group of most vocal champions. The common platform was that of abstention from *daru* and toddy. The Indian National Congress had from its earliest years put forward the view that the chief concern of the British in their excise policy was to raise as much revenue as possible in a manner which went against the best interests of the people.[263] It was argued that, although officials claimed that high prices discouraged drinking, in practice the local revenue officers did their utmost to stimulate the consumption of liquor. The nationalists favoured complete prohibition. The argument put forward by them for prohibition was that drinking was 'contrary to the sentiment of the great majority of the people of India'.[264] Demands for complete prohibition became more vociferous after the highly successful First All-India Temperance Conference held in Bombay in 1904. This brought together 301 temperance associations which already existed scattered over India.[265] These associations were, however, largely urban-based, with a predominantly high caste membership. They showed little interest in the popular temperance movements which were becoming increasingly important; instead they preferred to lobby the government for a change in policy.[266] It was only with the emergence of Gandhi within the Congress after 1918 that positive attempts were made to link the temperance activities of the middle classes with the anti-liquor movements of the masses. In 1921 Gandhi gave his blessings to a campaign to picket liquor and toddy shops. As a result, sales of drink decreased significantly in many areas.[267]

The nationalists, while appealing for prohibition, put forward the argument that drinking was a vice and the government had no right to derive revenue from it. They said that the majority of Indians did not drink as the traditions, customs, sentiments and religions of India were opposed to it. Drinking was looked upon by them as an exotic habit—not indigenous. They also linked up the issue of liquor boycott with religion and *sanskar.* They said that all the religious scriptures prohibited consumption of liquor because it destroyed one's *dharma* and *sanskar*. They also pointed out that earlier drink was found only in some aristocratic or lowest caste houses but under colonial regime a network of liquor shops were spread over the whole length and breadth of the land, taking it to the very doors not only of the village people but even to the hill tribes. They said a village would be without a school or *sarai* but there was scarcely a cluster of villages where there would be no liquor shop.[268] The nationalists said that the implementation of greater restrictions or, ideally, prohibition would be in the best interests of the 'drinking classes', most of whom were poor people and were ruined by their craving for liquor. They said that the liquor shops provided a temptation for all and since the masses were 'illiterate' they could not withstand the temptation.[269]

The nationalists also highlighted the adverse impact of liquor on health.[270] They said that the government was only interested in taxes and least concerned with its adverse impact on people. They also highlighted how the drinking 'evil' was a potent factor in promoting crime, in ruining happy homes, in causing perpetual indebtedness and consequent bondage and misery, and in the steady deterioration of the moral, mental and physical condition of the nation. They were also in pain as they had expected India, the sacred land, to have set an example to the rest of the world of complete eradication of the evil of drink. [271]

The Congress had been working hard to demonstrate that there was a mass demand for prohibition. They had been particularly successful in linking up with the tribal abstainers and then leading a powerful anti-drink movement. Thus the nationalist leaders' demand for total prohibition became linked, during the Gandhian era, with popular temperance movements. The popular movements for temperance were related to the general pauperization of peasants and workers under colonial rule and the impact of reform movement on the consciousness of the leaders of low-status communities. These movements were fuelled in part by resentment against the colonial excise laws, but were also a part of a widespread movement throughout India in which low-status communities began to demand to be considered equal to those of higher social status. The real dynamics of the movement lay in such popular initiatives. However, the historiography so far has not given due weightage to the popular dimensions of the campaign. [272]

However, the Excise Commissioner did not see liquor boycott as a purely social reform movement. For him, this movement was a clear form of political protest. According to him, its main object 'was to habituate the minds of the people to resistance to government'.[273] He also looked at this movement as a great threat to the government's resources. He feared that the attack upon excise revenue, if successful, would paralyse the administration, which was dependent upon excise for one-third of its resources. Excise receipts in April 1921 fell by 30 per cent. There was a huge decline of liquor revenue in the Tiṛhut Division. In Muzaffarpur, the revenue fell by Rs. 1.5 lakh. In Chapra, it fell by Rs. 1 lakh.[274] The loss to the local revenues amounted to around Rs. 20 lakh. Attack on the excise revenue was perceived by the Excise Commissioner as an immediate way of embarrassing the local government by the leaders of the movement. The Excise Commissioner felt that the local government in the face of a genuine temperance movement would have been prepared to make good that loss by some new form of taxation but the present loss, according to him, was caused without any permanent advantage to the cause of temperance.[275]

Campaign Against Liquor Boycott

The campaign against liquor boycott took a very intensive form. Local seva samitis and volunteers played a very crucial role in this campaign. A large number of meetings were held where leaders advocated liquor boycott. Liquor stores were picketed.[276] In Tirhut Division, picketing was very strong in Sitamarhi, Champaran, Hajipur, Sasaram, Bettiah and Muzaffarpur.[277] Liquor sale declined considerably. In Sasaram, one liquor vendor surrendered his licence as sale declined considerably.[278] When volunteers were arrested for picketing, there were strong protests. In Muzaffarpur, in September 1921, 400 people followed to the court the volunteers of Gandhi Ashram of Nawadah, who were arrested for picketing liquor and *ganja* shops.[279]

In Bhagalpur Division, northern Bhagalpur and Monghyr were strongly affected by the liquor boycott movement.[280] In Patna Division, the areas most affected were Gaya and Shahabad.[281] In Gaya, a person who had visited a liquor shop, was threatened by some non-cooperators. When he lodged a complaint against them, during the trial, around 500 people, most of whom were poor and of low-caste background, gathered at the court shouting *Gandhi ki jai*. When the accused were sent to the jail, the crowd followed them. The Congress leader Krishna Prakash Sen Sinha addressed the crowd. No one came forward to give evidence against those accused non-cooperators in the court.[282] Picketing was also strong in Buxar. Many volunteers in Buxar were arrested for picketing.[283] In Chotanagpur Division, the movement was most intense in Hazaribagh. The non-cooperators had considerable success in stopping drinking and in many places the liquor shops were not opened since the beginning of the official year 1921.[284] Another strong belt in Chotanagpur was Chakradharpur, where the volunteers were very well organized and posted at different shops for picketing. The liquor sale in Chakradharpur went down considerably.[285]

There was also protest at the time of auction for the settlement of excise shop in March 1921. In Manbhum, Purulia and Ranchi, there was a massive opposition from the local non-cooperators when the annual auction was held.[286] The day auction was to be held public meetings were held outside the excise office, where nationalist leaders strongly advocated boycott of the auction. In one such meeting in Manbhum on 4 March, the nationalists narrated the story of a Muslim kalal, how he died on the same night when he did not heed to the request made by the nationalists not to bid at the auction sale at Ranchi. After the meeting, when the auction commenced in Manbhum, 'a noisy crowd' invaded the auction tent and tried to dissuade the people from bidding. The government forbade the holding of any public meeting near excise shops under Section 144. In protest, the non-cooperators held a meeting in the town in the evening. This meeting was attended by 2,000 'bazaar' people. Many of the kalals, who had bid on the previous day, submitted petitions withdrawing their contracts.[287] In Purulia, the nationalists planned to hold a public meeting on 4 March in the immediate vicinity of the excise office compound to obstruct the excise settlement. When the government prohibited the holding of such a meeting, the people in protest observed a complete hartal. All the shops in the town were closed and all business was suspended.[288] In Ranchi also, the excise settlement could not take place. The Deputy Commissioner of Ranchi, who had made arrangements for kalals to bid for the outstills, did not succeed in his plan.[289]

There was also opposition to the *tari* settlements in many districts. The Pasis in many districts were unable to get settlement from the zamindars.[290] The Pasis were also intimidated, assaulted and prevented from tapping palm trees.[291] In Anandpur village in Monghyr, the non-cooperators beat the Pasis for not stopping the tapping of *tari* trees. In Patna, the Pasis and those who drank at *tari* shops were assaulted. The volunteers in Patna also prevented the Pasis from tapping palm trees. There was also a case of a woman, who owned some trees, assaulted.[292] *Tari* trees were damaged in many places. If any action was taken against the non-cooperators, people expressed strong anger. In Sitamarhi, in November 1921, a large crowd with drums, trumpets and flags escorted some persons accused of damaging *tari* trees to the subdivisional officer's camp.[293] Pressure was also built up on zamindars to damage all *tari* trees on their estate so that the *tari* vendors were not able to obtain *tari* from them. On 24 October 1921, Maulavi Muhammad Jalil, the vice-chairman of Darbhanga Municipality, visited Murli Matha, an influential zamindar of Jalley, and tried to persuade him to damage the palm trees growing on his estate but he refused to do that.[294] In many places, the Pasis did not take settlement.[295] In Sitamarhi, in April 1921, 14 *tari* shopkeepers put in applications to cancel their licences as there was no demand for *tari*.[296]

Liquor boycott was marked by intimidation and social ostracism.[297] Liquor vendors and customers were subject to severe social boycott. In a number of places, excise officials were also socially boycotted.[298] In Gaya, where a servant of a liquor seller had died, nobody came forward to assist in his burial for twenty-four hours. In Monghyr, a midwife refused to attend to a woman in labour till she was able to extract an assurance from her husband that he would give up liquor.[299] There was another incident in Ranchi in March 1921 where a kalal, who had taken to bidding, faced opposition in his dead son's burial. The non-cooperators of the area tried to obstruct his family from buying cloth for the corpse and the tailor from sewing the shroud. Only when the deceased's relatives admitted to the non-cooperators that they had committed a mistake by taking to bidding, they were allowed to bury the corpse.[300] In another incident in Ranchi, when a Muslim liquor vendor died in December 1921, he was refused burial. His burial could take place only with police assistance. But in the night his body was exhumed, his face mutilated and placed on the road.[301] Members of the Phulwari Seva Samiti boycotted a local liquor vendor and prevented him from getting the lease of a house.[302] In Chakradharpur, washermen were boycotted for not giving up drinking. The Marwaris of this town went round from shop to shop persuading the shopkeepers not to supply any article to the washermen. The washermen could get access only to those shops after they (the washermen) had proclaimed by beating of a drum in a procession that they would neither consume liquor nor wash clothes of those who consumed liquor.[303] Anyone who provided any provision to liquor vendor, who was under social boycott, was also boycotted. In Monghyr, a fruit-seller was confined for supplying fruit to a liquor vendor, who was under social boycott.

In many districts, especially Gaya, excise vendors who took settlement of the shops for the year, 1921–2, were subjected to severe boycott and refused any sites for shops.[304] If any one found drunk he was likely to be painted with tar and paraded with ignominy round the villages and bazaars. Members of the Khagoul Seva Samiti painted the face of a man, placed him on a donkey, and walked him through the streets because he had visited a liquor shop.[305] In many places in Muzaffarpur, Doms were posted outside liquor shops with sweepers' brooms to disgrace any possible customer.[306]

The non-cooperators in the campaign also played upon people's fear of gods and goddesses and superstitions to promote liquor boycott. Rahul Sankrityayan narrated one of his experiences while campaigning in village Parsa in Chapra. One of the youths in this village complained to Sankrityayan that people had not given up liquor and *ganja*. One day Rahul Sankrityayan pretended that he was possessed by a god. In the possessed form, he declared that all the gods were with Gandhi Baba and that Gandhi Baba did not want any kind of sacrifice, *ganja* or liquor. He threatened that any body offering these to gods would be destroyed.[307] This had a good impact. The campaign in the village after this picked up.[308] Rahul Sankrityayan narrated another incident of Chapra where there was a dharna in front of a liquor shop. Rahul Sankrityayan was also standing in front of the shop and requesting the customers to give up drink. But one customer despite his request went inside. The next day that customer's house was drowned in a flood. People spread the rumour that his house was drowned in flood because he had incurred the wrath of the saint, Rahul Sankrityayan, by pushing him in front of the liquor shop.[309]

Many times the movement went beyond the parameters defined by Gandhi. Although Gandhi insisted that only legitimate and courteous means should be used to persuade people to give up drink, picketing was often forcible and vendors were frequently assaulted and their shops looted and burnt. The customers, who visited the excise shops, were intimidated and assaulted. There were as many as five cases of arsons against liquor shops in a single subdivision of Hazaribagh district in April and May 1921.[310] In a village in Samastipur, the liquor shop of Bachu Lal, who had been warned not to take contract, was burnt by the punches and volunteers. The volunteers obstructed the transport of spirit from the warehouse to the shops and damaged *tari* trees. In Muzaffarpur, in January 1922, a salesman of a *ganja* shop was stabbed and robbed of his cash as well as of the *ganja* in stock.[311] At Basatpur in the same district, a salesman of the country spirit shop was belaboured and robbed in the same month.[312] In January 1922, in Monghyr, a *ganja* shop at Balha was looted.[313] Some people of village Jalapur in Bahwa in Santhal Pargana entered a liquor vendor's shop on 13 July night and broke the liquor container. They beat the vendor, the seller and others including the cook. They warned the liquor vendor not to sell liquor otherwise, they threatened, he might be killed. However, they did not touch any money—sale proceeds of the shop, utensils or clothes.

Thus, the liquor boycott was an issue that got the widest support from most sections of people. The moral element associated with drinking made the protest against liquor very strong. Many among those who had not supported other boycotts of non-cooperation, sympathized with this issue. The government also found it very hard to carry propaganda against liquor boycott. In dealing with the picketing of liquor shops, government was in a somewhat difficult position, as any strong action on their part might have been represented as hostility to the cause of genuine temperance reforms. The government could find no reason in defence of the promotion of liquor sale. As far as other boycotts like education, foreign cloth and courts were concerned, the government tried to highlight the adverse impact of such boycotts on people. There was not any moral or religious objection to the use of foreign cloth. But in the liquor boycott campaign, the government could not give any such rationalization.[314]

'Illicit' Distillation: Empowered by Gandhi

Another strong trend, particularly in tribal areas, was the 'illicit' distillation of liquor. This activity appears as contradictory to the liquor boycott trend but both the trends, the liquor boycott and the 'illicit' distillation of liquor, were the two sides of the same coin. To a large extent, the main force behind 'illicit' distillation was also anger against the British excise policy. This can be seen as an assertion of people's customary right to distil liquor, which was taken away by the new excise policy. It was also a subversion of the government's new excise policy. One of the government reports stated that the 'temperance workers openly advocate defiance of the excise authorities rather than abstinence'.[315]

A rumour that was very prevalent in the tribal areas was that 'everybody is empowered by Gandhi to distil liquor as they please'. [316] Often a strong rumour, in some areas, that swaraj was imminent led to rampant distillation in some areas. Swaraj meant being no longer under the British law and freedom for people to revive their customary right of distilling liquor. The Deputy Commissioner of Palamau reported in April 1921 that 'a rumour had been circulated amongst the nuniyas of the colliery areas that British Raj would cease on the 1st of April and on that day all the Deputy Commissioners and Deputy Magistrates would leave their posts, after which the people would be free to distil at their pleasure'.[317] The result of the rumour was that the whole countryside of Palamau started distilling liquor.[318] In the Santhal Pargana and Hazaribagh, in October 1921, a rumour had spread that everybody was empowered by Gandhi to distil liquor as they pleased.[319] 'Illicit' distillation was very rampant in Hazaribagh. Mahua trees grew freely all over the district.[320] In Muzaffarpur, there was an increase in the sales of country liquor.[321] 'Illicit' distillation had the tone of breaking British policy and evasion of British laws with impunity. It expressed the discontentment with British Raj. Amongst the poor and landless, no stigma was attached to breaking the law in this manner; rather, it was considered admirable to thus outwit the liquor vendors and the police. Where security was lax, peasant distillers made a large amount of *daru.* The people did not consider 'illicit' distillation a crime. In some cases, it was considered to be an order of Gandhi.[322]

'Illicit' distillation was rampant even when the Non-Cooperation Movement went through a low phase in June, July and August 1921.[323] 'Temperance workers' continued to advise the people to distil liquor themselves. In August 1921, there were 42 prosecutions for 'illicit' distillation in Ranchi district and 22 cases in Manbhum district.[324] The rampant 'illicit' distillations gave the impression to the government that the liquor boycott was not a 'temperance movement' in the true sense because the supporters of the liquor boycott promised cheap liquor, once the movement was successful, and advocated 'illicit' distillation to both vendors and consumers.[325] The consumption of government spirit in Hazaribagh district dropped by 90 per cent and there was heavy 'illicit' distillation all over the district to supplement shop liquor.[326] The Excise Commissioner stated that the incitement to defiance of the excise laws would lead to increased consumption and intemperance in many districts of Bihar and Orissa, where materials for 'illicit' distillation were easily attained and malpractices were prevalent. According to him, while a few of the initiators of this movement were undertaking it as a step towards genuine total prohibition, the majority of the supporters were prompted by no such reasons. The Excise Commissioner supported his argument by explaining how during the settlement of excise shops the agitators of the movement urged both vendors and consumers to abandon licensed shops and, in defiance of the excise law, start 'illicit' distillation and sell and buy cheap liquor, and pay no duty to government. He said that promises were also made by the agitators that, with the coming of swaraj, drink, like all other articles, would be cheap.[327]

One other major way, people often circumvented British liquor was by resorting to smuggling of liquor and toddy from other territories. Poor peasants were prepared to walk miles to obtain cheap liquor in this manner. As the borders of the different territories were very intermingled, it was impossible to prevent such smuggling. In North Tirhut, country spirit and *ganja* were smuggled from Nepal.[328]

Thus, a strong protest centring on liquor emerged in Bihar during the Non-Cooperation Movement. This protest ranged from boycott of liquor and 'illicit' distillation of liquor to smuggling from outside the province. Although these trends of protest may appear contradictory, the underlying thread was defiance of British authority and its excise policy, thereby undermining government revenue.

Extension of Liquor Boycott to Dietary Purity

The liquor boycott was often extended to dietary purity. People also gave up *ganja* and tobacco, and in many areas, people also started abstaining from the consumption of meat and fish. There was a strong rumour in many places in Ranchi that the consumption of meat and alcohol would be forbidden under Gandhi raj.[329] In Ranchi, there was a widespread belief that Gandhi, who was invested with divine attributes, was already enthroned as King or was just going to be. Many tribals from the northern parts of Ranchi district rushed to the markets in February 1921 and disposed of their goats and sheep at very low prices. The price of goat meat fell in Ranchi from 12 to 4 annas a seer. Pigs were also sold in some of the localities.[330] Another rumour widespread in Ranchi in March 1921 was that goats, pigs, hens, sheep and other live stock, if not got rid of instantly, would turn to stone or the owners would die. As a result, in some districts, hens and goats were sold at very low prices in haats, and in many cases, people were compelled to turn them out loose into the jungle.[331]

In 1921, the Bhumijs of Madhupur heard of a divine Raja and disposed of their chickens and goats. Then they realized that the Raja they had heard about was Gandhi. A rumour was afloat among the Bhumij tribes of Dhalbhum and Manbhum that a new Raja, who was an incarnation of God, appeared on the scene. When the Mahatma's chelas or disciples appeared, these tribals started leading a clean life.[332]

Thus, one notices a concern for dietary purity in the phase of Non-Cooperation Movement. Why was this concern for dietary purity? We have no evidence to enable us to fully answer this question. However, some plausible explanations may perhaps be suggested. Even prior to the Non-Cooperation Movement trends in favour of giving up not only liquor but also meat and fish had picked up momentum in these areas. Some of the purification movements among the Oraons, the Mundas and the Santhals had already started in the pre-Gandhian period. For example, the Tana Bhagat Movement laid great stress on simplicity and purity of life. There was an incident in Ranchi in 1915, when a supposed supernatural mandate for the prohibition of drink was followed by the abstention of hundreds of Oraons from their favourite beverage. It was finally revoked by a placard posted on some trees in the market place by a subordinate of the excise department. It appeared to be an order from the deity that the people should resume their drinking.[333]

The trend of giving up meat and liquor that had been going on before the movement got further entrenched during the Non-Cooperation Movement. The Non-Cooperation Movement gave impetus to the ongoing process of social reforms. The religious and moral overtone underlying the movement and the Gandhian notion of self-purification, which began to include in itself liquor prohibition, practice of vegetarianism, etc. strengthened the ongoing trend. Amongst the Bhumij community in Madhupur, even before the Non-Cooperation Movement, Sankritization was going on for a considerable time. They were claiming to belong to the kshatriya status. They tried to initiate changes in their dietary habits. They also created many restrictions on the movement of their women.[334] Non-Cooperation Movement accelerated this process.

The reformatory trend of the movement throws light on an important aspect of the Non-Cooperation Movement. The movement does not only remain a fight for extermination of foreign power but its character had broadened. The comment of Rambriksha Benipuri on the movement is quite telling on this character of the movement. For Benipuri, the movement ranked with religious reform movements of the world as it shook the Indian society to its roots, bringing about fundamental changes in the lives of millions of people. He remarked that unprecedented examples of self-purification were manifested where people not only gave up *ganja* and liquor but even gave up tobacco. According to Benipuri, one could see the spirit of Buddhist and early

Christian missionaries in this movement of twentieth century also. For him, the movement inspired the people to lead a pure and simple life where artificiality in all aspects of lives were shunned. Glamorous clothes and luxuries were looked upon with contempt and people made bonfire of costly foreign clothes and started wearing simple khadi cloth happily. Though, according to Benipuri, people did not get the swaraj but for him what is significant is that they had found themselves, that oneness, which they had lost, i.e. people got the 'self' even if they did not get Raj.[335]

Thus, through these various boycotts the nationalists succeeded in undermining British power and eroding its hegemony. The Raj's ground of collaboration started cracking under the impact of an upsurge against it. The various boycotts exposed the political, economic and ideological interests and policies of British rule. The boycott campaigns had strong social sanction, which put the government in a difficult position. Social sanction was such as to make it very difficult for any court to take cognizance of the boycotts in legal terms. Many of these symbols of protest were multi-vocal in meanings. In fact, the strength of these symbols lay in their varied interpretations by the people. It has been argued that a political symbol is powerful precisely because of its ambiguity, which allows a number of different people to respond to a single unified form without necessarily sharing a single interpretation of it.

Boycott had expanded to encompass broad cultural symbol of swaraj. At the core of the fight were issues like self-respect, Indian identity and moral independence. National struggle was also a contest to redefine and retrieve Indian cultural space vis-à-vis British cultural and ideological onslaught. In fact, the contest between nationalism and the colonial state inseparably intertwined historically with the contest for hegemony within society. However, the hegemonic project of nationalism was that of cultural normalization, drawing heavily from the Brahminical tradition and obliterating the popular traditions. Women got tied to this hegemonizing project which subordinated their position. In the nationalist's agenda, women's political role dovetailed with her traditionally accepted role in society.

Notes

1. *CWMG*, vol. 18, pp. 18–19, 31, 102; vol. 21, pp. 60, 195.
2. Ranajit Guha, 'Discipline and Mobilize', in *Subaltern Studies VII,* ed. Partha Chatterjee and Gyanendra Pandey, New Delhi: Oxford University Press, 1992, p. 73; *CWMG*, vol. 18, p.102.
3. Datta, *History of the Freedom Movement in Bihar,* pp. 317–19.
4. Prasad, *Autobiography,* p. 116. This whole paragraph is based on this source.
5. Fortnightly Report of Bihar and Orissa for the first half of November 1920, Government of India, Home Department (Political) File no. 74/1920, NAI.

6. Fortnightly Report of Bihar and Orissa for the second half of November 1920, Government of India, Home Department (Political) File no. 33/1920, NAI.
7. Ibid.
8. *Searchlight,* November and December 1920; Bihar and Orissa Political Special File no. 346/21.
9. Ibid., 'D.I.G. to Chief Secretary, 22 November 1920'; *Searchlight,* 1 December 1920.
10. Bihar and Orissa Political Special File no. 346/1921.
11. *Searchlight,* 26 November 1920.
12. Bihar and Orissa Political Special File no. 346/1921.
13. Ibid.
14. *Searchlight,* 22 December 1920.
15. Ibid., 12 November 1920; Bihar and Orissa Political Special File no. 346/1921, 'Note—Sd/- J.E. Brown, 16 November 1920'.
16. *Searchlight,* 17 November 1920.
17. Ibid.
18. Ibid.
19. Bihar and Orissa Political Special File no. 346/1920, 'Khilafat and Non-Co-operation'.
20. Ibid., 'Copy of a Special Branch Officer's Report dated the 28 January 1921'.
21. *Searchlight,* 12 and 17 November 1920; Bihar and Orissa Political Special File nos. 346/1921 and 44/1921.
22. *Searchlight,* 19 November 1920; Bihar and Orissa Political Special File no. 346/1921, 'Khilafat and Non-Cooperation'.
23. Ibid.
24. Ibid.
25. Ibid., File nos. 346/1921 and 44/1921.
26. Ibid., File no. 346/1921. This entire paragraph is based on this source.
27. Fortnightly Reports of Bihar and Orissa of November and December 1920, Government of India, Home Department (Political) File nos. 74/1920, 33/1920, 35/1921 and 77/1921, NAI.
28. Fortnightly Report of Bihar and Orissa for the first half of December 1920, Government of India, Home Department (Political) File no. 77/1921, NAI.
29. Ibid.
30. Ibid
31. Ibid.
32. Fortnightly Report of Bihar and Orissa for the second half of January 1921, Government of India, Home Department (Political) File no. 42/1921, NAI.
33. Ibid.
34. Ibid.
35. Ibid.
36. Ibid.
37. Bihar and Orissa Political Special File no. 12/1921, 'District Magistrate, Darbhanga, to the Commissioner, Tirhut Division, 11 January 1921, Fortnightly Confidential Report'.
38. Ibid.
39. Ibid.

40. Fortnightly Report of Bihar and Orissa for the second half of January 1921, Government of India, Home Department (Political) File no. 42/1921, NAI. The entire paragraph is based on this source.
41. Fortnightly Report of Bihar and Orissa for the second half of November 1920, Government of India, Home Department (Political) File no. 33/1920, NAI.
42. Fortnightly Report of Bihar and Orissa for the second half of February 1921, Government of India, Home Department (Political) File no. 43/1921, NAI, 'From Secretary to the Government of Bihar and Orissa, Education Department to the Secretary to Government of India, Department of Education and Health, 15 July 1922—Effect of the Non-Cooperation Movement on educational institutions'.
43. Bihar and Orissa Political Special File no. 357/22, 'From Secretary to the Government of Bihar and Orissa, Education Department, to the Secretary to Government of India, Department of Education and Health, 15 July 1922—Effect of the Non-Cooperation Movement on educational institutions'.
44. Sankrityayan, ed., *Rahul Vanmay*, pp. 258–9.
45. Bihar and Orissa Political Special File no. 357/1922, 'From the Secretary to the Government of Bihar and Orissa, Education Department, to the Secretary to the Government of India, Department of Education and Health, 15 July 1922—Effect of the Non-Cooperation Movement on educational institutions'; Ibid., File no. 35/1922.
46. *Searchlight,* 16 March 1921; Datta, *History of the Freedom Movement in Bihar,* pp. 324–5.
47. Bihar and Orissa Political Special File no. 357/1922, 'From the Secretary to the Government of Bihar and Orissa, Education Department, to the Secretary to the Government of India, Department of Education and Health, 15 July 1922—Effect of the Non-Co-operation Movement on educational institutions'.
48. Ibid.
49. *Searchlight,* 16 March 1921.
50. Ibid., 8 December 1920.
51. Ibid., 12 January 1921.
52. Ibid., 16 March 1921.
53. Datta, *History of the Freedom Movement in Bihar,* p. 311.
54. Bihar and Orissa Political Special File no. 346/1921, 'Note—Sd/- J.E. Brown, 16 November 1920'.
55. Ibid., 'DIG to Chief Secretary, 19 November 1920'.
56. Ibid., 'Khilafat and Non-Cooperation'.
57. *Searchlight,* 28 January 1921; Bihar and Orissa Political Special File no. 346/1921, 'Copy forwarded to Chief Secretary from DIG, 31 January 1921'.
58. Ibid., File no. 117/1921, 'Progress of the Non-Cooperation Movement in Bihar, from DIG to Chief Secretary, 8 March 1921'.
59. Ibid.
60. Ibid., File no. 346/1921, 'National Education Movement, Bihar and Orissa'. The rest of the paragraph is based on this source.
61. Ibid., File no. 44/1921, 'Speeches delivered by Gandhi, national leaders and others on the occasion of the visit of Mr. Gandhi to the Province in Bihar'. The rest of the paragraph is based on this source.

62. *Searchlight,* 11, 13 and 19 November 1920; 16, 28 and 30 January 1921.
63. Ibid.
64. Ibid.
65. Bihar and Orissa Political Special File no. 44/1921, 'Speeches delivered by Gandhi, national leaders and others on the occasion of the visit of Mr. Gandhi to the Province in Bihar'; *Searchlight,* 11 March 1921.
66. Ibid.
67. Ibid.
68. *Searchlight,* 17 November 1920.
69. Ibid.
70. Bihar Special Branch, 1921, proscribed pamphlet, 'Bharat Mata Ka Sandesh', CID Record Room, Patna.
71. *Searchlight,* 19 November 1920.
72. Ibid., 23 February 1921.
73. Bihar and Orissa Political Special File no. 346/1921, 'Khilafat and Non-Co-operation, Patna, 18 January 1920'.
74. Bihar and Orissa Political Special File no. 346/1921, 'Copy of a Special Branch Officer's Report, 28 January 1921'.
75. Krishna Kumar, *Political Agenda of Education: A Study of Colonialist and Nationalist Ideas,* New Delhi: Sage, 1991, p. 61.
76. Ibid., p. 160.
77. Ibid.
78. Bihar and Orissa Political Special File no. 44/1921.
79. Rajendra Prasad, *Satyagraha in Champaran,* Ahmedabad: Navajivan, 1949, p. 198.
80. *CWMG,* vol. 61, p. 212.
81. *Searchlight,* 19 November 1920.
82. Ibid., 17 November 1920.
83. Datta, *History of the Freedom Movement in Bihar,* pp. 311–12.
84. Bihar and Orissa Political Special File nos. 44/1921 and 346/1921.
85. Kumar, *Political Agenda of Education,* pp. 127–43, 192–203.
86. C.A. Bayly, 'The Origins of Swadeshi (home industry): Cloth and Indian Society, 1700–1930' in *Social Life of Things: Commodities in Cultural Perspectives,* ed. Arjun Appadurai, London: Cambridge University Press, 1986, pp. 309–17.
87. *CWMG,* vol. 23, p. 106; Bayly, 'The Origins of Swadeshi', pp. 311–13.
88. *CWMG,* vol. 23, p. 106.
89. Ibid.
90. *Bihar and Orissa Annual Administration Report,* 1921, p. 151; Prasad, *Autobiography,* p. 139.
91. Bamford, *Histories of the Non-Cooperation and Khilafat Movements,* p. 35.
92. *Searchlight,* 31 August 1921; Fortnightly Report of Bihar and Orissa for the second half of August 1921, Government of India, Home Department (Political) File no. 18/August/1921, NAI.
93. Freedom Movement Papers SCRO 56, BSA; *Searchlight,* 26 August 1921.
94. Bihar and Orissa Political Special File no. 410/1921, 'Copy of D.O. letter No. 150, 14 August 1921, from the Superintendent of Police, Gaya, to the D.I.G of Police, Crime and Railways, Bihar and Orissa'. This whole paragraph is based on this source.

95. Ibid., File no. 538/1921.
96. Ibid., File no. 400/1921.
97. Ibid., 'Copy of a report of M. Md. Kabir, S.I., Begusarai, 4 September 1921'. This whole paragraph is based on this source.
98. Ibid., '5 September 1921, Gogri'.
99. Ibid.
100. Ibid., '5 September, Jamalpur—S.I., H.N. Sinha, 6 September 1921'.
101. Ibid.
102. Ibid.
103. Ibid., 'Copy of a Special Branch Officer's Report, 11 September 1921, regarding the meeting held at Monghyr on the boycott of foreign cloth and Report of Speeches delivered at a meeting held at Monghyr on 11 September 1921'.
104. Ibid.
105. Ibid.
106. Ibid.
107. Ibid.
108. Ibid., 'Copy of a Special Branch Officer's Report dated the 11 September 1921 regarding the meeting held at Monghyr on the boycott of foreign cloth and Report of Speeches delivered at a meeting held at Monghyr on 11 September 1921'.
109. Ibid., 'Copy of D.O. letter no. 1256/17, 22 September—From the Superintendent of Police, Bhagalpur, to the 2nd Assistant to the D.I.G. of Police, Crime and Railways, Bihar and Orissa'. The rest of the paragraph is based on these sources.
110. Ibid., File no. 477/1921.
111. Ibid.
112. Fortnightly Report of Bihar and Orissa for the first half of October 1921, Government of India, Home Department (Political) File no. 18/October/1921, NAI.
113. Ibid.
114. Bihar and Orissa Political Special File no. 339/1921, 'Extract from the Confidential Diary of the Superintendent of Police, Bhagalpur, for the week ending 8 August 1921'.
115. Datta, *History of the Freedom Movement in Bihar*, p. 394.
116. *Searchlight*, 28 September 1921; Bihar and Orissa Political Special File nos. 339/1921, 477/1921, 400/1921 and 410/1921.
117. Ibid.
118. AICC Papers, File no. 6/1921.
119. Bihar and Orissa Political Special File no. 159/21 K.W.
120. Badrinarayan, *Lok Sanskriti Mein Rashtravad,* New Delhi: Radhakrishna, 1996, p. 74.
121. Bihar and Orissa Political Special File no. 538/1921.
122. Ibid.
123. *Searchlight*, 12 February 1922.
124. Ibid., 10 February 1922.
125. Ibid., 11 December 1921.

126. Ibid., 11 September 1921.
127. Bihar and Orissa Political Special File no. 410/1921.
128. *Searchlight*, 7 October 1921.
129. Ibid., 26 October 1921.
130. Ibid., 19 February 1922.
131. Ibid., 10 February 1922.
132. Ibid., 18 January 1922.
133. Bihar and Orissa Political Special File no. 400/1921.
134. Ibid., File no. 410/1921.
135. Datta, *History of the Freedom Movement in Bihar*, p. 394.
136. *Searchlight*, 22 July 1921; AICC Papers, File no. 6/1921.
137. *Young India*, 12 February 1925.
138. Ibid.
139. Bihar and Orissa Political Special File no. 291/1922, 'Note on the results of searches in connection with the Government, Notification No. 4609-C, 10 December 1921, under the Criminal Law Amendment Act'.
140. Ibid.
141. Ibid.
142. Ibid.
143. Ibid.
144. Ibid.
145. *Motherland*, 15 November 1921.
146. Bihar and Orissa Political Special File no. 477/1921.
147. *Searchlight*, 7 October 1921; Bihar and Orissa Political Special File no. 477/1921, 'Copy of a Special Branch Officer's Report dated 30 September 1921'.
148. Ibid.
149. *Searchlight*, 7 October 1921.
150. Ibid., 3 August 1921.
151. Ibid., 18 and 30 November 1921.
152. Ibid., 14 December 1921.
153. Ibid., 23 November 1921.
154. Datta, *Freedom Movement in Bihar*, p. 491.
155. K.K. Datta, *The Writings and Speeches of Mahatma Gandhi in Bihar, 1917–1947*, Patna: Government of Bihar, 1969, pp. 197–212.
156. Ibid.
157. Datta, *The Writings and Speeches of Mahatma Gandhi in Bihar, 1917–1947*, p. 172.
158. Datta, *Gandhiji in Bihar*, p. 211.
159. Ibid.
160. David Hardiman, *Peasant Nationalists of Gujarat: Kheda District 1917–1934*, New Delhi: Oxford University Press, 1981, p. 125.
161. *Report of the Indian Famine Commission 1901*, p. 78.
162. Datta, *Writings and Speeches of Mahatma Gandhi in Bihar*, p. 220.
163. Gyan Pandey, *The Ascendancy of the Congress in Uttar Pradesh 1926–34*, New Delhi: Oxford University Press, 1978, pp. 62–5.

164. Ghoors were a common mechanism through which village women gathered to carry on rituals and discuss their affairs. Wendy Singer, *Creating Histories, Oral Narratives and the Politics of History-Making,* New Delhi: Oxford University Press, 1997.
165. Ibid.
166. Ibid.
167. Ibid.
168. Ibid.; Sumit Sarkar, *Modern India*, New Delhi: Macmillan, 1983.
169. Bayly, 'The Origin of Swadeshi', pp. 311–15.
170. Bihar Special Branch, 163L/1921, proscribed song, 'Charkha Vinode', CID Record Room, Patna.
171. Sharma, ed., *Benipuri Granthavali*, p. 40.
172. Ibid.
173. Bihar Special Branch, L72A/1922, proscribed song, 'Rashtriya Bhajan', CID Record Room, Patna.
174. Ibid.
175. Ibid., proscribed pamphlet, 'Bharat Mata Ka Sandesh', CID Record Room, Patna.
176. Ibid., proscribed song, 'Bharat Udhar', CID Record Room, Patna.
177. Sharma, ed., *Benipuri Granthavali,* p. 60.
178. Ibid.
179. *CWMG*, vol.10, p. 19.
180. Bihar Special Branch, 163L/ 1921, proscribed song, 'Charkha Vinode', CID Record Room, Patna.
181. Ibid., proscribed leaflet, 'Bharat Mata Ka Sandesh', CID Record Room, Patna.
182. Bayly, 'The Origin of Swadeshi', pp. 312–14.
183. Gandhi, *Khadi: Why and How,* pp. 104–5.
184. Ibid.
185. Ibid.
186. Bihar Special Branch, 37L/ 1921, proscribed leaflet, 'Igarah Pai', CID Record Room, Patna.
187. Rajiv Nain Prasad, 'The Champaran Satyagraha', in *History of Indian National Congress in Bihar, 1885–1985,* ed. P.N. Ojha, Patna: K.P. Jayaswal Research Institute, 1985, p. 178.
188. Tarlo, *Clothing Matters*, pp. 94–6.
189. Ibid., pp. 94–6. This entire paragraph is based on this source.
190. Ibid.
191. Ibid.; *CWMG*, vol. 20, p. 386.
192. Home Department (Political) File no. 290/1921, NAI.
193. Bernard Cohn, *Colonialism and its Forms of Knowledge: The British in India*, Princeton: Princeton University Press, 1996, pp. 148–9.
194. Tarlo, *Clothing Matters*, pp. 96–101; Home Department (Political) File no. 290/1921, NAI.
195. Tarlo, *Clothing Matters*; *CWMG*, vol. 20, p. 105.
196. Tarlo, *Clothing Matters*, pp. 96–101; K.K. Datta, *History of the Freedom Movement in Bihar,* vols. 1–3, Patna: Bihar Government Press, 1957.

197. Tarlo, *Clothing Matters*, p. 100.
198. Ibid.
199. *Motherland*, 1 November 1921 and 23 June 1922.
200. Sumit Sarkar, 'The Conditions and Nature of Subaltern Militancy: Bengal from Swadeshi to Non-Cooperation, 1905–22', in *Subaltern Studies*, vol. III, ed. Ranajit Guha, New Delhi: Oxford University Press, 1984, pp. 301, 312–19.
201. *CWMG*, vol. 16, pp. 79–80, 168.
202. Geraldine Forbes, 'The Politics of Respectability: Indian Women and the Indian National Congress', in *The Indian National Congress*, ed. D.A. Low, New Delhi: Oxford University Press, 1988, pp. 54–97.
203. Radha Kumar, *History of Doing*, Delhi: Kali for Women, Delhi, 1993, pp. 42, 57–8.
204. Bihar Special Branch, proscribed leaflet, 'Bhanda Phore', LIII/21; 'Charkha Vinode', 163L/1921, CID Record Room, Patna.
205. Bihar Special Branch, LIII/1922, proscribed song, 'Charkha Vinode', CID Record Room, Patna.
206. Bayly, 'The Origins of Swadeshi', p. 293; Meredith Borthwick, *The Changing Role of Women in Bengal, 1849–1905*, Princeton: Princeton University Press, 1984, p. 348.
207. Bayly, 'The Origins of Swadeshi', p. 293; Borthwick, *The Changing Role of Women in Bengal*, p. 348.
208. Kumar, *History of Doing*, p. 66.
209. Datta, *Writings and Speeches of Mahatma Gandhi in Bihar*, pp. 223–4.
210. Mahatma Gandhi, *Women and Social Justice*, Ahmedabad: Navajivan, 1958, pp. 112, 164; Maria Mies, *Indian Women and Patriarchy*, New Delhi: Concept Publishing Company, 1980, p. 126.
211. Kumari Jayawardena, *Feminism and Nationalism in the Third World*, London: Zed Books, 1986, p. 95.
212. Bihar Special Branch, proscribed leaflet, 'Charkha Vinode', 163L/1921, CID Record Room, Patna.
213. Ibid.
214. Singer, *Creating Histories*, p. 43.
215. Bihar Special Branch, proscribed leaflet 'Bideshi kapro ka bahishkar', 71L, 1921, CID Record Room, Patna.
216. Datta, *Gandhi in Bihar*, pp. 95–6.
217. Chatterjee, *Nation and its Fragments*, p. 125.
218. Forbes, 'The Politics of Respectability', p. 70.
219. Tarlo, *Clothing Matters*, p. 110.
220. Himani Banerji, *Inventing Subjects: Studies in Hegemony, Patriarchy and Colonialism*, New Delhi: Tulika, 2001, pp. 99–134.
221. Tanika Sarkar, 'Politics and Women in Bengal—the Conditions and Meanings of Participation', in *Indian Economic and Social History Review*, vol. XXI, no. 1, January-March 1984, pp. 98–9.
222. Bihar Special Branch, L38/1921, proscribed pamphlet, 'Swaraj Ke Faede', CID Record Room, Patna.
223. Henningham, *Peasant Movements in Colonial India*, p. 22.

224. Bihar and Orissa Political Special 1921, proscribed pamphlet, 'Bharat Mata Ka Sandesh', CID Record Room, Patna.
225. To name some of the lawyers, Mazharul Haq, Rajendra Prasad, Anugrah Narayan Singh, Chandra Bansi Sahay, Bajrang Sahay, Jagat Narayan Lal, Ambica Prasad, Bipin Bihari Varma, Krishna Sen Sinha from Patna.
226. *Searchlight*, 16 March 1921; Bihar and Orissa Political Special File no. 117/1921, 'Progress of the Non-Cooperation Movement in Bihar, from DIG to Chief Secretary, 8 March 1921'.
227. Bihar Special Branch, proscribed song, L149/1921, proscribed leaflet 'Vakilwa', CID Record Room, Patna.
228. Ibid.
229. Ibid., proscribed song, L38/1921, proscribed leaflet 'Swaraj Ke Faede', CID Record Room, Patna.
230. Ibid., proscribed pamphlet, 'Bharat Mata Ka Sandesh', CID Record Room, Patna.
231. Ibid., proscribed pamphlet, L149/21, CID Record Room, Patna.
232. Ibid., proscribed pamphlet, 'Bharat Mata Ka Sandesh', CID Record Room, Patna.
233. Ibid.
234. Ibid., L149/1921, CID Record Room, Patna.
235. Prasad, *Autobiography*, pp. 134–5.
236. Evidences comes from the novel *Dhorai Charitmanas* of Satinath Bhaduri, Allahabad: Lokbharati, 1981.
237. This has been discussed in Chapter 2 'Contouring the Non-Cooperation Movement in Bihar: 1920–1922'.
238. Ibid.
239. Bihar and Orissa Political Special File no. 117/1921, 'Progress of the Non-Co-operation Movement in Bihar, from DIG to Chief Secretary, 8 March 1921'.
240. *Searchlight*, 16 March 1921.
241. Sahajanand Saraswati Papers, Personal Diary 1921, NMML.
242. Fortnightly Report of Bihar and Orissa for the second half of February 1921, Government of India, Home Department Political File no. 43/April/1921, NAI; Bihar and Orissa Political Special File no. 117/1921, 'Progress of the Non-Co-operation Movement in Bihar, from DIG to Chief Secretary, 8 March 1921'.
243. Ibid., File no. 37/1921; Ibid., File no. 69/1921, 'Extract from Hon. Mr. McPherson's note dated 5 July 1921'.
244. Ibid.
245. Prasad, *Autobiography*, pp. 134–5.
246. Ibid.
247. K.K. Datta papers, 'Statement of Shri Bajrang Sahay', Manuscript, NMML; Fortnightly Report of Bihar and Orissa for the second half of February 1921, Home Department (Political) File no. 43/April/1921, NAI.
248. In fact the *Panch Parmeshwar* story of Premchand highlights how god presides in *panches* and their judgements are always fair. *Panch Parmeshwar*, Premchand Rachna Sanchayan, ed. Nirmal Verma, Kamal Kishore Goyanka, New Delhi: Sahitya Akademi, 1994, pp. 66–75.

249. This is very well reflected in *Dhorai Charitmanas*, where the protagonist comes from the lower class and finds himself marginalized in such panchayats.
250. K.K. Datta papers, 'Statement of Shri Bajrang Sahay', Manuscript, NMML; Fortnightly Report of Bihar and Orissa for the second half of February 1921, Home Department (Political) File no. 43/April/1921, NAI.
251. Bihar and Orissa Political Special File no. 113/1921.
252. Fortnightly Report of Bihar and Orissa for the first half of June 1921, Home Department (Political) File no. 64/June/1921, NAI.
253. David Horton, 'The Functions of Alcohol in Primitive Societies: A Cross-Cultural Study', in *Quarterly Journal of Studies on Alcohol*, vol. 4, no. 2, September 1943, p. 246.
254. Ibid., pp. 106–10.
255. Ibid.
256. Ibid.
257. *Excise Administration Report, Bihar*, 1880–90.
258. Ibid.
259. Ibid.
260. Dwight B. Heath, 'Comment on David Mandelbaum's "Alcohol and Culture"', in *Current Anthropology*, vol. 6, no. 3, June 1965, p. 20.
261. M.N. Srinivas described the process as Sanskritization. In Sanskritization, a low-caste Hindu or tribal or other groups change their customs, rituals, ideology and way of life in the direction of a high, and frequently, twice-born caste, to claim higher position in social hierarchy than that traditionally conceded to the claimant group by the local community. See M.N. Srinivas, *Social Change in Modern India*, Bombay: Allied, 1972, p. 6. Others like David Hardiman see assertion in it. He says the lower caste or tribals by appropriating and democratizing the reserve of higher-caste values sought to deprive them of their power of domination. See David Hardiman, 'Adivasi Assertion in South Gujarat: The Devi Movement of 1922–23', in *Subaltern Studies III: Writings on South Asian History and Society*, ed. Ranajit Guha, New Delhi: Oxford University Press, 1984, pp. 11–19.
262. S.C. Roy, *Oraon Religion and Customs*, Calcutta: Industry Press, 1928, p. 251.
263. Bipan Chandra, *The Rise and Growth of Economic Nationalism in India*, New Delhi: Vikas, 1988, pp. 556–61.
264. David G. Mandelbaum, 'Alcohol and Culture', in *Current Anthropology*, vol. 6, no. 3, June 1965, pp. 281–94.
265. Presidential address to the Second All-India Temperance Conference, Benares, 26 December 1905; Hardiman, *The Politics of Drinking*, p. 216.
266. Chandra, *Economic Nationalism*, p. 560.
267. Brown, *Gandhi's Rise to Power*, pp. 315–16.
268. Bihar Special Branch 1921, proscribed pamphlet, 'Bharat Mata Ka Sandesh', CID Record Room, Patna.
269. Ibid., 181L/1921, proscribed song, 'Shri Gandhi Chalisa', CID Record Room, Patna.
270. Ibid.
271. Ibid.

272. This has been extensively studied by David Hardiman in *The Coming of the Devi: Adivasi Assertion in Western India*, New Delhi: Oxford University Press, 1987.
273. Bihar and Orissa Political Special File no. 309/1921.
274. Ibid., File no. 256/1921, 'From Excise Commissioner, Bihar and Orissa, to the Secretary to the Government of India, Department of Commerce'.
275. Ibid.
276. Ibid.
277. *Searchlight*, 18 May, 16 and 21 September 1921; Home Department (Political) File no. 49/1921, NAI.
278. *Searchlight*, 13 May 1921.
279. Ibid., 7 October 1921.
280. Bihar and Orissa Political Special File no. 400/1921.
281. Fortnightly Report of Bihar and Orissa for the first half of October 1921, Home Department (Political) File no. 18/October/1921, NAI.
282. Bihar and Orissa Political Special File no. 214/1921, 'Extract from a D.O. letter, 6 May 1921, from the Superintendent of Police, Gaya'.
283. Fortnightly Report of Bihar and Orissa for the second half of September 1921, Home Department (Political) File no. 18/September/1921, NAI.
284. Fortnightly Report of Bihar and Orissa for the first half of May 1921, Home Department (Political) File no. 63/June/1921, NAI.
285. Bihar and Orissa Political Special File no. 478/1921.
286. Ibid., File no. 153/1921, 'Extract from the confidential report of the Superintendent of Police, Manbhum, for week ending 5 March 1921'; Fortnightly Report of Bihar and Orissa for the first half of March 1921, Home Department (Political) File no. 65/1921, NAI.
287. Bihar and Orissa Political Special File no. 153/1921, 'Extract from the confidential report of the Superintendent of Police, Manbhum, for week ending 5 March 1921'.
288. Ibid.
289. Ibid., File no. 113/1921, 'Extract from demi-official letter No. 108-T.C., 12 March 1921, from F.F. Lyall, Chief Commissioner, Chotanagpur Division'.
290. Fortnightly Report of Bihar and Orissa for the second half of April 1921, Home Department (Political) File no. 13/June/1921, NAI.
291. Fortnightly Report of Bihar and Orissa for the second half of January 1921, Government of India, Home Department (Political) File no. 42/April/1921, NAI; Bihar and Orissa Political Special File no. 256/1921.
292. Ibid., File no. 65/1921, 'Some instances of the highhanded methods of Non-Cooperation'.
293. Fortnightly Report of Bihar and Orissa for the first half of November 1921, Government of India, Home Department (Political) File no. 18/November/1921, NAI.
294. Fortnightly Report of Bihar and Orissa for the second half of October 1921, Government of India, Home Department (Political) File no. 18/October/1921, NAI.
295. *Searchlight*, 18 May 1921.
296. Ibid., 13 April 1921.

297. Fortnightly Report of Bihar and Orissa for the second half of April 1921, Government of India, Home Department (Political) File no. 13/June/1921, NAI.
298. Bihar and Orissa Political Special File nos. 113/1921, 6/1921 and 65/1921.
299. Fortnightly Report of Bihar and Orissa for the second half of December 1921, Government of India, Home Department (Political) File no. 18/December/1921, NAI.
300. Bihar and Orissa Political Special File no. 113/1921, 'Extract from demi-official letter No. 108-T.C., 12 March 1921, from Commissioner, Chotanagpur Division'.
301. Fortnightly Report of Bihar and Orissa for the second half of December 1921, Government of India, Home Department (Political) File no. 18/December/1921, NAI.
302. Bihar and Orissa Political Special File nos. 113/1921, 6/1921 and 65/1921; Fortnightly Report of Bihar and Orissa for the second half of December 1921, Government of India, Home Department (Political) File no. 18//December/1921, NAI; Bihar and Orissa Political Special File no. 113/1921, 'Extract from demi-official letter No. 108-T.C., 12 March 1921, from Commissioner, Chotanagpur Division'; Ibid., File no. 65/1921, 'Some instances of the highhanded methods of Non-Cooperation'.
303. Ibid., File no. 478/1921.
304. Fortnightly Report of Bihar and Orissa for the first half of April 1921, Home Department (Political) File no. 51/June/1921, NAI.
305. Bihar and Orissa Political Special File no. 65/1921, 'Some instances of the highhanded methods of Non-Cooperation'.
306. Ibid., File no. 12/1921, 'From Commissioner, Tirhut Division, to the Chief Secretary, 20 January 1921'.
307. Sankrityayan, ed., *Rahul Vanvay*, p. 254.
308. Ibid.
309. Ibid., pp. 254–5.
310. Fortnightly Reports of Bihar and Orissa for April and May 1921, Government of India, Home Department (Political) File nos. 13/1921, 51/1921, 63/1921 and 46/1921, NAI.
311. Fortnightly Reports of Bihar and Orissa for January 1922, Government of India, Home Department (Political) File no. 18/January/1922, NAI.
312. Ibid.
313. Ibid.
314. Home Department (Political) File no. 170/1921, NAI.
315. Fortnightly Report of Bihar and Orissa for the second half of September 1921, Government of India, Home Department (Political) File no. 18/September/1921, NAI.
316. Fortnightly Report of Bihar and Orissa for the first half of October 1921, Government of India, Home Department (Political) File no. 18/October/1921, NAI.
317. Fortnightly Report of Bihar and Orissa for the second half of April 1921, Government of India, Home Department (Political) File no. 13/June/1921, NAI.
318. Ibid.

319. Fortnightly Report of Bihar and Orissa for the first half of October 1921, Government of India, Home Department Political File no. 18/October/1921, NAI.
320. Fortnightly Report of Bihar and Orissa for the second half of April 1921, Government of India, Home Department (Political) File no. 13/June/1921.
321. Ibid.
322. Ibid.
323. Fortnightly Reports of Bihar and Orissa for June, July and August 1921, Home Department (Political) File nos. 64/1921, 1/1921 and 18/August/1921, NAI.
324. Fortnightly Reports of Bihar and Orissa for August 1921, Home Department (Political) File no. 18/August/1921, NAI.
325. Bihar and Orissa Political Special File no. 256/1921, 'From Excise Commissioner, Government of Bihar and Orissa to the Secretary to the Government of India, Department of Commerce'.
326. Ibid.
327. Ibid.
328. Fortnightly Report of Bihar and Orissa for the second half of September 1921, Government of India, Home Department (Political) File no. 18/September/1921, NAI.
329. *Bihar and Orissa Annual Administration Report 1921*, pp. 148–9.
330. Ibid.
331. Freedom Movement Papers, SCRO 51, BSA, 'Commissioner, Ranchi, to all Deputy Commissioner, 19 March 1921'.
332. J.C. Jha, 'The Tribals of Bihar and the Indian Freedom Movement: 1920–1942', in *Indian Historical Review,* July 1985–January 1986, vol. XII, nos. 1–2, p. 285.
333. *Bihar and Orissa Annual Administration Report 1921*, pp. 148–9.
334. Jha, 'The Tribals of Bihar', p. 286.
335. Sharma, ed., *Benipuri Granthavali*, p. 219.

CHAPTER FOUR

Popular Protests: Peasant and Tribal Struggles

In the past two decades, there have been a large number of studies on peasant movements. There have also been a few studies on the Bihar Kisan Sabha.[1] However, these studies on Bihar have focused mostly on the relationship between the Kisan Sabha and the Congress/national movement. There has relatively been fewer works aiming to understand the nature of popular protest within the nationalist agitation, which was not merely correlated to nationalist agitation but was an essential part of it.[2]

Historians have long debated the question of how mass mobilization occurred during the course of the nationalist struggle. In nationalist and colonialist historiography, there is a serious underestimation of the extent of popular initiative in nationalist politics. The masses were viewed as essentially inert. The emergence of nationalist consciousness among the masses is seen exclusively or predominantly as an elite achievement. In colonialist and neo-colonialist historiography, these achievements are credited to British colonial rulers, administrators, policies, institutions and culture;[3] in nationalist and neo-nationalist writings, to the Indian elite, institutions, activities and ideas.[4] Even in Marxist historiography, the credit for mass mobilization and growth of radical consciousness is given to party programmes, leadership and organization.[5]

Of late, there have been a large number of studies highlighting the role of elites or dominant sections of villages in the mobilization of nationalist agitation.[6] These works underline how the agrarian base of the Congress, which was constituted of dominant and rich peasants, played important role in mobilization. Pouchepadass' work on Bihar emphasizes the role of dominant peasantry at local level in initiating the movement and transformig it into broad-based mass movement. He attributes significant role to caste panchayats of dominant peasants for this.[7] However, the emphasis on elite's role in his work overlooks the role of lower-caste panchayats.[8] Besides, as this study has shown, Gandhian panchayats, which played a significant role, was not exclusively under the domination of upper castes and a large number of lower castes were its members. Hence, one needs to problematize the relationship between the dominant peasants and the village community. Elite initiative paradigm neither captures the broad appeal and diverse receptions of nationalism by the masses nor gives political agency or autonomy to the masses.

The study of popular participation in nationalist agitation should also take into account the thoughts, feelings and aspirations of the subordinate sections. Stephen Henningham's study on rural Bihar also assigns political role to village elite. However, he does not see politics as linked only to economic factors. But he does not consider non-elites' response as political but primarily looks at it as the rebellion of desperation, for they are victims of economic diversity.[9] Even though the economic factor cannot be underplayed, one needs to look at the larger political context for understanding the participation of masses. Anand Yang's work also highlights how, at the fundamental level of agrarian society, the village-level controller was the key to both control and conflict.[10] Thus, these works, by giving importance to the agrarian base of the Congress and elite initiative, throw significant light on the class interest of the Congress movement: the domination of elites. But one needs to move beyond the paradigm of 'interests', 'initiative', 'betrayal' and highlight the complexity of the mass-based nationalism. Such paradigms keep out of purview a large range of mass movements from nationalist agitation. Popular participation cannot merely be dovetailed to elite initiative. There were varied popular responses and translations of nationalism. One needs to map peasant consciousness in its relation with nationalism at different levels, thus delineating the complex relationship of masses with nationalism.[11]

In recent years, subaltern studies have brought about a major shift in the historiography of the Indian national movement. It dismisses all previous writings including those based on Marxist perspective, as elite historiography which see mass political awareness and mobilization as the exclusive handiwork of the elite. According to the subaltern school, any peasant insurrection in such historiography is regarded as external to the peasants consciousness where explaination has often been sought in an enumeration of causes, say, factors of economic and political deprivation which do not relate at all to the peasants consciousness or do so negatively triggering off rebellion as a sort of reflex action, i.e. as an instinctive and almost mindless response to physical suffering of one kind or another (e.g. hunger, torture, forced labour, etc.) or as a passive reaction to some initiative of his superordinate enemy. Historians have been content in dealing with the peasant rebel merely as an empirical person or member of a class but not as an entity whose will and reaction constituted the praxis called rebellion. According to the subaltern studies, what is clearly left out of this unhistorical historiography is the politics of the people, the contributions made by the people on their own, i.e. independently of the elite, to the development of nationalism. Subalternists emphasize that parallel to the domain of elite politics there existed throughout the colonial period another domain of Indian politics of the subaltern classes and groups constituting the mass of the labouring population and the intermediate strata in the town and the country, i.e. the people. This was an autonomous domain, for it neither originated from elite politics nor did its existence depend on the latter. The experience of exploitation and labour endowed this politics with many idioms, norms and values which put it in a category apart from elite politics.[12]

One cannot overlook the significant contribution made by subaltern studies in widening the scope of nationalism. They bring to the centre the politics of the people and their contribution and help in understanding and assessing mass articulation of nationalism. They highlight the need to examine the thoughts, feelings and aspirations of the subordinated. The role of the village community in these agitations is highlighted. They point out that the popular agitation which sharpened during the Non-Cooperation Movement were prior to the year 1921. Thus, one can see agitation over certain popular issues as a continuity, rather than disjunction, between forms of struggle and mobilization that were traditional, and those that were adopted in the course of the anti-colonial movement in this region and not a total break or rupture. So one has to look beyond the paradigm of locating the previous movement and nationalism as binary dichotomy, such as 'political'/'pre-political': 'mature'/'primitive' with 'true consciousness'/'false consciousness'. The distance between 'modern' and 'primitive' forms of mass protest gets bridged by highlighting the interplay between 'traditional' and 'modern' elements in the constitution of popular political consciousness.

Despite the significant contribution of subaltern studies, there are certain serious problems in this historiography. There is far too much emphasis on the autonomous nature of the subaltern movement vis-à-vis the nationalist movement. It is true that 'urban nationalism' did not take the initiative in organizing popular protest. Popular protest on some of the issues had preceded the year 1921 and was shaped by organizational structures that were independent of the nationalist organization. There is sufficient justification for the view that there already existed a subaltern consciousness which was seized upon by the nationalist elite. But, the question is whether the widespread political ferment at the time affected the movement at all. The ferment is, of course, not the same thing as the role of a specific group of individuals. The peasants may also have interpreted in their own way the political message that created the ferment. In fact, the scope of the popular movement became broader as a result of its interaction with the Non-Cooperation Movement. One cannot overlook the atmosphere of non-cooperation which was writ with general defiance of authority and contempt of the government. Slogans in praise of Mahatma Gandhi and 'Swatantra Bharat' and cries that the *government was anniyayi* rent the air during the Non-Cooperation Movement. Swaraj was projected as a panacea for all grievances.

In fact, the bland formulation that peasants 'were clearly not derivative of the politics of urban nationalism' precludes consideration of their possible links with the nationalist movement of the time. There is no denying the fact that popular protest was not the exclusive handiwork of Congress politics, but one cannot overlook the role of the nationalist organization or the importance of the local nationalist organization in the campaign. One cannot also disregard the influence of the 'less' important Congress leadership at the local level. The popular protest, as discussed in the chapter below, proves beyond any doubt that the local non-cooperators were scarcely peripheral to the resistance and advanced their cause. Subaltern historians with their overemphasis on continuity rather than on disjunction in forms of protest and mobilization do not address the question of the new forms of peasant protest.

The rebels had, for the first time, the vision of a 'free India'. Idioms used for articulating the popular politics were strikingly new. Previous protests were sporadic, isolated and often spontaneous, qualitatively different from organized resistance. Certainly, there is clear evidence that the popular protest intensified or radicalized during the Non-Cooperation Movement.[13] The question arises: why did the radical tone of the movement become most pronounced in the year 1920–2. The subaltern historians do not quite explain the radicalization. In fact, there was a dialectical linkage between the call for struggle and the slogans given by the Gandhian nationalists and the masses with their problems, who believed that in swaraj their grievances would be redressed.

The Congress became a symbol of struggle for the masses, although the latter's responses to swaraj and the Mahatma had their own specificity. Thus, even while acknowledging the specificity of different class interests, it is difficult to accept the duality of the insurrection consisting of an elite nationalist uprising and the subaltern revolt. This work neither accepts some of the basic paradigm of subaltern historians, i.e. 'duality of the nationalism' ('elite' and 'subaltern' nationalism) nor the 'popular autonomy'. Although it does accept the specificity of the popular level and popular translations of swaraj, but it highlights the complexity of relationship between the Congress and the masses.[14] Sumit Sarkar in his study has highlighted the subaltern participation in the anti-imperialist struggle as a subset within the broader theme of subaltern awakening: the one does not automatically lead to the other without a variety of complex mediations in which the specific socio-economic structure of a region, historical traditions, efforts at mobilization by the elite—nationalist groups and ideologies—and British strategies all play a part.[15]

It is against this background that this chapter examines the nature of popular protests in the planters' and tribal belt. Popular protests in these belts sharpened during the Non-Cooperation Movement. The first section traces the nature of protest in the planters' belt and the following section deals with the protest in the tribal belt. Both belts had a strong tradition of protest. An attempt has been made to provide an overview of the nature of popular protest that preceded the Non-Cooperation Movement in these areas.

The Movement in the Planters' Belt of North Bihar

Position of Planters in Society

In order to understand the strong discontentment that was building up against the planters, it is necessary to examine the position of the European planters in society, their relationship with peasants and some of the peasants' grievances. By the late nineteenth century, the planters were well entrenched in the northern belt of Bihar—200 to 300 of them were spread across north Bihar. Their largest concentration was in Champaran where they held proprietary leases over half of the land.[16] In order to make adequate profit by legitimate means, a planter had to be active both as a landlord and as a supervisor of indigo production. The planters assumed zamindari rights as lessees acquiring total control over the land. They entered into agreements with the Bettiah raj, the Hathwa raj and the Darbhanga raj, to act as lessees over substantial areas with rights of rent collection from the tenants.[17]

Taking advantage of their position, the planters forced every one of their tenants to cultivate indigo on three kathas of their best land, out of every 20 kathas of land. This was known as the tinkathia system.[18] The successful cultivation of indigo demanded close supervision, thereby leading to greater intervention of the planter. As a landlord, the planter had to ensure that all arable land was under cultivation and that his rights in trees, hides, fishing and other miscellaneous products were protected.[19] The planters depended on tenants for the supply of labour and for the provision of carts and bullocks for transportation.[20]

The planters were an alien elite group, predominantly European, who had few ties with the local population. They often developed strong ties with the district level officials because of their similar ethnic background, mutual support and common social interests. Officials and planters interacted with each other socially at the club and on hunting expeditions. Planters derived many benefits because of this affinity.[21] In proportion to their numbers, the planters held a large number of seats on the district boards. In Muzaffarpur, they held one out of every four presidencies of the chaukidari unions.[22] They had charge of cattle pounds and were even given the contracts for the maintenance of roads in an area.[23]

Raj Kumar Sukul, the man who persuaded Gandhi to visit Champaran, talked of the pervasive hold of the planters in Champaran district in his account to the Champaran Agrarian Enquiry Committee. Champaran district had 70 factories, situated at a distance of 2 to 5 miles from each other. Almost the whole of the district was in the hands of the factory owners. The factory 'sahibs' did what they liked. It seemed as if there was no Raj of the British government.[24]

Planters status and position had both political and economic ramifications. In course of time, the planters or Gora Sahibs emerged as an important force in many kinds of activities in the local area. The planters had hegemonic hold on the villages. In Purnea district there are many villages that were named after planters, haunting reminders of the forgotten stories of the planters' age. The old names of the villages before the planters' regime had to be eroded from the memory of the villagers. Anybody who by mistake took the old name of a village was beaten and tortured by the planters. Bungalows of the planters in such villages were looked upon with awe and fear. The fear of the villagers was mixed with certain element of pride: if there was a Sahib's *kothi* near the village, a new villager would be shown the bungalow with great pride. Thus, there was among the subordinate sections of villages the coexistence and complex interpenetration of extremely varied types of sentiments towards the planters: these ambivalent responses from the subordinate sections reflected respect and affection for, as well as resentment of, and rebellion against, the planters.[25]

The nature of the terms and conditions as also the high costs of indigo production made its cultivation very unpopular amongst the peasants.[26] They were forced to grow indigo on the best parts of their land and at a low price. Besides, they had many other grievances, such as high rents, various kinds of threats and tyranny, and they were forced to do what is called *begari*, the obligation to work for some days for which they were not paid. They were paid meagre wages or often no wages at all for their labour, on top of forcible realization of heavy fines. They had to pay a number of *abwabs*. The planters commanded free use of their carts and ploughs. The *amlas*, appointed by the planters for managerial assistance, also oppressed the peasants. Those peasants who refused to cultivate indigo on their land, had to pay fines, contribute some free labour at the factories, pay *abwabs*, were sometimes framed in false cases, dispossessed of their land, boycotted by the service-castes, and their cattle prevented from grazing on the common land. All this created bitter resentment among the peasants, and they became increasingly reluctant to cultivate indigo. As free-market relations, in these circumstances, did not ensure the cultivation of indigo, the planters resorted to extra-economic coercion: as lessees of proprietary rights, the planters were in a position to force the peasants to cultivate indigo.

A de facto alliance emerged between the government, the administration, the indigo planters and the big Indian landlords in the northern districts of Bihar.[27] The indigo planters also founded the Bihar Planters' Association to protect their interests.[28] Officials regarded the planters as a useful protector of British rule. In fact, the planters assisted in the process of colonization in the initial stages at the grass roots level. They came to be regarded as an important symbol of British power.[29]

Tradition of Protest Preceding the Non-Cooperation Movement

Till the late nineteenth century, peasant protests against the planters were intermittent.[30] It was only during the 1905–8 period that widespread resistance was seen in the Motihari-Bettiah region, affecting an area of 400 square miles. After this, a section of the peasantry continued the struggle over the next decade through petitions, court cases and making contacts with the Congress leaders and journalists. Local lawyers, journalists and teachers highlighted the peasants' grievances through the medium of newspapers. They described their deplorable conditions in the Bihar Provincial Conference, and pressed for an official enquiry by the Bihar and Orissa Legislative Council. The peasants themselves made several petitions for relief to the District Magistrate of Champaran and the Divisional Commissioner of Tirhut. But all these efforts were in vain. Finally, in response to a resolution passed at the Lucknow Session of the Indian National Congress in 1916, Gandhi undertook a tour of Bihar to investigate personally the causes of agrarian unrest in north Bihar. His visit proved to be very significant as it took the form of an agitation against the planters.

Gandhi's arrival in Champaran raised the hopes of many and sparked off a string of rumours. These rumours reflected expected solutions to the continuing peasant-planter conflicts. In fact, in peasant politics rumours play very significant role. Many studies have shown how rumour is a language of collective dreams and aspirations to construct a political collectivity which would be more confident and directly confrontational in nature. When circumstances are alien, discriminating and repressive, rumour is a very effective weapon in the hands of the weak to air their political desires. As a social text without an individual author, rumour functioned as a script of 'public opinion'.[31] One of the rumours was that Gandhi had been especially appointed by the Viceroy in supersession of local officials to redress peasants' grievances. Gandhi was seen as the 'naya malik' and 'ishwar ka avtar', sent to free Bharat Mata from the whites.[32] In the context of long-standing grievances against the planters, Gandhi's presence aroused visions of an early millennium. A peasant compared Gandhi to Ramchandra and declared before the Enquiry Committee that 'the tenant would not fear the Rakshasa-planters now that Gandhi was there'.[33] The peasantry believed that Gandhi was a 'bhagwan' who challenged the administration as well as the planters and enlisted the support of the 'barka vakil log', who till then had listened to their grievances only in return for high fees.[34] Before Gandhi's visit, the peasants were so demoralized that they did not approach the Magistrate for their grievances or give evidence against the indigo planters. But the presence of Gandhi in Champaran heartened the peasants and made them fearless. Around 25,000 peasants gave evidence against the planters. There was hardly any planter whose peasants did not appear before the Enquiry Commission to give evidence.[35]

A wave of defiance swept the entire district, and peasants believed that they had the sanction of Gandhi.[36] They asserted that Gandhi had ordered them not to cultivate indigo. In many places, they stopped paying rent. Cattle were allowed to graze on indigo lands. Trees were cut and sold in defiance of the proprietary rights of planters. The haat settlements of the planters were challenged. The peasants even took possession of the wastelands, asserting that Gandhi had ordered free grazing. These wastelands had been enclosed and appropriated by the planters for cultivation. Indigo factories were attacked and there were cases of 'incendiarism'. All these actions were done in Gandhi's name. It is improbable that the peasants would have known the order of Gandhi as in many situations the peasants did not know who Gandhi was, as indicated by intelligence reports. They must have often supposed what his orders were. Gandhi's name was used by the peasants, without any specific instructions from Gandhi, to deliver justice from the landlords. Supremacy of Gandhi throws light on the nature of the peasant movement.

Gyan Pandey's study on peasant movement in Awadh has highlighted how the peasants, who were scattered and isolated by the conditions of their existence, found it difficult to mobilize themselves for political action. A need was felt for an outside leader—a peasant king or a modern substitute to deliver the people from their thrall. In fact a just and usually distant ruler had often been known to provide the necessary inspiration for peasant revolt. The belief in an 'outside leader' can be seen as the obverse of a belief in the breakdown of the locally recognized structure of authority; and rumour serves the function of spreading such a notion as efficiently as the leader from the town. The significance of the myth of the Great Man is that 'someone' had challenged the powers that be, 'someone' had come to deliver. As indicated in the intelligence report that the reverence shown to Gandhi was partly due to the belief that he had influence with the government had some truth. For the peasants, Gandhi was not a distant, western-educated lawyer-politician; he was a mahatma, a pandit, a brahmin, even a merchant from nearby.[37]

The anti-planter protest in Champaran in 1917–19 marked the high point of a series of protests, which occurred intermittently during the preceding decades. The Champaran agitation pressurized the British administration to intervene and enact the Champaran Agrarian Act. This Act outlawed the tinkathia system, lowered the rents which were raised in lieu of indigo cultivation, and enforced that the peasants be returned the money taken as a fee for their release from the obligation to grow indigo. Though this legislation was not a lasting solution, it placated the peasants somewhat by giving them concessions.[38]

However, the dissidence continued because many planters reacted to the legislation by seeking new means to extract income from their peasants. In doing so, they took advantage of their status as long-term lessees of proprietary rights, which endowed them with a wide range of rights and privileges, some of which they had not previously exercised. One of these relatively neglected rights was their proprietary control over much of the wasteland, which the peasants used for grazing. The planters also began to take advantage of their rights as landlords to appropriate timber, hides and extra rent payment for land on which houses were built. Some of the peasants had entitlements, but to prove this, they had to engage in expensive and prolonged litigation. In addition, the planters could extract extra income by imposing *abwabs*.[39] Throughout 1918 and 1919, many peasants of Champaran expressed their dissatisfaction with the Act. They delayed the payment of rents and refused to cooperate with the officials, who were in the process of finalizing the survey and settlement operations in the district. They used Gandhi's name to rally support.[40] In March 1919, three activists, who had returned from the Congress session in Delhi, informed the peasants of Gobindganj thana that Gandhi had given instructions that rent was not to be paid. They added that Gandhi had promised to visit the area in the near future.[41] In the ensuing months, resentment against the planters continued to simmer in Champaran, as well as in other parts of north Bihar, where the new legislation did not apply.

Anti-Planter Protest during the Non-Cooperation Movement

During the Non-Cooperation Movement, the agitation against the planters intensified. The widespread spirit of defiance aroused hostility against the planters, giving a fillip to the peasants' protest. In north Bihar, the planters were largely concentrated in the districts of Muzaffarpur, Champaran and Purnea. The local non-cooperators in these districts played a leading role in the protest and addressed peasants' problems vis-à-vis planters. There was a convergence between local pressures and the national movement. In response to the local situation and needs, the protest assumed varied forms: petitions, organizing demonstrations, boycotting factories, refusing to pay rent, boycotting planters' haats and establishing alternative haats. The protests often turned violent and peasants resorted to 'arson'. The next section delineates the nature of anti-planter protest in different districts of north Bihar.

Muzaffarpur

Many factories in Muzaffarpur district faced problems as employees and contract labourers went on strike in January 1921. They pressed for higher wages and even threatened to quit if their demands were not met.[42] The factory manager of Belwa had to deal with labour boycott.[43] The planter of Motipur factory also faced tension.[44] This factory was located in Bariarpur, where the Non-Cooperation Movement had made much impact under the leadership of Raghunath Gir (a mahant), Jhapo Rai and Kishun Rai. A non-cooperation sabha was formed with Raghunath Gir as the president and Jhapo Rai as the secretary. Many villagers enlisted themselves as volunteers. Most of the villagers' sympathy had turned in favour of the movement. 'Lecturers' and 'preachers' were invited to speak on non-cooperation. The local leaders, in their campaign, primarily addressed peasants' grievances against the planters. They projected swaraj as a goal which would mark the end of all hardships faced by the villagers. Raghunath Gir promised the villagers that once they attained swaraj, he would become the headman of Bariarpur and as headman he would divide the factory land amongst them. Under swaraj, he added, they would have to pay annually only two paisa per bigha to the government. The non-cooperators dissuaded the tenants from paying rent and supplying labour or carts for factory work. Factory employees and labourers were exhorted to leave the factory and were threatened with social boycott if they refused to comply. For example, when the two factory tokedars, Ramdhari Rai and

Bahari Rai, refused to leave the service, they faced social boycott. Even washermen and barbers refused to attend to them. To persuade these tokedars to join the movement, Raghunath Gir even joined the factory. Gradually, most of the employees of the factory came under the influence of the movement. The whole taluka combined forces against the factory. No carts, coolies, labourers or ploughs were available for the factory work. The tenants stopped paying rents and the arrears amounted to Rs.1,200. A large number of factory workers, most of whom came from the lower castes, resigned and joined the movement. Two new peons, Ram Charan Pande and Rajdeo Rai, were appointed and their appointment sparked off violence in August 1921. These new peons were sent to Bariarpur taluka to collect rent arrears from the tenants, but when they reached Paharchak, where Raghunath Gir had his *math,* they were forcibly detained there in the *math.* A large crowd assembled and the peons were abused and beaten to death for joining the factory.

The Belsand factory in Muzaffarpur also faced opposition from its tenants.[45] The factory had more than a 1,000 bighas of land under the tinkathia system in Muzaffarpur district. The tenants of this factory were not happy with the terms and conditions for growing indigo. Besides, they were paid extremely low rates for the use of their carts and labour. Criminal cases were often instituted against them when they lodged a complaint. They submitted a petition to the governor in August 1921 highlighting their problems but it went unheeded.[46]

There was also tension at Karnoul indigo factory which erupted into violence when a group of tenants, including local leaders of the Non-Cooperation Movement, gathered at the factory and threatened to assault the factory *amlas.*[47]

In January 1922, when the Non-Cooperation Movement was at its peak, the anti-planter campaign intensified. Volunteers in large numbers organized demonstrations against the factories and shouted slogans.[48] On 4 January 1922, a large crowd surrounded the Belsand factory shouting *Gandhiji ki jai.*[49] In January, nearly 1,000 men surrounded the Mia Chapra factory in Patepur thana in Muzaffarpur shouting *Gandhiji ki jai.* The owner of the factory took refuge with his family inside the bungalow. The crowd destroyed a considerable stock of the factory's sugar crop before dispersing. 'The ring leaders' of the crowd were prosecuted under Sections 143 and 379 of the IPC. In retaliation against this prosecution, the villagers picketed the factory, boycotted the factory manager and forbade his servants to work for him.[50] The Shahpur Maricha factory in Muzaffarpur also faced boycott in January 1922. This factory was owned by Shyamnandan Sahay and managed by Captain Harvey. The villagers had stopped paying chaukidari taxes. Shyamnandan Sahay, who was also the president of the chaukidari union, issued warrants against them.

In retaliation, the villagers boycotted the factory. They tried to pressurize the factory *amlas* to stop working in the factory and even attempted to stop the postmen from making deliveries to the factory.[51]

The intensification of the Non-Cooperation Movement in Muzaffarpur increased the militancy of the peasants. *Gandhi ki jai* became an important rallying cry for the peasants emboldening them to retaliate against the planters. However, the movement often overstepped Gandhian parameters and took a violent form.

Champaran

The Non-Cooperation Movement had a strong impact in Champaran, especially in the villages of Madhubani and Bagaha where most of the factories were located.[52] As in Muzaffarpur, the movement in this district, too, gave a fillip to the peasants' struggle against the planters. The local leaders of the non-cooperation campaign primarily addressed peasants' grievances against the planters. Swaraj raised the people's hopes that their grievances would be redressed and inspired them to struggle against the planters.[53]

Resistance against the planters intensified in many areas in January 1921. The labourers of the Sirha factory went on strike and returned to work only when they were given higher wages.[54] In the Patahi factory, the non-cooperation sabha members approached the *amlas* and urged them to resign from their service to the factory. In Padumkair, both the personal and factory employees of the planter demanded higher wages. The non-cooperators urged the tokedar of Byre factory to resign from service. Holthum of the Loheria factory informed the government that his factory employees had been threatened. Those who refused to resign were threatened with social boycott.

In the Piprasi factory in Madhubani there was tension between the peasants and planters over the cattle grazing rights.[55] The local leaders in Madhubani, particularly Baiju Gir, campaigned against the planters. Violence broke out in June 1921, when a factory peon discovered a herd of nearly 100 cattle of a tenant grazing on an uncultivated tract, which the factory owner claimed as his. Assisted by two *amlas* of the factory, the peon tried to steer the cattle to the pound. They had succeeded in steering half the animals into the pound, when around 100 villagers led by Baiju Gir attacked them. The villagers beat the peon with lathis till he was unconscious. The other two fled and the villagers released their cattle. They also set fire to the quarters of the *amlas*. The police, without specifically naming any of the Congress leaders, linked the incident to the Non-Cooperation Movement which, it stated, had unleashed forces leading to the protest. According to a police official, 'Baiju Gir, who was the leader of this village, was not likely to have countenanced anything more than the rescue of the cattle but would have been quite unable to control the crowd once they began to do so.' The militant mood of the peasants may be seen in the context of their translating the Non-Cooperation Movement into defiance against their exploiters.

There was tension in Dhanaha, another strong belt of Non-Cooperation Movement, in June 1921.[56] The tenants of Mackinnon, a planter in Dhanaha, refused to supply him carts and labour.[57] The planter asked for police help to threaten the tenants. A force of mounted troopers, accompanied by Mackinnon and two of his *amlas*, marched through the villages of Dhanaha. Some of the policemen, encouraged by the *amlas*, looted goods and money from the villagers' houses. A large crowd of villagers immediately surrounded them and threw clods of earth at them. They jostled the factory *amlas* and did not disperse until the police returned their looted goods.[58]

The Chauterwa factory in the north-west of Champaran also faced problems.[59] On the morning of 1 November 1921, a crowd of around 150 to 200 people from Patilar and Lagunaha villages gathered a few hundred yards away from the factory shouting *Gandhi ki jai*, marched past the main buildings of the factory and surrounded the houses of the *amlas*. On seeing the hostile attitude of the crowd, the *amlas* hid inside their houses. The crowds broke the windows and doors and asked the *amlas* to step outside. When the *amlas* refused to come out, the crowd set fire to their houses forcing them to leave their houses, whereupon they were attacked. An old servant of the factory, Jamuna Lal, was severely beaten up. The crowd attacked the head *amlas*' house, then it directed its fury against the sugar factory, grain godowns, the cutchery, small bungalows and the big bungalow. The Head *Amla* Kali Singh, was the first to be attacked because he refused to come out of his house. Encouraged by the ease with which it entered the factory, the crowd set fire to around eight to ten houses and sheds, leaving only a few small sheds and the cookhouse of the bungalow. Property worth more than Rs.1,00,000 was damaged. The local head panch, accompanied by some villagers and three chaukidars, tried unsuccessfully to control the crowd which had increased to 5,000. Poor peasants, largely of lower castes, played a significant role in the 'riot'.[60]

Such protest, as the study of Ranajit Guha has highlighted, had the characteristic of *atidesa* function, i.e. to the manner in which rebel violence tended to spread analogically developing its initial attack on any particular element among the peasant's enemies into a general attack on all or most of them. It was a process by which insurgency came to permeate an entire domain constituted by such authorities, institutions and groups as were antagonistic to the subaltern population. Thus whatever might have been the immediate cause of any particular outbreak, the rebels, almost invariably, enlarged the scope of their operations, hitting out against all classes and sections of the population hostile to the peasantry. Even though the attack had expanded there was discrimination in attack, the violence selectively directed by the peasants at particular targets.[61]

Attack on the bungalow was a very marked feature of this assault. The attack on bungalow could also be seen as contest over status symbol. The authority that elite had over the peasantry was symbolized by many objects and the subaltern by destroying the symbol of his enemy's power hoped to abolish the marks of his own subordination. Studies have highlighted that the power of the rural elite in all pre-industrial societies is prominently exhibited by the size and style of their residence and when the antagonisms get sharpened in the countryside, this provokes a lot of hostility amongst the peasants. Difference in types and styles of resident houses indicates the difference in status, marks the distinctions between the rulers and the ruled as well as of those between the indigenous castes and classes themselves. Bungalows, the traditional house-type, as a space was adopted by the colonial governing elite to demarcate itself politically and culturally. Bungalows emerged as a symbol of the authority of the whites and the Raj. Hence, in all hostile demonstrations against the government or its European associates, such as planters and railway officials, it featured almost inevitably as a target of popular anger. Hence it is in this context that the attack on planters' houses becomes meaningful.[62]

The protest against Chauterwa factory was a direct outcome of the long simmering grievances of the peasants against the planters.[63] The Non-Cooperation agitation precipitated the situation. For some time, there had been tension between the planters and the tenants over the issue of cattle grazing. The tenants persistently grazed their cattle on land which the planters claimed were their reserve. The tenants beat a factory guard, who had tried to impound cattle grazing on the land, which the factory claimed was their reserve. A case was instituted against these tenants. Tenants of this factory also had resentment against the *amlas*, particularly the Head *Amla* Kali Singh, who was very oppressive. There was also strong resentment against the appointment of some Magahiya Doms as chaukidars. The Magahiya Doms were appointed to deal with the growing tension and to keep the cattle off the lands that belonged to the factory. The Non-Cooperation Movement also gave fillip to the unrest. In the large number of non-cooperation meetings held in the villages, the local leaders primarily addressed the peasants' grievances against the planters. In these meetings, it was decided that the villagers should retaliate against the appointment of Magahiya Doms as chaukidars. The peasants even tried to pressurize the labourers and the factory servants to boycott the factory.

The burning of the Chauterwa factory created considerable tension in the surrounding areas. Rumours spread of impending attacks on other indigo factories. There were minor cases of arson in a couple of other factories.[64] Cases were reported of secret incendiaries against the factories at Narainpore, in the Bagaha elaka, and Sirkiah (Lauria thana), where a straw shed was set on fire. Illegal grazing of the factory Rakhawats on an extensive scale was becoming a general practice. Tirhut Commissioner sent a telegram to the Chief Secretary on 28 November underscoring the fear which gripped local officials after the Chauterwa incident. The telegram stated how the state of feeling in the district was very tense and that defiance of authority, contempt of government and its servants, and attack on property were on the increase. He further stated how haats were still a source of anxiety and that the District Magistrate had applied for the quartering of the additional police at Gorasahan haats, owing to the continuance of dispute over haats tax.[65]

The planters considered these activities as open defiance of law and order and were surprised that the government had not taken any action. A deputation of planters met the Tirhut Commissioner expressing their apprehension. They asked whether the government would keep silent until some more factories were burnt and wiped out.[66] Fifty Mounted Police were posted at Bagaha and they patrolled the villages of Patilar and Madhubani. The District Magistrate issued an order that a sum of Rs. 3 lakh was to be realized from the villagers as compensation for burning and providing security for 18 months. It added that those who had contributed the most to the Tilak Swaraj Fund and the Khilafat Fund would have to pay a sum proportionate to it to the planter.[67] However, the police, who came to conduct an investigation against the 'rioters', did not get any cooperation from the local people.[68]

The Chauterwa incident is an example of the popular translation of nationalism. The movement did not remain confined to the parameters of strict non-violence as laid down by the Congress. The district Congress leaders of Bettiah strongly disapproved of violent action. In fact, immediately after the Chauterwa incident, the Congress leaders rushed to the factory and warned the villagers against such 'indiscreet and hasty acts'.[69] They reiterated that the success of the movement would depend on following the path of total non-violence.[70] Deep Narayan Singh, who presided over the District Congress Committee meeting held at Bettiah on 12 November, highlighted the need for adhering to non-violence.[71]

Many haats in Kesaria, Gobindganj, Seguli and Ghorasan owned or leased by the European planters were boycotted in October 1921 and alternative haats were established in the vicinity.[72] This action was a direct challenge to the planters. The regular haats, which were held on the lands owned by the planters, were a consistent source of income of the planters. The planters levied a fee on those merchants and vendors who offered goods for sale at these haats. The setting up of rival haats had an adverse impact on the income of the planters.[73] In the new haats, the merchants had to pay lower or no fee at all. Merchants, who did not abide for selling his goods at the rival haats, were socially pressurized.[74] The boycott of the haats was the result of local initiative, where the local non-cooperators were very active. The district Congress leaders were not involved in it and wanted to disassociate themselves from such activities. They disclaimed any role in the boycott and establishment of rival haats. Debi Lal Sao and other leaders of the non-cooperation even visited Gobindpur to dissuade the people from establishing haats on the new site but failed in their efforts.[75]

Purnea

In Purnea district, too, the peasants had been struggling against the planters,[76] especially against the Shillingford brothers, who owned the indigo factory. As in other districts, the tenants of this factory were also dissatisfied with the terms and conditions under which they had to cultivate indigo. The tenants were forced to pay different kinds of *abwabs*: fees for permission to dig wells on their lands, tax on the sale of grain, fees at the time of marriage, etc.

During the Non-Cooperation Movement, a strong campaign built up against the Shillingfords in April and May 1921. There was a total boycott of the factory. The peasants stopped cultivation of indigo and refused to pay rent and as a result work in the factory came to a halt. For a short time, even the personal servants of the Shillingford brothers refused to work for them.[77] The District Officer of Purnea argued that it was not so much the anti-European propaganda as the exploitation of the planters that led to the tenants' protest.

The Bhagalpur Commissioner said that there was a certain amount of anti-European propaganda connected with the movement but it was neither very pronounced nor did it find open expression against factory except in the case of the Shillingfords and Thomas of Kolassi factory. He said that the reason for animosity against these factories was that the factory landlords treated their tenants very harshly. Their peasants were subjected to large numbers and varieties of illegal exactions, *abwabs* and disabilities and oppressions. He said that other indigo planters like Crow and Forbes and the biggest European zamindar of the district and also Pyne, a small zamindar in Araria, had no trouble with their tenants.[78]

Hence the main thrust of the official argument was that the movement was primarily directed against the landlords and that the latter were largely responsible for bringing it upon themselves. The notion that peasants were hostile against only the zamindars, takes the teeth away from the anti-imperialist wave. It also reveals a notion of a peasantry incapable of acting on their own and when they are impelled to rise, and they do, that is only because of economic motivation. Hence its action were perceived as non-political or at best 'pre-political'. It also absolves the colonial government of playing a role in precipitating any conflict. However, such protests cannot be merely looked upon as a rebellion of mere desperation. Economic factors were important but one cannot explain the agitation as a mere reaction to economic hardships. In fact there was nothing in the militant movements of the rural masses that was not political. The collusion between sarkar and zamindar was indeed a part of the common experience of the poor and the subaltern at the local level nearly everywhere. The hitherto discrete powers of the landlord and the official came to form, under colonial rule, a composite apparatus of dominance over the peasant. Peasants subjection to this was primarily political in character, economic exploitation being only one, albeit the most obvious, of its several instances.

For the appropriation of peasant's surplus was brought about by the authority wielded over local societies and markets by the landlord-moneylenders and a secondary capitalism working closely with them and by that encapsulation of that authority in the power of the colonial state. Indeed, the element of coercion was so explicit and so ubiquitous in all their dealings with the peasant that he could hardly look upon his relationship with them as anything but political. By the same token too in undertaking to destroy this relationship he engaged himself in what was essentially a political task, a task in which the existing power nexus had to be turned on its head as a necessary condition for the redress of any particular grievance.[79] Besides, one cannot overlook the influence of the Non-Cooperation Movement in intensifying the anti-planter protest. The mood of defiance that the Non-Cooperation Movement aroused made the tenants more rebellious. Swaraj raised people's expectations. Gandhi's word was considered supreme and his orders must be followed. Gandhi raj implied that the peasants would be free from all kinds of exploitation by the planters.[80]

In May 1921, around 500 tenants met the District Magistrate to apprise him of their grievances. The District Magistrate heard the grievances of both the tenants and the factory owners, and tried to negotiate a compromise between them. The Shillingford brothers had to accept many of the demands of the tenants. There was a reduction in pasture fee, homestead rent, interest on arrears of rent and in *nazrana* paid for securing permission to dig wells. Certain taxes like marriage tax and tax on sale of grain and cattle were remitted. Tenants were free to build houses on their land. They were also free to plant trees and bamboo clumps, gather honey, grow lac, etc., on their land. Indigo no longer had to be compulsorily grown. Rents were not to be increased any further. Once the settlement took place, the tenants paid their arrears and ended the boycott of the factory.[81]

Erosion of Planters' Hegemony

It is clear that during the Non-Cooperation Movement, the planters faced a series of attacks in north Bihar. Not only their employees and labourers went on strike demanding higher wages, their tenants also refused to pay rent and, in many places, they stopped providing carts, coolies and ploughs to the planters. Their haats were also boycotted. The protest against the planters broadened its base, involving a wide cross-section of peasants. An increasing solidarity of the poorer sections of villagers was visible in many protests. In view of this solidarity, even the servants of factories, armed with lathis, did not dare to confront them.

In most cases, the local leaders of the Non-Cooperation Movement were in the forefront of the agitation. The Chauterwa incident brings to light how the movement took shape at the local level and did not remain confined to the parameters laid down by the Congress. The aspirations and desires of the masses were linked with the Non-Cooperation Movement. The movement derived its organizational strength from the peasant sabhas and seva samitis. Those who did not join the movement were socially boycotted. Since the protest mainly derived its strength from sabhas and seva samitis, and social boycott, it became very difficult for the planters to take any action against the peasants.

The movement eroded the hegemony of the planters. In fact, after these protests, the planters never regained their former position. Their initial confidence was shaken as they became vulnerable to attack. In the past, they had felt secure because of the 'prestige of the Saheb, their wielding of considerable local power and local beliefs that their interests were the special care of government and local officials and the goodwill of their Indian neighbours'.[82] In the light of the changing circumstances, the planters became aware of the dangers 'to which a small and scattered European population was exposed, isolated as they were amidst a vast Indian population, amongst whom the doctrine of race hatred was being constantly inculcated'.[83] A delegation of the Champaran branch of the Bihar Planters' Association and the Muzaffarpur branch of the European Association met the Governor on 22 January 1921 and drew his attention to the threat posed by the movement.[84] The delegation expressed concern about the impunity with which an agitation directed against the very basis of the government had been allowed to continue and the widespread unrest and tensions caused by the apparent inaction of the government in the face of open advocacy of sedition. They also expressed their disappointment with the government for having failed to take stern action against the movement. They demanded that the government take strict measures to suppress lawlessness and intimidation, so as to bring it home to the local leaders and the people that their activities had not gone unnoticed, and that the government had not abdicated its duty but was prepared to enforce its will.[85]

The planters became increasingly aware that they no longer enjoyed the government support that they had once taken for granted. An exchange between the planters and the Governor revealed to some extent the denial of special support by the government. When the delegation of planters met the Governor to express their anxieties, he told them that they were not the only special target and that the movement was not solely directed against the Europeans but against the entire propertied classes, including Indian zamindars. When the Tirhut Commissioner pointed out that the movement in his division was particularly directed against the European community, the Governor informed him that this was probably so because of the fact that the grievances against the planters in Champaran had not been completely resolved. The Governor reiterated that the movement was not confined to any one division or province but had spread all over the country.[86] Thus, the kind of support and assurance, which the planters had expected, was not forthcoming from the government. Even before the Non-Cooperation Movement was launched, there was a distinct shift in official attitude towards the planters. During the initial phase of colonization, planters were perceived as a significant support to British rule. However, by the mid-nineteenth century, planters were no more proving to be crucial for imperial power.

By 1860, the rapacious phase of British rule in India came to an end as most of the important strategic annexations had been made. Colonialism had by then found its social base in an Indian neo-feudal class.[87] For the consolidation of Britain's power base in India, it was essential that the government should acquire the image of a well-run concern based on legality, order and responsibility. In this process, the indigo planters were no longer of any help. On the contrary, they were discomfiture for the imperial power. The planters often flouted laws whenever it suited them and openly subverted its processes. The private armies of the planters weakened the standing of the official law and order at the local level. Their resorting to different kinds of oppressions and torture had made the Indians question the superiority of the white man's civilization and morality. For the long-term interests of the imperial power, it had become necessary to discipline the planters.[88] Local officials acknowledged that the grievances of the tenants were genuine and that the planters were exploitative. The District Magistrate of Purnea admitted that it was the exploitation of the planters which had compelled the tenants to agitate against them. He even tried to intervene between the planters and tenants and forced the planters to grant certain concessions to the tenants.[89]

The Movement in the Tribal Belt

The impact of the Non-Cooperation Movement was felt in Ranchi amongst the Tana Bhagats, in Kolhan amongst the Hos, in Santhal Paragana amongst the Santhals and in Palamau amongst the Kherwars and Cheros. Beginning with the impact of colonial rule in the tribal belt, the discussion focuses on the spread of the Non-Cooperation Movement in different areas and the relationship between the tribals and the national movement. The Non-Cooperation Movement precipitated to a climax some of the issues over which the tribals had been agitating for long. This study of the national movement in the tribal belt also provides an insight into the popular perception of nationalism.[90]

There had been a strong tradition of agrarian protest in these areas. However, to understand the various aspects and forces of tribal protest against landed elements, one needs to look into the structure of landed power and the internal structure and dynamics of tribal society. In fact, the oppressive landlord structure, which the tribals were confronting, was further refurbished under colonialism. Colonialism, with its capital and market, generated new socio-economic forces in tribal society and economy. It not only transformed the agrarian relations but also reinforced the existing hierarchies in tribal society. The tribal grievances needs to be located within the changing context of tribal world.

The major grievances of the tribals centred around rent and *begari*. A large part of produce, in the different existing forms, were appropriated as rent. Besides rent, the raiyats also had to offer praedial service, which entailed rakumats and begaris. Rakumats required various payments in kind and miscellaneous cesses or *abwabs. Abwabs* were offered to landlords for different purposes and on various occasions. In *begari* the raiyats had to provide a number of day's labour to the landlords for the cultivation of their private estate or for their personal service. However, *begari* was very inequitable, with some privileged castes being exempted from it and for certain castes it was lighter as compared to the tribes. The landlords also resorted to various mechanisms to enhance rent and *abwabs. Salami*, which was sanctioned by custom, was also imposed on raiyats. This was a payment made by the raiyats to the landlords for the settlement of zamindar's bakasht land. Zamindar's previous permission was required by the raiyats to reclaim jungles and wastelands. This was paid as *salami*. Often outsiders, by paying more *salami*, got control over the land for their cultivation. This was in disregard of the custom, i.e. the original residents having the first right over the settlement of these lands.

Another area of contestation was the right over forests. Forest plays a very significant role in tribal's life. The multiplication of tenures, the increasing population and opening of roads and railways under colonialism led to gradual decrease of forests. The landlords also stressed their rights as proprietors over the forests. The tribals were imposed fees for the exercise of their customary rights over the forests. The colonial state also brought a large area of non-culturable forest under its control, as reserved forest. The tribals forfeited all their customary rights over these reserved forests. The zamindars, disregarding the recorded rights of tenants, often sold the forest or else gave unlimited forest cutting leases to timber merchant.

These grievances led to a series of protests in tribal belt. The tribals considered themselves as the original owner of the land and held 'outsiders'/ non-tribals responsible for the appropriation of their land. The 'outsiders' could be zamindars, moneylenders, merchants, Hindus, Babhans and Muslims. The tribals resented the imposition of rents, *begari* or *abwabs* by the 'outsiders'.

The colonial state absolving itself of exploitation held landlords responsible for the tribals' oppression. In the eyes of colonial state, the tribals and zamindars were 'natural' enemies and the conflict between them was seen as irreconcilable. British initiated certain legislative enactments to redress agrarian grievances. In 1869 Bhuinhari Act II was passed. The Act proposed to settle land disputes and agitations. It promised to protect the tribals from the oppression of landlords and also ensure the rights of zamindars. However, the Act did not address the grievances of cultivating tenancies. Besides, the commutation of praedial services and *begari* into money payments was also not taken up. Between 1902 and 1910, there was a survey and settlement operations in Ranchi, which tried to settle the record of rights so as to settle the grievances of praedial dues and services. In 1908 Chotanagpur Tenancy Act was passed. It granted occupancy rights to the tenants and protected them from arbitrary rent enhancements and ejectments at will by zamindars. It approved individual property rights on land, thus widening land market base. This resulted in land price rise, which further resulted in greater land transactions. Besides, once enhancement of rent was made illegal by the Act, the landlords resorted to other methods of extraction. One was to increase *salami*. As land emerged as a gainful investment, moneylenders (sahus) and village merchants (Banias) entered the land and credit market. Moneylenders and zamindars were not exclusive category. Many zamindars also engaged in moneylending activities. One can see a kind of nexus emerging between the sarkar (colonial power), the zamindars and the moneylenders.

However, the conflict cannot merely be seen as between the sarkar-zamindar-moneylenders and the tribals. Recent studies on tribals' protest have been trying to problematize the contradictions. Earlier writings on tribals glossed over the hierarchy and differentiation within tribal community, underlining the tribe as a homogeneous category. Tribals, being a monolithic category, are absolved of being exploitative and the conflict is attributed to as between 'insiders' and 'outsiders', i.e. between tribals and non-tribals.[91]

Some studies on tribals in Bihar attribute economic factors to the protest, some characterize it as class struggle and some highlight 'peasant consciousness' as marking the tribal protest.[92] Sangeeta Dasgupta's study of Tana Bhagat's protest highlights its complexity. Although Dasgupta's study recognizes the importance of tracing tribal opposition to the zamindars, banias and the British state, it also suggests that conflict need to be located within the internal hierarchy of the Oraon community. The study emphasizes how the world of sacred and secular remains linked in tribal society. Bhuinhars, the dominant section of the Oraon, derived its power from both. They belonged not only to privileged tenure section but were also the holder of traditional positions of the *pahan*, the *pujar* and the *mahto*. The *pahan* was responsible for making sacrifices to the *bhuts, nads* and *deotas* on behalf of the Oraons. The *pujar* helped the *pahan* in the exercise of his official duties. The *mahto*, being the village representative, dealt with the landlord, the government authorities and other non-Oraon elements.

The British looked upon the *pahan*, *pujar* and *mahto* as the natural leaders of the tribals, hearing their voice and authenticating them as informants of custom and tradition. The British's administrative and agrarian intervention by making the bhuinhars (dominant stratum) leaders of administration reinforced the existing hierarchy in the Oraon tribal society. *Mankis* (headman of a group of Oraon villages) and *mundas*, coming from bhuinhars, were restored in their particular villages. They also had to pay reduced rents. The agrarian Act had benefited the bhuinhars. The landlords were prevented from encroaching on their lands. The property of bhuinhars, who were dispossessed of their lands within a period of 20 years before the Act II of 1869 was passed, would be restored. Thus the Act by privileging the position of the bhuinhars in Oraon society, bestowed social, economic and political power to them. But a large number of tribals remained untouched by the reforms. The Tanas, who belonged to 'non-occupancy' and 'under-raiyats' category, were the disprivileged section, and under the social and economic control of the bhuinhars. The Act further underlined the division between the bhuinhars and the raiyats, reinforcing the hierarchy and intensifying their conflicts. Hence, the conflict between the privileged and the disprivileged sections of the Oraon community sharpened during colonialism. Thus the Tana Bhagat Movement marked not only the Oraon protest against the non-Oraons but was also a manifestation of the conflicts of the emerging hierarchies within Oraon society.[93]

Movement in the Tana Bhagat Belt

THE TANA BHAGAT MOVEMENT

The Tana Bhagat Movement began among the Oraons in the Gumla sub-division of Ranchi district in April 1914. Its leader Jatra Bhagat claimed to have received a divine message choosing him to lead a movement for religious revitalization and cultural and moral regeneration of the Oraons. The Tana Bhagats believed that the Oraons could be a match for their adversaries only through such a revitalization.[94] It established a new sect, the Tana sect, which was markedly different from the Oraon community. Tana faith was marked by some important features. Ghosts, spirits, *dains* (witches), *matis* and *ojhas* were to be purged. *Matis* and *ojhas* dealt with the spirit world. *Pahans*, *pujars* and *mahtos* played central role in the festivals, rituals and propitiation of spirits through sacrifices. Austerity and sobriety were emphasized. Socio-religious festivities were prohibited. Household utensils, agricultural tools and ornaments were to be thrown into the river for purification. Even relations between men and women outside marriage were discouraged. Violence, sacrifices and non-vegetarianism were despised. The Tanas had to give up eating fowl and pig, and drinking liquor. They were asked not to use red coloured articles as red was identified with British. German Baba emerged as an important symbol of the Tana protest. But there was no consistency in their observations of Baba. For some Baba was one of their deities, for some an external agent who would confront the forces which had set in their miseries, and for others Baba was a mighty power which would help the Oraons to come to power by defeating the British. Thus, German Baba was represented as an influential saviour who would usher in a new age for the Oraon.[95]

The movement challenged the traditional authority in the Oraon community. Opposition to the Oraon popular practices and spirit entailed rejection of the traditional authority of the *pahans*, *pujar* and *mahtos*, who belonged to the bhuinhari in the Oraon community. Tanas also defied the power of the panch, formed by the bhuinhars. There differences were to be settled by the *mandali* and later by the panchayat. Anybody who did not support these bodies were excommunicated. Dharmesh or Bhagwan emerged as the supreme of the community, and it was he who would ensure the prosperity and welfare of the community. The Tana Bhagat Movement was said to be authorized by Dharmesh (supreme god). Thus the movement was broadly a manifestation of the challenge of their subordination to dominant local groups. The leaders of Tana Bhagats came from the marginal section of the Oraon society. Jatra was a Mati, Sibu a Dhangar. The dominant sections of the Oraons not only distanced themselves from the movement but were opposed to it.[96]

The Tanas believed that the land belonged to them. They challenged the authority of zamindars, illaquadars and banias. They resisted payment of rent to landlords and *begaris*. They attributed their subjugation and impoverishment to the transformation of agrarian economy from shifting cultivation to plough agriculture, and dreamt of returning to the 'golden past' of shifting agriculture and forest dwelling. The Tana Bhagat Movement's relation with colonial state varied from invoking colonial power for redressal of their grievances to antagonism. The Tanas invoked the colonial state as the custodian of law and order, considering the state's judgement to be fair. Appeals were made to the state through pamphlets, petitions and memorials. Often the Tanas' protest against the landlords was articulated in the name of colonial Raj. They believed that zamindari raj had come to an end and the colonial state would hand over the Raj to them. But the Tana Bhagat Movement simultaneously had the trend of opposition to colonial state. The Tanas refused to pay chaukidari tax and to work as coolies for the government and other castes, as that entailed their subordinate relationship with the dominant sections, the 'outsiders'. Such labour was seen as disgraceful to their social status and dignity. Thus the Tana Bhagat Movement, representing the voice of the marginal section, challenged both the 'insiders', the privileged section of Oraon community, and the outsiders, the non-tribals, who had been responsible for their subjugation and oppression.[97]

The Tana Bhagats and the Non-Cooperation Movement

The Non-Cooperation Movement was initially confined to urban pockets in Ranchi and did not have much impact on the tribals.[98] In November 1920, several Congress leaders—Padam Raj Jain, Bhola Nath Burman, Maulvi Zakaria, Abdul Razak and Sunder Dutt Seobi—arrived in Ranchi to celebrate Pijrapole, a local festival. These leaders wanted to use the occasion to spread the movement.[99] There was a large gathering at the station to receive the leaders. A procession up to the upper bazaar was followed by a series of meetings, processions and hartals.[100] People attended these meetings in large numbers. At one meeting, nearly 6,000 people were present.[101] On 20 November, Padam Raj Jain, Bhola Nath Burman and Maulvi Zakaria reached Lohardaga to address a non-cooperation meeting. They appointed local office holders like Secretary and President to supervise the non-cooperation campaign in Lohardaga. In Dorand, a panchayat was formed.[102] It was under the influence of these non-cooperators that school boys in Ranchi went on strike.[103] The local people of this belt emerged as Congress leaders and played important role in the spread of the movement. Prominent amongst them were Usman, the head Maulvi in the Anjuman Islamia Madrasa and a protege of Maulvi Kalam Azad, Ram Tahal Brahmachari, Gulab Tiwari, Ram Chandra Prasad, Nagar Mal, Mohammad Ishaq, Mohammad Alam and Ali Fan Saudagar.[104]

When the movement spread in this belt initially, non-tribals, chiefly Marwaris, Banias, Goalas and Kahars, were involved in it.[105] However, by the end of January 1921, attempts were made to mobilize the tribals.[106] The first meeting of the tribals that was addressed by Congress leaders was a meeting of the Oraons in Ranchi district on 31 January 1921.[107] Within a month, the movement gained momentum amongst the tribals and a large number of meetings were held in the Tana Bhagat belt.[108] On 1 February, Usman, Gulab Tiwari, A.K. Azad and Ram Tahal Brahmachari addressed a meeting of the Oraons, Mundas, Bhuiyas and Ghasis in Ranchi. Many non-tribals, including barbers and Chamars, were also present at this meeting.[109] On the same day, a meeting was held in Sinha village in Lohardaga. Sri Kishun Sahu addressed this meeting.[110] On 2 February, meetings were held at Jamchua Madhukam, Itki and Ghagra in Sadar. More than 4,000 people attended the meeting at Jamchua Madhukam. People came from twelve villages. Gulab Tiwari, Usman and Ram Tahal Brahmachari addressed these meetings.[111] On 12 February, a meeting was held at Kuru, a storm centre of the Tana Bhagats. 8,000 tribals attended this meeting.[112] On 28 February, a meeting was held at Rahlih, which was addressed by the Congress leaders as well as by Keshri Pandey of Palamau.[113] The initial attempts at mobilization by the Congress were followed by the initiative of Tana Bhagat leaders to organize meetings.[114] The official notices issued under Section 144 of the Criminal Procedure Code failed to deter the tribals from attending these meetings in large numbers.[115]

As part of their campaign in the tribal belt, the Congress leaders emphasized programmes like the boycott of liquor.[116] The formation of panchayats was another programme of the Congress that became immensely popular. The tribals were familiar with this institution as they had a tradition of local panchayats. The tribals were often ruined by a kind of legal device which used the civil courts against them and then suppressed the processes to get an ex-parte decree that deprived them of their land and occupancy holdings. They were also tricked by a play on legal terms which were entirely alien and mysterious to them. A deep distrust of the law courts found imaginative expression in tribal folklore. Courts were described as corrupt and creating misunderstandings so that 'only a fool makes use of them'.[117] The feeling of helplessness in face of this incomprehensible and brutal process was aggravated by a systematic destruction of the indigenous forms of justice under the colonial rule. The conceptualization of an oppressive, alien government was powerfully conveyed through the workings of *bideshi bichar* or foreign law.[118] The Congress leaders dissuaded them from taking recourse to courts and stressed that they settle their differences through panchayats.[119]

The leaders reiterated that the tribals, who were once the true rulers of the region, had been reduced to coolies.[120] While addressing a meeting in Ranchi on 1 February 1921, Ram Tahal Brahmachari said that the Kols were the true rulers of Chotanagpur.[121] The same idea was expressed by him at another meeting. There, he explained, how they were the 'original Rajas and had now become coolies and if they followed the advice of giving up drinking and using foreign food, they would once again become Rajas. By giving up European thing, they would save 90 crores of rupees in the country, which would enable them to become Rajas again and then the government would have to leave of its own accord'.[122]

One finds a strong undertone of the contrasted pair of times (then/now), i.e. a good past negated by a bad present. However, what is debatable is whether the harping on past was a return to the 'ideal' past. In addition to the symbol of Raja, the representation of desh (homeland) was a theme that was mentioned time and again in the speeches. The fight for land merged in the general struggle for a homeland. In their minds, Raj or desh was inseparably associated with the golden era of their history, i.e. when they enjoyed absolute freedom and did not pay any rent or tribute but only made a small annual offering to their leaders. There would be no *hakim* (ruler) or thana or zila, no zamindar or zamindar's rent. The new Raj, the recovered desh, implicitly referred to a certain traditional and deeply-rooted idea of a lost golden age.[123]

After the initial campaign by the Congress, the movement assumed a local character. The campaign at the local level was addressed by leaders, who were largely Tana Bhagats and they primarily focused on issues related to land, such as payment of rent to the landlords. They argued that the landlords had no right to rent as the land belonged to them because their ancestors had cleared the jungles and brought the land under cultivation.[124] In fact, the spread of the Non-Cooperation Movement brought forth tribals' conflict with the landlords.

Police officials cautiously observed the proceedings of the meetings organized by the local Tana Bhagat leaders[125] and warned them not to discuss non-payment of rent to zamindars at these meetings. For instance, a sub-inspector, who was present at a meeting of the Tana Bhagats at Nagar in Sisai on 3 March, threatened the leaders that if they discussed the issue of non-payment of rent to zamindars, he would report the matter to the higher officials.[126]

Even the Congress leaders were concerned about agrarian tension in this belt. They apprehended that the Non-Cooperation Movement would intensify the tenants' conflict with the landlords and they wanted to avoid such escalation of tension. They appealed to the tribals to live peacefully with the landlords and resort to arbitration (along with the village mahto and pahan) in their disputes with the landlords.[127] The Tana Bhagats, however, argued out that they could not live peacefully with the landlords as the landlords had usurped their ancestral lands, and given them to tenants of 'non aboriginal castes'. According to them, the landlords had no right to rent or other dues, as the lands originally belonged to them.[128]

Following the spread of the Non-Cooperation Movement, the conflict with the landlords came to the forefront.[129] In February 1921, in a village in Kuru, a group forcibly ploughed the field of a landlord, Janki Dusadh of Kolsundi, and insisted that the land belonged to them. They added that they were following the orders of their guru Bundhu Oraon Mahato who was a resident of the village. According to the Deputy Inspector General of Police, 'this guru would not reply to any question put to him by the sub-inspector. He talked of cow worship, dharam and made reference to France, Germany and Hindustan'.[130] In Sarsari village, the leader of the Tana Bhagats, Danreya Oraon, refused to pay the dues to the zamindars and his land was auctioned off for non-payment of rent.[131] In a village in Mander a peon was threatened by the Tana Bhagats when he attempted to hand over possession of land that had been sold for failure to pay rent.[132] Rumours were afloat that the Tana Bhagats had secured exclusive rights to some of the villages, and that the transfer of lands of these villages in the Tana Bhagats' name would be recognized with the establishment of Gandhi raj.[133] In many places, the villagers refused to pay chaukidari tax.[134] The villagers of Karu decided not to pay more than 2 'pailas of dhan' to the zamindars and 3 'pailas of dhan' as chaukidari tax.[135]

The spread of the movement in this belt and the mounting tension against the zamindars were sufficient grounds for government's concern. Administrative and police officials toured these areas to dissuade the people from participating in the protest.[136] The Tana Bhagats informed these officials that they did not have any dispute with the sarkar who was their *mai-baap*, and that it was not their intention to go against the government. They added that they were compelled to stop paying rent or tax because of the untold exploitation and oppression by the zamindars, darogas, chaukidari tehsildars, constables and chaukidars, who had reduced them to penury. They said that they had been paying chaukidari tax regularly, and under ordinary circumstances would have remained steadfast in their loyalty to the government and would also have paid their just or prescriptive dues, but the 'incidence of chaukidari tax in the village was unequal and pressed hard on the poor tenants'.[137] Despite vouching their loyalty and faith to the sarkar, the Tana Bhagats were determined not to pay any dues to the landlords even if it was 'sarkar ka hukum'. The Superintendent of Police warned them that their refusal to pay rent would reduce the tenants to penury and starvation, but they refused to be intimidated to change their decision.[138] They informed the Superintendent of Police that they would not pay more than '3 pailas of dhan' unless, otherwise ordered by their guru.[139] They added that bhagwan, who resided inside them and whom they recognized as their only guru, forbade them to pay more.[140] Turia, a Tana Bhagat said, 'Bhagwan, who was speaking within him, declared that the land was theirs first'.[141] At Son, the Deputy Inspector General of Police tried unsuccessfully to convince the Tana Bhagats to come to terms with the zamindar. The villagers of Son refused to pay rent and chaukidari tax and declared they would not give up their land, even if they were dispossessed by the landlord.[142] Even though the language of protest was couched in deference to colonial authority and bound within legality or legitimate expression, there was a strong element of resistance which contested colonial power. The context and consequences following such actions render them contestory.

The Non-Cooperation Movement provided an opportunity to the Tana Bhagats to vent their anger against the banias. The Tana Bhagats attempted to regulate prices and to close down large markets in some areas.[143] In Palkot market, in February 1921, they issued orders that rice was to be sold at 16 *seers* per rupee instead of eight, paddy at 32 *seers* and cloth at half price. The Sub-Inspector of Police sent them to the Sub-Divisional Officer at Gumla, who gave them stern warning to stop indulging in such activities. Upon their return, they informed the other villagers that the Sub-Divisional Officer had admitted that the present Raj had collapsed and that he would soon hand over charge to them.[144]

An incident of 'looting and uproar' was reported from another market in Lohardaga in April 1921.[145] The banias of this market purchased locally produced goods from Tendar and sold them at Lohardaga and other areas at exorbitant prices. The people of the neighbouring villages resented this. A few days before the looting, the villagers decided at a meeting that if at the next haat the banias sold the local goods at higher prices to make a huge profit, they would beat them. Many villagers came to the haat 'armed with sticks' on the day of the looting. They found to their dismay that the banias had bought up the entire stock of ploughshares. The local price of a ploughshare was 7 *annas*, whereas at Lohardaga it was sold for Re.1, which meant at a profit of more than 100 per cent. Within a few moments of arriving at the haat, there was an 'uproar'. The stalls of the banias and other vendors were looted. Several persons were badly beaten. Hundreds 'participated in the general melee and looted freely, not only from the vendors, but also from each other. Grain, salt, tobacco, cloth, utensils, spice and thread disappeared from the haat'. In the midst of the looting, they shouted that the British Raj was over and Gandhi was in power. The Congress leaders of Lohardaga condemned such looting and appealed to the people to adhere to non-violence.

The local officials expressed concern about the form of the movement amongst the Oraons. As long as the movement was confined to non-tribals, they were not worried and hoped that it would fizzle out soon. When it began to spread amongst the Oraons, they feared that it would acquire 'a fanatical and religious form, involving attacks upon life and property, which could only be suppressed by force'.[146] The Deputy Commissioner of Ranchi was concerned over the large number of meetings held in this belt. According to him, the speeches delivered to a crowd of very 'excitable' tribals in the heart of the country in which the Tana Bhagat Movement had started were intended to work on the feelings of the Oraons and resuscitate their movement. He was anxious that violence originally directed against the zamindars under the influence of the present propaganda would be directed against the government, as the Tana Bhagats, who had already got a grievance, were gradually made to believe that the government, being bad, was responsible for their troubles. A rumour floated that the Tana Bhagats had asked Gandhi to visit them. All this made the official very anxious.[147]

It was defiance of government authority that the officials feared most. They blamed 'outsiders'—the Congress leaders—for creating a disturbance in the tribal belt. One of the local officials reported how outsiders 'had come round to make collections of rice and encouraged them in their beliefs, which had the support of Gandhi'.[148] They viewed the tribals as ignorant people, who were easily 'excited and provoked under the influence of outsiders'.[149] In fact, the external manipulation thesis was dear to the heart of colonial officials. It was a stereotypical belief that illiterate villagers egged on by self-seeking politicians perform destructive acts in a fit of mindless fury. In this belief not only is the possibility of any independent initiative on the part of the peasant/tribal denied, even his actions are depoliticized and rendered free of any underlying rationale. This view consistently refuses to acknowledge both the logic of peasant/tribal resistance and its impact on the process of colonial rule.[150] According to the officials, it was only under provocation that the tribals confronted the landlords and stopped paying rent to them.[151] It is not appropriate, however, to view the tribal protest as merely motivated by 'external factors'. It is true that the Congress leaders, whom the local officials referred to as 'outsiders', gave an impetus to the unrest but the tribals responded to the movement with their own beliefs, aspirations and desires. The complex interaction between the Congress and the popular agitation shaped the movement at the local level.

The spread of the movement was seen as an erosion of the government's hegemony over the tribals. District officials stressed that the government's ability to maintain law and order should be clearly established. They wanted their presence to be made visible.[152] In order to counter the propaganda of the 'outsiders', district administrative and police officials toured many villages in Ranchi, Boro, Lohardaga, Kuru and Mandar Thanas in the Tana Bhagat belt. They spoke to hundreds of Oraons and addressed informal meetings, highlighting the benefits of British rule. They tried to impress upon the Oraons that the sarkar was willing and ready to redress their just grievances, and they would bring ruin to themselves, if they paid heed to any wild talk of outsiders to rebel against the sarkar. They also reminded them that the sarkar had reached a settlement at an enormous cost and had prepared a record of rights for their benefit. They explained to them that the tenancy law was periodically revised in accordance with their interests. The local officials assured them of all kinds of help. They urged the Tana Bhagats to discuss with them their grievances and difficulties, including cases of excessive taxation.

The local officials made certain suggestions to win over the confidence of the people. They recommended the distribution of free medicines amongst the villagers.[153] They added that loyal educated Oraons, who wielded considerable influence in the community, should be given a suitable allowance and deputed to go round the villages preaching loyalty to and cooperation with the government. They suggested the distribution of pamphlets in Hindi and Oraon in the villages to inculcate faith in the government.[154] The Deputy Commissioner of Ranchi deputed S.C. Roy, an anthropologist, to rally the support of the Tana Bhagats for the government. Roy advised that 'the intention of government to enforce the law and to suppress illegal movements should be emphasized'.[155] He simultaneously emphasized that 'no promise of special assistance to the landlords should be given and nothing should be said which might convey the impression to the Tana Bhagats that all the rights were on one side and all the wrongs on the other'.[156] According to Roy, the Tana Bhagats would agree to pay some revenue directly to the government but were determined to die, rather than pay a farthing to the landlords, whom they regarded as their greatest enemy. His suggestion was that the government should buy up the landlords' rights in their villages and settle the villages with the respective 'aboriginal' village communities on a fixed rent. He feared that so long as this was not done permanent solution to the Tana problem could not be arrived at. He said that the villages inhabited by the class of 'extreme' Tanas would not be more than fifty and the total cost of buying up the villages would not exceed Rs. 2 lakh. In his opinion the peace and contentment likely to result from such a measure was worth the expenditure.

Thus there is attempt to gloss anti-colonial character of the Tana Bhagat Movement. Many observers registered these as nothing but a conflict between some of the exploiting and exploited sections of the Indian population itself. The colonial power by this time had come to believe strongly in its role as the protector and supporter of the peasantry. Hence whenever any rebellion occurred the government was contented to look upon it simply as a revolt of the underdog against his native oppressor rather than against the colonial government. The colonial power absolved itself of bringing the tribals to their miserable condition. However, such perception was not limited to colonial discourse. Even Indian scholars like S.C. Roy ignored the anti-colonialist content of these uprisings.

Kolhan

The Impact of British Rule in Kolhan

Kolhan, in Singhbhum district, was once described by the British administrators as the 'Tibet of Chotanagpur', because of its total inaccessibility to outsiders.[157] The Hos constituted the majority in Kolhan and because of their fighting prowess were popularly known as 'Larka Kols' or 'Larka Hos'. The Mughals failed to subjugate them, and the British were able to bring this area under their control with much difficulty and after a series of protests. In spite of having established their control over this area, the British were forced to constitute the 'Non Regulated Province of Kolhan' in accordance with Wilkinson's rules. Under these rules, even if the Hos were subject to British administration, they were allowed some degree of internal autonomy and self-rule. Their traditional social and administrative system was retained, and the Hos could also hold their land at preferential rates. The Manki-Munda system was retained. The Manki headed a cluster of villages and the Munda headed a village. They were responsible for revenue collection and maintenance of law and order.

Although the Wilkinson system preserved the traditional social and administrative system of the Hos to some extent, colonial intervention led to many administrative and economic changes. It introduced a hierarchy based on authority, with powers and responsibilities defined at each level. The British agent was at the apex of the hierarchy. The agent of the British Governor General at Calcutta communicated with the Mankis. The Mankis and Mundas became accountable to the administrative officers for the continuance of their posts. Thus the British incorporated the upper echelons of the community. Being no longer dependent on the goodwill of the people, the Mankis and Mundas often abused their increased judicial and executive responsibilities to further their own interests. Colonial intervention led to several socio-economic changes. With the imposition of the new revenue system, the Hos were forced to pay a regular land tax instead of the primitive plough tax. Rent was high and it was frequently revised. Mankis and Mundas were allowed to keep a portion of rent as remuneration for assisting in rent collection. Linking of the tribal economy with the outside world adversely affected them. The establishment of a large number of haats by the British was not viewed favourably by the Hos, who resisted bringing their produce to the market. They fiercely resented the intrusion by outsiders in their economy; indebtedness increased and their lands passed into the hands of outsiders.

Non-Cooperation Movement in Kolhan amongst the Hos

In the Kolhan belt, the Non-Cooperation Movement was initially confined to Chakradharpur and Chaibasa, and did not spread amongst the tribals.[158] Being geographically closer to Orissa, most of the nationalist leaders in Kolhan were from Orissa.[159] A large number of volunteers, who were recruited in Chakradharpur, participated in the boycott of liquor campaign and made efforts to transform Chakradharpur into a dry area. Picketing affected the sale of liquor, opium, *ganja* and *bhang* in Chakradharpur and Chaibasa.[160] From these centres the movement gradually spread to some of the villages around Chakradharpur.[161] Initially the Hos were not involved in the movement. In April 1921, attempts were made by the Congress leaders to mobilize the Hos: a Congress leader, Gopabandhu Das, addressed a meeting at Bari haat in Chaibasa and made a special appeal to the Hos to join the movement. On 23 May, Godavaris Misra, another Congress leader, visited Chaibasa and, during a meeting at a haat, he made an appeal to the Hos to join the movement but was not successful. He visited Chaibasa again in the second week of June, and urged not only the Hos, but Kulu Manki, an influential leader of the Hos, to join the movement. A few days after his visit, the Superintendent of

Police of Kolhan noted 'attempts made to spread Gandhi's name throughout the Kolhan by the distribution of rice'. This indicates the use of some traditional forms in mobilization. In fact, such signs had meaning assigned to it by convention, i.e. as a symbol and as such was evocative of the most celebrated symbol of that kind within their own tradition. Moreover, such signs for mobilization become necessary in an age of poor communication and nearly total illiteracy. By the end of June, the government learnt that small sums had been collected from the Hos by the non-cooperators near Tantnagar.

In July 1921, Haji Abdullah, a prominent non-cooperator, faced a trial for charges of sedition at Chaibasa.[162] The non-cooperators used this situation to mobilize the Hos to join the movement. Congress leaders, Godavaris Misra and Anant Misra, arrived from Puri and appealed to the Hos in a meeting to join the movement. A Ho youth also addressed this meeting.[163] Anant Misra appointed Bishun Mahuri, an influential member of the Ho community, to enrol the Hos as Congress members. Bishun Mahuri visited all the haats in Chaibasa and urged the people to stop paying haat fees. On the day of verdict in Haji Abdullah's case, around 15,000 Hos collected outside the jail and Bishun Mahuri addressed them primarily focusing on the Non-Cooperation Movement. Several Hos and volunteers also spoke on this occasion and they appealed to the Hos to actively participate in the movement. By August, the movement had made a strong impression on the Hos. Bishun Mahuri succeeded in persuading Phulchand Dusadh, an influential person from Chittimitti, to join the movement.

Chittimitti gradually emerged as the centre of the movement and Phulchand Dusadh played an important role in this. A vendor of patent Indian medicines, he was educated and had a knowledge of English and, because of his background, he enjoyed considerable influence in the community. He persuaded Gardi Manki, the leader of the village community, to join the movement. Being the leader, Gardi Manki would have succeeded in spreading the movement amongst the villagers.

Phulchand Dusadh went around the villages declaring that swaraj had been attained. He persuaded students to quit the government schools. He said that under Gandhi's swaraj, government schools would be taken over. In one of the meetings, he said that 'all the pupils are leaving the Zila and Mission schools in Chaibasa. New schools will be constructed with the order of Gandhi and the government schools will be abolished. No school fees should be paid. Oriya language will be spoken in the Kolhan. Cutcheries should be closed. People should not take any flesh'. He also said that in Gandhi's raj, no rents will be paid. There will be only a poll tax of two pice per head, of which one pice will go to the Manki and the other pice to the Munda.[164]

Phulchand distributed pamphlets and pictures of Gandhi and Bharat Mata among the villagers and told them that Gandhi was their Raja and Bharat Mata was the mother of Lakshmi. He instructed them to hang the picture of Bharat Mata and worship her daily by lighting a lamp. Urging the people to obey Gandhi's orders,[165] he said:

> If the people do not obey Gandhi's orders rakshasas and devils will come, people will get no food or drink, and rakshasas, devils and worms will eat them and they will become lame.... The English are leaving the country and the few Englishmen, who are left behind, are hiding in Chaibasa and will run away in three or four months time. 40 crores of Habsi, who are the soldiers of Gandhi, will come to Chaibasa and fight with the sahibs. The sahibs will run away to their own country.[166]

In Chittimitti, a large number of Hos joined the movement and described themselves as 'chelas' of Gandhi.[167] Every Wednesday evening, they met at Phulchand's house where Gardi Manki and Phulchand's brother Ganga Ram would be also present.[168] They led a procession to the Mahadeo temple chanting slogans, *Ho Hari, Hari, Hari, Radha Gobind, Gandhiji ki jai, Hari Hari Hari Nath*. Phulchand shouted *Gandhiji ki jai* and the others repeated it in chorus, thumping the ground with their lathis. They danced about shouting *Mahatma Gandhi ki jai*. At the end of the sankirtan, they returned to Phulchand's house, where Phulchand talked about swaraj and Gandhi. His speech was punctuated with shouts of *Gandhiji ki jai*. He also showed the crowd pictures of Gandhi and Kasturba Gandhi. This sankirtan was repeated every Wednesday evening. The entire meeting had a sacred aura and the air resonated with political slogans interspersed with religious symbols and slogans.

Thus the language of politics was overwhelmingly religious. In political meetings there was constant invocation of religious idioms. Ranajit Guha's study has not only thrown light on such religious invocation but he has also commented on it. According to Guha, in peasant insurgency politics appears to have taken on the appearance of Providence, its routine of rituals, its temporal articulations of a kind of timeless sacred history. There is a pervasive religiosity in almost all that happens in every day life of a peasant or tribal. Their understanding of the relations, institutions and processes of power were identified with or at least considered over determined by religion. During an uprising, that most political of all events, he was led spontaneously to interpret its vicissitudes by the quasi-religious code. At a time of quickening mass anxiety these figments of popular imagination had translated politics instinctively by a religious code and came to express an antagonism towards the Raj as a fear of the cultural hegemony of the Christian rulers, a sense of loss of freedom as an apprehension about loss of faith. What was political came to be regarded as religious. But one cannot overlook the fact that in the course of making politics sacred, the tribals did not miss the chance of airing their mundane, everyday suffering. The religious language is employed to emphasize the political economy of the time: the cruelty of the master of the village (the zamindar), the difficulty in obtaining loans, the state of perpetual hunger and so on.[169]

By August 1921, the movement spread to Jaintgarh and Gamaria.[170] Godavaris Misra undertook a tour of these areas. Another Congress leader from Orissa, Satyabadi, also visited Jaintgarh and addressed a large crowd of 2,000 tribals at a haat. He referred to the government as *rakshas* (demon) and descendant of Ravan and as a *shaitan* (devil), who had killed hundreds of people in the Punjab. The government was called a dacoit, who is said to have extracted heavy taxes and crores of rupees from the people, who paid under fear. The government also took away the forests of the people. Satyabadi gave hope to the people that the British government was being overthrown and Gandhi raj was coming. Under swaraj, he said, there would be no rent, no income tax, no protected forests, no forest rules and no haat dues and people would settle their disputes amongst themselves and they would not go to the court.

The nationalist propaganda highlighted the exploitative character of British rule. The imageries used for the British, such as *shaitan*, *rakshas* and Ravan, evoked a strong emotional response. In Jaintgarh, many tenants joined the Congress by paying a fee of 4 *annas*. Defying the Manki's order, the Mundas of this village also joined the Congress. The nationalist campaign gained momentum in Gamaria, where many Hos joined the Congress.

Although the Congress had not given the call for civil disobedience, the local non-cooperators began to campaign for it. They announced that by paying 4 *annas* as Congress members they would regain their lands. They declared that the British would soon leave the country as swaraj had been attained. Under swaraj, they claimed, there would be no rent or tax, apart from a head tax of two pice, one pice would be given to the Manki and the other to the Munda.

The nationalist leaders took advantage of large gatherings at the haats to address meetings.[171] In fact, haats emerged as the main centres of the movement. It is at the marketplace, where perhaps more than anywhere else in a pre-industrial society, people gather regularly at frequent intervals and en masse for trade and certain forms of folk entertainment. In fact, throughout history these local bazaars have provided not only listeners and gossip mongers, but also a gathered audience. These local bazaars were sites for a free trade in ideas. The socializing process of rumour too tends to operate most actively in such places where people assemble in large numbers. In fact, in India the bazaar was clearly identified in colonialist thinking with the origin and dissemination of rumours. All the intelligence records of the Raj so amply testify how official espionage kept its 'ears firmly glued to the bazaars throughout India and at all levels from the village upwards. For much more than in the Council Chambers and lecture halls ringing with elite voices it was there that the government could get some idea of the standpoint from which they (the masses) regard the actions of their foreign rulers'. Sensitivity to 'bazaar gup' was, of course, at its most acute among the officials when the regime felt threatened by enemies abroad as in times of war or by those within as in times of popular revolt.[172]

The district officials looked at the holding of a large number of nationalists meetings in haats with increasing concern. They apprehended that a small incident in haat could easily flare up and involve many people. Nationalists put pressure on those who visited haats to follow the orders of the Congress and join the movement. An incident took place in the Serangil haat in Tantnagar near Chittimitti on 15 August 1921 which alarmed the officials. The Hos of Tantnagar 'were ordering the women, who had come to the haat, to pull off their ornaments and with *Gandhiji ki jai* on their lips pay obeisance to him'. Another incident took place on the same day. A group of men from Chittimitti drew the attention of the Hos in the haat to some schoolteachers, who had not resigned from their jobs, saying, 'here are the Chittimitti pandits who will not obey Gandhi's orders'. The Hos immediately 'attacked the pandits, broke their umbrellas and assaulted them'. These Hos were subsequently arrested by Gardi Manki and taken to Chaibasa. This incident, according to the Superintendent of Police, was 'the most distressing example of the effect on the untrained minds of simple tribals of doctrines which they were unable to appraise at their true value'. He added that during the hearing of the case one of the accused told him that 'it was owing to the proceedings of Gardi Manki of Pulaohi, who had shown him pictures of Gandhi, that his mind had been upset and he had resorted to such action'. The Kolhan official blamed Phulchand Dusadh for this outbreak.

The administrative and police officials were apprehensive of the spread of the Non-Cooperation Movement amongst the Hos, especially the preaching of local non-cooperators urging the tenants to withhold the payment of rent. They feared that the Hos, who were 'ignorant and incapable of distinguishing truth from falsehood, would get excited, passionate and violent in the process'.[173] Thus these officials of Kolhan, like those of Ranchi, shared the same perception of the tribals, which denied them a consciousness of their own. Police officials in Kolhan feared that if the movement was allowed to continue, it would erode the government's hegemony. Expressing apprehension about the kind of nationalist propaganda the Hos were exposed to, the Kolhan Superintendent of Police wrote that even the most loyal Ho would lose confidence in the government, unless the lies were nailed to the counter. The Police Superintendent said that if a Ho was asked whether he paid a subscription to Congress, he made no attempt at concealing it. However, when the police official explained that he made an error by paying a Congress subscription, a Ho would admit that he made a mistake but then he would ask the extremely pertinent question: why, when the people tell them that Gandhi had gained a great victory and the sahibs were running away was not true, did the sarkar allow them to talk in that manner. They further asked, why did the government allow such people to come into the Kolhan and speak lies to the people.[174]

The local officials wondered why the government had not taken any action against the movement, which was aimed at subverting the government. They believed that it was government inaction that emboldened the people to such an extent. They requested the government to take action against the movement and put an end to all kinds of propaganda. They wanted officials to regularly visit the haats.[175]

Santhal Pargana

The Santhal Pargana was another belt where the Non-Cooperation Movement had tremendous impact. It was particularly intense in Damin-i-Koh area which had a strong tradition of protest. Damin-i-Koh, which adjoined the Rajmahal Hills, was the centre of the Santhal Rebellion of 1855–6.[176] It was a forested area which the Santhals had cleared and brought under cultivation. As in other tribal belts, the Santhals were gradually deprived of their land and were reduced to labourers. This aroused bitter resentment amongst them, and it led to a series of protests. The turning point in their struggle was the involvement of the Sidhu and Kanhu brothers, who claimed to have had experienced a divine revelation. The movement strengthened under them. Under their leadership around 30,000 Santhals marched to Calcutta and submitted a petition of grievances to the Governor General. The police attempted to terrorize them on the way but they failed and this marked the beginning of the struggle against authority. Policemen were attacked, villages were burnt and property pillaged. Many moneylenders were killed. Although Damin-i-Koh was the centre of the rebellion, the protest spread to Bhagalpur, Birbhum and Giridih. The Santhals established control over the area between Berio and Colgong. The government declared martial law on 19 July 1855. The protest had acquired a broad base, with other communities joining it.

Another area in the Santhal Pargana, where the movement made considerable impact, was the belt of the Kherwar Movement in Godda, that had started amongst the Santhals of this region in early twentieth century.

The discontentment against the oppression of landlords and moneylenders, loss of their lands, excessive rent and debt bondage were largely responsible for the emerging protest. The Kherwar Movement had element of religious and cultural revivalist movement.[177] The Santhals in Kherwar Movement believed that their oppression was divine retribution for abandoning the worship of God. Bhagirath Manjhi, a resident of Tardiha in Godda, declared that he was ordained by God to redress the grievances of the Santhals, to fight for their rights and to lead them as king. He proclaimed that the land the Santhals cultivated belonged to them and that no government could impose any taxes on them. Once appointed as the king of the new Santhal raj at Baunsi, Bhagirath Manjhi promised that his first act would be to abolish all rent, to ban the slaughter of pigs and fowls, and to prohibit drinking and dancing. It is in the background of such strong tradition of popular protest that one can understand the Non-Cooperation Movement in this belt.

The Non-Cooperation Movement had a strong impact in this belt since the beginning. A large number of Congress leaders visited this district and Swami Darshanand also was very active here.[178] Sasi Bhusan Roy was appointed Secretary of the District Congress Committee. He was a schoolmaster in a local high school but resigned from the teaching job when he assumed his new responsibility. He was assisted by Abdul Gafur and Baidyanath Jha. Sasi Bhusan Roy invited many leaders from outside the district, including Rajendra Prasad, to intensify the movement in this belt. Rajendra Prasad's appeal to the people to join the movement evoked a wide response. Congress activities in this belt were primarily confined to the towns.[179] Offices of the Congress were set up in Deoghar, Maheshpur and Dumka. The office in Rajmahal was subordinate to the one in Deoghar. Abdul Mean was its President and Chandra Narain Sahu its Secretary. A volunteer corp was attached to it. A large number of non-cooperators from Bengal, Bhagalpur and Monghyr toured Rajmahal to give a boost to the campaign.[180]

A large number of volunteers, most of them from lower classes, played a major role in the spread of the movement in this district. Many of these volunteers courted arrest and were subject to rigorous punishment. Whenever any action was taken against the volunteers, others would offer themselves as volunteers.[181] Many youths and schoolchildren were actively involved in the campaign; Marwaris and banias also extended support to the movement.[182] The most popular form of fund-raising was the *muthia* collection.[183]

Picketing of liquor shops was one of the main activities of the campaign. Excise settlement was boycotted. This led to a drastic reduction in the excise collections of the government.[184] Khadi-related activity was also very popular amongst the Santhals.[185] Wearing khadi cap was a popular activity. Khadi became almost a creed for the Santhals. Many popular perceptions got associated with it. The Gandhi cap became a sort of a talisman, capable of protecting its wearer against the government's bullet. It was an important symbol of defiance. The government took strong action against anyone wearing khadi cap.[186] When the excise shops were to be auctioned on 20 February at Dumka, the authorities in an attempt to prevent the protest against liquor, ensured that no volunteer, Congress worker or khadi worker was anywhere in the town. Policemen were posted at Jermundi, midway between Dumka and Rampurhat, and every car going to Dumka was searched at Jermundi and Sikaripara, and those wearing khadi were served with notices under Section 144 of the Criminal Procedure Code which were not even signed by any authorized officer, but carried a photocopy of the signatures of officers. Khadi caps and badges were seized and the distribution of cotton for spinning was viewed as an offence.[187]

The movement had a strong impact in Dumka where it was a common sight to see people carrying the national flags in hand and shouting anti-British slogans and *Gandhiji ki jai*.[188] In Pakur too, the movement established a stronghold where many non-cooperators from Bengal were active.[189] A swaraj ashram was established at Pakur. The non-cooperators planned to appoint their own swaraj officials. Robin Saren and Shyama Charan were actively involved in the movement.[190] In Deoghar, excise shops were picketed and Sasi Bhusan Roy played an active role in it. Volunteers who actively campaigned for the movement were convicted and sentenced to rigorous imprisonment.[191]

The Santhals attended political meetings in large numbers. They enrolled as volunteers and played an active role in haats and fairs.[192] *Muthia* collection became very popular. The national flag-carrying-Santhals tried to enter the Damin-i-Koh area.[193] The idea of swaraj had aroused great expectations amongst the Santhals. They believed that under Gandhi raj they would not have to pay any rent and would also regain their lands. In many places, non-payment of rent also started. The movement intensified in the bazaar area of Bero. A local official described the movement in Bero as 'some sort of minor revolution where bands of volunteers, who had taken possession of the bazaar, were building a house for themselves and had defied the Santhal officials and bazaar officials. They were promising Santhals and paharias free drink, no rent and Rs.12 a month'.[194]

As the campaign against the zamindars intensified, the zamindars played a crucial role in assisting the government in suppressing the movement. The inspector of Pakur and the sub-inspector of Maheshpur held an enquiry at the zamindar's *kachahari* against the tribal tenants. After consulting the local zamindar, the armed police of Dumka raided the Congress office and arrested the leader, Promotho Nath Sinha. On the zamindar's advice, Promotho Nath

Sinha was taken to the thana, handcuffed and a rope tied around his waist. This sight terrified the people to such an extent that when they saw the zamindar passing by the bazaar, they fled in fright and the haat was dissolved.[195]

The Non-Cooperation Movement was very strong in Godda which had a large number of Kherwars, who joined the movement and enrolled as volunteers. Khadi was very popular in Godda as was the campaign against liquor. The local Marwaris helped the movement financially. The movement raised the expectations of the Kherwars that under swaraj they would not only regain their land but would also not have to pay rent. There was bitter antagonism against the landlords. The Kherwars invaded a Damin bungalow, hoisted a swaraj flag and sacrificed a goat and a fowl. This was hailed as a sign of victory by the Santhals in Godda.

The district administrative and police officials expressed increasing concern over the spread of the movement in this belt. They regarded the Kherwars as 'prone to sudden outbreak of emotion' without any apparent cause. Memories of the Santhal Rebellion of 1855–6 still haunted them. Like the local officials of Ranchi and Kolhan, they too believed that the movement derived its 'origin and force almost entirely from outside the district'.[196] According to them, 'the few non-cooperators hailing from Birbhum and other places were misleading the ignorant and inflammable Santhal population by their mischievous activities'.[197] They kept a close watch on the people visiting this area and did not allow 'outsiders' to enter.[198] Thus there is a suggestion in official records of externality of its agent. In a sense the impression that one gets of rebellion is that of contagion and infection, of a virus hitting the countryside and destroying the peasants' healthy sense of loyalty to his lord, eroding the moral base of his authority. Peasants are said to have lost their innocence due to 'outsiders influence'. This purports to a conspiracy theory and image of an innocent tenantry happily reconciled to landlord rule. In fact, the notion of suddenness, speed and simultaneity is a convenient narrative on which is based a conspiracy theory. It is based on elitist perception and psychology, the elitists who are taken aback on the sudden revolt of those whose loyalty they had taken for granted. However, the uprising on such a scale do not require secret conniving but it is the open and domineering colonial power and its alliance with feudal forces, the landlords and money-lenders, that led to it. The subjection of the rural masses to a common source of exploitation and oppression makes them rebel.[199]

The government took strong action against the movement. Orders under Section 144 of the Criminal Procedure Code was passed which not only banned public meetings, gagged particular individuals, prohibited people from entering the subdivision, but also directed them to leave particular areas within a specified time. Punishment included rigorous imprisonment for the maximum period accompanied by heavy fines. The Congress offices were searched and papers seized. Volunteers were arrested without a warrant. They were insulted and their khadi caps and badges were seized. Nationalist activities like hoisting of the national flags, picketing, collection of *muthia* and observance of hartal were not tolerated. Externment order was served on Congress leaders. They were ordered to leave the subdivision immediately. Binodanand Jha was sentenced to six months' rigorous punishment for continuing to stay at Dumka despite an order to leave Dumka. The officials held meetings in which they ordered the people not to associate with the Congress. Fines were imposed on those who did not report to the authorities of the visit of any non-cooperator in their areas. Any kind of support to the non-cooperators, like providing food, receiving them and renting premises to them, was a punishable offence. The guilty were evicted from their homes and deprived of their lands. In Hajipur *diara*, many people were issued show cause notices in which they were asked to explain why they should not be compelled to furnish bonds of security for being one of the co-villagers of a village where the movement had spread. There were cases of eviction against the tenants of Damin-i-Koh. Even acts like helping pilgrims to the Basukinath Temple on Shivratri and banning gambling at the Karmatar Fair in Jamtara on Sankranti Day were disapproved by the government.[200]

Palamau

In Palamau, there was a strong tradition of protest amongst the Cheros and Kherwars, who constituted a considerable proportion of the population in this district. They considered themselves to be the original owners of Palamau and resented their marginalization from land and forest resources. However, the Non-Cooperation Movement had made little impact in this district as compared to Civil Disobedience Movement, when it was in the forefront of the agitation.

Numerous meetings and processions were organized in Palamau during the Non-Cooperation Movement despite government ban on such activities. The widespread organization facilitated the meetings. The meetings and processions were attended by large numbers from various parts of the district, which included a large number of Cheros and Kherwars.[201]

In this belt the initial campaign was by the Congress leaders, but soon the movement took on local forms. There emerged many local Congress leaders who campaigned in different areas: Dildar Hussain in Gardwa, Amrit Math and Ramdhani Sahu in Karso of Sadar, Matukdhari Sahu in Nagar

Untari, and Mahabir Lal in Chattarpur.[202] These leaders toured different areas and made consistent efforts to enrol the Kherwars and Cheros as volunteers: Dildar Hussain in Gardwa, Amrit Math and Ramdhani Sahu in the villages of Daltonganj and Ranka, and Matukdhari Sahu in Bagar. They enrolled a large number of Kherwars as volunteers, particularly in the Ranka and Untari areas of the south and west of Palamau district. Once the Kherwars were mobilized, they motivated others to become volunteers and thus developed a strong network of volunteers in Palamau district.[203]

The liquor boycott was also very successful. Many outstills were raided and destroyed. Consequently, many outstills closed down.[204] In Garhwa, Dildar Hussain was successful in closing down the outstill.[205] Volunteers also forcibly prevented the people from entering the outstill. Liquor shops were picketed in Nagar. The Non-Cooperation Movement was very intensive in Balumath.[206]

As elsewhere, the movement raised the expectations of the Kherwars. They began to think that the days of their oppression were numbered and that the era of swaraj would lead to restoration of their rights to land and forest. There was a defiant mood and a strong pressure to launch civil disobedience. Bidya Dhar Dubey, an ex-pupil of the Zila School in Daltonganj, toured round the villages along with Amrit Math and Ramdhani Sahu of Karso in Sadar, and organized many meetings. They openly advocated that after 31 January 1922 government laws should be defied.[207] At a meeting in Saradih Bazar on 13–14 January 1922, people were instructed not to pay chaukidari and other taxes.[208] Preparations were made for the non-payment of rent. Tenants in the government estate were openly defiant. The situation, according to one government official, in Chainpur, Ranka and Ladi was one of 'alarm and despondency'. Non-cooperators made earnest attempts to 'stir up trouble amongst the tenants and inculcate in them the beginning of civil disobedience'.[209] Firangi Kherwar and Parmeshwar Barhi were actively involved in the non-payment of rent propaganda in the government estate.[210] In Khas Mahal, the campaign focused on the issue of non-payment of rent.[211]

The struggle over forests was a significant aspect of the Non-Cooperation Movement in this belt. Many Kherwars participated in this movement, demanding the restoration of the customary rights of tribals to extract timber and collect forest produce for their own consumption. In fact, swaraj meant restoration of their right to the forests, the most important resource, next only to land. The non-cooperators drew the attention of the tribals to the depletion of their forest resources through commercial exploitation by the British.[212] Tenants were 'incited and instigated' to cut down the jungles on the grounds that only they were entitled to these jungles.[213] Reserved forests were destroyed. There were cases of 'illicit cutting' in the government reserved forests. The hill side jungle in Ranka, which had not been cut for twenty years, was cleared for jhum cultivation. The tenants justified their actions saying that swaraj had come and now the jungle was theirs.

The local officials were also concerned over the spread of the movement in this belt. The strong tradition of protest in this belt haunted them. Expressing their apprehension, they said that 'past traditions form a very favourable bed for agitators to drop seeds of sedition, non-cooperation and civil disobedience'. Reiterating this fear, the Chotanagpur Commissioner wrote to the Chief Secretary that the movement would bolster the 'hot-headed aboriginals', who had a long tradition of protest to defy authority.

Thus, this chapter examines the tribal and peasant protests during the Non-Cooperation Movement. The popular struggles, which converged with the Non-Cooperation Movement, moved beyond the parameter of Congress programme and threw up their own agendas. This study throws light on the popular perceptions and translations of nationalism, which were linked up with the desires and aspirations of the tribals and peasants. The popular translations of nationalism had pitted the tribals and peasants not only against the colonial exploiters but also against their internal exploiters. In effect, these were the deep-seated grievances, over which protests had been going on for long, and which sharpened during the Non-Cooperation Movement. Though the actions of the peasants and tribals were framed in terms of what was popularly regarded to be just, fair and possible, they derived and insisted on deriving the legitimacy for all their actions from the supposed orders of Gandhi. Everything that was unjust, cruel and oppressive was fought against in Gandhi's name, who emerged as the symbol of their hopes and aspirations. It marked the inversion of power relations that were deemed inviolable. This study thus highlights the complex relationship between popular struggles and nationalism, moving beyond the binaries of elite and subaltern nationalism.

Notes

1. These works include those of A.N. Das, Stephen Henningham, Walter Hauser and Rakesh Gupta—The Kisan Sabha as an organization; Swami Sahajanand as a charismatic leader of kisans in twentieth-century Bihar; the uneasy relationship between the Kisan Sabha and the Indian National Congress, are some of the themes explored in these works.
2. Shahid Amin, 'Agrarian Bases of Nationalist Agitations in India: An Historiographical Survey', in *The Indian National Congress: Centenary Hindsights,* ed. D.A. Low, New Delhi: Oxford University Press, 1988, pp. 98–128.
3. A. Seal, *The Emergence of Indian Nationlism,* Cambridge: Cambridge University Press, 1977; J. Gallagher, G. Johnson and A. Seal, eds., *Locality, Province and Nation,* Cambridge: Cambridge University Press, 1973.

4. Bisheswar Prasad, *Changing Modes of Indian National Movement*, New Delhi: People's Publishing House, 1966; B. Pittabhi Sitaramayya, *The History of the Indian National Congress (1885–1935),* Bombay: Padma Publications, 1946.
5. R.P. Dutta, *India Today*, Calcutta: Manisha Granthalaya, 1979.
6. These works include those of Stephen Henningham, D.A. Low, Chris Baker, D. Washbrook, Anand Yang, Jacques Pouchepadass and Walter Hauser.
7. Jacques Pouchepadass, 'Peasant Classes in Twentieth Century Agrarian Movements in India', in *Peasants in History: Essays in Honour of Daniel Thorner*, E.J. Hobsbawm et al., eds., Calcutta: Oxford University Press, 1980, p. 149.
8. Bhaduri, *Dhorai Charitmanas.*
9. Stephen Henningham, *A Great Estate and its Landlords in Colonial India: Darbhanga, 1860–1942*, New Delhi: Oxford University Press, 1990.
10. Anand Yang, 'Agrarian Origins of Crime: A Study of Riots in Saran District, India, 1886–1920', in *Journal of Social History*, vol. 13, no. 2, 1979, pp. 289–306.
11. Amin, 'Agrarian Bases of Nationalist Agitations'.
12. Ranajit Guha, ed., *Subaltern Studies I,* New Delhi: Oxford University Press, 1982; Ranajit Guha, *Elementary Aspects of Peasant Insurgency in Colonial India,* New Delhi: Oxford University Press, 1983.
13. B.B. Chaudhary, 'Subaltern Autonomy and the National Movement' in David Ludden, ed., *Reading Subaltern Studies: Critical History, Contested Meaning and the Globalization of South Asia*, New Delhi: Permanent Black, 2003, pp. 120–32; Mridula Mukherjee, 'Peasant Resistance and Peasant Consciousness in Colonial India: Subalterns and Beyond', in *Economic and Political Weekly*, vol. 23, nos. 41 and 42, 1988, pp. 2109–20, 2174–85.
14. The complexity of relationship between masses and nationalism has been delineated in Biswamoy Pati's *Resisting Domination: Peasants, Tribals and the National Movement in Orissa 1920–50*, New Delhi: Manohar, 1993.
15. Sarkar, 'The Conditions and Nature of Subaltern Militancy', p. 276.
16. Girish Mishra, 'Indigo Plantation and the Agrarian Relations in Champaran during the Nineteenth Century', in *Indian Economic and Social History Review*, vol. III, no. 4, December 1966, pp. 332–57.
17. Frankel, 'Caste, Land and Dominance in Bihar', p. 59.
18. Henningham, *Peasant Movements in Colonial India*, pp. 38–9.
19. Ibid.
20. Ibid.
21. C.M. Fisher, *Indigo Plantations and Agrarian Society in North Bihar in the 19th and early 20th Centuries*, Cambridge University, D.Phil. thesis, 1976, pp. 55, 232.
22. L.S.S. O'Malley, District Gazetteer, Muzaffarpur, 1907, p. 126.
23. *Searchlight*, 31 December 1920 and 22 September 1922; O'Malley, District Gazetteer, Champaran, 1907, pp. 108–11.
24. Quoted in Papiya Ghosh, 'Peasants, Planters and Gandhi: Champaran in 1917', in *Peasant Struggles in Bihar, 1831–1992: Spontaneity to Organisation*, Kaushal Kishore Sharma et al., eds., Patna: Janaki Prakashan, 1994, p. 98.

25. Renu, *Maila Anchal*, pp. 12–13; Bhaduri, *Dhorai Charitmanas*; Sarkar, 'The Conditions and Nature of Subaltern Militancy', p. 274.
26. This paragraph is based on Girish Mishra, 'Socio-Economic Background of Gandhi's Champaran Movement', in *Indian Economic and Social History Review*, vol. V, no. 3, September 1968, pp. 245–76; Stephen Henningham, 'The Social Setting of the Champaran Satyagraha: The Challenge to an Alien Elite', in *Indian Economic and Social History Review*, vol. XIII, no. 1, January-March 1976, pp. 59–74.
27. Frankel, 'Caste, Land and Dominance in Bihar', p. 66.
28. Ibid., p. 59.
29. P. K. Shukla, *Indigo and the Raj: Peasant Protests in Bihar, 1780–1917*, New Delhi: Pragati, 1993, p. 9.
30. This paragraph is based on these sources, Girish Mishra, *Agrarian Problems of Permanent Settlement—A Case Study of Champaran*, New Delhi: People's Publishing House, 1978, pp. 231–94; Jacques Pouchepadass, 'Local Leaders and the Intelligentsia in the Champaran Satyagraha (1917): A Study in Peasant Mobilisation', in *Contributions to Indian Sociology*, n.s. no. 8, November 1978, pp. 67–88.
31. Kumar's work *Rewriting the Language of Politics* highlights this, pp. 78–109; Guha, *Elementary Aspects of Peasant Insurgency*, pp. 252–56.
32. B.B. Mishra, ed., *Select Documents on Mahatma Gandhi's Movement in Champaran, 1917–19*, Patna: Government of Bihar, 1963, p. 90.
33. Prasad, 'The Champaran Satyagraha', pp.161–2.
34. Ghosh, 'Peasants, Planters and Gandhi: Champaran in 1917', p. 99.
35. Prasad, 'The Champaran Satyagraha', pp. 163–4.
36. Ghosh, 'Peasants, Planters and Gandhi: Champaran in 1917', pp. 99–102. This entire paragraph is based on this source.
37. Gyan Pandey, 'Peasant Revolt and the Indian Nationalism: The Peasant Movement in Awadh, 1919–1922', in *Subaltern Studies I*, ed., Ranajit Guha, New Delhi: Oxford University Press, 1982, pp. 163–6.
38. Henningham, *Peasant Movements in Colonial India*, p. 49.
39. Ibid., pp. 49–50; Bihar and Orissa Political Special File no. 159/1922.
40. Henningham, *Peasant Movements in Colonial India*, p. 50.
41. Bihar and Orissa Police Abstract of Intelligence, 7 March 1919.
42. Bihar and Orissa Political Special File no. 12/1921, 'Fortnightly Confidential Report—To Commissioner Tirhut Division, 11 January 1921'.
43. Ibid.
44. This paragraph and the following are based on Bihar and Orissa Political Special File no. 462/1921, 'From DIG of Police, C.I.D., Bihar and Orissa, to Chief Secretary, dated 23/2/1922—A copy of the Judgement'.
45. *Searchlight*, 19 August 1921.
46. Ibid.
47. Bihar and Orissa Political Special File no. 93/1921, 'Tirhut FR (1), August 1921'.
48. Ibid.; Home Department (Political) File no. 75/1922, NAI.

49. Bihar and Orissa Political Special File no. 3/1922, 'Report for the week ending 5 January 1922'.
50. Ibid., File no. 37/1922, 'From Commissioner, Tirhut Division, to Chief Secretary, 24 June 1922'; ibid., File no. 3/1922, 'Report for the week ending 5 January 1922'.
51. Ibid.
52. Ibid., File no. 287/1921, 'Copy of demi-official letter dated 21 June 1921 from the Superintendent of Police, Champaran, to the 1st Assistant to the D.I.G. of Police, Crime and Railways'.
53. Ibid.
54. This whole paragraph is based on the source in Bihar and Orissa Political Special File no. 12/1921, 'To Commissioner, Tirhut Division, Fortnightly Confidential Report, 11 January 1921'.
55. Ibid., File no. 287/1921, 'Copy of demi-official letter dated 21 June 1921 from the Superintendent of Police, Champaran, to the 1st Assistant to the D.I.G. of Police, Crime and Railways'. The rest of the paragraph is based on this source.
56. Fortnightly Report of Bihar and Orissa for the first half of June 1921, Government of India, Home Department (Political) File no. 64/June/1921, NAI; Fortnightly Report of Bihar and Orissa for the first half of January 1922, Government of India, Home Department (Political) File no. 18/January/1922, NAI; Bihar and Orissa Political Special File no. 3/1922, 'Report for the week ending 5 January 1922'; *Searchlight*, 23 June 1921; Fortnightly Report of Bihar and Orissa for the first half of June 1921, Government of India, Home Department (Political) File no. 64/June/1921, NAI.
57. *Searchlight*, 18 and 29 January 1922.
58. Bihar and Orissa Political Special File no. 3/1922, 'Report for the week ending 5 January 1922'; *Searchlight*, 15 January 1922; Fortnightly Report of Bihar and Orissa for the first half of January 1922, Government of India, Home Department (Political) File no. 18/January/1922, NAI.
59. Fortnightly Report of Bihar and Orissa for the first half of November 1921, Government of India, Home Department (Political) File no. 18/November/1921, NAI.
60. *Searchlight*, 9 November 1921; Bihar and Orissa Political Special File no. 539/1921, 'Situation in Champaran up to 9.11.21 and S.R. 29 dated 2 November 1921, Report II—Copy forwarded to Chief Secretary, D.I.G., C.I.D., dated 8 November 1921'; Government of India, Home Department Political File no. 357/1921, NAI; *Motherland*, 8 and 15 November 1921.
61. Guha, *Elementary Aspects of Peasant Insurgency*, pp. 23–36.
62. Ibid.
63. Bihar and Orissa Political Special File no. 539/1921, 'Special Report Case no. 29, dated 19 November 1921, S.P., Champaran'. The rest of the paragraph is based on this source.
64. Ibid.
65. Ibid.
66. Ibid., 'Copy of letter no. 4354 C, dated 20 November 1921, from the Chief Secretary, Bihar and Orissa, to the Secretary to the Government of India, Home Department'.

67. *Searchlight*, 9 December 1921.
68. Home Department (Political) File no. 357/1921, NAI.
69. *Searchlight*, 9 November 1921; Bihar and Orissa Political Special File no. 541/1921, 'Champaran Political Conference, Successful Session at Bettiah'.
70. *Searchlight*, 9 November 1921.
71. Ibid., 20 November 1921; Political Special File no. 541/1921, 'Champaran Political Conference, Successful Session at Bettiah'; ibid., File no. 539/1921, 'Copy of Report dated 4/5 November 1921, from the S.P., Champaran'.
72. *Searchlight*, 9 November 1921; Bihar and Orissa Political Special File nos. 93/1921 and 534/1921.
73. *Searchlight*, 9 November 1921.
74. Bihar and Orissa Political Special File no. 93/1921.
75. Ibid., File no. 534/1921.
76. Ibid., File no. 184/1921, 'Bhagalpur Commissioner to Chief Secretary, 1 June 1921'. This paragraph and the following two paragraphs are based on this source.
77. Ibid.
78. Ibid.
79. Guha, *Elementary Aspects of Peasant Insurgency*, pp. 6–10.
80. Bihar and Orissa Political Special File no. 184/1921, 'Bhagalpur Commissioner to Chief Secretary, 1 June 1921'.
81. Ibid., 'District Magistrate to Commissioner, Bhagalpur Division, 30 May 1921'.
82. Ibid., File no. 12/1921, 'Commissioner, Tirhut Division, to Chief Secretary, 20 January 1921'.
83. Ibid., File no. 40/1921, 'Planters' Association and European Association meeting with his Excellency on 22 January 1921'.
84. *Searchlight*, 28 January 1921.
85. Bihar and Orissa Political Special File no. 40/1921, 'Planters' Association and European Association meeting with his Excellency on 22 January 1921'.
86. Ibid.
87. Ranajit Guha, 'Neel Darpan: The Image of a Peasant Revolt in a Liberal Mirror', in *Peasant Resistance in India, 1858–1914,* ed. David Hardiman, New Delhi: Oxford University Press, 1992, p. 73.
88. Ibid., pp. 73–4.
89. Bihar and Orissa Political Special File no. 184/1921, 'Bhagalpur Commissioner to Chief Secretary, 1 June 1921'.
90. This section is based on these sources, Sangeeta Dasgupta, 'Reordering a World: The Tana Bhagat Movement, 1914–1919', in *Studies in History,* n.s., vol. 15, no. 1, 1999, pp. 1–41; Sajal Basu, *Jharkhand Movement: Ethnicity and Culture of Silence,* Shimla: Indian Institute of Advanced Study, 1994; K.S. Singh, *Birsa Munda and his Movement, 1874–1901: A Study of Millenarian Movement in Chotanagpur*, Calcutta: Oxford University Press, 1983; Victor Das, *Jharkhand—Castle Over the Graves,* New Delhi: Inter-India, 1992; *Indian Historical Review,* vol. XXXIII, no. 1, January 2006, Special Issue on the theme 'Adivasis in Colonial India', Guest Editor, Biswamoy Pati.
91. Ibid.

92. B.B. Chaudhary, 'The Story of a Tribal Revolt in the Bengal Presidency: The Religion and Politics of the Oraons, 1900–1926,' in Adhir Chakrabarti, ed., *Aspects of Socio-Economic Changes and Political Awakening in Bengal*, Calcutta, 1989, pp. 55–8; Prabhu Prasad Mohapatra, 'Class Conflict and Agrarian Regimes in Chotanagpur, 1860–1950', in *The Indian Economic and Social History Review*, vol. 28, no. 1, 1991, pp. 1–42; K.S. Singh, 'Tribal Peasantry, Millenarianism, Anarchism and Nationalism: A Case Study of the Tana Bhagats in Chotanagpur, 1914-25', in *Social Scientist*, vol. 16, 1988, pp. 36–50.
93. Dasgupta, 'Reordering a World', pp. 7–8, 17–24.
94. Singh, 'Tribal Peasantry, Millenarianism, Anarchism and Nationalism, pp. 35–40.
95. Dasgupta, 'Reordering a World', pp. 7–8, 24–30.
96. Ibid.
97. Ibid.
98. Fortnightly Reports of Bihar and Orissa for December 1920 and January 1921, Government of India, Home Department (Political) File nos. 35/February/1921, 77/February/1921, 41/April/1921 and 42/April/1921, NAI.
99. Freedom Movement Papers SCRO 51, BSA, 'S.P. Report to Deputy Commissioner, Ranchi, dated 3.2.21'.
100. Ibid. It is important to note that slaughter of cows was suspended for sometime during this period and the movement.
101. Ibid.
102. Ibid.
103. Ibid.
104. Fortnightly Report of Bihar and Orissa for the second half of February 1921, Government of India, Home Department (Political) File no. 43/April/1921, NAI.
105. Freedom Movement Papers SCRO 51, BSA, 'S.P. Report to Deputy Commissioner, Ranchi, dated 3.2.21'; Fortnightly Reports of Bihar and Orissa for January 1921, Government of India, Home Department (Political) File nos. 41/April/1921 and 42/April/1921, NAI.
106. Ibid.
107. Freedom Movement Papers SCRO 51, BSA, 'Second note on the Non-Co-operation Movement reviewing the growth of the movement amongst the Uraons and other aboriginal tribes of Ranchi from 31 January to 13 February 1921'.
108. Ibid.
109. Ibid.
110. Ibid.
111. Ibid.
112. Ibid., 'Deputy Commissioner, Ranchi to Commissioner, Chotanagpur Division, 13/2/21'.
113. Ibid., 'Deputy Commissioner, Ranchi to Commissioner, Chotanagpur Division, 9/2/21'.
114. Ibid.
115. Ibid.

116. Fortnightly Reports of Bihar and Orissa for January 1921, Government of India, Home Department (Political) File nos. 41/April/1921 and 42/April/1921, NAI.
117. Tanika Sarkar, 'Jitu Santal's Movement in Malda, 1924–1932: A Study in Tribal Protest', in *Subaltern Studies IV*, ed. Ranajit Guha, New Delhi: Oxford University Press, 1985, pp. 146–7.
118. Ibid.
119. Pol. File nos. 41/April/1921 and 42/April/1921, NAI.
120. Freedom Movement Papers SCRO 51, BSA, 'D.C. Ranchi to Commissioner, 13/2/21'.
121. Ibid.
122. Ibid.
123. Sarkar, 'Jitu Santal's Movement in Malda', pp. 157–8.
124. Bihar and Orissa Political Special File nos. 50/21 and 75/1921; Freedom Movement Papers, SCRO 51, BSA.
125. Bihar and Orissa Political Special File no. 50/1921.
126. Ibid., 'Extract from the Confidential Diary of the S.P., Ranchi, for the week ending 5 March 1921'.
127. Ibid., File nos. 75/1921, 'Sadar S.D.O., Ranchi to D.C. Ranchi, 14.2.21' and 232/1921.
128. Ibid.
129. Freedom Movement Papers SCRO 51, BSA, 'D.C. Ranchi to Commissioner, 9.3.21'.
130. Bihar and Orissa Political Special File no. 50/1921, 'Copy of Ranchi Special Case No. 81 dated 27 February 1921'.
131. Ibid., File no. 50/21, 'Note by the Chaukidari Magistrate of Ranchi showing the attitude of the Tana Bhagats, Commissioner, Ranchi, to Chief Secretary, 6 March 1921'.
132. Ibid.
133. Ibid., 'Commissioner, Ranchi to Chief Secretary, 1 April 1921'.
134. Freedom Movement Papers SCRO 51, BSA, 'Ranchi Commissioner to Chief Secretary, 1 April 1921'.
135. Bihar and Orissa Political Special File no. 75/1921, 'To Deputy Commissioner, Ranchi, from Sadar S.D.O., 14/2/21'.
136. Ibid.
137. Ibid., File no. 50/21, 'Note by the Chaukidari Magistrate of Ranchi showing the attitude of the Tana Bhagats, Commissioner, Ranchi, to Chief Secretary, 6 March 1921'.
138. Ibid.
139. Ibid.
140. Ibid., File no. 50/1921, 'Commissioner, Ranchi, to Chief Secretary, 6 March 1921'.
141. Ibid., 'Extract from the Confidential Diary of the S.P., Ranchi, for the week ending 5 March 1921'.
142. Ibid.
143. Ibid., File nos. 219/1921 and 218/1921.

144. Ibid., File no. 218/1921.
145. Ibid., File no. 219/1921, 'Special Report Case no. 14, Report 2nd, dated 4 May 1921'. This whole paragraph is based on this source.
146. Freedom Movement Papers SCRO 51, BSA.
147. Bihar and Orissa Political Special File no. 50/1921, 'From Deputy Commissioner, Ranchi to Commissioner, 3 February 1921'.
148. Freedom Movement Papers SCRO 51, BSA.
149. Bihar and Orissa Political Special File no. 50/1921.
150. Guha, *Elementary Aspects of Peasant Insurgency*, pp. 1–17.
151. Bihar and Orissa Political Special File no. 50/1921.
152. Ibid., File no. 50/1921; ibid., 75/1921, 'D.C. from M. Hamid, Sadar S.D.O. to D.C., 14.2.21'; Ibid., 50/1921; Freedom Movement Papers SCRO 51, BSA. The entire paragraph is based on this source.
153. Ibid., File no. 50/1921, 'Note of Chaukidari Magistrate Commissioner, Ranchi to Chief Secretary, 6 March 1921'.
154. Ibid.
155. Ibid.
156. Ibid.
157. This section is based on these sources, C.P. Singh, *The Ho Tribe of Singhbhum*, New Delhi: Classical, 1978; Das, *Jharkhand—Castle Over the Graves.*
158. Bihar and Orissa Political Special File no. 478/1921.
159. Ibid.
160. Datta, *Freedom Movement in Bihar,* vol. I, p. 341; J.C. Jha, 'The Bihar Tribal and The Indian National Movement', in *Bihar: Past and Present,* ed. P.N. Ojha, Patna: K.P. Jayaswal Research Institute, 1987, pp. 220–34.
161. Bihar and Orissa Political Special File no. 478/1921, 'From District Magistrate, Singhbhum, to Lyall, Commissioner of the Chotanagpur Division, 2 September 1921'. The rest of the paragraph is based on this source.
162. Ibid., File no. 239/1921, 'Legal Remembrancer to Chief Secretary, 3.6.21'.
163. Ibid., File no. 478/1921, 'From District Magistrate, Singhbhum, to Lyall, Commissioner of the Chotanagpur Division, 2 September 1921'. The rest of this paragraph and the next paragraph are based on this source.
164. Ibid.
165. Ibid.
166. Ibid.
167. Jha, 'The Bihar Tribal and The Indian National Movement', p. 225.
168. Bihar and Orissa Political Special File no. 478/21, 'Judgement—Emperor versus Phulchand Dusadh of Chittimitti under section 108 C.P.C.—District Magistrate, Singhbhum, copy to Commissioner, Chotanagpur Division, 20.9.21'. The rest of the paragraph is based on this source.
169. Guha, *Elementary Aspects of Peasant Insurgency*, pp. 168–73; This has also been highlighted in Kumar's *Rewriting the Language of Politics*, pp. 110–61 and Bhaduri's *Dhorai Charitmanas.*
170. Bihar and Orissa Political Special File no. 478/21, 'Judgement in case Emperor versus Satyabadi Nand under Section 108 Cr.P.C.—copy forwarded to the Chief Secretary from D.I.G. of Police, C.I.D., Bihar and Orissa, 30.11.21'. This paragraph and the next two paragraphs are based on this source.

171. Ibid., 'Judgement—Emperor versus Phulchand Dusadh of Chittimitti under Section 108 C.P.C.—District Magistrate, Singhbhum, copy to Commissioner, Chotanagpur Division, 20.9.21'. This paragraph and the next paragraph are based on this source.
172. Guha, *Elementary Aspects of Peasant Insurgency*, p. 258; Kumar, *Rewriting the Language of Politics*, pp. 81–2.
173. Bihar and Orissa Political Special File no. 478/21, 'District Magistrate to Commissioner, Chotanagpur Division, 2 September 1921'.
174. Ibid.
175. Ibid.
176. Santhal Rebellion of 1855–6 is based on Suchibrata Sen, *The Santals of Jungle Mahal: An Agrarian History, 1973–1861*, Calcutta: Ratna, 1984; N.B. Roy, 'New Aspects of the Santal Insurrection of 1855-6', in *Indian Historical Records Commission Proceedings*, vol. XXXV, part II, February 1960.
177. Kherwar Movement is based on these sources, A.P. Jha, 'Nature of the Santhal Unrest of 1871–75 and Origin of the Sapha Hor Movement', in *Indian Historical Records Commission Proceedings*, vol. XXXV, part II, February 1960; Revd P.O. Bodding, 'The Kherwar Movement Among the Santals', in *Man in India*, vol. I, September 1921.
178. Bihar and Orissa Political Special File no. 643/1921; *Motherland*, 9 June 1922.
179. Bihar and Orissa Political Special File no. 643/1921, 'Letter of District Magistrate to Commissioner, Chotanagpur Division, 19 January 1922'; K.K. Datta Papers, 'Statement of Dr. H.R. Ghosal, Assistant Professor of History, Bihar University, Muzaffarpur, Non-Cooperation Movement at Dumka (1920–21)', Manuscript Section, NMML.
180. Bihar and Orissa Political Special File no. 643/1921; ibid., File no. 86/1922; *Motherland*, 9 June 1922.
181. Bihar and Orissa Political Special File no. 86/1922; ibid., 643/1921; *Motherland*, 9 June 1922.
182. Ibid.; Bihar and Orissa Political Special File no. 86/1922.
183. *Motherland*, 9 June 1922; Bihar and Orissa Political Special File no. 86/1922.
184. Bihar and Orissa Political Special File no. 86/1922, 'Letter of District Magistrate, Santhal Pargana, to Chief Secretary, Government of Bihar and Orissa, 11 April 1922'.
185. Ibid.
186. Tarlo, *Clothing Matters*, p. 100.
187. Prasad, *Autobiography*, pp. 176–7; *Motherland*, 9 June 1922.
188. Ibid.
189. Bihar and Orissa Political Special File no. 86/1922, 'Letter of District Magistrate, Santhal Pargana, to Chief Secretary, Government of Bihar and Orissa, 11 April 1922'; Ibid., File no. 643/1921, 'Letter of District Magistrate to Commissioner, Chotanagpur Division, 19 January 1922'. The rest of the para is based on Bihar and Orissa Political Special File no. 86/1922, 'Letter of District Magistrate, Santhal Pargana, to Chief Secretary, Government of Bihar and Orissa, 11 April 1922'.
190. Bihar and Orissa Political Special File no. 86/1922.

191. Ibid., File no. 643/1921, 'Letter of District Magistrate to Commissioner, Chotanagpur Division, 19 January 1922'.
192. Ibid.
193. Ibid.
194. Ibid.
195. *Motherland*, 9 June 1922; Prasad, *Autobiography*, pp. 176–7.
196. Bihar and Orissa Political Special File no. 86/1922; ibid., 643/1921.
197. Ibid.
198. Ibid., File no. 86/1922.
199. Guha, *Elementary Aspects of Peasant Insurgency*, p. 225.
200. Prasad, *Autobiography*, pp. 176–7; *Motherland*, 9 June 1922; *Proceedings of the Bihar and Orissa Legislative Council*, vol. V, 1922, pp. 940–50.
201. Bihar and Orissa Political Special File no. 85/1922, 'Letter of Deputy Commissioner of Palamau to Commissioner of the Chotanagpur Division, dated 23 January 1922'.
202. Ibid., 'Commissioner, Chotanagpur Division, to Chief Secretary, 8 February 1922, and Letter of Deputy Commissioner, Palamau, to Commissioner, Chotanagpur Division, 4 February 1922'. The entire paragraph is based on this source.
203. Ibid., 'Commissioner, Chotanagpur Division, to Chief Secretary, 8 February 1922, and Letter of Deputy Commissioner, Palamau, to Commissioner, Chotanagpur Division, 4 February 1922'. The entire paragraph is based on this source.
204. Ibid., 'To the Officer Incharge, Manatoo Police Station, from Amarnath, Inspector, 16 February 1922'.
205. Ibid.
206. Ibid., 'From Deputy Commissioner, Palamau to Commissioner, Chotanagpur Division, dated 4 February 1922'.
207. Ibid., 'Letter from Deputy Commissioner, Palamau, to the Commissioner, Chotanagpur Division, 7 February, 1922'.
208. Ibid., 'Fortnightly Confidential Report, From Commissioner, Chotanagpur Division, to Chief Secretary, 26 January 1922'.
209. Ibid., 'From Deputy Commissioner of Palamau to the Chief Secretary, dated 23 January 1922'.
210. Ibid., 'Commissioner, Chotanagpur Division, to the Chief Secretary, dated 5 February, 1922', 'From Deputy Commissioner, Palamau, to Commissioner, Chotanagpur Division, dated 2/3 February 1922'.
211. Ibid.
212. Bihar and Orissa Political Special File no. 85/1922.
213. Ibid., 'From Deputy Commissioner, Palamau, to Chief Secretary, 10 February 1922', 'From Deputy Commissioner, Palamau, to Commissioner, Chotanagpur Division, 2/3 February 1922' and 'From Commissioner, Chotanagpur Division, to Chief Secretary, 5 February 1922'. The rest of this paragraph and the next paragraph are based on this source.

CHAPTER FIVE

Exploring the Margins of Resistance: The Bihar Constabulary, 1920–1922

THIS CHAPTER examines the interface of the subordinate police force—the constables, who formed the bulk of the police force—with the first mass-based national movement, i.e. the Non-Cooperation Movement. The police constituted an important symbol of British authority and power, and served as a metaphor for the colonial regime as a whole. In fact, the modern police had been shaped by the developing needs of the colonial state and reflected its specific requirements. The development of institutions like police demanded total subservience from the subject people in order to maintain law and order, and was also indicative of society rapidly coming under a regime of discipline and surveillance.[1]

This image of the police was largely altered in the 1919–21 phase. In fact, the importance of the Non-Cooperation Movement lay precisely in building up an atmosphere of defiance against British authority. The general disrespect for law and order and contempt for authority during the movement undermined the respect for legal authority, the police, thana and jails—all symbols of British authority. These symbols of authority and terror were transformed into sites where nationalist forces routinely mocked the imperial order. This weakening of the legitimacy or hegemony of the existing order provides clues for an understanding of the impact of certain phases of the nationalist agitation on the lives of the common people. What emboldened the masses was the diminishing fear of British institutions of authority, which gave them a new self-confidence in their ability to successfully defy the government and resist oppression. This erosion of respect for authority became a major concern of the government. The government emphasized that successful administration depended as much on the maintenance of a general atmosphere of obedience to authority and acceptance of the existing order of society, as on the definite enforcement of law or the working of the administrative machinery.

Hence, a significant development of the Non-Cooperation Movement was the extent to which it became a vehicle for the expression of popular hostility against the police, who were frequently defied and attacked. However, a closely related trend visible in the movement was the nationalists trying to befriend the police. The movement succeeded in striking a sympathetic chord amongst the lower rungs of the police force. There were also police protests during the movement. In many places, the subordinate policemen went on strike, demanding better service conditions. How does one view these varied trends during the Non-Cooperation Movement? Why did the nationalists try to befriend the police, regarded as agents of the state? Does it indicate the existence of another identity of the police to which the nationalists made an appeal? Under what conditions did this identity assert itself? Besides, how does one look at the police protest during the Non-Cooperation Movement when their loyalty was most crucial for the government? In fact, why did their protest sharpen during the Non-Co-operation Movement?

Unfortunately, episodes such as police protest have never been a major concern of historians. The study of resistance has largely focused on the development of nationalist challenges to colonial rule and, more recently, on the struggles and insurgencies of subaltern groups. In fact, the lack of such concern gives an impression that the state subordinates were normally very effectively integrated into the structure of the colonial state that was a formidable, autonomous force, when it came to controlling subordinate groups. This study explores some of the imperfect aspects of colonialism in sharp contrast to such claims. The colonial administration was constrained by many complexities, viz., the social organization and cultural traditions, by its own financial stringency, the state subordinate, etc.[2] Moreover, this study highlights how its agendas were constantly stalled and altered by everyday struggles of colonial subjects.

There is a dearth of studies on the relationship between the bureaucracy and the national movement. Some scholars who have examined the last phase of the national movement have focused on the demoralization of the British officials and the changing loyalties of Indian officials. Nevertheless, the references they contain are very general.[3] Moreover, the impression that one gets is that till the 1940s the hegemony of the British over its bureaucracy remained intact. However, it is argued here that during the Non-Cooperation Movement there was a strong feeling in government circles that the lower rungs of the police could not be trusted or relied upon to deal with the national movement.

Further, in most of the available works the focus has been on the very small and exclusive administrative elite, the Indian Civil Services (ICS), the 'heaven-born service' much vaunted as the 'steel frame' of the Raj.[4] The demise of British rule has been directly attributed to the dwindling European recruitment into and progressive Indianization of the ICS.[5] Thus, in these studies, the history of the colonial state has been virtually equated with that of the ICS and there is no discussion of the origins, outlook and careers of the far greater numbers of Indians who occupied the subordinate ranks of the colonial bureaucracy. According to David Arnold, 'in celebrating the ICS, historians have either altogether ignored or relegated to the obscurity of a minor supporting role the many thousands of subordinate state employees without whom there could have been no colonial bureaucracy at all'.[6] His study seeks to correct the elitist bias and balances it by a broader analysis of the economic and political bases of the colonial state. According to him, one can arrive at a greater understanding of the actual character and operation of the colonial state by examining the means by which it recruited and disciplined its subordinate personnel. He also underscores the importance of exploring the relationship between subordinate and dominant groups within the bureaucracy and between state subordinates and various social groups, outside the state structure. Arnold examines some of the more salient ambiguities of the constabulary in a colonial situation.[7]

The significance of David Arnold's pioneering work lies in his highlighting the subordinate base of the colonial bureaucracy. But there are some problems at the theoretical and analytical levels. Two assumptions underpin his arguments: (a) the existence of a 'distinct subaltern identity active within the institutions of state control'; and (b) the subordinated constabulary's 'analogies and parallels with other subaltern groups'. Can one overlook the implications of his arguments? Could there by any meaningful analogies and parallels between subordinated workers of the coercive colonial state apparatus and oppressed subaltern classes, just because the former were the low paid employees of the state?[8] Besides, the main concern of Arnold's work is to highlight the subaltern identity of constabulary and not so much its interface with nationalism and its varied trends, which is the main focus of this study. However, one cannot understand the different trends without taking into account the conditions of the constables.

Locating the Constabulary

The colonial authorities primarily determined how the police department should be structured and staffed, since the police system was an object of colonial discourse and was created to serve colonial needs. It was generally accepted that there could be no large-scale European colonization and settlement in India for a variety of political, social, economic and environmental reasons. European manpower, though valued, would always be scarce and expensive. Its utmost utility was to be obtained, therefore, by freeing it from purely menial and routine servile tasks and assigning to it the responsibility of directing and disciplining the Indians. The belief that Europeans should occupy a supervisory position was further supported by a basic mistrust of Indians and a low perception of their abilities and character, except within a system of European direction and supervision. By ensuring that the Europeans occupied a commanding position the colonial state provided a distinctly racial rationale to the bureaucracy's functional hierarchy.[9]

In this hierarchy the position of the constabulary was one of extreme subordination as it occupied the lowest tier of the extended police hierarchy, subject to the directives and scrutiny of their institutional superiors. The pay of the constables were extremely low. Prior to 1920, their pay ranged from Rs. 6 to Rs. 8. In 1920, their pay was revised to Rs. 11–Rs. 14 scale. However, even this revised scale was very low.[10] Most of the constables were in debt with the exception of those who had some ancestral property and other sources of joint family income. Housing was another problem. There was a shortage of police quarters. Moreover, the residential houses provided in police lines were often cramped: the families lacked privacy as well as space. Despite government promises, constables lived in dilapidated huts. They were even forced to take rooms on rent, often at rates that exceeded departmental allowances.[11] The constables were not happy with their white drill uniforms which became dirty easily and were expensive to clean.[12] In addition to their expenditure on house rent and washermen, they had to meet other expenses like charges for water and scavenging in the police lines, which they considered unfair.[13] Furthermore, their services did not offer any opportunity for promotion. In the initial phase, some of them were promoted to the post of inspectors but later this had been curtailed because of the direct recruitment to the posts of sub-inspectors and inspectors. Even the post of the Station House Officer, formerly the great prize of a constable's career, was entrusted to sub-inspectors. Howsoever impeccable his record, a head constable could not become a sub-inspector. This was equivalent to a downgrading of the constabulary, which thereafter became a dead end in terms of career.[14]

The conditions of employment of constables were also very miserable. They were posted to cholera- and plague-infected areas, where they were exposed to great health risks.[15] Besides, allowances for travel, food and accommodation for those serving away from home were very meagre. Moreover, during the First World War, they were expected to work long hours, perform extra duties, and go without holidays and festival leave.[16] The duties of the lower echelons of the police were menial and purely mechanical in nature requiring no intelligence or judgement. The higher police officials held them and their work in contempt. The general impression of these officials was that their professional association with crime and violence contaminated the constables.[17] These officials also believed that the lower rungs of the police were corrupt, coward, vicious and mean.[18] Corruption among the constables was a major concern of the officials and the declining respect and confidence of the public in the police were attributed to this aspect. This provided the rationale for imposing discipline among them, through a harsh system of departmental punishments, largely in terms of fines and demotions. The parade and drill at the police lines were very tough. However, such measures proved to be counterproductive, driving many constables to quit the police force.[19]

Everyday Resistance

The strong discontentment among the constables over their job conditions took the form of an organized protest in 1921, during the Non-Cooperation Movement, when they went on strike in a number of places. However, even earlier during 'normal' times, they had expressed their antipathy to the nature and terms of their employment in various ways. Of late, many studies have highlighted the importance of focusing on the 'normal or dormant' moment that constitutes the quotidian world of the subordinate. Revolt is considered as an extreme and exceptional pole in the continuum of attitude of subordinate groups. The tendency to focus on periods, when confrontational protest and organized struggles directly and consciously challenge the social order, has frequently allowed two assumptions to reassert themselves: first, relations of power enjoy a rather uncomplicated and unchallenged life until moments of societal upheaval, and second, in 'normal' times, the cultural practices and identities of the dominated remain firmly grounded in a terrain mapped by the dominant. However, social structures rather than being a monolithic autonomous entity, unchallenged except during dramatic instances of revolt, appears more commonly as a constellation of contradictory and contestory processes where power is constantly fractured by the struggles of subordinate groups.[20] Thus, this study has also turned its gaze towards the examination of more enduring, 'everyday' forms of resistance manifested in the behaviours, traditions and consciousness of subordinate police officials.

One form of resistance was the reluctance of the upper caste/class and educated sections to join the police force as constables as long as other work was available, especially in the initial years of the force.[21] Police authorities preferred to recruit constables from among the upper castes/classes which were perceived as respectable, because they believed that would enhance the prestige of the government and strengthen the authority of the colonial police.[22] Official returns emphasized the communal and caste composition of the constables. A close scrutiny of the social base of the constabulary reveals a predominance of Rajputs, Brahmins and Muslims. In 1913, of 238 men recruited by the Principal of the Constable's Training School in different districts of Bihar, 74 were Rajputs or Chattris, 64 Brahmins and 35 Muslims. Perhaps, the social composition reinforced some of the traditions, customs, occupations and self-image of these communities. For the Rajputs, for example, service in the colonial police and army not only appeared to be an appropriate and attractive occupation but also one that reinforced and revitalized their 'old warrior' ascendancy. To the Brahmins, who were preferred for the clerical and bureaucratic aspects of police work, it offered vocation suited to their literacy and traditions of state service. Muslims were preferred in the police force because of the perception that they were 'tough', 'hard-working' and 'courageous', 'beef-eating descendants of the warriors' who had 'conquered the effete, timid, vegetarian Hindus'.

However, a claim to a military tradition or Kshatriya status did not guarantee admission to the force, since the British had their own criteria of eligibility. The police officials did not prefer the low ranking and educationally and economically backward caste and so only a small number from among them were recruited. In fact, the British were not only looking for recruits from only the upper castes but also from the educated, upper classes. However, they were unable to attract and retain such men because of their refusal to pay more than an absolute minimum.

The educated and upper classes did not consider a constable's job honourable and remunerative, particularly before the First World War. It was viewed as a means of staving off unemployment, hunger and poverty.[23] The police officials repeatedly expressed their concern about the unavailability of the 'right stamp' of recruits.[24] 'Quick intelligence, sound physique and education' were considered to be the basic qualities. The officials voiced their concern that the majority of the new recruited constables were far below the desired standards insofar as class, social standing, physique and education were concerned.[25] Besides, it was also believed that the frequent removal or dismissal of policemen on charges of corruption deterred candidates of the 'superior' classes from seeking a career in the force. The officials regretted that these factors 'compelled [them] to take undersized, ignorant, low caste, stupid recruits who they felt did the service no credit'.[26]

The constables expressed their dissatisfaction with the service in other ways as well, i.e. by resigning from their jobs, taking sick leave frequently, performing their duties in slipshod manner that led to their dismissal. Absenteeism was high. Resignations and desertions were also rampant, as, for example, in the districts of Patna, Muzaffarpur, Ranchi and Manbhum.[27] In an attempt to improve the record in this respect, the Lieutenant Governor in

Council introduced a reform which granted local allowances to constables of the armed reserve in 14 districts.[28] Despite this, the situation did not improve.

However, such resistance was generally at an individual level, disorganized and sporadic. There was no concerted effort by the constables to press for higher pay and improved working conditions. Organized police protest was first seen only in 1921; a combination of various factors intensified this protest. After the First World War, the conditions of the police deteriorated further. The end of the war saw acute scarcity conditions and soaring prices. The low paid policemen were among the worst hit. The War also led to an increasing burden of work.[29] Besides, the political and economic conditions of the immediate post-War years gave the constables an unprecedented leverage over their employers. This was also the period when trade unions were formed and labour unrest was on the rise. The railway, post, telegraph and dockyard staff, to mention only a few, were resentful and restless, and were influenced by trade union consciousness.[30]

The constables likened their position similar to that of other poorly paid, ill-housed, over-worked factory hands and municipal workers. This was evident from the constables' petitions and demands drawn up in 1920–21.[31] By 1921, the police subordinates found a collective voice of their own to express their grievances. Till now, in official literature, the police subordinates had appeared merely as statistical and communal categories. However, in 1921, the Police Association was formed and its objectives were to improve, by all legitimate means, the pay, status, conditions of service and morale of its members, to create and foster an esprit de corps amongst the members, to deal with issues affecting the general interests of its members and to safeguard them.[32] It is important not to overlook the context of nationalism in fomenting police protest. Many nationalists in Bihar evinced a keen interest in the problems of police subordinates.[33] The ongoing national movement emboldened the constables as their protests could not be easily isolated and suppressed. It may be surmised that the constables participated in the collective protest confidently because they knew that they had the support of a larger movement and a well-developed nationalist organization. The impression that the government was too afraid and weak to do anything at that time further encouraged them.

Stages and Forms of Protest

Discontentment among the constables was evident from November 1920 onwards in most of the districts, even though there was no concerted action. Initially, the constables made submissions orally and in writing to the District

Superintendents of Police, with a plea that these be forwarded to the Inspector General of Police and the government. They demanded a pay scale revision of Rs. 25–Rs. 40 scale. They even asked the government to provide them food and clothing. They drew attention to their housing problems and demanded casual and medical leave.[34] Senior police officials did not regard these constables as agitators but merely supplicants because they found them to be 'polite, nay docile, in their speech and behaviour throughout'.[35] The concern of the government to determine whether the constables were mere petitioners or agitators is evident throughout the protest. Their language of protest was couched in deference and loyalty to the government and made them appear as petitioners.[36]

However, the constables' petitions went unheeded and they were forced to protest by resorting to strikes. The first reference to rumours about the possibility of mass resignations appears in a confidential letter written by the Superintendent of Police, Hazaribagh, dated 28 December 1920, and addressed to the Assistant Inspector General of Police. The letter reads, '42 more memorials have been received and are being forwarded. There is a wide spread rumour that Ranchi constables have given an ultimatum that they will resign their posts and go in for a strike, if their pay is not increased by January 1921'.[37] Till December 1920, the constables had not taken any collective decision regarding the strike and mass resignations.[38]

By January 1921, the policemen became more organized and began to communicate with each other, both within and outside their districts.[39] The initial organized meetings of constables were held in Patna, Chapra and Arrah on 2 January 1921.[40] In Patna, the meeting was held at the *diara* to ensure privacy and it was attended by 400 constables. A Mahavir Jhanda was planted at the site of the meeting. This site had a sacred significance as the oath taken between the two streams of the Ganga and in front of a Mahavir Jhanda became a solemn vow for the Hindus. The constables also referred to cow touching in that meeting to lend further sanctity to the oath. A resolution was passed demanding Rs. 30 per month pay hike. They declared that if their demands were not met by 5 March, they would submit their resignations. The resolution was to be followed up by a detailed petition from the constables to the higher authorities. Representatives from Saran, Gaya and Shahabad districts also attended this meeting. After this *patias* (letters) were sent to many districts recommending similar action.

The Patna meeting clearly revealed that the constables had moved on from the stage of petitioning and had begun to assert their right to protest. At the meeting, they took an oath that, if the authorities punished any of them for attending the meeting or for demanding an increase in pay, they were duty-bound to help such men and protest collectively.[41] A week later, meeting of head constables and constables was held in Gaya, on the banks of the river Phalgu. Writer head constable, Damodar Prasad, presided over the meeting.[42] After the meeting, a group of writer head constables led by Damodar Prasad, Ali Habib, Ram Balak Ram and Mohammad Bashir called on the Superintendent of Police of Gaya, Lloyd Williams, with as many as 300 signed petitions. They were determined that if their demands were not considered they would resort to strike.[43]

A common theme in all the petitions and resolutions was the constables' demand for a 'living wage'. They considered the 1920 revised pay scale (Rs.11–Rs.14) too low. They argued that when it cost Rs.14 to Rs.15 per month to feed one man, the revised pay did not make provision for their families. They added that even the postal peons and the railway khalasis (peons), who were not full-time government servants, drew Rs.18 and Rs.20 per month, respectively. Highlighting their housing problems, they pointed out that they were forced to maintain two establishments as they were not provided accommodation for the family at the place of their posting. Sharing a mess with other constables could have been a cheaper option but the men of the District Armed Police and the Ordinary Reserves available in the police lines insisted on separate caste- and community-based kitchens. They complained that they did not get leave to spend time with their families and they also demanded medical and casual leave. They wanted the government to provide them food and clothing at cheap rates and restore the grain compensation allowance. They even urged a reduction in the period of mobilization and non-recovery of hospital diet from pay. They demanded a pay scale ranging from Rs. 25 to Rs. 40 a month and daily allowance ranging from 8 to 12 *annas* (50–75 paise).[44] Thus, they fought for certain basic demands and sought redressal for specific grievances over pay, housing and other service conditions. They did not contest the institutional subordination or the nature of departmental discipline. But their threat to go on strike during the nationalist agitation, when their support was very crucial to the government, was not looked upon favourably by the government. The Inspector General of Police, with a force far below the sanctioned strength, needed every constable on duty. The Congress under Gandhi's leadership launched the campaign of non-cooperation that included a call for resignation of Indians from the army and police.[45] Alarmed at the prospect of widespread 'disaffection' among the police, the Bihar government saw the necessity of conceding some of the constables' demands. Emphasizing the urgency of the situation, the Chief Secretary sent a letter to the Government of India that 'it was imperative, however, that whatever further increase might be granted should be given at the earliest possible moment'.[46]

Thus, the constables' threat to go on strike at the time when the Non-Cooperation Movement had gathered momentum forced on the government a novel appreciation of the political importance of maintaining the loyalty and morale of the constabulary by attending to some of its material needs. Previously their demands had been virtually ignored by the government. They were given an extremely low priority in government expenditure. Economizing on the constable's pay was an easy way of curtailing the state expenditure. As long as there were enough constables to do the job, there was little inducement to face the consequences of state parsimony. It was only in moments of a political crisis, i.e. when the government was confronted with the Non-Cooperation Movement, that it was forced to recognize the grievances and make some concessions to ensure the continuing obedience of its subordinate employees. A new scale of pay—Rs. 15 to Rs. 20—was sanctioned in January 1921.[47] Thus, the government only partially considered the constables' demand for an increase in salary. The other demands were not even considered.[48] The constables were not happy with the new pay scale. They were determined to struggle and they were not intimidated by the government's warning. The Superintendent of Police of Purnea attributed many reasons behind the determination of the constables to go on protest. According to him, the apparent finality of the recent orders led the constables to believe that they had no more hope. Besides this, he said that a large number of constables were persuaded to join because the petitions and constitutional methods had failed and the other methods proposed could only be successful if every constable joined the protest. He also pointed out that there was a general impression amongst the constables that government was too weak and afraid to do anything. Besides, there was a strong belief amongst the constables that the government was willing to give them Rs. 30 but the orders sanctioning it had been withheld by the Inspector General. The Purnea Police Superintendent had a strong belief that the non-cooperators were behind fomenting unrest amongst the constables.[49]

Though the government sanctioned a new scale of pay for the constables, it was not prepared to accept their threat to go on strike as it was read as a sign of defiance. It wanted to bring home to the policemen that their defiance would not be taken lightly. Immediately after announcing the new pay scale in January 1921, the Inspector General of Police instructed the Superintendents of Police of different districts that each constable, who sent the memorial, should be asked to confirm or deny having submitted the memorial. If the constable admitted that he did so, he should be told that if he still desired to resign, he would be discharged from the force, and if he preferred to withdraw his resignation, he could do so provided he apologized for the breach of discipline. The constable was also to be informed that if he resigned, he would not, on any account, be allowed to re-enter the service.[50]

The Superintendent of Police of Purnea circulated an order stating that the constables' decision to go on strike was tantamount to being disloyal to the government and through such action they would lay themselves open to prosecution which would even mean their exclusion from government service for all times. He also reminded them that they were government servants and were not entitled to resign from service without giving two months' notice. The constables were determined to hand in their kits, i.e. their duty charge on 5 March. In fact, they took this decision after fully considering the consequences of the order of the Superintendent of Police.[51]

The constables of Gaya went on strike on 8 February. The strike also spread to a few police stations in the interior of the district.[52] Around 170 constables and a head constable submitted their resignations as a mark of protest.[53] The Superintendent of Police of Gaya claimed that non-cooperators were behind this agitation.[54]

The constables of Patna, Purnea, Monghyr and Champaran went on strike on 5 March. They deposited their kits and refused to take their discharge certificates.[55] In Patna, 235 constables and in Champaran, 33 men of the armed police deposited their kits. In Monghyr, 20 constables were prepared to deposit their kits but eventually reconsidered their decision.[56] In Purnea, 77 men deposited their kits.[57] The date fixed for the strike, i.e. 5 March was a day when, the railway employees and jail wardens had also decided to go on a strike. There was organized planning behind this move.[58] Secret communication links were established for intra- and inter-district coordination. Some letters and telegrams intercepted by the government revealed the use of code words.[59] The Superintendent of Police of Purnea received information that the constables in Bahadurganj and Rupauli were secretly corresponding and planning to go on strike from 5 March. On 25 February, the constables in Katihar even recorded an entry in the station diary to this effect. When the information that the policemen of Gaya, Patna and Muzaffarpur were organizing a strike reached Purnea, it strengthened the resolve of the constables in Purnea to go on a strike too.[60] In fact, it was the wide support that gave confidence to the constables to go on strike.

The senior police officials were sympathetic to the constables' demands. They realized that even with the new pay scale the constables would not be able to maintain their families and so would be forced to resort to underhand means. Despite their sympathy, they strongly objected to their method of protest. Strikes were perceived as open defiance of and contempt for the government, a breach of discipline, a deliberate attack on authority, a sign of disloyalty, and a symptom of a possible insurrection and subversive behaviour.[61] It was also apprehended that the strike by policemen—regarded as an important pillar of the government—during the national movement, would be interpreted by the people as indication of weakening and crumbling of the government. Senior police officials decided to take strong action against them.

The Inspector General of Police sent a circular to the Superintendents of Police of different districts stating that the policemen's 'conduct has amounted to a public scandal and that they have publicly shown contempt for authority, disgraced themselves, their officers and the police generally'.[62] The circular further stated that any application for reconsideration of the order of dismissal should be accompanied by an act of genuine contrition. In Patna, the constables who participated in the strike were dismissed.[63] On the other hand, in Purnea the Superintendent of Police allowed the constables to resume duty unconditionally but he was reprimanded by the Inspector General of Police for encouraging breach of discipline.

The Superintendent of Police of Purnea justified his action for allowing the constables to resume duty without giving them punishment. He said that the constables did not have the intention to tender their resignations either in writing or verbally, but had deposited their kits merely to draw attention to their grievances. According to him, the constables only wanted to strike but when told that to do so was tantamount to resigning and once the realization came to them that a temporary strike was out of the question for them, the battle for the government was over. The Police Superintendent further said that it would not have been in the best interest of government to have forced an issue before the true issue had time to sink into the constables' minds. According to him, the constables 'were sound at heart' and had taken such steps because they were in a state of exaltation, ready for martyrdom, and later realized their foolishness. He further said that amongst the constables were a large number with excellent records and long service, and that is why he took great pains to make the constables see the error of their ways. For him it would have been a great catastrophe that constables with many years of excellent service should be lost to the government and their future irretrievably ruined through their one day's 'foolishness' and a mistaken sense of loyalty to their comrades. The Police Superintendent further said that if he had treated the constables with less patience and sincerity, they would have marched off in body and that the discharge of the whole force would have created troubles in other districts also.[64]

The District Magistrate of Purnea did not agree with the rationale provided by the Superintendent of Police that the constables had not resigned on 5 March. According to him, their leaving duty without permission and depositing their kits was tantamount to resigning.[65] Thus one can see that the issue of loyalty was at the core of senior police officials' concern. Even in Purnea, where the Superintendent of Police succeeded in persuading the constables to withdraw their resignation, an appeal was made to their sense of loyalty to the government.[66]

How should such resistance of the police force be viewed? If one examines their demands, one finds that they fought for certain basic issues and did not contest institutional subordination. They believed that all their actions were consistent with an attitude of deference to the colonial rulers and loyalty to the Empire. The Superintendent of Police of Purnea maintained that the constables had not shown any sign of insubordinate spirit but throughout had been respectful and disciplined. According to him, they endeavoured all along to make the point that their intention of depositing their kits was merely to call attention to their grievances. They had not come to give resignations and none was prepared to put in a written resignation. The police official further said that the constables vouched that they were ready to give their lives for [the] government but were merely asking for a living wage.[67]

Thus, rarely did the constables seek in their resistance a more abstract liberation by which they posed a direct challenge to the dominant ideology of the state. Their resistance generally constituted 'contests within hegemony', i.e. struggles whose claims to justice were grounded in the dominant group's principles and moral categories.[68] Despite this, even such resistance was significant because it is the context and the consequences that render certain actions contestory. Seemingly innocuous behaviour and commonplace actions, within the bounds of legality or legitimate expressions, can have unintended yet profound consequences for the objectives of the dominant social order. In the context of the constables' protest, what was of great significance was their assertion to voice their demands and that too, at a time when the government had to deal with the national movement and when their support would have been very crucial for the government. This shook the government as the police was primarily seen as one of its main pillars of support. To confine the understanding of resistance to its more traditional sense would mean not to consider the very processes by which power is often tested and eroded by the actions of the subordinate sections in society.

Police Protest: Context of the Non-Cooperation Movement

Policemen went on strike for the first time. It was not easy for them, being an important pillar of British authority, to go on strike, and that too, at a time when the government needed their support most. Why did the police protest sharpen during the Non-Cooperation Movement? The police officials account highlighted the significance of the context of the Non-Cooperation Movement in fomenting police unrest. The note of the Deputy Inspector

General of Police to Chief Secretary, dated 4 March 1921, revealing the extent to which unrest among the police was fomented by the non-cooperators, read: 'even though the main cause of police unrest was economic, the general excitement and unrest created by the Non-Cooperation agitation had done a good deal to render the discontent more acute'.[69] The note further pointed out that the 'police unrest on the question of pay had been fomented by non-cooperation agitators working in the background in the same manner in which similar unrest has been stirred up in labour areas throughout the province'. It added that 'some of the constables, who had been taking active part in the agitation, had been secretly in sympathy with the Non-Cooperation Movement'.

The constables and non-cooperators were in communication with each other, and the latter took an interest in the constables' problems, supporting their agitation and urging them to join the national movement. Many non-cooperators attended the constables' meeting held in the *diara* in Patna on 2 January 1921. Pandit Jewanand, a non-cooperator, addressed this meeting. In the meeting of the head constables in Patna on 9 January 1921, Tulsi Singh, a noted non-cooperator, played an active role. Some Muslim constables of Patna approached Mazharul Haq and other nationalist leaders 'for advice as to their course of action before and after the meeting held on the diara'. In Gaya, writer head constable, Damodar Prasad (who had been dismissed) and others were in contact with Congress leaders like Krishna Prakash Sen Sinha. On his return from Patna, Damodar Prasad stayed with Rai Hari Prasad, one of the non-cooperation leaders from Gaya. Many non-cooperators joined Damodar Prasad to convince the constables to resign. They carried out their propaganda work amongst the police at night. In Champaran, some constables of the Motihari Reserve were in contact with the local non-cooperation leaders. They visited these leaders at night. According to the Superintendents of Police of both Darbhanga and Purnea, 'in the background of the agitation were non-cooperators'. The Champaran police official reported that in his district the 'Purbia members of the Mounted Military Police, who mostly came from Chapra, Shahabad, Ballia, Ghaziapur and neighbouring districts, were sympathetic to the Non-Cooperation Movement'.

Why did the nationalists show an interest in police problems? This can be better understood in the context of the broader aims of nationalist policy. The nationalists wanted to establish their hegemony over what had hitherto been an emphatically colonial bureaucracy. They wanted to win over the support of the subordinate bureaucracy so as to isolate the colonial regime.[70] Hence, they looked for opportunities to interpose themselves between the colonial state and the subordinate police.[71] The Congress, at its special session in Calcutta in September 1920, adopted a programme of non-cooperation which also included a call to Indians to withdraw from the police and army. This gave impetus to the attempts of the nationalists to gain a hold over the subordinate police.[72] In December 1920, the Nagpur Session of the Indian National Congress ratified the non-cooperation decision and made an appeal to the police and army, saying that the Congress recognized the growing friendliness between the police and soldiers and the people, and hoped that the former would refuse to subordinate their creed and country to the fulfilment of orders of their officers. It further hoped that the police and soldiers by courteous and considerate behaviour towards the people would remove the reproach levelled against them that they were devoid of any regard for the feelings and sentiments of their own people.[73]

In Bihar, the nationalists empathized with policemen, especially the subordinate ranks, as fellow Indians even prior to the launching of the Non-Cooperation Movement. As early as March 1920, the Bihar Special Branch came across an anonymous letter addressed to the sub-inspector of Bankipore (Patna) Police Station. Similar letters were received in other districts.[74] The letter made an appeal to all Hindu and Muslim constables, chaukidars, daffadars, head constables, sub-inspectors and inspectors that the time was not to sit quietly but to weep and mourn. Addressing the Hindus as brothers the letter further said that the government was trying to do *zulum* in connection with the religious concern of their Muslim brothers and when government was presently interfering with the Muslims they would be sure to do *zulum* against the Hindus later. So the Hindus should stand by their Muslim brothers and help with their property, strength, life, swords and guns without fear as both Hindus and Muslims belonged to the Indian Army. Since the Hindus had guns, they should always be present to help the Muslims. Finally, the letter derided the police, saying that do they want always to remain slaves and have their heads beaten with shoes. The letter was to be sent to every District Police Office.[75]

When the Khilafat Movement intensified in 1920, the government was apprehensive that it may be exploited to create 'disaffection' among the army and police personnel, particularly Muslims. The Government of India addressed a secret D.O. letter to the Provincial governments on 12 June 1920 which, inter alia, stated that it had information that efforts had been, or shortly would be, made to organize Khilafat or anti-government propaganda in rural areas amongst the sepoys and police constables, while they were at their homes on leave, and to foment 'disaffection' amongst the classes from which the army and police were primarily recruited. The Government of India wanted all efforts to be made by the provincial governments to ascertain whether such propaganda was carried and to bring to trial those who were conducting or instigating it.[76]

Nationalist involvement in the issues of the subordinate police intensified during the Non-Cooperation Movement. Some leaders in Bihar wanted to use the opportunity of discontentment amongst the constables to draw them into the movement. They expressed concern over the dismal conditions of work and the low wages of constables. Deep Narayan Singh, a leader of the Non-Cooperation Movement from Bhagalpur, while addressing a meeting in February 1921, urged the nationalists to take advantage of police discontentment to increase their influence among them.[77]

While addressing meetings in different parts of Bihar, some nationalist leaders reiterated that the final phase of the Non-Cooperation Movement would be the withdrawal of the police and military from government service. They expressed the hope that policemen would eventually resign from the service and join the movement.[78] At a public meeting held in Patna on 6 January 1921, Muhammad Ali said, 'if the parents removed their children from schools and people gave up drink, then the police and sepoys would also eventually leave their barracks'.[79] At another meeting held at Jharia on 5 February, Muhammad Ali reiterated that 'the day schools got vacated, on the very next day the police and army would also leave their service'.[80] Speaking at Jharia on 20 February, J.L. Banarji, a nationalist leader, argued that the main support to the British government was provided by the Indian police, army and magistrates, and once Indians withdrew their support the government would be paralysed.[81] At another meeting held in February, Chandra Bansi Sahay said that 'the nationalist leaders were now busy in the spread of the movement amongst the students and in the opening of national schools for them. As soon as this task was complete, the nationalists would focus their attention on the police and army, for which task they were making some provisions'.[82]

Leaflets carrying an appeal to the police to join the movement were distributed by the local nationalists.[83] According to the nationalists, it was the moral duty of Indian policemen to free themselves from service under the British and their slavery and to identify with the cause of national freedom. They firmly believed that nationalism commanded a loyalty superior to that of the colonial state. Policemen were severely reprimanded for betraying their motherland and countrymen. One such pamphlet, 'Police Bhaion se Namr Nivedan' highlights how on one hand police were addressed as brothers to serve the country and on the other hand they were derided for their deeds. It reprimanded them for having taken the path of sin, fallen in love with slavery and 'sucking the blood of their own brothers', for their sycophancy and dishonesty. It rebuked them by saying: how deliverance of India was expected from them but they let down the name of their nation. It appealed to them to give up the path of sin, saying that when the whole country was sacrificing its life for Desh raj, they should also lend their help. It asked them to give up looting and regard Gandhi as a true rishi (saint) and remove the handcuffs from India's hands. It said that if they followed good path their progeny would be happy.[84]

In another pamphlet, 'Sipahiya', the policemen, while being addressed as brothers, were portrayed as brutal and strongly condemned for killing and torturing their own countrymen. They were exhorted in the name of religion not to commit atrocities against their own countrymen, to resign from their service, which had enslaved them, and to serve their country.[85] They were rebuked for firing shots and killing their own people and imposing *challans* on their own brothers for small matters. It said that all such torture by them was perpetrated for the sake of bread and when that service merely gave them a salary of Rs. 5 or Rs. 10. They were requested to go back to their homes and maintain their children by taking to agriculture.[86]

Such appeals to the police alarmed the government as it feared that the national movement would influence the police force. To estimate the extent to which the national movement had influenced the police force, the Inspector General of Police instructed the Superintendents of Police of different districts to report on the attitude of the police towards the Non-Cooperation Movement. All of them were of the view that the higher ranks of police officials were loyal to the government and were opposed to the movement.[87] But, they were not so confident about the loyalty of the lower ranks such as sub-inspectors and writer head constables. According to Superintendent of Police of Purnea, some of his sub-inspectors and writer head constables were disloyal. The Superintendent of Police of Monghyr estimated that 20 per cent of his sub-inspectors were not only disloyal but also sympathetic to the movement, 20 per cent were absolutely loyal and the remaining 60 per cent were neutral. He also added that a number of sub-inspectors in the Jamalpur subdivision sympathized with the movement. The Superintendent of Police of Darbhanga did not trust his Muslim officers, whom he described as 'fanatical' on the Khilafat question. Some of the Muslim officers, according to him, secretly sympathized with the non-cooperation propaganda because they wanted the Turkish Peace Treaty to be amended. The Superintendent of Police of Muzaffarpur reported that a number of sub-inspectors and writer head constables 'were sitting on the fence and some of them even visited extremist leaders'.

However, all the Superintendents of Police categorically pointed out that the lowest echelons in the police force were not trustworthy; the constables were not as dependable as in the pre-War period. They added that 'the constables revered Gandhi and looked upon him as a divinity'. As far as the Armed Police was concerned, they pointed out that there was loyalty in those districts where the Armed Police comprised tribals but not where the Armed Police consisted of 'Biharis'. The Superintendent of Police of Monghyr reported that two months ago he would have answered that members of the Armed Police were unreliable and that if ordered to 'fire on a mob with the shout of Gandhi on their lips, they might have refused'. But he believed that the situation had improved since then. However, the Superintendent of Police of Muzaffarpur was not confident about the loyalty of the Armed Police in his district. His idea was that 'under circumstances such as rioting his men would not disobey an order to fire but he said that if they were called on to answer the call of duty or the call of the nation, they would refuse'.

In July 1921, a new challenge faced the government. Muhammad Ali, at the All India Khilafat Conference held at Karachi on 8 July, declared that it was 'religiously unlawful for the Muslims to continue in the British army' and instructed that his message be conveyed to every Muslim in the army. Consequently, Muhammad Ali and some other leaders were immediately arrested. In protest, the speech was repeated at innumerable meetings all over the country. On 4 October, 47 leading Congressmen, including Gandhi, issued a manifesto repeating whatever Muhammed Ali had said and added that every civilian and member of the armed forces should sever connections with the repressive government. This made the government doubt the loyalty of the police as well.[88] Besides, the fatwa issued by the Ulema on the Khilafat question deepened the feelings of animosity among the police force all over the country.[89] Secret meetings held between the non-cooperators and policemen and between the policemen themselves were reported from many districts of Bihar.[90] Many Muslim constables resigned on the grounds that their religious convictions prohibited them from serving the government. They added that to serve in the police was haram. Writer head constable, Ishwari Prasad of the Hazaribagh Sadar Court, resigned and was appointed Tehsildar of the *muthia* on behalf of the Khilafat Committee. Constable Abdul Ghaffar of Darbhanga district resigned, saying that the Maulana influenced him to leave government service.

A police officer reported that the 'Calcutta Police comprising a large number of constables from Bihar and U.P. were stirred up by upcountry agitators, especially by the receipt of letters from their homes telling them to resign from service, otherwise, their families would be put to shame'. Towards the end of November 1921, the Bihar Special Branch received information that 11 discharged constables of the Calcutta Police would visit Patna to prevail upon the local officers and men to resign from the force.

A number of rumours were floating. One such rumour was that the court sub-inspector of Jamui in Monghyr district and several other Muslims met at the house of a Muslim *mukhtar* 'to weep and wail their sorrow on the arrest of the Ali Brothers'. A strong rumour in Tirhut Division was that 55 Muslim constables of Saharanpur district had resigned and others would follow suit. Another rumour was that a deputation of ten men, each from Raghunathpur and Siwan in Saran district, would press upon the local sub-inspectors to resign or else face social boycott.

In Jamui and Jamalpur, both in Monghyr district, appeals were made to the police to resign in response to Mahatma Gandhi's call. An inspector in Monghyr made an attempt to spread non-cooperation amongst the police. In Kharagpur, a Muslim sub-inspector stated on one occasion that it was unfortunate that Indians in the police had to report the speeches of those who worked for the good of the country to the higher police officials. In Monghyr, police were vacillating, whether they should resign following the example of the Calcutta men. A constable of Jamalpur outpost was found wearing a Gandhi cap and later submitted his resignation. In Jamalpur town, there was a move amongst the Muslim constables to resign in a body but it did not materialize. A head constable of the Champaran District Armed Police admitted before his superintendent that he was upset and could not decide how to react to the situation. At a meeting in Muzaffarpur, an appeal was made to all Muslims to resign from government service. Following this, two constables resigned. The Deputy Commissioner of Hazaribagh expressed concern as to how the Non-Cooperation Movement had impacted the police in Chatra where one sub-inspector and six constables had resigned. In Giridih, too, police constables resigned. Many constables applied for three to four months' leave. In Ranchi, a writer head constable resigned. His son was very active in the Non-Cooperation Movement. Around 50 constables in Bihar submitted their resignations. Muzaffarpur and Monghyr districts topped the list of resignations.

Thus, the Non-Cooperation Movement struck a sympathetic chord amongst the lower rungs of the police force. The government was apprehensive about the efforts made by the nationalists to establish moral and political ascendancy over the police. Despite the government's apprehension, the threatened collapse of police morale did not materialize and the colonial state was able to retain effective control over the police.[91] Nevertheless, one cannot overlook the symbolic importance of police resignations. The movement partially succeeded in neutralizing the lower echelons of the police force. The British could not even play one religious community of police against the other because Khilafat issue brought a large number of Muslims into the movement.

The nationalists' appeals to the police force, the striking of a sympathetic chord among the lower sections and the resignation of constables would compel one to rethink about their 'other' identity. Thus, this study questions the way the police have been located as agents of the state and as embodiments of state power. This study delineates how this identity of the police obscures more than it illuminates, since it excludes alternative, possibly intersecting, identities and relationships. As emphasized, one cannot view the police only in terms of dichotomies such as 'friend' or 'enemy' of the colonial regime or in terms of 'loyalty' or 'disloyalty'. At certain historical junctures, state subordinates discard their allegiance to the state in order to associate with the people and their movement. In spite of their outward appearance, such shifts cannot be seen as abrupt or spontaneous. They should perhaps be interpreted as indicative of the existence of a distinct identity normally submerged but at times clearly visible.

The subordinates could not be reduced to a mere mechanized and dehumanized agent of colonial control. Despite their training and duties, they remained a part of society with strong social ties and affinities. The off-duty constables were engaged day-to-day in the social and cultural life of the community around them. These lateral ties and affinities often inhibited or negated institutional subordination and the efficiency of the colonial police. Even the very nature of police work as conceived by the British precluded the total isolation of the constabulary from the public. There were many duties that brought policemen, singly or in small groups, into direct contact with the people. Even when they lived in the police lines with their families, an important link with the outside world was maintained. Colonialism could not sever this relationship.

The constabulary was not that effectively disciplined, supervised and isolated from external influence as to be entirely subordinate to colonial control. Moreover, the British neither had the capacity nor the inclination to enforce a more vigorous system of control over the rank and file of the police. They were not prepared to allocate the funds necessary to accommodate all the subordinates in the police lines, where they could be kept under closer supervision. Nor was the government prepared to pay higher wages to attract and retain the kind of policemen it wanted, or to free them from the temptation of petty corruption.

Besides, the ideological integration of the constables with the colonial regime was not that very strong. By virtue of their background, education and limited contact with Europeans even within the force, constables were hardly ideologically integrated with the western culture. During the early years of the force, constabulary training received little attention. Recruits were given no more than a rudimentary introduction to their duties at the district headquarters before they were sent to their stations. Following the recommendation of the Police Commission of 1902–3, the government sanctioned the establishment of training schools to impart a more thorough and specialized training to the newly enlisted constables. During their six months recruits at training schools they were primarily instructed in the law and departmental procedures, besides concentrating on physical training and arms drill. But in this training ideological thrust was not very important.[92] In this respect, the colonial state had only limited expectations of its police subordinates. It had a low opinion of their mental capacities. Besides, unquestioned loyalty could not be expected from this section of police force, as it has already been discussed how subordinate their position was and how much discontented and dissatisfied they were with their service conditions. Many constables entered the service on little more than a labourer's wage not because they subscribed to the objectives of the colonial state but because many of them could not find alternative or more remunerative employment.

The 'Other Side': The Non-Cooperation Movement and Popular Hostility Against the Police

In this section the intense animosity against the police will be discussed. Deep-seated anger and hostility against the police were strong undercurrents of the national movement. Even though hostility against the police had been simmering for a long time, it was only during the Non-Cooperation Movement that criticism against the police became more sharp and sustained. The prevailing mood created by the Non-Cooperation Movement was one of defiance and strong contempt of colonial authority. The local police were the most visible representatives of state authority, standing at the critical point of intersection between the state and the people. They were among the few agents of the state with whom the masses had direct contact. Through the police, the priorities and principles of the colonial administration were institutionalized and enacted. The executive authority of the state was channelled through them. The role of the police was not restricted to that laid down by the lawmakers. Police power was often used to circumvent or supplement the legal process for the sake of prompt retribution and collective punishment. The more resolutely colonial control was challenged, the greater the willingness of the colonial authorities to authorize police action that went beyond both the letter and the spirit of the law. Police action represented the arbitrary and cruel nature of colonial rule and its unaccountability to Indian people. The lathi-wielding policemen beating a defenceless satyagrahi became an emotive symbol of India's freedom struggle. That it was usually an Indian constable who flogged the satyagrahi under the direction of an European officer made the role of the police appear both divisive and brutal.[93]

Besides, regarding the police as the coercive agent of the state, the general public also took an intense dislike to them because of their unlicensed petty tyranny and corruption. Their persistent *zulum* and everyday oppression alienated them from the people. Though the constables were low-paid and had many similarities with the masses yet their role as police clearly set them apart from the masses. Policemen were aware of their superior power and status which they derived from their official position and used it to extort bribes and favours from anyone who was too weak to resist their demands.[94]

In most instances, constables revered men of wealth and power: they protected the interests of the landlords, wealthy peasants and village heads against the poor and the weak. This can be explained on the grounds that most of the constables belonged to the locally dominant communities of the village.[95] The subordinate police, even though cast in a colonial mould as servants of the colonial state, were most often absorbed into the pre-colonial pattern of subordination of peons and retainers to feudal landlords and rajas. They assisted the landlords in collecting rent from refractory tenants. The police in Bihar generally protected the interests of the planters against their tenants. They assisted the Darbhanga raj in containing the peasant agitation in 1919–20. [96] Whenever the police came to investigate any case in the villages, they sided with the planters and their *amlas* against the villagers. For example, the policemen, who had come to investigate a case in a village in Dhanaha in Champaran, where the mounted troopers were accused of looting in December 1921, sided with the planters and their *amlas* against the villagers.[97] Similarly, the policemen who investigated the 1921 riots in Sonbarsa and Chauterwa in 1921, supported the planters.[98] Thus, the subordinate policemen, who rose from the peasantry to a position of power, instead of showing solidarity with the peasants, exploited them.

It is in this context one can understand the frequent anti-police riots, arising out of the anger caused by police activities or their execution of government's unpopular policies. It was the high-handedness and *zulum* of policemen that often transformed a dispute from a minor fight into a violent confrontation with the police. There are innumerable such examples. On 10 February 1922, at the Tarhasi haat in Palamau district, the police, who were attempting to check the picketing of an outstill, were assaulted by a large crowd and had to flee for their lives.[99] Several other cases were reported from Muzaffarpur and Hazaribagh where the police were either resisted or assaulted while attempting to execute distress warrants.[100] In Rupauli, the police were openly defied by one of the parties in a land dispute in January 1921.[101] There was a confrontation with the police in Kateya in Saran district in February 1922 where the police were investigating a case in which it was alleged that the non-cooperation panchayat had treated a Koeri woman unjustly and cruelly. While the police were interviewing witnesses, a large crowd shouting *Gandhi ki jai* arrived armed with sticks, lathis and spears. They ordered the policemen and chaukidars to kneel down and proclaim their acceptance of swaraj by shouting *Gandhi ki jai*. When the police refused, the crowd showered them with clods of earth and attacked them with lathis, forcing them to retreat.[102]

The police station which had emerged as a site of coercive colonial state was often besieged and picketed. In December 1921, 200 men attacked the Sonbarsa thana in Muzaffarpur district. They had been encouraged by the All India Congress Committee's announcement of 4 November that non-cooperation had reached a stage at which its climatic phase of full civil disobedience could be launched in selected and carefully prepared areas. After attacking the police station, the non-cooperators demanded that the police relinquish control and resign from government service because their continuing in service was tantamount to Hindus eating beef and Muslims eating pork.[103] On 23 December 1921, 100 Sevak Dal volunteers paraded in front of the Hajipur Police Station hurling abuses at the police and shouting slogans like *sarkar ki nokri karni haram hai.*[104]

Often the attempt to rescue non-cooperators imprisoned in police custody resulted into violent confrontations between the police and the masses. At such times, it was in opposition to the police that the masses defied authority. For instance, on 5 February 1922 in Araria thana in Purnea, some policemen and chaukidars arrested three picketers for assaulting and robbing a liquor shop customer. The police station was then attacked by a mob of a thousand people shouting slogans in support of non-cooperation. The crowd thrashed the policemen forcing them to release the prisoners.[105] In another incident in Dhanaha in January 1922, the police could arrest some persons accused of demolishing the cattle pound only with much difficulty, amidst hostile demonstration. Hence, a strong hatred developed against the police.[106] People refused to report crimes to the police in Bagaha in Champaran district. Police officials touring Purnea found it difficult to get any accommodation.[107]

During their conflicts with the police, masses often stripped off the latter's uniforms, which were paraded by them or even burnt. Their *pugris* were also pulled off and thrown away.[108] There were several such incidents. For example, one of the shopkeepers, Bhokari Koer, of Bagajan Bazaar in Damgara had a dispute with a constable. The constable had forcibly taken away a few sweet potatoes from the shopkeeper, and when he was asked to pay for them, he thrashed the shopkeeper. Following this, a large crowd surrounded the constable and snatched his *pugri* shouting what was the use of any constables and chaukidars when swaraj had been obtained.[109] The red turban was particularly offensive to the people. An extract from the pamphlet 'Policewa' brings out the strong contempt against their dress:[110]

Putting on uniform and belt he walks in the streets;
The policeman speaks with great pride
The day the red pugree is taken away,
The policeman will be reduced to nothing.

Why did their uniform become a target of attack? Bernard Cohn has highlighted how dress emerged as an important symbol of British power and authority. According to him, when the British established themselves as the new rulers of India, they constructed a system of code of conduct which constantly distanced them physically, socially and culturally from their Indian subjects and the dress was one such important code. The British constructed a new kind of dress for the police to establish their distinct separation from others.[111] The earlier blue dress of the police was later changed to khaki.[112] Apart from khaki, another distinctive feature of their dress was the red *pugri*.[113] Because of its association with the colonial constabulary, khaki colour has since come to represent formal organization, discipline and exercise of paramilitary force. Once khaki was chosen as the police uniform, there was a strict control over its distribution, use and maintenance. In 1902, an order was promulgated deprecating the growing tendency in several departments to prescribe a dress for their subordinates that was similar to the uniform worn by the police. The government directed that employees of other departments should not be allowed to wear khaki clothes, along with a red *pugri*, which was to be worn only by members of the police force.[114] It was the turban and its distinctive red colour that proclaimed the constables and the chaukidars as a composite coercive force of the state.

Other significance was also attached to the *pugri*. In most parts of rural India, great weight is attached to the *pugri* as headgear. With some communities, it is the headman alone who may wear the headdress.[115] It was a significant gesture, then, to have conferred the *pugri* on the lowly chaukidar along with the policeman proper. It was this four-yard strip of red cloth that the constables flaunted and it was that which was often attacked. Consequently, during the movement the extent of popular hatred to all that symbolized police power was very noticeable. The police were frequently threatened, abused, insulted, boycotted, and made the object of bawdy songs. Sometimes request and appeal was also made to the police to leave their service. The 'Sipahiya' leaflet brings out some of these responses. It depicted the police as dishonest, liar and a creator of quarrels amongst the people. It revealed their level of corruption, how they extorted money from their fathers and mothers, the extent of their brutality was shown in their beating their fathers with shoes and kicking their brothers. They were reprimanded by drawing their attention to think why God had brought them into this world, and chastised them saying that Hindus and Muslims were brothers but whose sons would they be called. It rebuked them saying how they were kicked daily and lost their *izzat* for the sake of merely 2 *annas*. It asked as to why did they get so less salary when even the cooks got Rs. 7 and khansamas Rs. 10. Finally an appeal was made to them to give up their police service and take to cultivation with the farmers.[116]

The sustained hostility towards, and frequent attacks on, the police demoralized the police force and greatly undermined the prestige of the government. A note of the Commissioner of the Tirhut Division underscoring the concern for the constant erosion of British authority explained how in the past the establishment had been able to meet the requirements of the district because of its great prestige and the prestige of the government behind it. But he felt that presently because of the result of organized agitation against the police and the government the prestige had 'temporarily' greatly diminished. The police therefore, he said, had to rely on a show of strength where, formerly, prestige alone precluded opposition and that presently the strengthening of the armed guard had become an unavoidable necessity.[117]

Thus, this study by examining the relationship of constabulary and the Non-Cooperation Movement throws significant light on the police protest, the impact of nationalism on police and simultaneously the increasing defiance by the masses of police authority during the movement. These different trends during nationalism bring into prominence the other identities of police, which generally get little attention in the over-determined paradigm of seeing state subordinates as only agents of state and as effectively integrated into the state structure, consolidating its power. The police, who were one of the main pillars of British power and whose assistance was most crucial during the movement, themselves went on strike. Even though they fought for the redressal of their basic grievances, their decision to go on strike during the movement had much significance.

This chapter broadens the way the concept of nationalism has been located. Nationalism was not merely a struggle with masses arrayed against the state and its apparatus. By foregrounding police protest it seeks to re-locate the scope of resistance itself. The conventional understanding of resistance is that it is always overt and conscious. But to adopt the term resistance in its more traditional sense would mean to ignore the very processes by which power is often tested and eroded by the actions of the subordinate sections or classes of society. Resistance may be defined as those behaviours and cultural practices of the subordinate groups that contest hegemonic social formations, that threaten to unravel the strategies of domination; 'consciousness' or dramatic action need not be essential to its constitution. Commonplace actions, often within the bounds of legality or legitimate expression, may undermine hegemonic projects and ideological presumptions. In short, it is the context and the consequences that render certain actions contestory. If seen from this perspective, the significance of police protest can be appreciated seriously. After all, their resistance rarely sought a more abstract liberation or posed a direct challenge to the dominant ideology of the state.

Notes

1. Michel Foucault, *Discipline and Punish: The Birth of the Prison*, New York: Vintage Books, 1979.
2. This has been underscored in David Arnold's study, *Police Power and Colonial Rule: Madras, 1859–1947*, New Delhi: Oxford University Press, 1986.
3. Sumit Sarkar, 'Popular Movements and National Leadership, 1945–47', in *Economic and Political Weekly*, vol. XVII, nos. 14–16, April 1982; Sucheta Mahajan, 'British Policy, Nationalist Strategy and Popular National Upsurge, 1945–5', in *Myth and Reality: Struggle for Freedom in India, 1945–47*, ed. A.K. Gupta, New Delhi: Manohar, 1987; Subrata Banerjee, *The R.I.N. Strike*, New Delhi: People's Publishing House, 1981.
4. Philip Woodruff (Mason), *The Men Who Ruled India: Volume II, The Guardians*, London: Jonathan Cape, 1954; B. Spangenburg, *Bureaucracy in India: Status, Policy and the ICS in the Late 19th Century*, New Delhi: Manohar, 1976; H.M.L. Alexander, 'Discarding the "Steel Frame": Changing Images Among Indian Civil Servants in the Early Twentieth Century', in *South Asia*, n.s., vols. 1–12, 1982; T. Beaglehole, 'From Rulers to Servants: The Indian Civil Service and the British Demission of Power in India', in *Modern Asian Studies*, vol. 11, no. 2, 1977; B.B. Misra, *The Bureaucracy in India: An Historical Analysis up to 1947*, London: Oxford University Press, 1971; J. Gallagher, G. Johnson and A. Seal, eds., *Locality, Province and Nation: Essays on Indian Politics, 1870–1940*, London: Cambridge University Press, 1973; C. Baker, G. Johnson, and A. Seal, eds., *Power, Profit and Politics: Essays on Imperialism, Nationalism and Change in Twentieth-Century India*, London: Cambridge University Press, 1981.
5. David C. Potter, 'Manpower Shortage and the End of Colonialism: The Case of the Indian Civil Service', in *Modern Asian Studies*, vol. 7, no. 1, 1973, pp. 47–73.
6. David Arnold, 'Bureaucratic Recruitment and Subordination in Colonial India: The Madras Constabulary, 1859–1947', in *Subaltern Studies IV*, ed., Ranajit Guha, New Delhi: Oxford University Press, 1985, pp. 1–2.
7. Ibid.

8. Murali Atlury, 'Subaltern Studies IV: A Review Article', in *Social Scientist*, vol. 16, no. 3, March 1988, pp. 24–7.
9. Arnold, 'Bureaucratic Recruitment', pp. 4–5.
10. S.K. Jha, *Raj to Swaraj, Changing Contours of Police*, New Delhi: Lancer, 1995, p. 406.
11. Deplorable conditions of constables have been highlighted in Arnold's study, 'Bureaucratic Recruitment'; Bihar and Orissa Political Special File no. 115/21.
12. *Bihar and Orissa Police Administration Report*, 1913, p. 25; Ibid., 1915, p. 2; Ibid., 1916, p. 2.
13. Ibid., 1918, p. 24.
14. *Report of the Indian Police Commission, 1902–1903*, Simla, 1903, pp. 37–8, 140; *Bihar and Orissa Police Administration Report*, 1915, pp. 34–5.
15. Ibid., 1913, p. 25.
16. Ibid., 1917, p. 1.
17. *Report of the Indian Police Commission, 1902–1903*, pp. 37–8, 140; *Bihar and Orissa Police Administration Report, 1918*, p. 19.
18. Ibid.
19. Ibid., 1913, p. 25; Ibid., 1915, p. 2; Ibid., 1916, p. 2; Ibid., 1918, p. 24.
20. James C. Scott, *Weapons of the Weak: Everyday Forms of Peasant Resistance*, New Haven: Yale University Press, 1985; James C. Scott and Benedict J. Tria Kerkvliet, *Journal of Peasant Studies*, vol. XII, 1986; Douglas Haynes and Gyan Prakash, *Contesting Power: Resistance and Everyday Social Relations in South Asia*, New Delhi: Oxford University Press, 1991.
21. *Bihar and Orissa Police Administration Report*, 1915, pp. 34–5; Ibid., 1918, pp. 1, 17, 24.
22. Ibid., 1915, pp. 34–5; Ibid., 1918, pp. 1, 24.
23. Ibid., 1910, 1911, 1912.
24. Ibid., 1915, pp. 34–5; Ibid., 1918, pp. 1, 24.
25. Ibid., 1918.
26. Ibid.
27. Ibid., 1913, p. 25; Ibid., 1917, pp. 1–2; Ibid., 1915, p. 27.
28. Ibid., 1917.
29. Jha, *Raj to Swaraj*, p. 407.
30. Ibid.
31. Bihar and Orissa Political Special File no. 115/1921.
32. Ibid., File no. 263/1921.
33. Ibid., File no. 102/1921.
34. Ibid., File no. 1/1921.
35. Ibid.
36. Ibid., File no. 115/1921.
37. Ibid., File no. 130/21.
38. Ibid.
39. Ibid.
40. Ibid.
41. Ibid.
42. Ibid., File no. 102/1921.

43. Ibid., File nos. 51/1921 and 102/1921.
44. Ibid., File no. 115/1921.
45. Fortnightly Report of Bihar and Orissa for the second half of December 1920, Government of India, Home Department (Political) File no. 77/February/1921, NAI.
46. Ibid.
47. This has been brought in the study of David Arnold, *The Congress in Tamilnad: Nationalist Politics in South India, 1919–1937*, New Delhi: Manohar, 1977, pp. 98–149. Fortnightly Report of Bihar and Orissa for the second half of January 1921, Home Department (Political) File no. 42/1921, NAI.
48. Fortnightly Report of Bihar and Orissa for the second half of December 1920, Government of India, Home Department (Political) File no. 77/February/1921; Bihar and Orissa Political Special File no. 115/1921.
49. Ibid., File no. 115/1921, 'Copy of a demi-official letter, dated 2 March 1921, From Superintendent of Police, Purnea, to the Inspector-General of Police, Bihar and Orissa'.
50. Ibid.
51. Ibid.
52. *Searchlight,* 20 February 1921.
53. Ibid., 27 February 1921.
54. Bihar and Orissa Political Special File no. 102/1921.
55. Ibid., File no. 130/1921; Fortnightly Report of Bihar and Orissa for the first half of March 1921, Government of India, Home Department Political File no. 65/1921, NAI; *Searchlight*, 11 March 1921.
56. Fortnightly Report of Bihar and Orissa for the first half of March 1921, Government of India, Home Department Political File no. 65/1921, NAI; *Searchlight,* 11 March 1921.
57. Bihar and Orissa Political Special File no. 130/1921; *Searchlight,* 11 March 1921.
58. Bihar and Orissa Political Special File no. 115/1921.
59. Ibid.
60. Ibid.
61. Ibid., File no. 130/1921.
62. Ibid., File no. 115/1921.
63. Ibid.
64. Ibid., 'Purnea S.P.'s letter to Inspector General of Police, dated 8 March 1921'.
65. Ibid., 'Inspector General of Police's letter to Chief Secretary dated 24 April 1921, Purnea Constable Strike'.
66. Ibid.
67. Ibid.
68. Scott, *Weapons of the Weak*, pp. 335–40.
69. Bihar and Orissa Political Special File no. 102/1921, 'Deputy Inspector General of Police's note to Chief Secretary, dated 4 March 1921—The extent to which unrest among the police was fomented by non-cooperators'. The rest of this section is based on this source.

70. Ibid., File no. 144/1921.
71. Ibid.
72. Bamford, *Histories of the Non-Cooperation and Khilafat Movements*, pp. 15–18.
73. Ibid.
74. Jha, *Raj to Swaraj*, p. 342.
75. Ibid., pp. 342–3.
76. Bihar and Orissa Political Special File no. 102/1921.
77. Ibid., 'Letter of Inspector General of Police, Bihar and Orissa, to the Chief Secretary, dated 4 March 1921—Extent to which unrest among the police has been kept up by Non-Cooperation'.
78. Ibid.
79. Ibid.
80. Ibid.
81. Ibid.
82. Ibid.
83. *Searchlight*, 20 February 1921.
84. Bihar and Orissa Political Special File no. 191/1921.
85. Bihar Special Branch, File no. 144L/1921, proscribed leaflet, 'Policewa', CID Record Room, Patna.
86. Ibid.
87. Bihar and Orissa Political Special File no. 102/1921, 'Note on the attitude of the Police towards the Non-Cooperation Movement, dated 8 July 1921'. This and the next paragraph are based on this source.
88. Low, 'The Government of India and the First Non-Cooperation Movement', p. 306.
89. Bihar and Orissa Political Special File no. 541/1921.
90. Ibid., File no. 49/1921. This paragraph and the following three paragraphs are based on this source.
91. *Bihar and Orissa Police Administration Reports, 1921–22.*
92. This paragraph and the earlier two paragraphs are based on Arnold, 'Bureaucratic Recruitment and Subordination in Colonial India'; Report of Indian Police Commission, Simla, 1903.
93. This has been highlighted in Arnold's study, *Police Power and Colonial Rule*, pp. 190–206.
94. Ibid.; Home Department (Political) File no. 159–170, August 1910, NAI; *Bihar and Orissa Annual Administration Report, 1922,* pp. 89–92; *Bihar and Orissa Police Administration Report, 1915,* pp. vi, vii, viii; ibid., 1918, p. 19.
95. Henningham, *Peasant Movements in Colonial India,* p. 24.
96. Ibid., p. 88.
97. Bihar and Orissa Political Special File no. 69/1922; *Motherland*, 9 January 1922.
98. Bihar and Orissa Political Special File no. 539/1921; Home Department (Political) File no. 315/1922, NAI.
99. Bihar and Orissa Political Special File no. 85/1922.
100. Ibid., File nos. 3/1922 and 85/1922.
101. Ibid., File no. 146/1922.

102. Ibid., File no. 58/1921.
103. Ibid., File no. 3/1922.
104. Ibid.
105. Ibid., File no.146/1922.
106. Ibid.
107. Ibid., File no. 184/1921.
108. Ibid., File no. 213A/1922.
109. Ibid., File no. 213A/1922.
110. Bihar Special Branch, File no. 144L/1921, proscribed leaflet, 'Policewa', CID Record Room, Patna.
111. Cohn, *Colonialism and its Forms of Knowledge,* pp. 111–13.
112. Jha, *Raj to Swaraj,* pp. 67–8, 75–6, 210–14.
113. Ibid., p. 212.
114. Ibid.
115. Guha, *Elementary Aspects of Peasant Insurgency,* p. 66.
116. Bihar and Orissa Political Special File no. 32/1921.
117. Ibid., File no. 586/1921, 'Copy of a Note by the Commissioner of the Tirhut Division'.

Epilogue

THE NON-COOPERATION Movement was very significant as it proved to be a turning point in the national movement. After this, the national movement no longer remained confined to the educated sections only but witnessed the broadening of popular participation. The Non-Cooperation Movement in Bihar witnessed mass articulation of nationalism, unleashing a variety of protests and arousing feelings in many directions. As the movement spread it took diverse shapes and forms in different areas. In Tirhut Division, the movement primarily intensified the struggle against the planters. In Purnea and Saran districts tensions mounted against the landlords, where the tenants disputed and delayed payment of rent. In some places, the settlement operations elicited hostile reactions. There were cases of haat lootings in Darbhanga and Muzaffarpur. In the tribal belt, animosity built up against the landlords and traders. In many districts, the police force went on strike. In Purnea and Shahabad, cattle pounds were boycotted. Tensions mounted against the chaukidars and in some districts attempts were made to stop payment of chaukidari tax. The movement received impetus from local social and agrarian tensions and agitations and became a vehicle of expression for a variety of discontents. In north Bihar, the movement not only drew strength from the agitations that had crystallized during the anti-indigo agitation and peasants' protest preceding the Non-Cooperation Movement, but also sharpened the struggle against the planters and landlords.

The peasants were in the forefront of the movement. In fact, the movement derived its strength from the peasant base. This study sheds interesting light on the Gandhian politics of the peasants and attempts to reconstruct the world of peasant nationalists. This has been examined in the context of the thoughts, feelings and aspirations of the subordinate as there is complex relationship between popular culture, religiosity and inchoate political consciousness. Popular protest on some of the issues had preceded the year 1921 and was shaped by organizational structures that were independent of nationalist organization. However, the widespread political ferment of 1921–2 affected the popular agitation which intensified during the Non-Cooperation Movement. Radicalization and intensification of popular protest can be located within the general atmosphere of Non-Cooperation Movement which was writ with general defiance of authority and contempt of the government. At the regional level the local non-cooperators primarily took up agrarian issues in their campaign, emphasizing that peasants' grievances would be redressed in swaraj. The nationalist ideology was given a particular flavour in the course of its assimilation by the tribals and peasants to meet their social and political aims. The popular translations of nationalism pitted the peasants not only against the colonial but also against their internal exploiters.

In north Bihar, anti-planter protests sharpened. Relations between the planters and tenants became strained and the planters faced a series of attacks. Their employees and labourers went on strike, demanding higher wages; their tenants did not pay rents, they even stopped supplying carts, coolies and ploughs. In many areas, the bazaars and factories of the planters were boycotted. The personal servants of the planters ceased to work for them. A wide cross-section of the peasantry were involved in these protests. The trend of increasing solidarity of the poorer sections of villagers was discernible in many rebellions. The protest derived its organizational strength from the peasant sabhas and seva samitis. The social boycott, as a weapon, was also resorted to against those who did not join the protest, which made it difficult for the planters to take action against them. Militant mood of the peasantry could be seen in the context of their translating the Non-Cooperation Movement into defiance against their exploiters, i.e. the planters. The Non-Cooperation Movement had succeeded in eroding planters' hegemony in north Bihar.

In certain regions, peasants' tensions mounted against the zamindars. In some places, a proposal to start a campaign for non-payment of rent to the landlords was openly discussed. Tenants in many areas disputed payment of rent and refused payment of other claims of the zamindars. Rents were withheld on a large-scale in the Hathwa estate in the district of Saran. The tenants of the Muhammadia zamindar in the district of Purnea refused to pay rent in some villages. A large number of panchayats were held in villages which settled disputes amongst the villagers over land, loans and grazing. This eroded the hegemony of the zamindars, who saw it as a threat to their power and authority.

As the Non-Cooperation Movement made inroads in the tribal belt, it intensified agrarian agitation. The Non-Cooperation Movement had made considerable impact on the Tana Bhagats in Ranchi, the Hos in Kolhan, the Kherwars and Cheros in Palamau and the Santhals in Damin-i-Koh in Santhal

Pargana. These areas had a strong tradition of tribal protests. The Damin-i-Koh belt was well known for the Santhal Rebellion of 1855–6. Rent and land issues were in the forefront of the agitation in these belts. In Palamau, forest satyagraha was prominent, with tenants cutting down the forests and claiming their right to them. The movement also brought forth tribal animosity against the traders. The Tana Bhagats made attempts to prevent traders from increasing the prices of goods. In fact, tribal movement like that of the Tana Bhagats' expressed not only protest of the Oraons against the non-Oraons, but it also was a response to the tensions and hierarchization which arose within the Oraon society. The Tanas articulated the ideology of a marginal group within the Oraon society and challenged those elements, tribal and non-tribal, that had forced them into dependence and subordination.

Tribal and peasant agitations shed light on the popular perceptions of Indian nationalism. They often translated the codes of their leaders on the basis of their own world views and experiences to their own social and political needs. A millenarian trait was evident in the movement. Peasants and tribals perceived swaraj as a millennium which would end all their exploitations and oppressions. Under swaraj, it was believed, they would regain their land and would not have to pay rent, chaukidari tax, haat fees; there would be no protected forests and no forest rules. These were deep-seated grievances of peasants and tribals around which they had been agitating for long and which surfaced sharply during the Non-Cooperation Movement. The popular struggles converged with the Non-Cooperation Movement, and threatened the power relations deemed inviolable until then, especially landlord/peasant relations.

Peasant and tribal actions were framed in terms of what was popularly regarded to be just, fair and possible. However, peasants and tribals derived legitimacy for their actions from the supposed orders of Gandhi. There was a popular tendency to look upon Gandhi as an alternative source of authority. Gandhi became the symbol of their hopes and aspirations. Everything that was unjust, cruel and oppressive was fought in Gandhi's name. The peasantry looted bazaars in Gandhi's name; the tribals distilled liquor on 'his orders', and the peasants burnt planters' factories to the 'jaikar' of Gandhi. In effect, the 'jaikar' of Gandhi became a militant avowal of the organized strength of peasant volunteers, a rallying cry for direct action, a cry that mobilized and struck terror in the hearts of planters. In fact, in the whole phase of the Non-Cooperation Movement, it was Gandhi, and not Congress, whose name was frequently invoked. The organizational hold of the Congress at the local level during the non-cooperation was not yet strong as the Congress was still emerging as an organization. It was Gandhi who emerged as a phenomenon and an aura was getting created around him. Lots of rumours centred around

Gandhi and he was elevated to a higher moral pedestal and divinity. In actuality, Gandhi emerged as an alternative power vis-à-vis the British.

Thus, the movement marked popular translation of nationalism. Once the desires and aspirations of the masses got linked with swaraj, the Non-Cooperation Movement developed its own rhythm and dynamics, bringing forth its own agenda, which often ran independent of the Congress leaders. The Congress and the colonial power feared this the most. The movement had not drawn much response from the educated section, and the official programme of the Congress, i.e. the various boycotts, had elicited lukewarm response. The movement had drawn strength from the popular agrarian protests, which was not a part of the Congress programme. The movement brought to the forefront peasants' and tribals' conflict with the landlords and planters over agrarian issues. However, the Congress did not approve of confrontation with the landlords and appealed to the peasants to live with them (landlords) peacefully by resorting to arbitration in disputes with them. The apprehension of the Congress to launch civil disobedience was that with strong tradition of agrarian protest the peasants, who formed the mainstay of the Non-Cooperation Movement, would translate the call of civil disobedience to air their grievances against the zamindars. The Congress did not approve of the boycott of planters' bazaar and haat lootings, and publicly disclaimed of having any role in such activities. It also did not approve of direct confrontation with the British, such as picketing of thanas and demonstrations outside the courts or police stations. However, the Congress leaders' advice to the masses in the movement to 'restraint' often went unheeded and they were unable to control the masses. The movement did not remain confined to the parameters of non-violence as laid down by the Congress.

Thus, the phase of non-cooperation, when the movement moved out of the confines of educated sections to assume a mass character, becomes very significant in revisiting historiography on nationalism. This study questions the binary paradigm of elite/subaltern nationalism and charts out the complexities of the process. In fact, the way the masses had been denied any political agency or subjectivity in the earlier existing historiography that there was now a need to underline the subjectivity of subalterns and give them political voice, independent of elites. This study of popular struggles questions the nationalist historiography which looks at the Non-Cooperation Movement as the creation of a few charismatic leaders. It was not the nationalist elites which had taken initiative to organize popular protests. In fact even preceding the Non-Cooperation Movement, there was a strong tradition of popular protests in Bihar, which were shaped by organizational structures that were independent of the nationalist organization. But, at the same time, one cannot overlook the widespread political ferment at the time of Non-Cooperation

Movement, which was writ with general defiance and contempt of authority that affected the movement. Popular protests intensified and radicalized as a result of its interaction with the non-cooperation. Thus this study does not accept some of the basic premises of subaltern historians like the duality of nationalisms (i.e. elite and subaltern nationalism), and popular autonomy. Although it accepts the specificity of the popular level and popular translations of swaraj, it highlights the process of interaction of nationalism with popular struggles.

Again the whole mobilization process was very complex and does not fit into the binary paradigm of mobilization from above or below. Apart from the role of the Congress leaders, it was furthered by the efforts of thousands of grass root nationalist workers—the city-based as well as the village-reared. The popular protest proves beyond doubt that the 'less' important Congress leadership and the local non-cooperators were scarcely peripheral to the resistance and advanced their cause. A large number of people, mostly from the lower class and caste, had offered themselves as volunteers and they played a crucial role in mobilization. However, the Congress leaders were very apprehensive of these volunteers, whom they did not consider to be 'disciplined' soldier of the movement.

The nationalist propaganda and campaigns took place at various levels through meetings, speeches, nationalist songs, pamphlets and newspapers. A strong network of organizations, such as peasant sabhas, panchayats and volunteer organizations, provided momentum to the movement. Social boycott was also resorted to against those who refused to join the movement by drawing upon the traditional institutions of social authority like caste strictures. For the government it was difficult to pass any seditious act against such social boycott. The movement evolved a new language and style of mass politics, new techniques of mass political organization and action. The political language and symbols of the campaign expressed the ethos and urges of the masses with which people could easily relate and identify with. Critique of nature of British rule and its impact was translated into popular idioms. Very often metaphors in campaign evoked powerful feelings of passion, anger or excitement, intensifying the identification with the Non-Cooperation Movement.

The Non-Cooperation Movement was a struggle in which people in a variety of positions took wide ranging steps, contributing to the disruption of the agenda of the colonial power. Many of the symbols of protest were multi-vocal in meanings. The strength of these symbols lay in their varied interpretations by the people. It has been argued that a political symbol is powerful precisely because of its ambiguity, which allows a number of different people to respond to a single unified form without necessarily sharing a single interpretation of it but all at the same time defying authority. Various dimensions and trends converged around the issue of liquor boycott. Protests around liquor ranged from liquor boycott to the 'illicit' distillation of liquor. This work highlights the popular dimensions of protests around liquor, which had not received due attention before. Besides, one finds that khadi did not remain merely a swadeshi symbol, linked with the drain of wealth, but a whole range of beliefs and popular aspirations got woven around it, thus providing a unifying ideology more powerful than any single call for political representation or independence. Khadi dress had emerged as an important political symbol and national identity. Nationalism had raised the issue of cloth to primary economic and political importance. Dress was an important symbol of British power and authority. When the British established themselves as the new rulers of India, they constructed a system of code of conduct which constantly distanced them physically, socially and culturally from their Indian subjects, and dress was one such important code. So the khadi dress had become an important symbol of assertion and defiance by the nationalists. In the dress, khadi cap became an obligatory part of Congress uniform, becoming a visible mark of swadeshi and swaraj.

This study also highlights how the Non-Cooperation Movement had marked erosion of colonial hegemony, which has not received due attention in studies on nationalism. What was breaking down, above all, under the pressure of mass militancy, was the legitimacy of foreign rule, its acceptance as sacrosanct. In fact, increasing popular resistance can be seen in this context. The diminishing fear of British institutions of authority during the Non-Cooperation Movement emboldened the masses, giving them a new self-confidence in their ability to successfully defy the government and resist oppression. The Non-Cooperation Movement was writ with atmosphere of defiance against British authority. There was general disrespect for law and order, and strong contempt for authority. Nationalist agitation undermined respect for legal authority, the police, thana and jail—all pillars of British authority. Large crowds demonstrated outside the courts when the non-cooperators were tried in the court or when they were taken from the court to the jail. It is interesting to see the erosion of the authority of prison in the popular psyche. People were no longer scared of jail, an important pillar of British power, but on the contrary routinely mocked this colonial authority. The jail began to be perceived as a place of pilgrimage. A significant development of the Non-Cooperation Movement was the extent to which it became a vehicle for demonstration of popular hostility towards the police. Frequent attacks on the police demoralized the police force and undermined the prestige of the government.

The lack of respect for authority, especially amongst the masses, was a major concern of the colonial government. Expressing concern about the undermining of respect for authority among the masses during the Non-Cooperation Movement, the local officials said that in the past a small police post was able to meet the requirements of the district because of the prestige and reputation of the government. But with the undermining of the government's authority, the officials said, the police had to rely more on a show of strength, when earlier its prestige alone precluded opposition. The government emphasized that success in administration depended as much on the maintenance of an atmosphere of obedience to authority and acceptance of the existing order of society as on the definite enforcement of statute law or the working of the administrative machinery.

This study also throws light on the colonial government's perception of the movement. There is nothing like monolithic colonial perception but only layered perceptions of the national movement. The local government's perception of the non-cooperation and its policy towards it was very different from the Government of India. Local government was not happy with the Government of India's policy of restraint towards the movement which it considered to be subversive in character. It considered Government of India's policy of restraint as having negative consequences that undermined the prestige and authority of colonial administration. The policy of restraint, according to the local government, besides raising doubt amongst their loyalists and servants, was giving rise to the impression amongst the 'ignorant' masses that the government was indifferent or too timid to take action against the movement. In the official discourse, masses were often invoked as 'ignorant' and were seen as being provoked by the 'outsiders'. Such discourse robbed the masses of any political agency and consciousness.

The movement not only undermined respect for colonial authority but also impacted the colonial state apparatus, the mainstay of British authority. The impact of nationalism on bureaucracy or state apparatus or resistance in the ranks of state personnel during the national movement has not attracted much scholarly attention. In the existing historiography on nationalism, the focus has been primarily on popular struggles. The general impression about nationalism is that it was a mass struggle against the British, with the masses arrayed against the state and its apparatus. The other kinds of resistance during the national movement have not attracted much attention. This study, however, alters such an image, pointing out that there was a strong protest among the police force, an important agent of the state apparatus. This study highlights that the lower ranks of the police personnel in many districts went on strike demanding better service conditions. Police subordinates began to find a collective voice of their own to express their grievances. The confidence to go on strike came from the atmosphere of Non-Cooperation Movement, as their agitation could not be easily isolated and suppressed. In fact, the constables joined the collective protest confidently as they knew that they had the support of a larger movement and a well-developed Congress organization. Even though they were seeking redress for specific grievances related to pay, housing and other conditions, and not contesting institutional subordination, their decision to go on strike at the time of the movement, would send the message of weakening of colonial authority. The colonial government looked upon constables resorting to strikes, even though for the redressal of their own grievances, as a sign of disloyalty to their authority. The issue of loyalty was at the core of colonial official concern.

However, it was not just the constables' protests over their own grievances that surfaced during the Non-Cooperation Movement, the protests were also getting influenced by nationalism. The nationalists, whose aim was to ultimately bring the bureaucracy within its fold, took the opportunity of discontentment amongst the lower rungs of the police to mobilize them in their favour. A number of constables resigned and joined the Non-Cooperation Movement. Reports of higher police authority from different districts underlined that the lower rungs of the police could not be trusted or relied upon to deal with the Non-Cooperation Movement. In fact, neutralizing the police force to some extent is one of the significant achievements of the Non-Cooperation Movement. Thus, this study questions state subordinates as being effectively integrated with colonial state and also their only identity being that of state agent. It throws light on the other identity of police, which is generally overlooked, since the police were also part of society, having strong ties and affinities with it. However, the other identity asserts in the context of nationalism.

Besides highlighting the popular and the different kinds of resistances, this study also foregrounds nationalism as a site of hegemonic contest. It is in this context that one can understand the significance of different boycotts. The boycotts were resorted to make the British governance impossible and cripple its resources. British rule in India had semi-hegemonic foundations. It was a rule that was buttressed by the ideology of Pax Britannica, law and order, the British officials as the *mai-baap* of the people, and also by educational, legal, judicial, constitutional and administrative systems which acted as the active purveyors of colonial ideologies. Boycotts were effective means of undermining the prestige of the Raj. It was a struggle to prove that coercion exceeded persuasion in the organic composition of British power over India. The British rulers emphasized and promoted the collaborative structure or constitutional reform. Legislative Councils and courts were presented as aspects of collaboration. The Non-Cooperation Movement stressed the alien and unrepresentative character of the British regime, exploding the *mai-baap* myth of a filial attachment on the masses to their rulers. All this helped to neutralize the promotion of collaborative structure or constitutional reform. Whatever institutional and ideological resources were at the disposal of the British to establish their hegemony began to crack down under the pressure from the movement. The Non-Cooperation Movement demolished the prestige of the courts, the hegemonic insignia of the colonial state, exposed that educational institutions were ideological apparatus in the hands of the government, it showed that the real interest in promoting foreign cloth was to advance British trade, which resulted in huge outflow of wealth from India, and that the main interest of the excise policy was to generate revenue for the government. The various boycotts thus exposed the political, economic and ideological agenda of the British rule.

The Non-Cooperation Movement exposed not only the unrepresentative character of the British rule but also highlighted the adverse impact of foreign rule on 'Indian society' and 'culture'. Hence nationalism also became an important agenda to retrieve 'Indian culture'. British ruler was depicted as devil, demon, irreligious, treacherous, looter, dishonest and responsible for the decline of the character of Indian people. It was said that British institutions, like education and courts, crushed people's soul, suppressed noble ideas, instigated evil passions and led to divisiveness in society and increased family disputes. Courts were projected as places of falsehood, treachery, deceit, dishonesty, human frailty, wickedness and meanness. It was highlighted that under the impact of British rule, India, which had a glorious civilization, had become devoid of its spirituality, individuality, manliness and strength. Hindu and Muslim religions were said to be under threat. Metaphors were frequently drawn from the *Ramayana* and the *Mahabharata*, and colonial power was often referred to as Ravan. Metaphor of the cow was frequently used and the nationalist fight was projected as a struggle to protect the sacred cow. The notion of purity and pollution were often invoked in the nationalist campaign. Brahmins and Kshatriyas were said to have fallen from their high pedestal.

Hence nationalism became a call to save the religion, culture, tradition, honour, spirituality and morality of the nation. At the core of boycott was the issue of moral independence and self-respect vis-à-vis the colonial power. By refusing to collaborate with an unjust and oppressive rule, the nationalists projected that Indians might recover some of their self-respect and moral purity which they had lost in the course of the last two hundred years. The nationalist education would be a panacea to salvage Indian culture, religion, tradition and morality. Liquor boycott would make India once again ritually pure, as drinking was considered to be against Indian 'tradition' and only the characteristic of 'lower orders' of society. Panchayats would be the saviour of people's dharma, *izzat* (honour) and wealth, and play a 'harmonious', and not a 'divisive' role in society and family. Handloom weaving gradually transformed from an endangered rural craft to a powerful symbol of the moral and spiritual regeneration of India. The country was elevated to the status of a mother goddess and the national movement had become a battle of dharma against adharma. Thus nationalism interjected into the public culture a vocabulary originating particularly in the domain of religious practice. Secular and sacred space intersected, not remaining exclusive.

Hence, nationalism did not remain confined merely to the extermination of the British, simply a political struggle for power, but broadened to become a cultural encounter with the British. It related the question of political independence of the nationalism to virtually every aspect of the material and spiritual life of the people. In the entire phase of the national struggle, the crucial need was to protect, preserve and strengthen the inner core of the national culture, its spiritual essence. No encroachments in it by the colonizers were to be tolerated. It can be seen as an attempt to create and revive national cultural identity, around the institutions of education, dress, judiciary through the medium of panchayats. The contest between nationalism and the colonial state inseparably intertwined historically with the contest for hegemony within society. However, the nationalist hegemonic project was that of cultural normalization. The domain of the 'national' was defined as one that was different from the western. It was necessarily built upon the privileging of an 'essential' tradition; self-purification, practice of vegetarianism, a concern for dietary purity, liquor prohibition, all deriving its legitimacy from Indian 'tradition' and religion. The discourse drew heavily from the Brahminical tradition, obliterating popular traditions, and had its implication for caste, class, minority and gender.

The nationalist discourse reinforced the patriarchal structure. Nationalism was constantly evoked as a call to protect the honour and chastity of women. The call for the participation of women in nationalism was to cleanse and add virtues to politics as women were perceived as the embodiment of virtuous qualities. Woman's image as a mother, sister, nurturer, sacrificer and sufferer was retained and went unchallenged. The nationalists particularly directed the khadi message to women and it became popular among women. This was an activity that did not violate women's domestic role. Women could spin khadi and contribute to the nationalist cause even while being at home. It also did not violate parda and many women from conservative families took to it. Hence the structures which developed to mobilize women can best be understood as a function of the limited autonomy allowed to women in a society which valued modesty and practised sex-segregation. White khadi was prescribed as dress for women and Gandhi thought that it would be a suitable mean of enabling women to enter the public political sphere without appearing sexually provocative or immodest. Thus, an 'ideal' image of woman was being constructed, endowed with attributes approved by patriarchal society. The male nationalists turned inward, reifying the home and women's place within it, as a spiritualized 'inner space' that contested colonial hegemony. Ideals of wifely domesticity marked the formation of a (male) nationalist subjectivity. This may be seen not only as a strategy for contesting colonial hegemony, but also as a strategy for the containment of women's agency. However, the nationalist's quest of dovetailing women's subjectivity comes under fissure by fore-fronting women's agency. Women's participation in public sphere to engage in political protest ultimately led to the erosion of the privacy of the female space. It became a galvanizing source for further politicization of women. As a result of this early political experience, many women continued to participate later in other forms of local politics. Many traversed their own independent courses. Women on public platforms, in demonstrations, while picketing or offering satyagraha, were defying and breaking their familiar and customary roles. Without speaking a word in favour of women's emancipation, they began the process by releasing themselves from exclusively home-bound functions and roles.

Thus this work on the Non-Cooperation Movement in Bihar throws significant light on the different facets of nationalism. The study draws attention to the view that nationalism was not only marked by a series of popular protests but was also a struggle where people, in a variety of positions, taking a wide range of steps, posed a severe challenge to the British authority and hegemony. It also highlights nationalism as a hegemonic encounter, where the question of retrieving 'Indian culture' becomes utmost important. What remains remarkable about the Non-Cooperation Movement was the simultaneous presence in it of so many trends and forces, which went on shaping later nationalist politics.

APPENDIX I

The Song 'Firangia'

The land of Bharat was good and fair but now,
O Firanghees, it has become a cremation ground.

Foodgrain, wealth, men, strength, and wisdom have all been destroyed
and there is no trace left of any of them, O Firangia.

At that very place where lacs of maunds of corn
and paddy used to be produced, the farmers now,
resting their hands against their head,
are weeping bitter tears, O Firangia.

For what sin of ours, O God,
have we been reduced to such state?
Seven hundred lacs of men starve both morning and evening,
and there is famine all the time, O Firangia.

And whatever remains, you put that into your ship
and take that across the seas, O Firangia.

What is this way of the world that, while people starve at home,
wheat is taken to foreign countries, O Firangia.

In a land where people lived in satisfaction and were quite rich,
and now cast your eyes anywhere
and you will see only poor men, exceedingly poor, O Firangia.

No trade and commerce have survived;
all have been destroyed.
Even for trifles, alas, O Firangia, we have to look up to the foreigners.

We keep our honour by wearing cloth,
only when it comes from foreign countries, and,
O Firangia, if cloth supply from outside is stopped, we will go naked.
O Firangia, you take cotton from us at cheap rates
which you weave into cloth and then sell that cloth to us.

In this and similar ways, you rob the wealth of India
and take it to foreign countries.

Forty crores of rupees of our country
goes to other countries every year, O Firangia.

Wealth, strength, wisdom and learning are all gone
and we have become extremely poor.
Though the country has become poor in every way,
you have increased the burden of taxes, O Firangia.

There is tax on salt, tax on cooly
and there is tax imposed upon every thing, O Firangia.[1]

Note

1. Bihar Special Branch, 132L/1921, proscribed song 'Firangia', CID Record Room, Patna.

APPENDIX II

The Pamphlet 'Bharat Mata ka Sandesh'

AFTER LISTENING to the call of the Bharat Mata, boys, who are over eighteen years, should withdraw immediately from their educational institutions because the kind of education given in these institutions strengthens your bond of slavery and destroys your self-help and self-reliance. The Indian history before the coming of the British has been painted dark. The coming of the British is viewed as the arrival of 'messiah'. So, if one reads this history, it gives one the feeling of helplessness and also a strong fear that if the British gives us swaraj or leaves us and goes away then we will start fighting among ourselves and die, and once again some other people from outside India will be called upon to rule over us. Apart from this, the present education is so costly that poor people cannot afford it. Even people with average background can afford it only with great difficulty. Even after receiving such costly education, one cannot get a job. The large universities, colleges and schools that you see have not been made for your good. They are machines for creating slaves, wherein boys are trained to be slaves, and after passing out from these institutions, they cannot do much but be slaves. That is why Mother has sent message through Gandhi that, as soon as possible, the boys should leave the educational institutions and join the national schools. In this way, they can be brave men and serve their country.[1]

Note

1. Bihar Special Branch, 1921, proscribed pamphlet, 'Bharat Mata ka Sandesh', CID Record Room, Patna.

APPENDIX III

Leaflet 'Swaraj ke Faede'

LITIGATION may die out soon; it may vanish out of the courts. The heart is rent to hear the costs of a suit of Rs.100 but I cannot help mentioning it. The touts embrace us by the neck in open courts and cheat us squarely. They take us by means of deception to the Bar library, where a pleader jumps up. The two (the tout and the pleader) whisper to each other and talk unintelligibly, and then the pleader realizes the shagun (the first fee). The suit costs Rs.7/8/- for (court fee) stamp, Rs.1/8/- as process fee and besides another stamp worth -/8/- for (vakalatnama). The pleader then goes with the petition to the Ijalas, where the Amla realizes Dakhla (illegal fee for admitting a petition). After several months, the chaprasi (peon) comes back with the report of the service of notice or summons; he eats and drinks and gets some money (from the party). The peshkar puts off four dates and then puts up the case before the court in the evening. He extracts peshi (illegal fee for putting up the case). We have to feed the witnesses and pay the vakils fees. Affidavit has also to be made. Cases are reversed, from 'Decree' and 'Dismiss' and vice versa. After a lot of bother, even if the decree is prepared, the execution gives immense troubles. Warrants of attachment are issued and houses are put up for sale by auction, when the Nazir calls on men to bid. The delivery of possession and mutation of names that are doubly difficult give rise to a fresh quarrel. Review and appeal make people insolvent May thy face burn, O litigation. Listen to what Gandhiji says; find out men fit to be panches and refer cases to them for arbitration: Let no suits go to the courts.[1]

Note

1. Bihar Special Branch, L38/1921, proscribed leaflet, 'Swaraj ke Faede', CID Record Room, Patna.

APPENDIX IV

Leaflet 'Sipahiya'

Alas! Alas! it is difficult to say,
why God has brought you into this world, O sipahi.
My heart breaks seeing my brethren in trouble.
Moreover the sipahis issue orders to them.
Having said something partly true and partly false
to the dishonest persons and government,
the sipahis create quarrels among ourselves.
Gandhiji and Shaukat Ali call out loudly to the sipahis:
Resign the service of the firangia.
Sipahis lose their izzat for the sake of 2 annas, and are kicked daily.
Cooks get seven rupees, khansamas rupees ten,
it is not understood why is your pay smaller, O sipahi.
O sipahis, when you become sipahis you extort money from your father.
You kick your brothers and beat your father with shoes
and extort money from your mother.
Hindus and Muhammadans are brothers in India.
Whose sons will you be called, O sipahi.
Oh sipahis, be you Hindus or Muhammadans,
Give up service and do cultivation with the farmers.[1]

Note

1. Bihar and Orissa Political Special File no. 32/1921.

APPENDIX V

Cotton Depots

Cotton depots were opened in following places in Bihar:

Districts	*Places*
Patna	Bihar, Bikram.
Gaya	Nawada, Palmerganj, Nabinagar, Arwal, Jehanabad.
Shahabad	Nasriganj, Semaria, Garbain, Bhabua, Sasaram.
Muzaffarpur	Hajipur, Lalganj, Mahua, Muzaffarpur, Katra, Bakhra, Sitamarhi, Sheohar, Sursand, Pupri.
Saran	Maharajganj, Mirganj, Sivan, Chapra, Mashrak, Daroli.
Champaran	Mehal, Jihuli, Bettiah.
Darbhanga	Madhubani, Samastipur, Rosra, Darbhanga.
Bhagalpur	Bhagalpur, Banka, Supaul, Madhipura, Nowgachhia, Amarpur, Sultanganj.
Monghyr	Monghyr, Luckesarai, Sheikpura, Barbigha, Jamui, Kharagpur, Khagaria, Gogri, Begusarai.
Santhal Pargana	Godda, Rajmahal, Jamtara, Dumka.
Hazaribagh	Chatra, Hazaribagh, Giridih, Dhanwar, Champaran, Barkagaon, Ramgarh, Kodarma, Kisgo.

Statements compiled by the BPCC in 1922 show the figures of charkha, looms, kargah, etc. in use in different districts.[1]

Districts	*Charkha*	*Kargah and loom*	*Daily quantity of yarn*	*Khadi*	*Foreign cloth shops closed*	*Shops stocking khadi*
Muzaffarpur	39,600	3,866	66 Mds.	16,880 Yds.	33	30
Saran	40,000	3,751	125 Mds.	1,875 Yds.	—	141
Palamau	3,000	2,000	—	—	—	—
Monghyr	10,000	8,500	—	—	7	81
Manbhum	15	1	—	—	2	6
Shahabad	—	3,110	—	100 Thans	2	10
Darbhanga	70,000	9,000	250	20,000 Yds.	—	Almost all
				30,000	—	—
				20,000	—	—
TOTAL	162,615	30,228	441	88,855 Yds. and Thans	44	268

Some of the district figures showed the following:

Districts	*Charkha*	*Kargah and loom*	*Daily quantity of yarn*	*Khadi*	*Foreign cloth shops closed*	*Shops stocking khadi*
Patna	10,510	5,040	500 Mds.	10 Yds.	212	—
Gaya	25,000	8,000	Not	(daily)	(signed)	100
Hazaribagh	300	4	ascertainable		2	—
			8 Yds. (daily)			

Note

1. Bihar and Orissa Political Special File no. 291/1922, 'Note on the results of searches in connection with the government, Notification No. 4609–C, 10 December 1921, under the Criminal Law Amendment Act'.

Select Bibliography

Primary Source Materials

Official Records

GOVERNMENT OF INDIA

Fortnightly Reports to the Government of India from the Government of Bihar and Orissa, National Archives of India, New Delhi.

Government of India, Home Department Political Files, National Archives of India, New Delhi.

GOVERNMENT OF BIHAR

Annual Report on the Vernacular Newspapers and Periodicals of Bihar and Orissa, Bihar State Archives, Patna.

Bihar and Orissa Special Section Files, CID Record Room, Patna.

Freedom Movement Papers, Bihar State Archives, Patna.

Bihar and Orissa Police Abstract of Intelligence, Bihar State Archives, Patna.

Bihar and Orissa Political Special Department Files, Bihar State Archives, Patna.

Official Publications

Bihar and Orissa Annual Administration Reports, Patna.

Bihar and Orissa Legislative Council Proceedings, Patna.

Bihar and Orissa Police Administration Reports, Patna.

Census of India 1911, Vol. V Bengal, Bihar and Orissa and Sikkim Part I Report, Calcutta, 1913.

Excise Administration Reports of Bihar and Orissa, Patna.

Bihar District Gazetteers: O'Malley, L.S.S., *Bengal District Gazetteers: Darbhanga, 1906; Gaya, 1906; Muzaffarpur, 1907; Palamau, 1907; Champaran, 1907; Singhbhum, Sarai Kela and Kharsainan, 1910: Purnea, 1911.*

Report of Indian Police Commission, Simla, 1903.

Report of the Public Service Commission, 1886–87, Calcutta, 1888.

Reports on the Land Revenue Administration of the Province of Bihar and Orissa, Patna.

Newspapers and Periodicals

Searchlight (microfilm), Nehru Memorial Museum and Library (hereafter NMML), New Delhi.

Motherland (microfilm), NMML, New Delhi.

Behar Herald (microfilm), NMML, New Delhi.

Indian Annual Register, Calcutta.

Young India (microfilm), NMML, New Delhi.

Private Collections

A.N. Sinha Papers (Manuscript Section), NMML, New Delhi.

K.K. Datta Papers (Manuscript Section), NMML, New Delhi.

Mazharul Haq Papers (Manuscript Section), NMML, New Delhi.

Ramnandan Mishra Papers (Manuscript Section), NMML, New Delhi.

Sahajanand Saraswati Papers (Manuscript Section), NMML, New Delhi.

Sahajanand Saraswati Private Papers (on microfilm), NMML, New Delhi.

Interviews

(Transcripts consulted at the Oral History Section, NMML)

Ramnandan Mishra

Syed Mahmud

Kishori Prasanna Sinha

Institutional Papers

Papers of the All India Congress Committee (Manuscript Section), NMML, New Delhi.

Report of the Bihar Vidyapith (Sadaquat Ashram, Patna).

Memoirs and Autobiographies

Gandhi, M.K., *An Autobiography or Stories of My Experiments with Truth*, Ahmedabad: Navajivan, 1927.

Mishra, Ramnandan, *Sansmaran*, Darbhanga: Nav Bharat, 1981.

Prasad, Rajendra, *Autobiography*, Bombay: Asia House, 1957.

Sahay, Bajrang, *My Reminiscences of the Freedom Movement in Bihar*, in K.K. Datta Papers (Manuscript Section), NMML, New Delhi.

Sankrityayan, Rahul, *Meri Jeevan Yatra*, vols. 2–5, Allahabad: Kitab Mahal, 1950–67.

Saraswati, Sahajanand, *Mera Jeevan Sangharsh*, Patna: Sitaram Ashram, 1952.

Shivpujan Sahay, *Mera Jeevan*, Patna: Paarijaat, 1985.

Sinha, A.N., *Mera Sansmaran*, Patna: Kusum, 1961.

CONTEMPORARY PAMPHLETS AND SONGS (IN HINDI) (BIHAR SPECIAL BRANCH, CID RECORD ROOM, PATNA)

Ankhon Ka Kanta, 1922.
Asahyog Bina, 1921.
Bhandaphore, 1922.
Bharat Durdasha, 1923.
Bharat Mata Ka Sandesh, 1921.
Bharat Uddhar, 1922.
Bideshi Kapron Ka Bahishkar, 1921.
BPCC and Government Circular, 1921.
Charkha Vinode, 1921.
Chhati Ka Peepar, 1922.
Darogwa, 1921.
Desher Pukar, 1923.
Deshghatia, 1921.
Desh Ki Pukar, 1921.
Dharma Ki Ter, 1921.
Din Pukar, 1921.
Firangia, 1921.
Gandhi Suyash Gazal, 1921.
Hinduon Ki Pariksha, 1921.
Igarahpai, 1921.
Jail Mahatmya, 1921.
Kisan Vinaya, 1921.
Luterwa, 1921.
Mahatma Ki Giraftari, Mukadama and Jail Jatra, 1922.
Mahatmaji in the Council, 1922.
Navin Gandhi Guna Gan, Part II, 1921.
Notice No. I of Swadeshi Preaching Society, Bihar and Orissa, 1921.
Policewa, 1921.
Police Bhaion Se Namr Nivedan, 1921.
Pratigyan, 1921.
Rashtriya Bhajan, 1923.
Rashtriya Tarang Mala, 1921.
Rashtriya Shabad, 1921.
Satyagraha Atharwa, 1921.
Shri Gandhi Chalisa, 1921.
Sipahia, 1921.
Sri Gandhi Updesh Bhajanavali, 1921.
Swaraj Ka Danka, 1922.
Swaraj Ke Faede, 1921.
Swaraj Pataka, 1921.
Vakilwa, 1921.
Zamindarwa, 1921.

Secondary Source Materials

Books

Ahmad, Qeyamuddin and Jha, Jata Shankar, *Mazharul Haq*, New Delhi: Publications Division, Government of India, 1976.

Ahmad, Razi, *Sadaqat Ashram*, New Delhi: Shabd, 1996.

Aloysius, G., *Nationalism without a Nation in India*, New Delhi: Oxford University Press, 1997.

Amin, Shahid, *Event, Metaphor, Memory, Chauri Chaura, 1922–1992*, New Delhi: Oxford University Press, 1995.

Anderson, Benedict, *Imagined Communities: Reflections on the Origin and Spread of Nationalism*, London: Verso, 1983.

Arnold, David, *Police Power and Colonial Rule, Madras 1859–1947*, New Delhi: Oxford University Press, 1986.

———, *The Congress in Tamilnad: Nationalist Politics in South India, 1919–1937*, New Delhi: Manohar, 1977.

Ayde, Shivaji Rao, *Gandhi Aur Mazharulhaq*, Chapra: Mazharulhaq Smarak Mandal, 1965.

Badrinarayan, *Lok-Sanskriti Mein Rashtravad*, New Delhi: Radhakrishna, 1996.

Baker, C., Johnson, G., and Seal, A., eds., *Power, Profit and Politics: Essays on Imperialism, Nationalism and Change in Twentieth-Century India*, London: Cambridge University Press, 1981.

Baker, Christopher John, *The Politics of South India, 1920–37*, New Delhi: Vikas, 1976.

Baker, D.E.U., *Changing Political Leadership in an Indian Province: The Central Provinces and Berar, 1919–39*, New Delhi: Oxford University Press, 1980.

Bamford, P.C., *Histories of the Non-Cooperation and Khilafat Movements*, New Delhi: Deep, 1974.

Banerjee, Subrata, *The R.I.N. Strike*, New Delhi: People's Publishing House, 1981.

Banerji, Himani, *Inventing Subjects: Studies in Hegemony, Patriarchy and Colonialism*, New Delhi: Tulika, 2001.

Basham, A.L., *The Wonder that was India*, London: Sidgwick and Jackson, 1954.

Basu, Sajal, *Jharkhand Movement, Ethnicity and Culture of Silence*, Shimla: Indian Institute of Advance Studies, 1994.

Bayly, C.A., *The Local Roots of Indian Politics: Allahabad, 1880–1920*, London: Oxford University Press, 1975.

Bhaduri, Satinath, *Dhorai Charitmanas*, Allahabad: Lokbharati, 1981.

Bhartiya Rashtriya Congress Ka Itihas (District Muzaffarpur, Bihar), Muzaffarpur: Congress Shatabdi Samaroh Samiti, 1985.

Bhattacharya, Sabyasachi, *The Contested Terrain: Perspectives on Education in India*, New Delhi: Orient Longman, 1998.

——— et. al., *The Development of Women's Education in India: A Collection of Documents 1850–1920*, New Delhi: Kanishka, 2001.

Borthwick, Meredith, *The Changing Role of Women in Bengal, 1849–1905*, Princeton: Princeton University Press, 1984.

Brown, Judith, *Gandhi's Rise to Power: Indian Politics 1915–1922,* London: Cambridge University Press, 1972.

Chanana, Karuna, *Interrogating Women's Education: Bounded Visions, Expanding Horizons,* Jaipur: Rawat, 2001.

Chandra, Bipan, *Indian National Movement: Long-term Dynamics*, New Delhi: Vikas, 1988.

———, *The Rise and Growth of Economic Nationalism in India*, New Delhi: People's Publishing House, 1966.

Chandra, Bipan et al., *India's Struggle for Independence 1857–1947,* New Delhi: Penguin, 1989.

Charan, Umeshwari, *Responsible Government: A Case Study of Bihar 1919–1933,* New Delhi: Classical, 1985.

Chatterjee, Partha, *Bengal 1920–1947: The Land Question in Bengal,* Calcutta: K.P. Bagchi, 1984.

———, *The Nation and Its Fragments: Colonial and Post Colonial Histories*, New Delhi: Oxford University Press, 1994

Chaturvedi, V., ed., *Mapping Subaltern Studies and the Postcolonial,* London, New York: Verso, 2000

Chaudhary, Prasanna Kumar, and Srikant, *Bihar Mein Samajik Parivartan Ke Kuch Ayaam (1912–1990),* New Delhi: Vani, 2001.

Chaudhary, V.C.P., *The Creation of Modern Bihar,* Patna: Yugeshwar Prakashan, 1964.

Chopra, P.N., ed., *India's Struggle for Freedom: Role of Associated Movements,* vol. II, New Delhi: Agam, 1985.

Cohn, Bernard, *An Anthropologist among the Historians and other Essays,* New Delhi: Oxford University Press, 1987.

———, *Colonialism and its Forms of Knowledge: The British in India,* Princeton: Princeton University Press, 1996.

Dalmia, Vasudha and Heinrich Von Stietencron, ed., *Representing Hinduism: The Construction of Religious Traditions and National Identity,* New Delhi: Sage, 1995.

Damodaran, Vinita, *Broken Promises, Popular Protest, Indian Nationalism and the Congress Party in Bihar 1935–1946,* New Delhi: Oxford University Press, 1992.

Das, Arvind N., ed., *Agrarian Movements in India: Studies on 20th Century Bihar,* London: Frank Cass, 1982.

———, *Agrarian Unrest and Socio-Economic Change in Bihar, 1900–1980,* New Delhi: Manohar, 1983.

Das, Victor, *Jharkhand: Castle Over the Graves,* New Delhi: Inter-India, 1992.

Datta, K.K., *Gandhiji in Bihar*, Patna: Government of Bihar, 1969.

———, *History of the Freedom Movement in Bihar,* 3 vols, Patna: Bihar Government Press, 1957.

———, *The Santal Insurrection of 1855–57,* Calcutta: Firma KLM, 1940.

———, *The Writings and Speeches of Mahatma Gandhi in Bihar, 1917–1947,* Patna: Government of Bihar, 1960.

Desai, A.R., ed., *Peasant Struggles in India,* Bombay: Oxford University Press, 1979.

Desai, Mahadev, *Gandhiji in Indian Villages,* Madras: S. Ganesan, 1927.

Dhanagare, D.N., *Peasant Movement in India 1920–1950,* New Delhi: Oxford University Press, 1983.

Forbes, Geraldine, *Women in Modern India,* The New Cambridge History of India, vol. 4.2, Cambridge: Cambridge University Press, 1998.

Foucault, Michel, *Discipline and Punish: The Birth of the Prison,* New York: Vintage Books, 1979.

Frankel, F.R., and Rao, M.S.A., eds., *Dominance and State Power in Modern India: Decline of a Social Order,* vol. I, New Delhi: Oxford University Press, 1989.

Fuchs, Stephen, *Rebellious Prophets: A Study of Messianic Movements in Indian Religions,* Bombay: Asia Publication House, 1965.

Gallagher, J., Johnson, G., and Seal, A., eds., *Locality, Province and Nation: Essays on Indian Politics 1870–1940,* London: Cambridge University Press, 1973.

Gandhi, Mahatma, *Khadi: Why and How,* Ahmedabad: Navajivan, 1959.

———, *The Collected Works of Mahatma Gandhi,* New Delhi: Publications Division, Ministry of Information and Broadcasting, Government of India, 1958–84.

Gandhi, Mahatma, *Women and Social Justice,* Ahmedabad: Navajivan, 1958.

Gender and Nation, Nehru Memorial Museum and Library, New Delhi, 2000.

Ghosh, Papiya, *The Civil Disobedience Movement in Bihar,* New Delhi: Manak, 2008.

Grierson, George, *A Bihar Peasant Life,* Patna: Superintendent, Government Printing, 1926.

Guha, Amalendu, *Planters' Raj to Swaraj: Freedom Struggle and Electoral Politics in Assam, 1826–1947,* New Delhi: Indian Council of Historical Research, 1977.

Guha, Ramchandra, *The Unquiet Woods: Ecological Change and Peasant Resistance in the Western Himalayas,* New Delhi: Oxford University Press, 1989.

Guha, Ranajit, *Elementary Aspects of Peasant Insurgency in Colonial India,* New Delhi: Oxford University Press, 1983.

Gupta, Rakesh, *Bihar Peasantry and the Kisan Sabha,* New Delhi: People's Publishing House, 1982.

Hardiman, David, ed., *Peasant Resistance in India 1858–1914,* New Delhi: Oxford University Press, 1992.

———, *Peasant Nationalists of Gujarat: Kheda District 1917–1934,* New Delhi: Oxford University Press, 1981.

———, *The Coming of the Devi: Adivasi Assertion in Western India,* New Delhi: Oxford University Press, 1987.

Hauser, Walter, ed., *Sahajanand on Agricultural Labour and the Rural Poor,* New Delhi: Manohar, 1994.

Haynes, Douglas, *Rhetoric and Ritual in Colonial India: The Shaping of a Public Culture in Surat City, 1852–1928,* New Delhi: Oxford University Press, 1992.

Haynes, Douglas and Prakash, Gyan, *Contesting Power: Resistance and Everyday Social Relations in South Asia,* New Delhi: Oxford University Press, 1991.

Henningham, Stephen, *A Great Estate and its Landlords in Colonial India: Darbhanga 1860–1942,* New Delhi: Oxford University Press, 1990.

———, *Peasant Movements in Colonial India, North Bihar, 1917–42*, Canberra: Australian National University, 1984.

Imam, Muzaffar, *Role of Muslims in the National Movement, 1912–1930: A Study of Bihar,* New Delhi: Mittal, 1987.

Jannuzi, F. Tomasson, *Agrarian Crisis in India: The Case of Bihar,* Austin: University of Texas Press, 1974.

Jayawardena, Kumari, *Feminism and Nationalism in the Third World,* London: Zed Books, 1986.

Jha, J.S., *Early Revolutionary Movement in Bihar, 1906-1920,* Patna: K.P. Jayaswal Research Institute, 1977.

Jha, S., *Political Elites in Bihar*, Bombay: Nora, 1972.

Jha, S.K., *Raj to Swaraj, Changing Contours of Police,* New Delhi: Lancer, 1995.

Joshi, Pushpa, *Gandhi on Women: Collection of Mahatma Gandhi's Writings and Speeches on Women,* Ahmedabad: Navajivan House and Delhi: Centre for Women's Development Studies, 1988.

Kumar, Arun, *Rewriting the Language of Politics: Kisans in Colonial Bihar,* New Delhi: Manohar, 2001.

Kumar, Kapil, ed., *Congress and Classes: Nationalism, Workers and Peasants,* New Delhi: Manohar, 1988.

Kumar, Krishna, *Political Agenda of Education: A Study of Colonialist and Nationalist Ideas,* New Delhi: Sage, 1991.

Kumar, Radha, *The History of Doing,* New Delhi: Kali, 1993.

Kumar, Ravinder, ed., *Essays in Gandhian Politics: The Rowlatt Satyagraha of 1919,* London: Oxford University Press, 1971.

Ludden, David, ed., *Reading Subaltern Studies: Critical History, Contested Meaning and the Globalization of South Asia,* New Delhi: Permanent Black, 2003.

Low, D.A., ed., *Congress and the Raj: Facets of the Indian Struggle 1917–1947,* London: Arnold-Heinemann, 1977.

———, ed., *The Indian National Congress: Centenary Hindsights,* New Delhi: Oxford University Press, 1988.

MacDougall, *Land or Religion? The Sardar and Kherwar Movements in Bihar, 1858–1895,* New Delhi: Manohar, 1985.

Mazumdar, Veena and Kasturi, Leela, eds., *Women and Indian Nationalism,* New Delhi: Vikas, 1994.

McLane, J.R., *Indian Nationalism and the Early Congress,* Princeton: Princeton University Press, 1977.

Menon, Nivedita, ed., *Gender and Politics in India*, New Delhi: Oxford University Press, 1999.

Mies, Maria, *Indian Women and Patriarchy,* New Delhi: Concept Publishing Company, 1980.

Minault, Gail, *The Khilafat Movement: Religious Symbolism and Political Mobilisation in India,* New Delhi: Oxford University Press, 1982.

Mishra, B.B., ed., *Select Documents on Mahatma Gandhi's Movement in Champaran, 1917–19,* Patna: Government of Bihar, 1963.

Mishra, Girish, *Agrarian Problems of Permanent Settlement—A Case Study of Champaran,* New Delhi: People's Publishing House, 1978.

Mishra, Girish, and Pandey, Braj Kumar, *Sociology and Economics of Casteism in India: A Case Study of Bihar,* New Delhi: Pragati, 1996.

Misra, B.B., *The Bureaucracy in India: An Historical Analysis up to 1947*, London: Oxford University Press, 1971.

Mittal, S.K., *Peasant Uprisings and Mahatma Gandhi in North Bihar,* Meerut: Anu, 1978.

Ojha, P.N., ed., *History of the Indian National Congress in Bihar, 1885–1985,* Patna: K.P. Jayaswal Research Institute, 1985.

Pandey, Gyanendra, ed., *The Indian Nation in 1942,* Calcutta: K.P. Bagchi, 1998.

———, *The Ascendancy of the Congress in Uttar Pradesh, 1926–34: A Study in Imperfect Mobilisation,* New Delhi: Oxford University Press, 1979.

Panigrahi, D.N., ed., *Economy, Society and Politics in Modern India,* New Delhi: Vikas for Nehru Memorial Museum and Library, New Delhi, 1985.

Pannikar, K.N., *Against Lord and State, Religion and Peasant Uprisings in Malabar 1836–1921,* New Delhi: Oxford University Press, 1992.

Parekh, Bhikhu, *Colonialism, Tradition and Reforms: An Analysis of Gandhi's Political Discourse,* New Delhi and London: Sage, 1989.

Pati, Biswamoy, *Resisting Domination: Peasants, Tribals and the National Movement in Orissa 1920–50*, New Delhi: Manohar, 1993.

Pinch, William R., *Peasants and Monks in British India,* New Delhi: Oxford University Press, 1996.

Pouchepadass, Jacques, *Champaran and Gandhi: Planters, Peasants and Gandhian Politics,* New Delhi: Oxford University Press, 1999.

Prasad, Rajendra, *Satyagraha in Champaran,* Ahmedabad: Navajivan, 1949.

———, *Mahatma Gandhi and Bihar: Some Reminiscences,* Bombay: Hind Kitab Limited, 1949.

———, *Bapu Ke Qadmon Me,* Aligarh: Anjuman Taraqqui Urdu, 1954.

Prasad, Ramchandra and Sinha, Ashok Kumar, *Shri Krishna Singh, Adhunik Bharat Ke Nirmata,* New Delhi: Publications Division, Ministry of Information and Broadcasting, Government of India, 1988.

Ranger, T. and Hobsbawm, E.J., ed., *The Invention of Tradition,* London: Cambridge University Press, 1983.

Ray, Bharati, *From the Seams of History,* New Delhi: Oxford University Press, 1995.

Ray, Rajat, *Social Conflict and Political Unrest in Bengal, 1875–1927,* New Delhi: Oxford University Press, 1984.

———, *Urban Roots of Indian Nationalism: Pressure Groups and Conflict of Interests in Calcutta City Politics, 1875–1939,* New Delhi: Vikas, 1979.

Renu, Fanishwar Nath, *Maila Anchal,* New Delhi: Rajkamal, 1954.

Roy, S.C., *The Mundas and Their Country,* Bombay: Asia House, 1970.

———, *Oraon Religion and Custom,* Calcutta: Industry Press, 1928.

Said, Edward W., *Orientalism,* New York: Pantheon Books, 1978.

Sangari, Kumkum and Vaid, Sudesh, eds., *Recasting Women: Essays in Indian Colonial History,* New Delhi: Kali, 1989.

Sankrityayan, Kamala, ed., *Rahul Vanmay: Jeevan Yatra,* vols. 1–2, New Delhi: Radhakrishna, 1994.

Sankrityayan, Rahul, *Mere Asahyog Ke Saathi,* Allahabad: Kitab Mahal, 1999.

Sarkar, Sumit, *Modern India,* New Delhi: Macmillan, 1983.

———, *'Popular' Movements and 'Middle Class' Leadership: Perspectives and Problems of a 'History from Below'*, S.G. Deuskar Lectures on Indian History, 1982, Calcutta, 1983.

———, *Swadeshi Movement in Bengal,* New Delhi: People's Publishing House, 1973.

Sarkar, Tanika, *Bengal 1928–1934: The Politics of Protest,* New Delhi: Oxford University Press, 1987.

Scott, James C., *Weapons of the Weak: Everyday Forms of Peasant Resistance,* New Haven: Yale University Press, 1985.

Sen, Suchibrata, *The Santals of Jungle Mahals: An Agrarian History, 1793–1861,* Calcutta: Ratna, 1984.

Shah, Ghanshyam, *Protest Movements in Two Indian States: A Study of the Gujarat and Bihar Movements,* New Delhi: Ajanta, 1977.

Sharma, K.K., Singh, Prabhakar Prasad, and Kumar, Ranjan, eds., *Peasant Struggles in Bihar, 1831–1992, Spontaneity to Organisation,* Patna: Janaki Prakashan, 1994.

Sharma, Kaushal Kishore, *Agrarian Movements and Congress Politics in Bihar,* New Delhi: Anamika, 1989.

Sharma, Suresh, *Ramvriksh 'Benipuri': Benipuri Granthavali,* 8 vols., New Delhi: Radhakrishna, 1998.

Shukla, P.K., *Indigo and the Raj: Peasant Protests in Bihar, 1780–1917,* New Delhi: Pragati, 1993.

Siddiqi, Majid, *Agrarian Unrest in North India, The United Provinces, 1918–22,* New Delhi: Vikas, 1978.

Singer, Wendy, *Creating Histories, Oral Narratives and the Politics of History Making,* New Delhi: Oxford University Press, 1997.

Singh, C.P., *Ho Tribe of Singhbhum,* New Delhi: Classical, 1978.

Singh, K.S., *Birsa Munda and His Movement 1874–1901: A Study of Millenarian Movement in Chotanagpur,* Calcutta: Oxford University Press, 1983.

———, *Tribal Society in India: An Anthropo-historical Perspective,* New Delhi: Manohar, 1985.

Singh, Radhey Shyam, *Constructive Programmes of Mahatma Gandhi (1920 to 1939),* New Delhi: Commonwealth, 1991.

Sinha, Bagishwar Prasad, *Sachidananda Sinha,* New Delhi: Publications Division, Ministry of Information and Broadcasting, Government of India, 1969.

Sinha, Mrinalini, *Colonial Masculinity: The Manly Englishman and the Effeminate Bengal in the late 19th Century,* Manchester: Manchester University Press, 1995.

Sinha, Sachidananda, *Some Eminent Behar Contemporary,* Patna: Janaki, 1944.

Sinha, Satya Narayan, *1921 Movement-Reminiscences,* New Delhi: Publications Division, Ministry of Information and Broadcasting, Government of India, 1971.

Sitaramayya, B. Pittabhi, *The History of the Indian National Congress (1885–1935),* Bombay: Padma Publications, 1946.

Spangenburg, B., *Bureaucracy in India: Status, Policy and the ICS in the Late 19th Century,* New Delhi: Manohar, 1976.

Srinivas, M.N., *Social Change in Modern India,* Bombay: Allied, 1972.

Tarlo, Emma, *Clothing Matters, Dress and Identity in India,* New Delhi: Penguin, 1996.

Thomson, Mark, *Gandhi and His Ashrams,* Bombay: Popular Prakashan, 1993.

Tinker, Hugh, *The Foundations of Local Self-Government, Pakistan and Burma,* Bomabay: Lalvani House, 1967.

Tomlinson, B.R., *The Indian National Congress and the Raj,* London: Macmillan, 1976.

Viswanathan, Gauri, *The Masks of Conquest: Literary Study and British Rule in India,* New York: Colombia University Press, 1989.

Washbrook, D.A., *Emergence of Provincial Politics: The Madras Presidency, 1870–1920,* New Delhi: Vikas, 1977.

Washbrook, D.A., and Baker, C.J., eds., *South India: Political Institutions and Political Change 1880–1940,* New Delhi: Macmillan, 1975.

Woodruff, Philip Mason, *The Men Who Ruled India: Volume II, The Guardians,* London: Jonathan Cape, 1954.

Yang, Anand, *Limited Raj: Agrarian Relations in Colonial India, Saran District 1793–1920,* New Delhi: Oxford University Press, 1989.

———, *Bazaar India: Markets, Society and the Colonial State in Gangetic Bihar,* Berkeley: University of California Press, 1998.

Articles

Adas, Michael, 'From Avoidance to Confrontation: Peasant Protest in Pre-Colonial and Colonial Southeast Asia', in *Comparative Studies in Society and History,* vol. 23, 1981.

Alexander, H.M.L., 'Discarding the "Steel Frame": Changing Images among Indian Civil Servants in the Early Twentieth Century', in *South Asia,* n.s., vol. V, nos. 1–12, 1982.

Amin, Shahid, 'Agrarian Bases of Nationalist Agitations in India: An Historiographical Survey' in *The Indian National Congress: Centenary Hindsights,* ed. D.A. Low, New Delhi: Oxford University Press, 1988.

———, 'Gandhi as Mahatma: Gorakhpur District, Eastern U.P., 1921–22', in *Subaltern Studies III: Writings on South Asian Society and History,* ed. Ranajit Guha, New Delhi: Oxford University Press, 1984.

Arnold, David, 'Bureaucratic Recruitment and Subordination in Colonial India: The Madras Constabulary, 1859–1947', in *Subaltern Studies IV: Writings on South Asian Society and History,* ed. Ranajit Guha, New Delhi: Oxford University Press, 1985.

———, 'Looting, Grain Riots and Government Policy in South India, 1918', in *Past and Present,* August 1979.

———, 'Rebellious Hillman: The Gudem-Rampa Risings 1839–1924', in *Subaltern Studies I: Writings on South Asian History and Society,* ed. Ranajit Guha, New Delhi: Oxford University Press, 1982.

Atlury, Murali, 'Subaltern Studies IV': A Review Article, in *Social Scientist,* vol. 16, no. 3, March 1988.

———, 'Non-cooperation in Andhra in 1920–22: Nationalist Intelligentsia and the Mobilisation of Peasantry', in *Indian Historical Review,* July 1985–January 1986, vol. XII, nos. 1–2.

Bagchi, J., 'Representing Nationalism: Ideology of Motherhood in Colonial Bengal', in *Economic and Political Weekly,* 20–27 October 1990, WS-65-71.

Baker, C.J., 'Non-Cooperation in South India', in *South India: Political Institutions and Political Change 1880-1940,* eds., Washbrook, D.A., and Baker, C.J., New Delhi: Macmillan, 1975.

Basu, Aparna, 'The Role of Women in the Indian Struggle for Freedom', in *Indian Women from Purdah to Modernity,* ed. B.R. Nanda, New Delhi: Radiant, 1990.

Basu, Mrinal Kumar, 'Regionalism Patriotism: A Study in Bihar Politics (1907-1912)', in *Indian Historical Review,* vol. III, no. 2, January 1977.

Bayly, C.A., 'The Origins of Swadeshi (home industry): Cloth and Indian Society, 1700–1930', in *Social Life of Things: Commodities in Cultural Perspectives,* ed. Arjun Appadurai, London: Cambridge University Press, 1986.

Beaglehole, T., 'From Rulers to Servants: The Indian Civil Service and the British Demission of Power in India', in *Modern Asian Studies,* vol. II, no. 2, 1977.

Bhattacharya, Sabyasachi, 'Cotton Mills and Spinning Wheels-Swadeshi in the Non-Cooperation Era', in *Economic and Political Weekly,* November 1976.

Bodding, Revd P.O., 'The Kharwar Movement Among the Santals', in *Man in India,* vol. I, September 1921.

Charlesworth, Neil, 'The Middle Peasant Thesis and the Roots of Rural Agitation in India, 1917-47', in *Journal of Peasant Studies,* vol. 8, no. 3, April 1981.

Chatterjee, Partha, 'Gandhi and the Critique of Civil Society', in *Subaltern Studies III: Writings on South Asian History and Society,* ed. Ranajit Guha, New Delhi: Oxford University Press, 1984.

———, 'The Nationalist Resolution of the Women's Question', in *Recasting Women: Essays in Colonial History,* eds. Kumkum Sangari and Sudesh Vaid, New Delhi: Kali, 1989.

Chaudhary, B.B., 'The Story of a Tribal Revolt in the Bengal Presidency: The Religion and Politics of the Oraons: 1900-1926', in *Aspects of Socio-Economic Changes and Political Awakening in Bengal,* ed. Adhir Chakrabarti, Calcutta: Government of West Bengal, 1989.

———, 'Agrarian Movements in Bihar and Bengal, 1919-1939', in *Socialism in India,* ed. B.R. Nanda, New Delhi: Vikas, 1972.

Das, Arvind N., 'Peasants and Peasant Organisations: The Kisan Sabha in Bihar', in *Agrarian Movements in India: Studies on 20th Century, Bihar,* ed. Arvind N. Das, London: Frank Cass, 1982.

Dasgupta, Sangeeta, 'Reordering a World: The Tana Bhagat Movement, 1914–1919', in *Studies in History,* n.s., vol. 15, no. 1, 1999.

Dasgupta, Swapan, 'Adivasi Politics in Midnapur, *c.* 1760–1924', in *Subaltern Studies IV: Writings on South Asian History and Society,* ed. Ranajit Guha, New Delhi: Oxford University Press, 1985.

Dhan, R.O. 'The Problems of the Tana Bhagats of Ranchi District', in *Bulletin of the Bihar Tribal Research Institute,* vol. II, no. 1, July 1960, Ranchi.

Dhanagare, D.N., 'Agrarian Conflict, Religion and Politics: The Moplah Rebellions in Malabar in the 19th and early 20th Century', in *Past and Present,* February 1977.

Dube, Leela, 'On the Applicability of the Concept of Sanskritization: Comment on Hetukar Jha', in *Indian Economic and Social History Review,* vol. XV, no. 4, 1977.

Forbes, Geraldine, 'The Politics of Respectability: Indian Women and the Indian National Congress', in *The Indian National Congress: Centenary Hindsights*, ed. D.A. Low, New Delhi: Oxford University Press, 1988.

Frankel, F.R., 'Caste, Land and Dominance in Bihar: Breakdown of the Brahmanical Social Order', in *Dominance and State Power in Modern India: Decline of a Social Order,* vol. I, eds. F.R. Frankel and M.S.A. Rao, New Delhi: Oxford University Press, 1989.

Freitag, S., 'Sacred Symbols as Mobilising Ideology: The North Indian Search for a "Hindu" Community', in *Comparative Studies in Society and History,* vol.22, no. 4, 1980.

Gender and History, Special Issue on Gender, Nationalisms and Identities, vol. 5, no. 2, 1993.

Ghosh, Papiya, 'Peasants, Planters and Gandhi: Champaran in 1917', in *Peasant Struggles in Bihar, 1831–1992, Spontaneity to Organisation et al.*, eds. Kaushal Kishore Sharma, Patna: Janaki Prakashan, 1994.

———, 'Rural Base of the Bihar Congress, 1920–36', in *Social Science Probings,* New Delhi, March 1986,

Guha, Ramchandra, 'Forestry and Social Protest in British Kumaun, *c.* 1893–1921', in *Subaltern Studies IV: Writings on South Asian History and Society,* ed. Ranajit Guha, New Delhi: Oxford University Press, 1985.

Guha, Ranajit, 'Discipline and Punish', in *Subaltern Studies VII: Writings on South Asian History and Society,* eds. Partha Chatterjee and Gyan Pandey, New Delhi: Oxford University Press, 1992.

———, 'Neel Darpan: The Image of a Peasant Revolt in a Liberal Mirror', in *Peasant Resistance in India 1858–1914,* ed. David Hardiman, New Delhi: Oxford University Press, 1992.

———, 'On Some Aspects of the Historiography of Colonial India', in *Subaltern Studies I: Writings on South Asian History and Society,* ed. Ranajit Guha, New Delhi: Oxford University Press, 1982.

Hardiman, David, 'Adivasi Assertion in South Gujarat: The Devi Movement of 1922–3' in *Subaltern Studies III: Writings on South Asian History and Society,* ed. Ranajit Guha, New Delhi: Oxford University Press, 1984.

———, 'From Custom to Crime: The Politics of Drinking in Colonial South Gujarat' in *Subaltern Studies IV,* Writings on South Asian History and Society, ed. Ranajit Guha, New Delhi: Oxford University Press, 1985.

Hauser, Walter, 'Swami Sahajanand and the Politics of Social Reform, 1907–50', in *Indian Historical Review,* vol. XVIII, nos. 1–2, July 1991 and January 1992.

Heath, Dwight B., 'Comment on David Mandelbaum's "Alcohol and Culture"', in *Current Anthropology*, vol. 6, no. 3, June 1965, p. 20.

Henningham, Stephen, 'Agrarian Relations in North Bihar: Peasant Protest and the Darbhanga Raj, 1919–20', in *Indian Economic and Social History Review,* vol. XVI, no. 1, January-March 1979.

———, 'The Social Setting of the Champaran Satyagraha: The Challenge to an Alien Elite', in *Indian Economic and Social History Review,* vol. XIII, no. 1, January-March 1976.

Horton, David, 'The Functions of Alcohol in Primitive Societies: A Cross-Cultural Study', in *Quarterly Journal of Studies on Alcohol,* vol. 4, no. 2, September 1943, p. 246.

Jha, A.P., 'Nature of the Santhal Unrest of 1871–75 and Origin of the Sapha Hor Movement', in *Indian Historical Records Commission Proceedings,* vol. XXXV, part II, File 1960.

Jha, Chetkar, 'Caste in Bihar Politics' in *State Politics in India,* ed. Iqbal Narain, Meerut: Meenakshi Prakashan, 1976.

Jha, Hetukar, 'Lower-Caste Peasants and Upper Caste Zamindars in Bihar (1921–1925): An Analysis of Sanskritization and Contradiction between the Two Groups', in *Indian Economic and Social History Review,* vol. XIV, 1977.

Jha, J.C., 'The Bihar Tribals and the Indian National Movement', in *Bihar: Past and Present,* ed. P.N. Ojha, Patna: K.P. Jayaswal Research Institute, 1987.

———, 'The Khilafat and the Non-Cooperation Movement in Bihar (1919–22)', in *History of Indian National Congress in Bihar, 1885–1985,* ed. P.N. Ojha, Patna: K.P. Jayaswal Research Institute, 1985.

———, 'The Tribals of Bihar and the Indian Freedom Movement: 1920–1942', in *Indian Historical Review,* July 1985–January 1986, vol. XII, nos.1–2.

Jha, Pankaj Kumar, 'Collaboration And Opposition: Darbhanga Raj's Response To The Non-Cooperation Movement (1920–22)', in *Proceedings of the Indian History Congress,* 60th Session, Calicut, 1999.

Katrak, Ketu H., 'Indian Nationalism, Gandhian Satyagraha and Representations of Female Sexualities', in *Nationalism and Sexualities et al.,* ed. Andrew Parker, New York and London: Routledge, 1992.

Kishwar, Madhu, 'Gandhi on Women', in *Economic and Political Weekly of India,* 5 and 12 October 1985.

Krishna, Gopal, 'The Development of the Indian National Congress as a Mass Organization, 1918–23', in *Journal of Asian Studies,* November 1965–August 1966, vol. XXV.

Kumar, Kapil, 'Baba Ram Chandra and Peasant Upsurge in Oudh 1920–21', in *Social Scientist,* June 1978.

Kumar, Ravinder, 'From Swaraj to Purna Swaraj: Nationalist Politics in the City of Bombay, 1920–32', in *Congress and the Raj: Facets of the Indian Struggle, 1917–1947,* ed. D.A. Low, London: Arnold-Heinemann, 1977.

Low, D.A., 'The Government of India and the First Non-Cooperation Movement, 1920–22', in *Essays on Gandhian Politics—The Rowlatt Satyagraha of 1919,* ed. Ravinder Kumar, London: Oxford University Press, 1971.

Mandelbaum, David G., 'Alcohol and Culture', in *Current Anthropology,* vol. 6, no. 3, June 1965.

Mahajan, Sucheta, 'British Policy, Nationalist Strategy and Popular National Upsurge, 1945–6', in *Myth and Reality, Struggle for Freedom in India, 1945–47,* ed. A.K. Gupta, New Delhi: Manohar, 1987.

Mahmud, Syed, 'Looking Back', in *1921 Movement Reminiscences*, New Delhi: Publications Division, Ministry of Information and Broadcasting, Government of India, 1971.

McDonald, G. 'Unity on Trial: Congress in Bihar, 1919-39', in *Congress and the Raj: Facets of the Indian Struggle 1917–1947,* ed. D.A. Low, London: Arnold-Heinemann, 1977.

Mishra, Girish, 'Indigo Plantations and the Agrarian Relations in Champaran during the Nineteenth Century', in *Indian Economic and Social History Review,* vol. III, no. 4, December 1966.

———, 'Socio-Economic Background of Gandhi's Champaran Movement', in *Indian Economic and Social History Review,* vol. V, no. 3, September 1968.

Mitra, Manoshi, 'A Review of the Role of Zamindars in Bihar vis-à-vis the Agrarian Economy', in *Proceedings of the Indian History Congress,* 37th Session, Calicut, 1976.

Mohapatra, P., 'Coolies and Colliers: A Study of the Agrarian Context of Labour Migration from Chotanagpur, 1880–1920', in *Studies in History,* n.s., vol. I, no. 2, July-December 1985.

Mukherjee, Mridula, 'Peasant Resistance and Peasant Consciousness in Colonial India: Subalterns and Beyond', in *Economic and Political Weekly*, vol. 23, issues 41 and 42, 1988.

Mukhopadhyay, Anandita, 'Jail Darpan: The Image of the Jail in Bengali Middle-Class Literature', in *Studies in History,* n.s., vol. 15, no. 1, 1999, pp. 108-44.

Natrajan, L., 'The Santhal Insurrection: 1855–56', in *Peasant Struggles in India,* ed. A.R. Desai, Bombay: Oxford University Press, 1979.

Pandey, Gyan, 'Peasant Revolt and Indian Nationalism: the Peasant Movement in Awadh, 1919–1922' in *Subaltern Studies I: Writings on South Asian History and Society,* ed. Ranajit Guha, New Delhi: Oxford University Press, 1982.

Patel, Sujata, 'Construction and Re-construction of Woman in Gandhi', in *Economic and Political Weekly,* 20 February 1988.

Potter, David C., 'Manpower Shortage and the End of Colonialism: The Case of the Indian Civil Service', in *Modern Asian Studies*, vol. 7, no. 1, 1973.

Pouchepadass, Jacques, 'Peasant Classes in Twentieth Century Agrarian Movements in India', in *Peasants in History: Essays in Honour of Daniel Thorner et al.*, ed. E.J. Hobsbawm, Calcutta: Oxford University Press, 1980.

———, 'Local Leaders and the Intelligentsia in the Champaran Satyagraha (1917): A Study in Peasant Mobilization', in *Contributions to Indian Sociology,* n.s., no. 8, November 1974.

Prakash, Gyan, 'Writing Post-Orientalist Histories of the Third World', in *Comparative Studies in Society and History,* vol. 34, 1992.

Prasad, Rajiv Nain, 'The Champaran Satyagraha', in *History of the Indian National Congress in Bihar, 1885–1985,* ed. P.N. Ojha, Patna: K.P. Jayaswal Research Institute, 1985.

Ray, Rajat, 'Masses in Politics—Non-Cooperation in Bengal 1920-22', in *Indian Economic and Social History Review,* vol XI, no. 4, December 1974.

Richard, Gordon, 'Non-cooperation and Council Entry 1919 to 1920', in *Locality, Province and Nation: Essays on Indian Politics 1870–1940,* eds., J. Gallagher, G. Johnson and A. Seal, London: Cambridge University Press, 1973.

Roy, N.B., 'New Aspects of the Santal Insurrection of 1855–6', in *Indian Historical Records Commission Proceedings*, vol. XXXV, part II, February 1960.

Sarkar, Sumit, 'Popular Movements and National Leadership, 1945–47', in *Economic and Political Weekly,* vol. XVII, nos. 14–16, April 1982.

———, 'The Conditions and Nature of Subaltern Militancy: Bengal from Swadeshi to Non-Cooperation, *c.* 1905–22', in *Subaltern Studies III: Writings on South Asian History and Society,* ed. Ranajit Guha, New Delhi: Oxford University Press, 1984.

———, 'Popular Culture, Community, Power: Three Studies of Modern Indian Social History', in *Studies in History,* vol. 8, no. 2, 1992.

Sarkar, Tanika, 'Politics and Women in Bengal—the Conditions and Meanings of Participation', in *Indian Economic and Social History Review,* vol. XXI, no. I (January-March 1984), pp. 98–99.

———, 'Jitu Santal's Movement in Malda, 1924-1932: A Study in Tribal Protest', in *Subaltern Studies IV: Writings on South Asian History and Society,* ed. Ranajit Guha, New Delhi: Oxford University Press, 1985.

Scott, James C., and Tria Kerkvliet, Benedict J., *Journal of Peasant Studies,* vol. XII, 1986.

Sengupta, Nirmal, 'Agrarian Movements in Bihar', in *Agrarian Movements in India: Studies on 20th Century Bihar,* ed. Arvind N. Das, London: Frank Cass, 1982.

Shah, Ghanshyam, 'Traditional Society and Political Mobilisation: The Experience of Bardoli Satyagraha (1920-1928)', in *Contributions to Indian Sociology,* n.s., no. 8, New Delhi, 1974.

Shukla, P.K., 'Patriotism and Socio-Economic Inequality as Reflected in the Writings of a Gandhian Poet—Ram Jeevan Sharma', in *Proceedings of the Indian History Congress,* 59th Session, Patiala, 1998.

Siddiqi, Majid, 'History and Popular Rebellion, Mewat 1920–33', in *Comparative Studies in History and Society*, vol. 28, no. 3, July 1986.

Singh, K.S., 'Tribal Peasantry, Millenarianism, Anarchism and Nationalism—A Case Study of the Tana Bhagats in Chotanagpur, 1914-25', in *Social Scientist,* vol. 16, no. 11, November 1988.

Singh, Sita Ram, 'Gandhi, The Colonial Middle Class and the Indian People', in *Proceedings of the Indian History Congress,* 56th Session, Mysore, 1993.

Viswesaran, Kamla, 'Small Speeches, Subaltern Gender: Nationalist Ideology and Its Historiography', in *Subaltern Studies IX: Writings on South Asian History and Society,* eds. Shahid Amin and Dipesh Chakrabarty, New Delhi: Oxford University Press, 1996.

Washbrook, D.A., 'Development of Caste Organisation in South India 1880–1925' in *South India: Political Institutions and Political Change 1880–1940*, eds. D.A. Washbrook and C.J. Baker, New Delhi: Macmillan, 1975.

Yang, Anand, 'Agrarian Origins of Crime: A Study of Riots in Saran District, India 1886-1920', in *Journal of Social History,* vol. 13, no. 2, 1979.

THESES AND DISSERTATIONS

Aturi, Murali, *Social Change and Nature of Social Participation in National Movement in Andhra, 1905–1934,* Ph.D. thesis submitted at the Jawaharlal Nehru University, New Delhi, 1985.

Fisher, C.M., *Indigo Plantations and Agrarian Society in North Bihar in the 19th and early 20th Centuries,* Ph.D. thesis submitted at the Cambridge University, 1976.

Hauser, Walter, *The Bihar Provincial Kisan Sabha, 1929–1942: A Study on Indian Peasant Movement,* Ph.D. dissertation, Department of History, University of Chicago, 1961.

Jha, Narendra, *Aspects of Regional Consciousness in Bihar, 1870–1912,* M.Phil. thesis submitted at the Jawaharlal Nehru University, New Delhi, 1991.

Mitra, Chandan, *Political Mobilisation and the National Movement in Eastern U.P. and Bihar 1937-42*, Ph.D. thesis submitted at the Oxford University, 1983.

Sharma, Haridev, *Non-Cooperation Movement 1919–1922,* Ph.D. thesis submitted at the Delhi University, New Delhi, 1969.

Roy, Ramashray, *A Study of the Bihar Pradesh Congress Committee, Bihar, India,* Ph.D. thesis submitted at the University of California, Berkeley, 1966.

Glossary

Abwab	Unauthorized cesses levied in addition to rent by the landlords
Adharmi	Irreligious
Amla	Employee of a landlord's establishment
Begari	One who renders unpaid service to the landlords
Bhang	A preparation of the leaves and flowers of the hemp plant
Chalisa	Eulogizing as divine
Chauk	Cross-road
Chaukidar	Village watchman
Daru	Distilled country liquor
Dharma/dharmic	Religious
Dharna	To sit in protest in order to enforce compliance of a demand
Diara	River bank or alluvial land gained by recession of a river
Ekka	Coach
Fatwa	Judicial judgement or decree passed by a Muslim judge
Ganja	Narcotic, usually smoked through a pipe, the kalki
Haat	A period village market
Haram	Sinful or prohibited by religion
Havan	Ritual of purifying surrounding/air by holy fire
Jhanda	Flag
Kachahari	A court house
Mufassil	The countryside
Mai-baap	Mother-father
Mukhtar	A person authorized to act or plead for someone in the court
Muthia	A system whereby a handful of grain was set apart everyday by a householder and this was collected once a week by the volunteers

Pugri	Turban
Salami	Landlord's fees
Tari	Palm liquor/toddy
Tehsildar	Assessment official
Zulum	Oppression

Index